The Quebec Democracy

STRUCTURES

PROCESSES

POLICIES

GUY LACHAPELLE
CONCORDIA UNIVERSITY

GÉRALD BERNIER
UNIVERSITÉ DE MONTRÉAL

DANIEL SALÉE
CONCORDIA UNIVERSITY

LUC BERNIER
ÉCOLE NATIONALE D'ADMINISTRATION PUBLIQUE

McGraw-Hill Ryerson Limited

TORONTO MONTREAL NEW YORK AUCKLAND BOGOTÁ CARACAS LISBON LONDON
MADRID MEXICO MILAN NEW DELHI PARIS SAN JUAN SINGAPORE SYDNEY TOKYO

The Quebec Democracy
Structures, Processes, and Policies

1 2 3 4 5 6 7 8 9 10 BG 2 1 0 9 8 7 6 5 4 3

Printed and bound in Canada.

SPONSORING EDITOR: Anne Louise Currie
COPY EDITOR: Rodney Rawlings
PERMISSIONS EDITOR: Norma Christensen
COVER DESIGN: Matthews Communications Design
TEXT DESIGN: Kim MacKillop (Heidy Lawrance Associates)
TYPESETTING: Heidy Lawrance Associates
PRINTING & BINDING: Best Gagné

Canadian Cataloguing in Publication Data

The Quebec democracy : structures, processes, and policies

ISBN 0-07-551394-3

1. Quebec (Province)—Politics and government. I. Lachapelle, Guy, 1955–

JL250.Q83 1993   320.9714   C92-094602-X

CONTENTS

PART III Politics and Policy in Quebec: The Policymakers

PART V   Conclusion

PREFACE

Two hundred years ago, on December 17, 1792, the first Quebec parliament opened in Quebec city, establishing the basis for both an eventual parliamentary government and a modern democracy. Both goals were to be achieved in 1848, with the acquisition of responsible government (see Chapters 1 and 9). Though it coincided with the French and American revolutions, the establishment of representative government in Quebec was not won by violence, but granted on simple petition. Analysis of Quebec government since 1791 to the present reveals a constant quest by the Québécois to improve the structures and practice of democracy. Throughout its history, but especially since 1970, Quebec governments have made tremendous efforts to democratize the political process, passing various acts to increase citizens' participation in politics. Few democracies have done so much in the past thirty years to reform voting procedures, party financing, party structure, and electoral behaviour. One of the most important documents of this period is the Charter of Human Rights and Freedoms, enacted on June 27, 1975. In 1982, the Government of Quebec gave the Charter precedence over all other legislation. Quebec's is widely recognized as one of the most progressive charters in the world.

An essential element of Quebec democracy is a fundamental attachment to community values. Over years and years of political debates, Quebecers have always sought a compromise between individual and collective rights: every citizen feels entitled to the advantages of belonging to the community, and to be a member of the community remains an individual right. Obviously, this "double contract" principle is a course of endless ambiguities and policy debates. Individual rights cannot exist without a state that promotes full democratic rights. Without democratic rights, what do individual rights mean? This attitude, peculiar to North America, explains why Quebecers believe so strongly that the State's key role is to implement programs that serve collective interests, and why they expect the private sector to respond to pressure for individual rights. In some situations, citizens expect the State to preserve the cultural integrity of the community; in others, citizens expect it to keep its distance from the economy.

By any standard, the Quebec democracy can be considered one of the soundest societies in the world. Quebec people understand that constitutional arrangements are not sufficient to guarantee democratic rights, and that government actions can infringe those rights. To build confidence between citizens and their institutions, it is essential that the political and policy process remain as transparent as possible, and permit free expression of citizens' opinions.

It is well known that Quebec politics is a difficult, complex subject. Having taught various courses on Quebec government over the past twenty years in the United States and Canada, we have each come to the conclusion that a major obstacle for those who want to fully understand Quebec is the lack of a textbook that presents the fundamentals of Quebec democracy from both a historical and a political perspective. Accordingly, we have tried to write a textbook that one can refer to for basic facts about Quebec politics and its evolution, especially since the 1960s. We also believe that an introductory text on Quebec government should go beyond basic information and offer a broad overview of the political process, structures, and public policies. We hope *The Quebec Democracy* will enable students to make connections, and more importantly enable them to put all the information about Quebec into a broader perspective.

We also think it important that students be apprised of the latest research; therefore, as much as space has allowed, we have tried to incorporate the contributions of the best political scientists in this area. Their various perspectives provide tools with which we can better analyze contemporary institutions and practices, and observe the ongoing development of Quebec democracy. Quebec politics, like politics everywhere, reflects competing value systems and the conflicts, controversy, and consensus that may result. No single thesis dominates these pages. We emphasize the interplay of four basic theories as they apply to Quebec politics: democratic theory, elite theory, class theory, and pluralism.

This book adopts a "policy" approach. The study of public policy is fundamental to understanding government and politics today. And more than ever, government influence in society, and more specifically in the policy process, is intertwined with broader changes in social and cultural values, education and technology, and the ethnic and religious makeup of the population.

This book was written, not only to inform, but also to stimulate today's students. Therefore, like other textbooks, this one includes as much material as possible about historical and constitutional issues, governing institutions and officials, political behaviour, and policymaking—all the key aspects of the subject. However, some hard choices had to be made to match this book as closely as possible to the needs of instructors. We think we have largely succeeded.

Each chapter of this book is designed to offer a good overview of Quebec's social evolution as it relates to the topic at hand, and concludes with a list of key terms and a bibliography. The four appendices provide the text of three basic historical documents—the Quebec Charter of Human Rights and Freedoms, the BNA Act and constitutional documents of 1982, and the Meech Lake accord—and a section called Benchmarks in the History of Quebec. A Glossary of the key terms and an Index end the book.

Note: For important titles of positions in the bureaucracy, names of corporations and organizations, and place names, we have usually given the French form (often with English translation). Otherwise we have used whatever form seemed more familiar or frequently used.

ACKNOWLEDGEMENTS

A great many people have contributed to this book. Catherine O'Toole, our sponsoring editor at the beginning of the project, deserves very special thanks; her keen judgement, steady encouragement, and endless patience have led draft by draft to a book we are proud to have authored. Anne Louise Currie, her successor, was no less diligent and vigilant in her efforts to make this the best book possible.

Ellen Vanstone also had major input into the book. Thought by thought and line by line, she spent weeks sharpening its points and improving its readability. In addition, we want to acknowledge our debt to the rest of the superb staff of McGraw-Hill Ryerson, and to copy editor Rodney Rawlings in particular. We would also like to thank Deborah Fahey, whose initial intervention was instrumental in initiating this project.

We have also been fortunate in receiving the help of many outstanding political scientists across North America, who gave generously of their time to review drafts of chapters and make suggestions. Their comments and advice were enormously helpful, thoughtful, and constructive. Our thanks to all of them.

We would also like to thank Harold Mailhot, Pierre Lavigne, and Jennifer Pasniack from the Department of International Affairs of the Quebec government, who believed in this project from the beginning and helped us financially. We also extend our gratitude to diligent research assistants Jean-François Fortin, David Irwin, and Tim Thomas.

Special thanks are due to *Le Devoir*'s Bernard Descôteaux, Chief Editor, who cordially allowed us access to their documentation centre, and librarian Gilles Paré, for the excellent work he did in finding many of the photos used in this book; and to Normand Charbonneau and the superb staff of the Archives nationales du Québec, who helped us to identify several photographs from various collections.

Lastly, we would like to thank the political science staff at Concordia University—Gail Trottier in particular, who spent hundreds of hours at the word processor working on our various drafts—and Louise Doré at École nationale d'administration publique.

ABOUT THE AUTHORS

Guy Lachapelle is Associate Professor with the Department of Political Science at Concordia University. He is the author of *Canada at the Polls* and *The Media in Canadian Elections: Taking the Pulse* (1992). He is co-editor of *Québec: un pays incertain—réflexions sur le Québec post-référendaire* (1980). His publications include contributions to the *Canadian Journal of Political Science, Revue québécoise de science politique, Quebec Studies,* and *Canadian Journal of Program Evaluation.* His recent work has focussed on public opinion theory, comparative voting behaviour, and Quebec public policy.

Gérald Bernier is Associate Professor In the Department of Political Science at the Université de Montréal. He is co-author with Robert Boily of *Le Québec en chiffres de 1850 à nos jours* (1986) and *Le Québec en transition* (1987). With Daniel Salée he has published *The Shaping of Quebec Politics and Society: Colonialism, Power, and the Transition to Capitalism in the 19th Century* (1992). He has contributed articles to several books on Quebec politics, and published several articles in Canadian and American journals on 19th century Quebec politics. He has been a frequent lecturer at American and British universities. His research interests are Quebec politics from a historical perspective and comparative subnational economic policies.

Daniel Salée is Vice Principal of the School of Community and Public Affairs at Concordia University. He is co-author with Gérald Bernier of *The Shaping of Quebec Politics and Society: Colonialism, Power, and the Transition to Capitalism in the 19th Century* (1992). He is co-editor of *Canada Under Mulroney: An End-of-Term Report* (1988). He has also published widely in scholarly journals on issues related to Quebec and Canadian politics and political development.

Luc Bernier is Professor at the École nationale d'administration publique (ENAP). He is co-author of *Introduction à l'administration publique* (1992). He has authored chapters in *Perforated Sovereignties: Quebec's Foreign Policy* and *La Communication avec l'électeur: les campagnes électorales dans les circonscriptions* (1992). He has published in *Politiques et management public.* His research interests include state-owned enterprises, public administration, and public policy.

PART I

The Constraints of History

CHAPTER 1

FROM NEW FRANCE TO CONTEMPORARY QUEBEC

This chapter focusses on Quebec economic and political history prior to the period under consideration in the rest of this book, namely 1960 to the present day. Though we will present only a brief overview, it is important to look at the formative years of French and British colonial rule, for ultimately these years shaped the form and practice of power in the modern Canadian and Quebec states, and also greatly influenced Canada's and Quebec's political culture.

In five sections, the chapter examines (1) the French regime (1608–1760), (2) the British regime (1760–1867), (3) early federalism (1867–1920), (4) conservatism and associated foreign-dependent development (1920–1960), (5) and, finally, in a brief introduction that outlines some of the themes to be reviewed at length in subsequent chapters, modern Quebec (1960 to the present).

This chapter, which embodies unconventional views and interpretations of the province's history, will seek to raise issues seldom addressed in Quebec historiography.

1.1 NEW FRANCE: 1608–1760

Quebec's modern history began with the "discovery" of New France by Jacques Cartier in 1534. Settlement did not start until 1608, when Samuel de Champlain established a post in Quebec City. In 1642, Montreal was claimed and developed by Chomedey de Maisonneuve. Note that these dates pertain specifically to the history of *white* settlement; North

America had been inhabited for thousands of years, of course, by native peoples (Trigger 1985).

At the height of the French presence in North America (i.e., before the Treaty of Utrecht in 1713), New France's geographical boundaries extended much farther than those of present-day Quebec. The total area under French control included, to the east, all of the St. Lawrence basin, French Acadia, Labrador, a portion of Newfoundland, and all of the coastal area between the Belle-Isle Strait to Hudson Bay. To the southwest, New France encompassed all of the Great Lakes region, the Ohio valley, the Mississippi and Missouri basins, and Louisiana. To the north and west, it reached as far as the plains of Saskatchewan and the Assiniboine river.

Because of limited French migration to New France, it was impossible for French nationals to settle such an extensive portion of North America. It is estimated that at the time of the British Conquest in 1760, New France had 80,000 inhabitants, 65,000 of whom resided in the St. Lawrence valley, i.e., more or less within Quebec's present boundaries. The resistance of the French population to the idea of emigrating to the New World was a continuing problem throughout the French regime. It is estimated that during the French regime (i.e., from 1608 to 1760), only 10,000 individuals (Hamelin and Provencher 1987: 28) crossed the Atlantic to settle in Canada. Consequently, by 1760 the majority of inhabitants of New France were native-born. This fact gave rise to a desire for autonomy at the end of the period, as more and more Canadian-born inhabitants of New France began to develop their own sense of identity. Frictions appeared between them and colonial administrators and recently arrived French settlers. (Berthet 1991).

The Catholic Church's virtual monopoly and privileged status in New France was a contributing factor in limiting immigration. While large numbers of religious dissenters helped to populate the 13 colonies of the United States, religious reformers, and especially the Huguenots, were barred from settling in New France, where the Catholic Church was enjoined by the King of France to evangelize the native peoples.

France established its North American colonies at the height of the mercantilist era, and sought to establish a monopoly on beaver pelts in the New World. A brisk trade sprang up as native peoples supplied the raw material to *coureurs des bois*, who travelled great distances to gather the pelts and bring them back to the merchants, by whom they were exported to France. The fur trade was an important external component of France's economy.

Pelts made up 70% of New France's exports (Hamelin and Provencher 1987: 30). It is estimated that between 1675 and 1760, 72% of fur trade revenues went to France, 14% went to Canadian merchants, 9% went to

New France or Canada in 1656. [Map by Nicolas Sanson d'Abbeville. Courtesy Bibliothèque nationale du Québec.]

the *coureurs des bois* and other intermediaries in the colony, and 5% was used to cover the administrative costs of the colony (Hamelin 1960: 55).

Over the years, trade monopolies were awarded to various companies by the King of France. In return, these companies were expected to foster settlement in the colony by bringing in immigrants and contributing to the creation of communication systems and the development of seigneurial lands. In view of the figures mentioned above, it would appear that the companies were hardly diligent in their efforts to populate New France.

Agriculture was the main occupation of 85% of the active population. Some farmers produced for local markets, but most practised subsistence farming. The agrarian society set up by the French was based on a feudal model called the *seigneurial* system in which a huge tract of land was granted by the King to a *seigneur*, who in turn granted plots to virtually anyone who asked. These individuals, called *censitaires*, and their heirs, had to pay in perpetuity annual fees known as *cens et rentes* to the seigneur. This annual rental amount was fixed for life under the *Coutume de Paris* (Custom of Paris). There were other charges and obligations such as *corvées* (free labour), whereby the censitaires built mills, canals, and bridges for the seigneurial domain. In return, the seigneur had certain duties, such as providing his censitaires with a grist mill. Perceived by many historians as a straightforward settlement system, the seigneurial regime revealed its true feudal nature after the British Conquest (Bernier and Salée 1992).

In essence, New France offered a two-tiered economy. In keeping with the logic of a mercantilist economic system, the external sector was controlled by and satisfied the needs and wants of the metropolis. The objective of the internal sector, characterized by agriculture, was to make the colony self-sufficient in order for the metropolis to run the colony at minimal cost. That is why, in contrast to the situation under British rule after 1760, New France had very few restrictions with respect to producing manufactured goods, for France itself was still in a pre-industrial stage during that period. This poses something of a theoretical problem in analyzing New France in terms of the dominant mode of production. According to a certain school of thought (Wallerstein 1974; Frank 1978), which dates the emergence of the capitalist mode of production as far back as 1460, most Canadian historiography of whatever ideological bent characterizes Canadian colonial ventures (French and British) as having taken place under the aegis of the capitalist mode of production. In short, the widely accepted interpretation of Canada is that it was "born" as a capitalist country.

The Wallerstein-Frank school links capitalism with the creation of an international market, thus tying its emergence to the development of the market. Maurice Dobb (1963), on the other hand, links capitalism with the development of the sphere of production, i. e., the investment of capital in the production of goods and services, and with the ensuing emergence of new relations of production. The case of New France is fertile ground for this intense debate. Was it a capitalist society, or did it develop in a pre-capitalist context—namely, mercantilism—during which the economy was driven by the exchange sphere and feudal relations of production?

Jean Hamelin (1960) has tried to demonstrate that during the French regime the essential ingredients of capitalist development were missing. First, there was an absence of indigenous capital accumulation, because most of the profits derived from the fur trade were returned to France. Second, the necessary conditions for the creation of a "free" labour force did not exist, because there was such easy access to small parcels of landed property. In these conditions, surplus labour did not exist, and it was impossible for capitalism to emerge. On the other hand, a prominent author, Cameron Nish (1968), has maintained that New France had an extensive bourgeoisie (the majority of whom returned to France after the Conquest, resulting in the longstanding economic weakness of French Canadians thereafter), and that therefore it was a capitalist society.

Throughout the New France era, France was engaged in endless wars with Britain both overseas and in North America. The war that started in 1756 and culminated in the British Conquest of New France was part of the Seven Year War, which France and England fought for international economic hegemony. Its battleground stretched from Europe to North America. Ultimately, France concentrated its efforts in Europe, while Britain sent more contingents to North America. In 1758 the British conquered French Acadia, and by 1760 they had made their way up the St. Lawrence, first to Quebec City, and then to Montreal, where the French capitulated on September 8, 1760. With the Treaty of Paris, signed on February 10, 1763, France gave up Canada, Acadia, and the left bank of the Mississippi. It retained only the islands of St. Pierre and Miquelon and fishing rights to the Newfoundland banks (Hamelin and Provencher 1987: 38).

1.2   THE CONQUEST AND THE BRITISH REGIME: 1760–1867

In a sense, there was continuity between the British and the French regimes. Quebec could still be characterized as pre-capitalist and pre-democratic up to the end of the 1840s. The guiding principles of economic development continued to be those of mercantilism; exchange of goods was still the raison d'être of the colony. At the same time, the list of natural resources exported to Britain in exchange for manufactured goods expanded over the years. Thanks to tariff barriers, Canadian merchants also benefitted from privileged access to British markets, until Britain's repeal of the Corn Laws in 1846. This repeal officially marked Britain's acceptance of the principle of free trade.

Until then, however, Britain exercised strict control over the colony's economic development. Various Navigation and Trade Acts protected Britain's monopoly on trade and banned the production of industrial goods within the colony. Certain types of machinery were banned from entering the colony, as were certain categories of skilled workers. Thus, many products could not be produced in the colony and had to be imported from Britain. And because it was still controlled from without, Quebec's economy remained more or less what it had been under the French regime: rooted in and dependent upon the sphere of exchange or circulation—as opposed to the sphere of production—of goods. In short, Quebec's economy remained pre-capitalist, and this structure was reinforced by the workings of the internal component of the economy.

Given the more advanced state and quasi-capitalistic nature of the British economy, one might have expected the British to be somewhat repulsed by the feudal overtones of the French seigneurial tenure, and seek to abolish it or at the very least refuse to support it. Exactly the opposite happened, however: British merchants were quick to buy seigneuries that came up for sale. Between 1782 and 1840 they purchased 52.7% of the seigneuries sold in Lower Canada (Ouellet 1977: 203); Filteau (1975: 53) estimates that by 1837 English Canadian merchants controlled nearly 50% of all seigneuries. Moreover, their management practices were more "feudal" than the rules and regulations contained in the Coutume de Paris. For instance, these merchants/seigneurs raised rents on a regular basis, whereas the Coutume specified fixed rents in perpetuity. When the peasants of the seigneuries fell into arrears in their rent, the seigneurs made them sign a new contract at a higher rent. In short the feudal nature of the system was actually reinforced after the Conquest, as various seigneurial rights that had never been used were put into effect. These consisted mostly of taxes paid for fishing and hunting rights on the seigneurial domain, the appropriation of timber by the seigneurs, and the renewed exploitation of corvées for the construction of infrastructures such as roads and bridges.

These practices and the widespread land speculation and monopolization of non-seigneurial land—i.e. Crown lands—made it difficult for new settlers and sons of peasants from seigneuries to establish themselves. Land could not be obtained at a reasonable price (Bernier and Salée 1992, ch. 2). This resulted in a surplus in the labour force, because individuals who could not afford to buy land moved to the cities only to discover that there were no jobs due to Britain's prohibition of manufacturing. This triggered a massive exodus of French Canadians to the United States, especially to the New England states, that peaked at the end of the 19th century and did not end until the Great Depression of the 1930s (Lavoie 1981; Roby 1990). It is estimated that between 1840 and 1930, 900,000 Quebecers, most of them of French origin, migrated to the United States.

Speculating as to the effect of this migration on present-day Quebec's French population, Yolande Lavoie (1981) has stated that, all else being equal, in 1971 Quebec's French population might have been around 9 million instead of 4.8 million. She also points out that this estimate depends on a number of assumptions, most notably the fertility rate, which might have been different had there not been the possibility of migrating to the United States, and should be used with caution. Nonetheless, there is no doubt that Quebec's French population was significantly depleted in the 19th and early 20th century due to British colonial policy, as expressed in land management practices and restrictions on the development of an industrial sector. (See Tables 1.1 and 1.2.)

Politically, Quebec went through several constitutional regimes before the creation of the Canadian federation in 1867 (see Table 1.3). None of

Table 1.1

Rates of Increase of Quebec Population
(various years and census years as of 1851)

	Quebec Population	% of Increase
1765	67,810	26.90
1784	113,012	61.88
1790	161,311	42.74
1806	250,000	54.98
1814	335,000	34.00
1822	427,465	27.60
1831	553,134	29.39
1844	697,084	26.02
1851	890,261	27.67
1861	1,111,566	24.86
1871	1,191,516	7.19
1881	1,359,027	14.06
1891	1,488,535	9.53
1901	1,648,898	10.77
1911	2,005,776	21.64
1921	2,361,199	17.72
1931	2,874,662	21.78
1941	3,331,882	15.91
1951	4,055,681	21.72
1956	4,628,378	14.12
1961	5,259,211	13.63
1966	5,780,845	9.92
1971	6,027,764	4.27
1976	6,234,445	3.43
1981	6,438,403	3.27
1986	6,532,461	1.50
1991	6,846,000	4.58

Sources: *Annuaire de la statistique du Québec, 1926*, p. 41;
Annuaire du Québec, 1977–1978, p. 253; Statistics Canada,
Census, 1981; Statistics Canada, *Census, 1986, 1991.*

these regimes could be termed a democracy by today's standards. True, in
1848, when the colony was granted responsible government, Cabinet
became accountable for its actions to the elected representatives of the
people, and it became possible for the House of Assembly to overthrow

Table 1.2

Net Migration to United States of Persons Born in
Province of Quebec
(approximate numbers, 1840–1930)

Period	Migration (in thousands)	Percentage of Total Population by Decade
1840–1850	35.0	5.4
1850–1860	70.0	7.8
1860–1870	100.0*	—
1870–1880	120.0	10.1
1880–1890	150.0	11.3
1890–1900	140.0	9.6
1900–1910	100.0	6.0
1910–1920	80.0	4.0
1920–1930	130.0	5.6
TOTAL	925.0	

Source: Lavoie (1981): 53.

*Gross estimate.

the government should a majority of members vote against legislation put
forth by the Cabinet or acquiesce to a motion of non-confidence. However, such instances would be rather rare under the two-party British parliamentary system, because the governing party usually has a majority of
representation and party discipline is strictly enforced and adhered to by
majority members of the House. Though the later Union Act regime
(1840–1867) was prone to political instability, with Cabinets regularly
being overthrown. This period was exceptional in Canadian history, and
was due to the nature of that constitutional system, which required a
majority vote from both the Assemblies (of Upper and Lower Canada—see
below) for the passage of any legislation—i.e., it operated under the so-
called *double majority principle*.

The Constitutional Act of 1791 had divided Quebec into two sections,
Upper and Lower Canada, roughly corresponding to present-day Ontario
and Quebec respectively. The main feature of this constitution was the
introduction of an elected House of Assembly. In the beginning of that
period, almost all family heads over 21 years of age had the right to vote;
for the time, it was tantamount to universal suffrage. In fact, however, the
system was democratic only in appearance. The elected representatives
were perennially held in check by members of the Legislative Council,
who had the right to veto any legislation passed by the Assembly. For a
bill to become law, it had to be passed by both the House and the

Table 1.3

Various Quebec Constitutions Under the British Regime
(1760–1867)

Year and Act	Political Institutions	Other Features
1763—The Royal Proclamation	• Governor • 12-member Council with executive and legislative powers	• Access to the civil service and to political functions contingent upon renouncing the Catholic faith under oath • Introduction of British Law
The 1774 Quebec Act	• Governor • Executive Council • Legislative Council composed of between 17 to 23 members	• Reestablishment of French civil law • British criminal law • Reestablishment of the Catholic faith with freedom of religion and the right of the Church to collect the tithe
The 1791 Constitutional Act	• Governor • 9-member Executive Council • 15-member Legislative Council • Creation of an elective House of Assembly	• Quebec divided into two colonies: Upper Canada (today's province of Ontario) and Lower Canada (today's province of Quebec) • Establishment of the Church of England and its granting of 1/7 of Crown Lands known as Clergy Reserves
The Union Act of 1840	• Governor • Executive Council • Legislative Council • House of Assembly • Equal representation of both provinces within the Councils and the House of Assembly, despite Quebec's population being considerably higher than that of Ontario until 1850.	• The two Colonies are reunited under the name "Province of Canada" or "United Canada" • Both provinces retain their legal systems • English declared the official language • In 1848, the province granted responsible government, whereby Cabinet responsible for its actions before the House of Assembly • In 1848, French reestablished as the second official language

Legislative Council. The Council was liable to block legislation emanating from the House; between 1822 and 1836, for example, it vetoed 234 bills proposed by the House (Ryerson 1972: 57).

This is hardly surprising, since members of the Legislative Council, often large land owners, were nominated to their position by the Governor subject to the approval of Imperial authorities. In many cases, the same individuals sat in the Executive and Legislative Councils or served in the civil service.

Up until 1848, then, Quebec's system of government had more in common with the absolutist governments of western Europe than modern democracies. It was clearly an *ancien régime* form of government, characterized by concentration of all powers in the hands of the executive branch, centralization of authority (e.g., there were no local governments), confusion and overlapping of powers, impunity of the civil servants, who were not accountable to the voters for their actions, and political domination of landed interests. The resulting supremacy of the landowning class was, in a sense, the logical counterpart of its hegemonic position in the economy.

The tumultuous decade of the 1830s had culminated in the populist uprisings of 1837–1838. These uprisings were the result of growing frictions caused by British colonial rule and exacerbated by land monopolization and speculation (Bernier and Salée 1992, ch. 4) Lord Durham, in his report on the causes of these uprisings, cited deep-seated antagonism between the two ethnic communities, and recommended a fusion of Upper and Lower Canada, with the intention of assimilating the French into the dominant British society. The Union Act of 1840 was an attempt at such assimilation. It was not successful, and the French started to develop a conservative defensive nationalism (i.e., the *survivance* ideology—see Chapter 3) and a siege mentality that set in shortly after confederation (1867) and remained until the end of the Duplessis era (1936–1959).

In many ways, British colonial rule ended with the attainment of responsible government in 1848, as the logical conclusion to the repeal of the Corn Laws in 1846, whereby Britain put an end to the protective tariffs granted to its colonies. With such economic links severed, it became less justifiable for Britain to exert political dominance, and by the end of the decade it was significantly lessened. In addition to responsible government, the Province of Canada acquired freedom of trade, and all restrictions on industrial production were lifted.

From this perspective, it is clear that the federal system established in 1867 was more the result of an internal arrangement among the elites of the British North American colonies (i.e., the two provinces of Canada, plus New Brunswick and Nova Scotia) than a dictate from Imperial authorities, even though Confederation formally came about through an act passed by the British parliament. This is why, in 1981, when the Trudeau government decided that the time had come to make fundamental changes to the Constitution, an act of the British parliament was required to patriate the 1867 constitution.

On July 1, 1867, modern Canada was born and Quebec was one of the four founding provinces. The federal arrangement of 1867 was founded both in political and in economic reality. The political reality dictated that Lower and Upper Canada be kept separate, as they had been under the Constitutional Act of 1791, so that each province could govern internal matters as it saw fit. On the other hand, the economic reality was the very costly ongoing construction of the railroads. All the British colonies were severely indebted to British investors and banks, and the completion of the east-west railroad system was in serious jeopardy. There was great pressure from British financial circles to consolidate the debts. One way of doing so, favoured by British authorities, was to create a federation. A strong centralistic structure was also preferred to avoid the centrifugal forces that were seen to be causing the breakup of the American federation in a civil war.

1.3 EARLY FEDERALISM: 1867–1920

While the Fathers of Confederation wanted a strong central government, they left matters of local or regional concern to the provinces. Little did they know that the powers given to the provinces in 1867 would work endless mischief for the central government in the 20th century.

Among the provincial domains enumerated in Article 92 of the 1867 constitution are health, education, and welfare— i.e., those fields of jurisdiction that form the basis of the modern welfare state. Yet the provinces are allowed only the power of direct taxation, whereas the federal government can draw its revenues from whatever sources it chooses. Eventually the federal government itself began to fund and initiate several social programs and involved itself in health care and higher education so that, to this day, the central government annually transfers billions of dollars to the provinces to help defray the cost of these programs.

This development and funding of social programs has been a constant source of friction between Quebec and Ottawa. From the days of Duplessis to the present, successive Quebec governments have denounced—though not always for the same reasons—what they perceived as an intrusion by the federal authorities into matters that officially concern the provinces.

Back in 1867, during the process of distributing respective powers, the provincial governments were seen as little more than modified municipal governments. Quebec's main source of revenue up until the 1920s—with the exception of 1900–1901—was transfers from the federal government. Right from the start of Canadian federalism, the notion of transfer payments was a fundamental principle of intergovernmental relations. The Constitution provided for the annual transfer of a lump sum of $70,000 plus 80 cents per capita based on population figures derived from the 1861 census (Hamelin and Provencher 1987: 72). The province's main internal sources of revenue were logging and mineral rights and the sale of Crown lands, and later on, Quebec developed additional sources, such as permits and licences, capital gain taxes, inheritance taxes, and so on. Overall revenues, however, proved insufficient. In 1887, in the first interprovincial conference, called by Honoré Mercier and attended by four other premiers, it was resolved to demand that: (1) the federal government raise the amounts transferred to the provinces, (2) the provinces have a say in the appointment of senators by the federal government, and (3) Ottawa give up its right to disavow provincial legislation. At least two of these themes resonate today: fiscal federalism and Senate reform.

This was also the period of Quebec's first steps toward an industrial economy. First came the transformation of agricultural products in the 1870s. Quebec agriculture had up to then specialized in dairy production, and the first rural industrial products were butter and cheese. Later on during this period, Quebec developed what are now known as the traditional or "soft" sectors of its economy. The availability of cheap labour enabled entrepreneurs to fully develop such labour-intensive sectors as leather, textiles, clothing, lumber processing, and furniture-making, the foundations of Quebec's first wave of industrialization. Toward the end of the period, the availability of inexpensive hydro electric power enabled the province to begin developing its natural resources sector (Piédalue 1976a, 1976b). Aluminum was the first heavy industry to emerge, followed by paper mills for the production of pulp and paper. Asbestos mining began to be exploited at the turn of the century. The transportation industry, mainly activities related to railway construction (e.g., train wagons), also became an important element of Quebec's manufacturing sector, boosting the steel industry as numerous foundries produced railroad tracks (Table 1.4).

During this period, Quebec society underwent a transition from rural to urban. The 1921 census showed that a majority of the population lived in urban centres and that Quebec had more or less the same urbanization rate as Ontario. However, there were fundamental differences between Quebec's and Ontario's urban population distribution. Whereas Ontario had numerous small and medium-sized urban centres, Quebec's urban population was concentrated in the Montreal metropolitan area. This phenomenon was quite significant; it meant that industrialization in Quebec was concentrated in the Montreal area whereas in Ontario it was spread throughout the province (Table 1.5). Thus, almost from the beginning, Quebec faced problems of regional economic disparity—uneven development—while Ontario experienced a developmental pattern of widespread industrialization.

The Church became a major social and political force during this period. It had faced a liberal lay challenge during the 1830s and 1850s. But

Table 1.4

Manufacturing Sector in Quebec, 1851–1901

(value of production in dollars)

Sector	1851	1861	1871	1881	1891	1901
Food	153,504	3,830,307	18,650,000	22,440,000	34,700,000	33,099,000
Tobacco		262,050	1,430,000	1,750,000	3,600,000	8,231,000
Rubber						39,000
Leather	103,720	1,206,527	14,330,000	21,680,000	18,900,000	20,325,000
Textile	46,528	788,316	1,340,000	2,400,000	4,300,000	12,352,000
Clothing		28,000	5,850,000	10,040,000	13,600,000	16,542,000
Wood	187,276	4,155,693	11,690,000	12,790,000	18,500,000	16,340,000
Pulp and paper		268,200	540,000	1,342,000	2,300,000	6,461,000
Iron and steel	45,200	1,472,680	3,130,000	4,220,000	7,600,000	12,842,000
Printing and publishing			1,250,000	1,830,000	2,300,000	3,510,000
Transportation equipment		648,041	2,910,000	3,600,000	9,900,000	8,058,000
Primary metals						1,497,000
Electrical products		47,300			400,000	1,815,000
Non-metallic mineral products		321,390				1,630,000
Petroleum and coal						245,000
Chemical products		130,600				4,138,000
Miscellaneous		35,750	1,510,000	2,490,000	4,270,000	1,342,000

Source: Jean Hamelin and Yves Roby, *Histoire économique du Québec 1851–1896* (Montreal: Fides, 1971), p. 267.

Table 1.5

Distribution of Urban Population

(according to size of towns)

1. Number of Towns

POPULATION	Quebec			Ontario		
	1850	1860	1870	1850	1860	1870
25,000+	2	2	2	1	1	2
5,000 to 25,000	0	1	3	4	8	10
1,000 to 5,000	14	18	22	33	50	69
TOTAL	16	21	27	38	59	81

2. Population Distribution, Urban and Rural (in thousands)

Towns with Population of	Quebec			Ontario		
	1850	1860	1870	1850	1860	1870
25,000+	100	141	167	31	45	83
5,000 to 25,000	0	6	20	41	83	95
1,000 to 5,000	31	39	42	67	108	149
Total urban	131	187	229	139	236	328
Total population	890	1,112	1,192	952	1,396	1,621
Percentage of urban	14.7%	16.8%	19.2%	14.6%	16.9%	20.2%

Source: John McCallum, *Unequal Beginnings* (Toronto: University of Toronto Press, 1980), p. 55.

3. Compared Urbanization Rates, Canada, Quebec, Ontario: 1851–1986 (in percentages)

	1851	1871	1891	1911	1931	1951	1971	1981	1986
Canada	13.1	18.3	29.8	41.8	52.5	62.9	76.6	75.8	76.5
Ontario	14.0	20.6	35.0	49.5	63.1	72.5	82.4	81.7	82.1
Quebec	14.9	19.9	28.6	44.5	59.5	66.8	80.0	77.6	77.9

Sources: Statistics Canada, *Census*, 1971 and 1981; L. O. Stone, *Urban Development in Canada* (Ottawa: Statistics Canada, 1967).

as of 1840, the clergy and religious orders experienced a formidable expansion, due to an influx from France where various religious orders were being banned. The ratio of priests to parishioners went from a low of 1:1,834 in 1830 to 1:578 by 1920 (Hamelin 1961: 238). The Church began to adopt more-modern means—such as a Catholic press—to challenge its critics, and increased the opportunity for public manifestations of faith by creating new religious ceremonies. Eventually, all dimensions of social and community life were carried out under the Church's aegis. The relationship between Church and State was characterized by a division of labour: education, health, and welfare institutions became the responsibility of the Church, which subsequently came to control all French schools, hospitals, and welfare agencies; on the other hand, the state was able to provide services without paying for labour (except for the few lay persons who worked in the system). Thus, until the Quiet Revolution of the 1960s, the parish formed the locus of all social organizations.

From the 1870s on, the Church also defined and controlled the dominant ideology, which frowned on industrialization and urbanization and viewed agriculture not only as the ideal activity around which to build a society, but also as the divinely ordained vocation of the French Canadian

The Church played a key role in the social development of Quebec. Shown here is the parent establishment of the Bon Pasteur sisters on rue de la Chevrotière in Quebec City. [Courtesy Archives nationales du Québec.]

people. The Church clung to this perspective well into the 1950s (Trudeau 1970), ignoring the fact that Quebec was not well suited to agriculture: aside from the inhospitable climate, only a small fraction of Quebec soil can be cultivated. The Church also failed to acknowledge that Quebec had irreversibly changed into an industrial, urban society. While influential politicians may have paid lip service to the Church's views, they continued to foster a modern, industrial Quebec through their actions.

1.4 CONSERVATISM AND DEPENDENCY: 1920–1960

Politically speaking, this period is essentially the story of two men, Louis-Alexandre Taschereau and Maurice Duplessis, except for two intervals (June–August 1936 *and* November 1939–August 1944) when a Liberal Premier, Adélard Godbout, led the government. Taschereau, also a Liberal, headed the government from July 1920 to June 1936. Duplessis, a Conservative who later created a new party known as the *Union nationale* (Quinn 1979), was Premier from August 1936 until June 1939, and again from August 1944 until his death in September 1959.

The two men and their governments had more in common than might be expected given their different political affiliations. Taschereau and Duplessis had a common view of Quebec society. They both presided over

Louis-Alexandre Taschereau, Liberal leader, and Premier of Quebec from 1920 to 1936. [Courtesy Bibliothèque nationale du Québec.]

Maurice Duplessis, Union nationale *leader, and Premier of Quebec from 1936 to 1939 and 1944 to 1959. [Courtesy Archives nationales du Québec. Photo: David Bier.]*

Quebec's second wave of economic development and industrialization, which rested on the exploitation of natural resources and the opening up of northern Quebec ("Le nouveau Quebec") under Duplessis. Their approach to economic development was based on pure 19th-century laissez-faire, and rested on the use of foreign capital, mainly American capital. This second wave of development involved three sectors: (1) pulp and paper mills, and the accompanying extensive exploitation of Quebec forests; (2) mining of all sorts (especially iron ore on Quebec's north shore after 1940); and (3) hydroelectric power, with its industrial spinoffs such as aluminum production and pulp and paper mills.

This development was essentially geared to an external market. It was a form of dependent development. Quebec's natural resources were exported to the United States, and to a lesser extent Ontario, and returned in the form of industrial goods. In order to attract necessary investments, both Taschereau and Duplessis implemented such policies as tax reliefs, subsidies, the construction of the necessary infrastructure at taxpayers' expense, concessions in perpetuity of Crown lands, the chartering of company towns, the sale of waterfalls to private interests at very low prices, and so on.

The justification for such measures was the belief that Quebec could not generate from within the huge amounts of capital necessary to develop its own natural resources. Of course, given their economic liberalism, Taschereau and Duplessis never considered that the State might help finance these large-scale projects. It was believed that the State had no business in the economic sphere—despite the advent of Keynesian economics —and that the overall role of the State should be as limited as possible.

The weakness of the Quebec government's position vis-à-vis foreign investors is put in proper perspective when government expenditures are taken into consideration. During the first year of the Taschereau regime, the provincial budget totalled only $26.2 million. When Duplessis first came to power in 1936, the budget was $72.2 million. In 1945, at the time of Duplessis' return to power, it was $108 million, and in 1959, when the regime ended, it had reached a mere $598 million. (Compare this to $35.3 billion for the fiscal year 1990–1991.) These governments adhered to the principle that the less you spend, the better off you are, and considered it unimaginable for a government to create a deficit.

Another reason for such solicitude toward American investments was the sheer necessity to create jobs for Quebecers. This point is often ignored when passing judgement on the Taschereau and Duplessis administrations. At times, Quebec has had the highest birthrate among the white population of the Western world; between 1761 and 1770, it went as high as 56.8 per thousand population. For the period under consideration, it was substantially higher than the Canadian average and the rate in Ontario. During this period, Quebec increased its population by only slightly less than 20% every decade, and most of this growth was due to natural reproduction. At the same time, migration to the United States had ceased, except for the decade 1920–1930. There was no external outlet for surplus population; moreover, Quebec had begun to receive its share of immigrants (although it was modest in comparison with Ontario's). The only alternative to job creation in the exploitation of natural resources and in the manufacturing sectors was to try to colonize remote regions such as the Abitibi, Témiscamingue, Lac St-Jean, Saguenay, and the Upper Laurentians, which were basically unfit for agriculture or cattle breeding. Both administrations resorted to such colonization schemes until the 1950s. Thus, as mentioned, the task of job creation should be taken into account in judging the economic policies of the Taschereau and Duplessis administrations.

The costs of these policies were borne mainly by the working class. In making their pitch to foreign investors, both Premiers stressed that Quebec had an abundant reserve of cheap and docile labour. A variety of laws made unionization difficult and when unionization did occur in a given industry or sector, it was often encouraged to be under the aegis of the Confédération des travailleurs catholiques du Canada (CTCC). It was well known that CTCC unions rarely went on strike, and that the "moral advisor" (i.e., a priest) had the right to veto a strike vote. For instance, between 1915 and 1936, the CTCC initiated only 9 of the 507 strikes that took place in Quebec. Analysts of the period are quick to criticize the CTCC for its submissiveness, if not outright collaboration, with employers and capital in general. There is no doubt that this occurred, but these same analysts often fail to observe that had it not been for the CTCC, thousands of small-shop employees in remote areas of the province would never have been unionized. These workers were of no interest to American affiliated unions, which went after the larger plants and skilled labour.

The working class was subjected to severe governmental repression on many occasions, especially when it went on strike in American-controlled plants (Dumas 1971; Rouillard 1989; FTQ–CEQ 1984). Among the most famous strikes were those that took place in asbestos mining (1949), textile production in Louiseville (1952), and iron ore extraction in Murdochville (1957). The provincial police acted in a repressive manner in all instances. They used the force of arms against the strikers and there were several casualties. These events gave rise to serious questions about Duplessis' mode of administration and economic policies, even in circles close to the Establishment.

The working class and the population in general suffered from these policies in other ways. In order to keep labour costs as low as possible, it was imperative that redistributive measures and other welfare-state initiatives be suppressed or kept at a minimum. Quebec therefore lagged behind the rest of Canada in health care, education, and social security. A contributing factor was the fact that most welfare-state measures had been introduced by the federal government, and Quebec, fearing impingement on provincial fields of jurisdiction, refused to participate in these programs (e.g., unemployment insurance, hospitalization costs, manpower training, technical schools, etc.).

Duplessis covered all this with talk of provincial rights and "autonomy." It is unclear whether this intelligent man believed his own rhetoric, or was simply caught in a bind, truly thinking that socioeconomic dictates (the need to create jobs) had to take precedence. Nevertheless, Duplessis-bashing has been a favourite sport among Quebec intellectuals for the past three decades; seldom have the overall societal circumstances under which his administration governed been taken into consideration. This is not to excuse the abuses, repressive measures, and corruption practices that took place during his administration, but merely to try to put this period in its proper perspective.

Thetford Mines, a company-owned asbestos city, circa 1971. The modern period of Quebec nationalism is often dated from the 1949 asbestos strike, which involved 5,000 workers and lasted four months. [Courtesy Archives nationales du Québec.]

Because welfare programs had been kept to a minimum, Quebec's urban centres, and especially Montreal, suffered under Third World conditions well into the 1950s (Roy 1976), with poor housing, high infant mortality rates, poverty, lack of proper medical care, an outdated school system, questionable sanitary conditions, etc. Of course, the Catholic Church continued to provide minimal health, social, and educational services, at no great cost to the State; however, these services became more and more outdated.

During the 1950s, progressive forces—among the unions, the intellectuals, the press (most prominently Montreal's *Le Devoir*), Laval University's Social Sciences Faculty, and even some segments of the Catholic Church—mounted an attack on the conservative forces and ills of Quebec society that the Duplessis regime had come to symbolize. They complained that Quebec was dragging its heels in every field (Behiels 1985). For instance, Quebecers had the lowest average number of years of schooling in Canada, despite Duplessis' insistence that Quebec had the best education system in the world; urban dwellers had been neglected by a Parliament whose majority represented rural electoral districts; there were no housing programs, sanitary conditions were abominable, vocational training was minimal, welfare programs run by the municipalities showed great discrepancies from city to city, medical facilities lacked modern equipment, the elitist school system allowed only those from private and tuitional classical colleges to attend university; the list went on and on. Partly due to this campaign, by the end of the 1950s there was so much discontent at every level of Quebec society, and the desire for change was so great, that the regime did not survive the death of its leader. In the June election of 1960, the Liberal party, headed by Jean Lesage, won handily – and the era known as the Quiet Revolution began.

1.5   THE QUIET REVOLUTION AND ITS AFTERMATH: 1960 TO THE PRESENT DAY

As the other chapters in this book deal in detail with the various aspects of the period from 1960 to the present, only a brief mention of certain events will be made here.

The Liberal victory of 1960 inaugurated an era of statism, as Quebecers came to realize that they had a collective instrument of development at their disposal and could use it to catch up with the rest of the industrialized Western world. This they did throughout the 1960s and until the end of 1970s, regardless of which political party happened to be in power. There was a political consensus that the State and the various state-owned enterprises created through the years should play a fundamental role in developing all sectors of Quebec society.

This developmental model had its limits, however. Revenue sources were limited, because of the division of fiscal powers between the federal government and the provinces. Most instruments of economic policy rested with the federal government, which controlled monetary policy, international trade, foreign investment, and a large part of fiscal policy.

Quebec had to confront these limits at about the time the Parti québécois (PQ) came to power in 1976. In fact, there is an intimate connection between these two events, in that State-building efforts had greatly contributed to the rise of nationalism in Quebec. Succeeding governments

Alcan Company in Arvida, 1966. [Courtesy Archives nationales du Québec.]

had begun operating under the often-unconscious assumption that Quebec was an independent country. State-building had fuelled nation-building and the rise and access to power of the Parti quebecois seemed, in this context, to be a logical conclusion to this process. Throughout the period, tensions grew steadily between the federal government and Quebec, as Quebec continually pressed for more and more powers.

At first, during the 1960s, the province was granted what it asked for. This sparked resentment in the other Canadian provinces and they too began to engage in a process of autonomization. However, the Quebec political class was slow to perceive fully these developments, continuing to view the rest of Canada as a unified monolith. Nothing better exemplifies this than the PQ's elaborations on the "association" component of its "sovereignty-association" project. For a long time, one was hard pressed to find any references to other provinces in PQ documents on the negotiation process; there were only references to the federal government, or use of the vague expression "the rest of Canada." The assumption was that Ottawa spoke for an English Canada that had but one voice. That perception was shattered during the Meech Lake accord ratification debate of June 1990.

Whether it remains within the Canadian federation or chooses to become an independent country, Quebec will be faced with crucial economic decisions over the next decade. Given its industrial structure, Quebec ought to be worried about extension of the U.S.-Canada Free Trade Agreement (FTA) to Mexico. Its traditional sectors are in risk of being seriously jeopardized. So far, the federal government has procured maximum protection for these sectors at various GATT[1] conferences; ultimately, however, this kind of protection may have done more harm than good, by preventing Quebec from pursuing the profitable course of diversifying its economy more rapidly over the past 30 years. One wonders if the political parties have any sense of urgency about these matters. The recession of the early 1990s has shown the vulnerability of Quebec's so-called economic giants, products of "Quebec's economic miracle," which in most instances were developed and sustained through governmental support in one form or another. In view of the North American Free Trade Agreement (NAFTA), Quebec ought to seriously examine the viability of its industrial and financial superstars without the state support they have received so far. Such an exercise might dampen the unmitigated support that has been given to the liberalization of trade on the North American continent.

KEY TERMS

Capitalism	**Disavow**
Capitalist mode of production	**Double majority principle**
Coureurs des bois	**Mercantilism**
Coutume de Paris	**Québécois or Quebecer**
Democracy	**Redistributive measures**

---

1. General Agreement on Tariffs and Trade.

REFERENCES AND FURTHER READING

Armstrong, Robert. 1984. *Structure and Change: An Economic History of Quebec.* Toronto: Gage Publishing Limited.

Behiels, Michael D. 1985. *Prelude to the Quiet Revolution: Liberalism Versus Neo-Nationalism, 1945–1960.* Montreal: McGill-Queen's University Press.

Bernier, Gérald. 1988. "Landownership and access to political power in Lower Canada, 1791–1838." *Quebec Studies*, 7: 87–97.

Bernier, Gérald and Daniel Salée. 1992. *The Shaping of Quebec Politics and Society: Colonialism, Power, and the Transition to Capitalism in the 19th Century.* Washington: Crane Russak.

Berthet, Thierry. "Le processus d'autonomisation dans les colonies de peuplement: le cas de la "Nouvelle-France." Ph.D. dissertation (Political Science). Montreal: Université de Montréal.

Brun, Henri. 1970. *La formation des institutions parlementaires québécoises, 1791–1838.* Quebec: Les Presses de l'Université Laval.

Brunet, Michel. 1957. "Trois dominantes de la pensée canadienne-française: l'agriculture, le messianisme et l'anti-étatisme." *Écrits du Canada français*, 3: 33–115.

Comeau, Robert and Paul-André Linteau. 1965. "Une question historiographique: une bourgeoisie en Nouvelle-France." In *Économie québécoise.* Ed. Robert Comeau. Pp. 311–323.

Dobb, Maurice. 1963. *Studies in the Development of Capitalism.* London: Routledge and Kegan Paul.

Dubuc, Alfred. 1966. "Une interprétation économique de la Constitution." *Socialisme 66*, 7: 3–22.

Dumas, Evelyne. 1971. *Dans le sommeil de nos os.* Montreal: Léméac.

F.T.Q.-C.E.Q. 1984. *Histoire du mouvement ouvrier au Québec.* Montreal: F.T.Q.-C.S.N.

Filteau, Gérard. 1975. *Histoire des Patriotes.* Montreal: L'Aurore.

Frank, André Gunder. 1978. *World Accumulation, 1492–1789.* New York: Monthly Review Press.

Gow, James Iain. 1986. *Histoire de l'administration publique québécoise, 1867–1970.* Montreal: Presses de l'Université de Montreal. P. 20.

Hamelin, Jean. 1960. *Économie et société en Nouvelle-France.* Quebec: Les presses de l'Université Laval.

Hamelin, Jean and Yves Roby. 1971. *Histoire économique du Québec, 1851–1896.* Montreal: Fides.

Hamelin, Jean and Jean Provencher. 1987. *Brève histoire du Québec.* Montreal: Boréal.

Hamelin, Louis-Edmond. 1961. "Évolution numérique séculaire du clergé catholique dans le Québec." *Recherches sociographiques*, 2 (2): 189–241.

Lavoie, Yolande. 1981. *L'émigration des Québécois aux États-Unis de 1840 à 1930*. Quebec: Éditeur officiel du Québec.

Linteau, Paul-André et al. 1989. *Histoire du Québec contemporain: Le Québec depuis 1930*. Revised and enlarged edition. Montreal: Boréal compact.

Miquelon, Dale. 1977. *Society and Conquest: The Debate on the Bourgeoisie and Social Change in French Canada, 1700–1850*. Toronto: Copp Clark.

Nish, Cameron. 1968. *Les bourgeois-gentilshommes de la Nouvelle-France, 1729–1748*. Montreal: Fides.

Ouellet, Fernand. 1977. "Proprieté seigneuriale et groupes sociaux dans la vallée du Saint-Laurent (1663–1840)." *Revue de l'Université d'Ottawa*, 47 (January–April): 183–213.

Piédalue, Gilles. 1976a. "Les groupes financiers du Canada 1900–1930: Étude préliminaire." *Revue d'histoire de l'Amérique française* 30 (1) (June): 3–34.

Piédalue, Gilles. 1976b. "Les groupes financiers et la guerre du papier au Canada 1920–1930." *Revue d'histoire de l'Amérique française*, 30 (2) (September): 223–258.

Quinn, Herbert. 1979. *The Union Nationale: Quebec Nationalism from Duplessis to Lévesque*. 2nd ed. Toronto: University of Toronto Press.

Roby, Yves. 1990. *Les Franco-Américains de la Nouvelle-Angleterre, 1776–1930*. Sillery: Septentrion.

Rouillard, Jacques. 1989. *Histoire du syndicalisme québécois*. Montreal: Boréal.

Roy, Jean-Louis. 1976. *La marche des québécois: Le temps des ruptures (1945–1960)*. Montreal: Léméac.

Ryerson, Stanley B. 1972. *Le capitalisme et la Confédération*. Montreal: Parti Pris.

Smith, C. D. 1974. "The role of land alienation, colonization and the British American Land Company on Quebec's development, 1800–1850." M.A. thesis (History). Montreal: McGill University.

Trigger, Bruce. 1985. *Natives and Newcomers: Canada's "Heroic Age" Reconsidered*. Kingston and Montreal: McGill-Queen's University Press.

Trudeau, Pierre E. 1970. "La province de Québec au moment de la grève." In Pierre E. Trudeau (ed.), *La grève de l'amiante*. Montreal: Éditions du Jour. Pp. 1–93.

Young, Brian and John A. Dickenson. 1988. *A Short History of Quebec: A Socio-Economic Perspective*. Toronto: Copp Clark Pitman.

Wallerstein, Immanuel. 1974. *The Modern World-System I: Capitalist Agriculture and the Origins of the European World-Economy in the Sixteenth Century*. New York: Academic Press.

CHAPTER 2

QUEBEC
AND
CANADIAN
FEDERALISM

The relationships between Quebec and Ottawa have been the subject of
much study and debate. To many observers, the nature of these relationships—and for that matter, relationships between Quebec and the rest of
Canada—are at the heart of the current constitutional quandary. Quebec,
it is argued, has been a disruptive force in Canadian politics for the past 30
years, forcing a redefinition of Canadian federalism. Though Quebec has
not been alone in calling for this redefinition. However, unlike the other
provinces—whose demands have generally centred on working out an
administrative equilibrium with Ottawa—the province of Quebec has,
through successive governments, sought to find for itself a legitimate and
comfortable place—either within the federation or outside it.

Quebec's aspirations have been and still are perceived as a threat to
Canada's integrity and legitimacy. The central question—What does Quebec
want?—remains a major cause of controversy, bewilderment, and anger.

In this chapter we will investigate relations between Quebec and Ottawa
from a historical perspective. We will try to show that these relations are
part of a complex sociopolitical and administrative dynamic , and not just
a question of Quebec capriciously and exasperatingly "begging to differ."

2.1 THE DYNAMICS OF
CANADIAN FEDERALISM

It is almost impossible to understand Quebec's specific motivations and
expectations vis-à-vis the Canadian constitutional arrangement without

first addressing the structural and political parameters within which Canadian federalism has evolved. True, Quebec's demanding stance undoubtedly stems partly from the emancipatory, assertive approach of its political leaders during the Quiet Revolution. But Quebec is also part of a larger political and administrative system that, more often than not, influences public policy issues. Quebec has been responding as much to the historical realities of Canadian federalism as to the tendencies of its own internal dynamics.

The history of Canadian federalism has been characterized by ambiguity from the beginning. It was never clearly established whether the Canadian federation rested on truly federal or only quasi-federal principles. The Constitution does indeed abide by certain basic criteria normally used to define the bounds of federalism: (1) the Constitution is supreme and cannot be amended by the federal authorities alone, at least in matters pertaining to the powers of the provinces; (2) the national territory is divided into inviolable geographic units, each with a defined and equal sphere of jurisdiction; and (3) judicial protection is guaranteed for the federal system. However, these are undermined by a number of provisions that give the federal government supervisory powers over the provincial governments: (1) the power to appoint both the Lieutenant Governor of the provinces and Superior Court judges responsible for the interpretation of federal and provincial laws; (2) the power exercised by the Lieutenant Governor to disavow (veto) or reserve provincial acts; (3) the subsidy provisions (Articles 118 and 119 of the British North America Act), whereby as much as 50% of provincial revenues comes from direct federal subsidies; (4) the overriding power of the federal parliament to legislate for "peace, order, and good government" (Fitzmaurice 1985: 152).

The ambiguity that has always characterized Canadian federalism stems from the resulting potential for either the provincial or federal government to dominate the management of public policy. Indeed, the history of Canadian federalism has oscillated between centralism and provincialism according to socioeconomic and political/administrative circumstances and judiciary interpretations of the Constitution.

The seemingly arbitrary distribution of powers has also contributed significantly to this ambiguity. There has been frequent confrontation between jurisdictions. Article 91 gives the federal government broad powers to legislate for "peace, order, and good government" in all matters not specifically assigned to the legislatures of the provinces; it indicates as well the precise jurisdiction of the federal government in a variety of areas such as the public debt, property, the regulation of trade and commerce, the postal service, navigation and shipping, and native reservations. Article 92, on the other hand, delineates provincial jurisdiction in areas such as direct taxation in order to raise revenues for provincial purposes, property and civil rights in the province, and most matters of a purely local or private nature; furthermore, the provinces have exclusive jurisdiction over non-renewable natural resources, forestry resources, and electrical energy (Article 92A). Article 93 confirms provincial jurisdiction over education subject to certain provisions that allow federal intervention when minority rights are at stake. Finally, immigration, agriculture, and old age pensions are areas of shared jurisdiction.

The Constitution Act establishes two distinct jurisdictions, provincial and federal. In theory, apart from the shared areas (agriculture, immigration, and old age pensions), each legislature is sovereign within its sphere of power. While the limitations introduced by the entrenchment of the Charter of Rights in 1982 take priority over provincial laws that might violate fundamental rights, provincial legislatures may, under Article 33 of the Constitution Act, 1982, declare a provincial law valid "notwithstanding" the provisions of the Charter—hence the term *notwithstanding clause*, which one hears frequently.

Practice, however, has often blurred the boundaries between jurisdictions. John A. MacDonald, the first prime minister of Canada, always favoured a more centralized system, and—so in spite of the intended structure of the new nation, which implied autonomy as well as unity—a centralizing spirit dominated federal-provincial relations in the first decades of Confederation. In the first ten years, 39 pieces of provincial legislation were reserved and 29 disallowed. In contrast, after thirty years, 51 bills had been reserved and 65 disallowed (Gagnon and Montcalm, 1990: 139).

Several factors may account for the federal tendency to disregard provincial autonomy during those years, and the provinces' disinclination to assert themselves. For the political movers and shakers of the time, Ottawa, not the provincial governments, was seen as "the place to be." Support for a centralist model was reinforced by a massive migration of political talent out of the provinces to Ottawa. The new provincial governments lacked the necessary political jurisdiction to challenge Ottawa's dominance (Gibbins, 1985: 226). In any case, the areas in which the provinces could have made claims, such as health and welfare or energy and resources, were then practically nonexistent or undeveloped. Another factor was the virtual dominance of the Conservative party in politics, which gave additional strength to the federal government (Adie and Thomas, 1987: 430).

But toward the end of the 19th century, Ottawa's stature began to erode as a result of sluggish economic growth. Greater equilibrium between federal and provincial jurisdictions was reached with agricultural settlement in the West and industrialization in central Canada after 1896. The new prosperity made it less essential for the national government to retain strict direction and control. Another significant factor was the policy of the Judicial Committee of the Privy Council (a body of the British Crown that until 1949 decided all constitutional issues in Canada), that usually favoured the provinces, leaving jurisdiction to the federal government in residual areas only. Strong provincial premiers, such as Ontario's Oliver Mowat and Quebec's Honoré Mercier, conducted provincial rights offensives that eventually led to the first interprovincial conference in 1887 and a First Ministers Conference in 1906. These meetings brought substantial increases in financial subsidies to the provinces and a reorganization of the financial arrangements of Confederation.

In fact, between the turn of the century and the onslaught of the Great Depression in 1929, a fairly decentralized version of the classical model of federalism evolved in Canada. Except during the First World War (when the decentralizing tendency momentarily stopped as Ottawa assumed sweeping control over the economy and matters of property and civil rights, hitherto a provincial jurisdiction), the period was characterized by the emergence of Canada as "a collection of smaller communities banded together for instrumental reasons" (Simeon and Robinson, 1990: 56).

Increased provincial autonomy was engendered by many societal forces. Growing urbanization and industrialization, for example, led to increased demands for those services that fell mainly within the provincial sphere (health, education, welfare, local roads). These demands forced provincial governments to seek new sources of revenue. They began to tap personal and corporate taxation in a much bigger way than ever before, and there were new revenues from automobile licensing fees, gasoline taxes, resource royalties, and controlled liquor sales. By 1929, provincial governments had reached "their highest historical level of fiscal autonomy: they received, on average, only 13% of their revenues from federal transfers" (Simeon and Robinson, 1990: 56).

On other fronts, regional collective identities developed in strong opposition to the central government. In the Atlantic provinces, the Maritime Rights Movement of the 1920s emerged largely against central interests. In Quebec, an isolationist, conservative French Canadian nationalism came into being in the aftermath of the conscription crisis of the First World War. By the time the Depression began, a consensus had emerged that Canada was basically an agreement among preexisting parties and no changes could be made without consulting the contracting parties.

Yet this consensus was short-lived. The Depression soon revealed the precarious finances of many provincial governments. The financial power acquired in the preceding years proved insufficient to meet the economic crisis of the 1930s. After the governments of the Prairies and the Maritimes almost went bankrupt, the federal government stepped in with relief measures (welfare and unemployment benefits) and funds for maintenance of the essential services—that is, the federal government began to intervene in areas of provincial jurisdiction. As the number of areas of mutual concern increased, all levels of government scrambled to find additional sources of revenue. Fiscal chaos and administrative competition reigned.

At this point, the 1940 report of the Rowell-Sirois Royal Commission on Dominion-Provincial Relations recommended a major overhaul of the system. Calling for a "unified effort in administration," the report suggested pooling administrative power in key economic and social areas under a single government. Two national economic functions were emphasized: the federally coordinated collection of progressive taxes (income tax, corporate tax, and succession duties) and the introduction of an equitable system of interprovincial redistribution based on equal access for all Canadians to comparable standards of government services at comparable levels of taxation. Similarly, it was suggested that two social policy areas be the exclusive responsibility of the federal government: (1) a national system of unemployment insurance and ancillary programs and (2) a contribution-based old age pension scheme. Ottawa was thus to be the initiator of universal social security. All other forms of social security were to remain provincial responsibilities provided they were offered in accordance with average Canadian standards (Simeon and Robinson, 1990: 106).

The Rowell-Sirois recommendations were not implemented immediately; there was much opposition to them from the wealthier provinces, who felt they would lose out under centralized financial schemes. But the situation created by the Second World War soon brought the federal system closer to the Commission's suggested restructuring. All the provinces were forced during the war to relinquish complete control over personal and corporate income tax fields to the federal government. The war also fostered a huge bureaucratic machine in Ottawa that regulated every aspect of Canadian society during those years. Its attractiveness to highly qualified people was comparable to that exercised by the new national government in 1867 (Gibbins, 1985: 227). The war also contributed to a new sense of national identity and pride that reinforced the role and influence of the federal government.

By war's end, the federal government was at the pinnacle of its power and prestige, while the provincial governments had fallen into comparative insignificance (Stevenson, 1984). Various schemes of fiscal and economic policy had made the federal government the main recipient and manager of public revenue in the country. By the mid-1950s, Ottawa was collecting 75% of all taxes paid by Canadians; the remaining 25% was collected by the provinces and municipalities.

The National Reconstruction Conference of 1945. The beginning of modern federal-provincial relationships. **Left to right:** *Hon. E. C. Manning, Alberta; Hon. J. Walter Jones, P.E.I.; Hon. S. S. Garson, Manitoba; Hon. A. Stirling Macmillan, Nova Scotia; Hon. George Drew, Ontario; Prime Minister W. L. Mackenzie King; Hon. Maurice L. Duplessis, Québec; Hon. J. B. MacNair, New Brunswick; Hon. John Hart, British Columbia; Hon. T. C. Douglas, Saskatchewan. [Courtesy Bibliothèque nationale du Québec.]*

Between 1945 and 1960, it was a heyday for federal centralism. Bolstered by its newfound bureaucratic and financial prominence, the federal government expanded its legislative reach into provincial fields. During the 1950s, drawing on tax money brought in by the booming postwar economy, Ottawa established a series of conditional grant programs or shared-cost agreements in the fields of health care, higher education, and social welfare. Funds for such programs were readily available through five-year tax-rental agreements between the provinces and the federal government, whereby— as during the war years—the federal government acted as the sole tax collector and redistributed the monies to the provinces. These agreements (also called *tax-sharing* agreements) have been renegotiated every five years since 1947; both Quebec and Ontario opted out of the first agreement, but Quebec has remained the only province to opt out continuously, thus establishing, starting in 1954, double taxation system on its territory.

André Laurendeau, Quebec leader of the Bloc populaire *in the early 1940s. In 1947, he had become associate editor-in-chief of the Montreal newspaper* Le Devoir. *In 1948 the* Bloc *dissolved. He advocated economic and social reformism of liberal Catholicism and greater state intervention in the economy. [Courtesy Archives nationales du Québec. Photo: André Laurendeau.]*

Federal participation in the conditional grant programs was essentially in the form of financial support, matching provincial expenditures in return for such conditions as universal accessibility. Although responsibility for choosing which programs to deliver remained with the provinces, conditional grants influenced provincial spending priorities in the direction of areas where matching federal funds were available. To protest federal intrusions, provinces could choose not to participate, as Quebec did on a number of occasions in the 1950s, but this carried a high political and financial cost. Caught between rising demand for services from a growing population and limited fiscal resources, the provinces often had little choice but to accept the grants. In fact, in the postwar period, federal largesse was generally welcomed without a fuss (Gibbins, 1985: 228).

On the face of it, in accepting these grants the provinces were merely retrieving what was rightfully theirs, but they were also enabling the federal government to exercise considerable influence over policy. "The extensive use of shared-cost agreements meant that the distinction between the jurisdictions formally assigned by the constitution was blurred. By incorporating fairly detailed conditions to federal grants, the federal government exerted considerable control over the size, scope and substance of policies, which, in a strict legal sense, fell within exclusive provincial jurisdiction" (Simeon and Robinson, 1990: 152).

The very success of federal dominance in postwar policymaking planted the seeds of federal-provincial tensions. First, negotiations over tax-rental agreements and shared-cost programs institutionalized certain aspects of federal-provincial relations, causing a large intergovernmental machinery to develop over the years. Soon, governmental officials were poised for confrontation over their respective turfs. Second, because provincial administrations were responsible for the implementation of shared-cost programs, the provincial component of government expenditures and government employees grew rapidly. By the 1960s, many provincial governments were ready to argue for administrative autonomy and the return of their jurisdictional territory. After 1960, the history of Canadian federalism is to a large extent that of the federal government's attempts to maintain its dominant position within the national decision and policymaking process in the face of mounting challenges from the provinces.

For a while, Ottawa's response to all this was one of accommodation. Opting-out provisions were introduced in federal-provincial programs— mostly to satisfy Quebec—allowing a province to withdraw without financial loss from programs, provided similar provincial ones were initiated. Eventually conditional grants were replaced with unconditional grants, and shared-cost programs no longer obligated the provinces to spend federal funds in ways determined by the federal government.

In fact, the federal dynamic was increasingly influenced by the provinces, and by the late 1960s a complete reversal of the fiscal balance had taken place: barely one-third of all governmental revenue in Canada went to the federal government, in contrast to nearly three-quarters in the postwar years. At the same time, combined provincial and local government expenditures surpassed federal expenditures. Admittedly, provincial expenditures were not without some elements of federal control. Also, it would be incorrect to conclude that there was a shift of the fiscal centre of gravity; the federal government still had the most financial and economic clout. What is significant, though, is that throughout the 1960s and 1970s the federal government was losing ground and provincial assertiveness was gaining.

Continuing postwar prosperity allowed the provinces to develop this socioeconomic capacity until the end of the 1960s. Secularization, urbanization, and a shifting balance of societal forces led to changing conceptions of the role of government. In the case of Quebec, statism at the provincial level was no doubt a major factor in shaping its more confrontational style.

In the 1970s and early 1980s, there was pressure for the pendulum to again swing the other way: economic stagnation and decline translated into structural and fiscal crises that hit both levels of government. Tensions arose between the provinces and the federal government over contradicting strategies as to how to deal with the problems.

For their part, the provinces sought to maximize their revenue and increase employment and population through industrial diversification, enhanced manufacturing and transformation of natural resources, and enlargement of their jurisdictional spheres—all with a view to promoting local and regional interests. The federal strategy, on the other hand, focussed on reducing the fiscal gap that gave an advantage to the provinces and restructuring the framework for economic power-sharing between jurisdictions. Ottawa sought economic union and continental integration, an objective for which it wanted to act as coordinator, and asked the provinces to downplay their parochial ambitions. The Canadian Charter of Human Rights and Freedoms and the Free Trade Agreement with the United States were both aimed at the achievement of such goals.

Clearly, by the early 1980s, the Canadian dynamic had become increasingly polarized between irreconcilable national and provincial visions of community. The remainder of the decade saw a search for constitutional and structural arrangements that would suit all parties. As the defeat of the Meech Lake accord and the ensuing constitutional tribulations has shown, Canadians are far from achieving a consensus on the ideal political and administrative framework.

2.2 AN OVERVIEW OF QUEBEC–OTTAWA RELATIONS

It would be a mistake, on the basis of the above discussion, to think of Quebec as the sole source of recent problems in Canadian federalism. To be sure, Quebec has been at the forefront of provincialist attacks on the legitimacy of the constitutional framework, but its assertive stance is by no means an aberration or whimsy. It is simply part of the natural historical logic of federal-provincial relations in Canada.

Though the Quebec-Ottawa rivalry intensified in the 1960s with the onset of the Quiet Revolution, confrontation with the federal government had always been more or less a permanent feature of Quebec's relations with Ottawa. Early on, Quebec governments crossed swords with Ottawa over its centralist policies. Honoré Mercier, Quebec's premier from 1887 to 1891, stands out as the first, and one of the most vocal, defenders of provincial rights and autonomy. Later, in the 1940s and 1950s, Maurice Duplessis vociferously tried to protect Quebec's jurisdiction against intrusion by the federal government, to the point of depriving it of federal grants and subsidies. The challenge to the existing constitutional framework was never expressed clearly, however, and the stance was often confused with a conservative and reactionary nationalism.

In spite of everything, a modicum of stability would continue to prevail in Quebec-Ottawa relations. Why? According to political scientist Don Smiley, the explanation lies in the so-called Canadian duality and in the peculiarities of French-English relations prior to 1960. The factors of stability, Smiley (1980: 219-221) says, included:

1. **The federal division of legislative powers**   Ottawa's involvement in provincial jurisdictions pertained mainly to national economic issues. Its involvement did not directly infringe on matters of provincial jurisdiction that were crucial to the French language and culture.

2. **Institutional self-segregation**   Quebec's institutions and underlying values did not challenge Anglo-Saxon economic and political domination in Quebec and in the rest of Canada. Anglophones and francophones have always been able to pursue their occupational and other objectives without much interference from one other.

3. **Cooperation among the elites**   Problems and conflicts between the two national groups have always been mediated at the summit. Leaders of the power elites in both communities have generally cooperated on the basis of an implicit but effective division of socioeconomic roles, regularizing the procedure for managing the reciprocal demands of each group.

4. **Traditional French Canadian distrust of the State**
   French Canadian political and religious leaders tolerated Anglo-Saxon
   economic power because of a predilection to the laissez-faire viewpoint. For example, pre-1960 Quebec resistance to federal policies
   was often based on the fear of expansion of state functions in Canada.

5. **The defence of historic, prescriptive rights**   From the
   1880s onwards, Confederation was defined as a compact either among
   the provinces or between the French and English communities.
   Implicitly, the idea of a compact meant that the terms of Confederation could not be modified without the consent of the original part-
   ners. It was also an affirmation of the continuing legitimacy within
   Quebec of the federal system.

The more-demanding and assertive stance of Quebec since the Quiet
Revolution, contends Don Smiley, stemmed from a breakdown of these
factors, which up to then had held sway over the evolution of Canadian
federalism. (1) Conflicts over the federal division of legislative powers
arose in response to Ottawa's encroachment into provincial areas of jurisdiction in the 1940s and 1950s (notably in health, welfare, higher education, and vocational training). (2) Institutional self-segregation vanished as
the new breed of political and socio-economic leaders sought to enhance
the presence of francophones in what had been the traditional preserves of
Anglo-Saxon capital. They turned to public institutions for more control
over the social and economic future of the province. Their drive to expand
the public sector and bureaucratize private and public institutions dis-
placed the traditional power elites and contributed to the construction of
a more interventionist and aggressive provincial state. (3) Cooperation
among the power elites was sabotaged by vigorous conflicts within francophone Quebec over the proper direction of the province that altered
Quebec's relations with the rest of Canada. (4) Finally, the historic, prescriptive rights that informed the compact theory, were increasingly challenged as of the 1960s, and the legitimacy of the Constitution was questioned (Smiley, 1980: 222–223).

Due to this breakdown, Quebec governments have sought since 1960
to maximize their jurisdiction in most fields of policy and minimize that
of the federal state; reduce the federal role in developing, delivering, and
financing provincial programs; enhance Quebec's say in the composition
and operation of federal institutions, and the implementation of provincial programs; and increase Quebec's visibility on the international scene
(Gagnon and Montcalm, 1990: 150).

Let us look at how the evolution of Quebec-Ottawa relations since
1960 has gone through various phases, each corresponding roughly to the
tenure of an elected government.

The Lesage Years: 1960–1966

Jean Lesage and the Liberal party initiated a major refurbishing of Quebec's social and political institutions. Though this administration pursued objectives in intergovernmental relations similar to those of Maurice Duplessis, the approach was qualitatively different. Whereas Duplessis promoted a strategy of isolationism, rejecting joint action and federal subsidies in order to protect Quebec's administrative autonomy, the Lesage government was resolutely proactive in pushing for the reform of intergovernmental relations in Canada. The general aim of the Lesage government was to strengthen Quebec's autonomy, while reactivating federalism in Canada. It was during the Lesage years that the province of Quebec successfully reclaimed territory lost to the federal government in the preceding decades (Morin 1976). For example, the Lesage government frequently opted out of shared-cost programs and established Quebec's own social welfare and economic development schemes. It was under the Lesage administration that Quebec set up a public pension plan of its own while all the other provinces participated in the federally run Canada Pension Plan. The Lesage government also sought to forge relationships with international organizations and other national governments, thus asserting its right to act abroad in areas of provincial jurisdiction. The government saw to it that Quebec was present at various international meetings of French-speaking countries and even opened a "Maison du Québec," a quasi-embassy in Paris.

Lesage was clearly bent on broadening the range and scope of the provincial government's policies, programs, and spending power—to the point, in fact, where it tried to influence federal policies and programs. The 1966 Quebec budget suggested that the province should participate directly in developing and executing fiscal, monetary, and trade policies—areas of exclusive federal jurisdiction—and successive Quebec provincial governments would ask for a similar role. (The idea, however, was always resisted by the federal government.)

Though relations with Ottawa were never free of acrimony, under Lesage's direction Quebec achieved some degree of reform of the federal system. In 1960, Lesage organized a conference of provincial premiers, one that has met in August of every year since, in the hope that interprovincial cooperation would lessen the chances of unilateral federal intervention in provincial concerns. He also pressed for more-frequent federal-provincial meetings to discuss mutual problems and administrative concerns. The Lesage government's insistence on a more-executive type of federalism in fact, led to development and expansion of the intergovernmental machinery.

The Lesage government's action in constitutional matters was less productive. Political pressures in the Legislative Assembly and within the Liberal party made it difficult to achieve a consensus on reform. Twice during his mandate, Lesage rejected formulas to amend the Constitution: the Fulton formula in 1961; and the so-called Fulton-Favreau formula in 1966. Fulton and Favreau were ministers of justice in two consecutive federal governments, Conservative and Liberal respectively.

The *Fulton formula* recommended that the consent of all provinces be necessary for any constitutional amendment of their jurisdiction. Quebec rejected it on the grounds that it did not sufficiently circumscribe the power acquired by the federal government in 1949 to unilaterally amend the Constitution in areas of exclusive federal jurisdiction. Interestingly, Saskatchewan also opposed this formula because it opposed the veto power granted to the provinces (Roy 1976: 24).

Five years later, the *Fulton-Favreau formula* proposed that on fundamental questions (e.g.,legislative powers and independence of the provinces, language) any modification to the Constitution would require the consent of both the federal and all the provincial governments; in fields of mutual concern, the approval of two-thirds of the provinces representing at least 50% of the Canadian population would be necessary. But Quebec rejected any formula based on unanimity, because it might discourage agreements between Quebec and the federal government in culturally sensitive areas such as language policy. Personally, Lesage was originally prepared to accept the formula, but in fear of being outflanked by his political opponents and by the nationalist wing of his own party, he gave in to political pressures from more nationalist and provincialist quarters.

The Return of the *Union nationale*: 1966–1970

In 1966, Lesage was defeated by the Union nationale (Maurice Duplessis' party), then under the leadership of Daniel Johnson. Lesage had set the tone and style of relations with Ottawa. Daniel Johnson, and Jean-Jacques Bertrand, who succeeded Johnson after his untimely death in 1968, pursued the push for constitutional reform and autonomy initiated by Lesage in fiscal and program areas. Unlike Duplessis, Johnson and Bertrand employed a more interventionist approach and focussed on the achievements of the Quiet Revolution.

In fact, Johnson went even further than Lesage, with a stronger appeal to nationalist sentiments. His campaign theme, "Egalité ou Indépendance," explicitly stated the extent to which Johnson was prepared to go if Quebec's basic demands were not met. For Johnson, the secession of Quebec was a distinct possibility, and "equality" meant not just equality among the provinces, but also equality between the two founding nations.

Johnson emphasized a "binational" perspective, seeing Canada as a compact between the French and the English. On this view, Quebec is the protector of the rights and interests of French-speaking Quebecers, and, to a lesser extent, of francophones outside Quebec.

In order to maintain the "dual alliance" of 1867 between the French and English—that is, in order to keep the integrity and dignity of the French within this alliance—Quebec had to be given greater powers. Failing that, it would have no other choice but to bow out. The Johnson-Bertrand regime thus called for the constitutional recognition of Quebec's distinctiveness and its claim to special status. In this, Johnson and Bertrand were in opposition to Prime Minister Trudeau, who denounced the parochialism and anti-liberal nature of Quebec nationalism. Thus during the Johnson-Bertrand years, Quebec and Ottawa remained at odds on the constitutional issue. The Union nationale refused to agree to patriation or an amending formula unless changes in the division of powers were effected; the federal government in turn rejected the Quebec government's view of the province's role and status.

The Johnson-Bertrand regime's aggressive style did much to antagonize the federal government. When the Union nationale pressed for an end to joint occupancy of tax fields, it went so far as to ask for federal withdrawal from social programs run on a shared-cost basis. It also argued that family allowances, pensions, social assistance, health services, and manpower training should be the sole responsibility of the province and governed by bilateral arrangements with Ottawa regardless of Ottawa's relations with the other provinces. This amounted to special status for Quebec, and Ottawa vehemently resisted.

In spite of these seemingly irreconcilable differences, some progress was made. The province was allowed to play an enhanced role in international relations, and to expand the small immigration bureau established under the Lesage administration into a full-fledged government department. These two policy areas were quite significant in terms of nationalist symbolism and the protection of French-language culture. Quebec would eventually gain near-special status in those policy fields at least.

The First Bourassa Government: 1970–1976

In 1970, the Liberal party was returned to power under the leadership of Robert Bourassa. This government also pursued the goal of a decentralized Canadian federalism, one that would make it more "profitable." Bourassa and his administration sought additional powers and the money to exercise them fully. In 1973, for example, Bourassa's government reached an agreement with Ottawa that allowed Quebec to run its own family allowance program and set the rate of benefits independently of the central government. Overall, however, Bourassa was more federalist than his predecessors. His government was more concerned with reforming the federal framework than with entrenching Quebec's national aspirations within the existing constitution. Essentially, his goal was the acquisition by Quebec of the powers needed to preserve the bicultural character of Canada.

Bourassa's first term is notable mostly for the Victoria Conference in 1971. In June of that year, this First Ministers Conference tentatively adopted a "Canadian Constitutional Charter." It included an entrenched bill of rights, provisions making English and French the official languages of Canada, and a set of more limited language rights (excluding education) applying to several individual provinces. In addition, by the Victoria Charter provincial governments would play a role in the selection of Supreme Court judges, and Quebec was guaranteed that at least three of nine judges would be chosen from that province. Other provisions included a commitment to equalization and provincial supremacy in family, youth, and occupational allowances. Finally, the formula for amending the Constitution required the assent of the federal government, together with all provinces with 25% or more of Canada's population, plus two Atlantic provinces and two western provinces, together comprising at least half these regions' population.

Pierre Elliott Trudeau and Robert Bourassa during the federal-provincial energy conference in Ottawa on January 1974. [Courtesy Archives nationales du Québec. Photo: Michel Elliott.]

Upon his return from Victoria, Bourassa faced vehement opposition from other political parties, the major unions, Quebec rights activists, and even the rank and file of his own party (Roy 1976: 267–277). The Victoria Charter, it was felt, did not explicitly guarantee Quebec control of cultural and social policy. Bourassa was left with little choice but to withdraw his original support of the Charter, much to the dismay and disappointment of the other participants at the Conference. The internal dynamic of Quebec politics had made constitutional reform virtually impossible. "The other provinces remained bystanders for the most part; they felt little pressure to come to agreement and were incapable of mediating what was essentially a battle among Quebecers, in Quebec City and Ottawa, about their future" (Simeon and Robinson, 1990: 208).

As the years went by, the gap between Quebec and the rest of Canada widened. On the eve of the 1976 election, Bourassa made Quebec's support of a new constitution conditional upon inclusion of the following: a Quebec veto over constitutional amendments; participation in Supreme Court appointments; provincial sovereignty in cultural and educational matters; the right to opt out of federal programs with compensation; provincial participation in the recruitment and selection of immigrants and control over their integration into Quebec society and placement in the labour market; and severe limitations on Ottawa's declaratory and spending powers in areas of provincial jurisdiction (Gagnon and Montcalm 1990: 158). But this new, more autonomous stance of the Bourassa government was not enough to guarantee reelection. In the fall of 1976, the Parti québécois (PQ), wholly committed to a deeply nationalist and sovereignist vision of Quebec, took power.

The Reign of the *Parti québécois*: 1976–1985

The objective of the PQ in terms of federal-provincial relations can be expressed in one key concept: "sovereignty-association."

The election of René Lévesque's PQ represented for many a dream come true: the opportunity to achieve a sovereign and possibly independent Quebec. But because the idea of independence itself was not popular with the majority of the Quebec electorate, the PQ often had to tone it down, pursuing what it called *sovereignty-association*—which implied full political sovereignty along with a possible economic association between Quebec and Canada as the most acceptable compromise.

The accession of the PQ marked a break in the traditional pattern of Quebec-Ottawa relations by opening up a full debate on Quebec's actual role and position within the federation. Until then, no government had seriously envisaged the desirability or feasibility of Quebec's withdrawal from Canada. Daniel Johnson's Union nationale had only toyed with the

The speech of René Lévesque on the eve of November 15, 1976 at the Paul Sauvé Arena. The PQ was elected with 41% of the popular vote. [Courtesy Le Devoir and Gilles Paré, Librarian.]

idea, exploiting it more as a guide to strategy than as a viable option. Whereas its predecessors merely sought increased provincial powers, the PQ wanted nothing less than a complete overhaul of the structures and principles by which Canadian federalism had operated since Confederation; more than ever before, Quebec and the federal government were opposed over constitutional issues. Until the defeat of the referendum in 1980, the PQ shunned all federal attempts to renew Canadian federalism.

Ottawa's main goal during the first term of the PQ was the patriation of the Canadian constitution with an amending formula much in the spirit of the Victoria Charter. The PQ resisted such a proposal, as it felt the question of the division of powers had to be given explicit attention before a reform constitution was assented to. Also, the proposal did not include a right for Quebec to veto constitutional amendments or to opt out of programs or policies that could jeopardize the province's interests and cultural integrity. The PQ was afraid that the entrenchment of a charter of rights and freedoms would override vital provincial legislations in the name of national principles. Finally, the PQ government felt that promises for decentralization were inadequate. Quebec would not accept Ottawa's proposals without a constitutional guarantee that it could act with full autonomy in areas of exclusive provincial concern (Gagnon 1990: 104–105).

In spite of the recommendations of the Federal Task Force on Canadian Unity (Pépin-Robarts Commission), which favoured increased decentralization, and supported special status and greater powers with respect to language policy for Quebec, the federal government stuck to its original agenda. Quebec, meanwhile, stepped up its efforts toward sovereignty-association and called a referendum on the question.

The victory of the No forces (60% of Quebec's population against sovereignty-association; 40% in favour) was construed by the federal government as a vote of confidence on the part of the Quebec population for a new federal order. The Trudeau government set to work, and in November 1981 presented a plan to unilaterally reform and patriate the constitution. The plan was opposed, not only by Quebec, but also by all other provinces except Ontario and New Brunswick. In the end, however, after backroom negotiations, Quebec was left alone in its opposition as its "allies" eventually sided with Ottawa in exchange for their preferred amending formula and the right to opt out of the secondary provisions of the Charter (Morin 1988).

The outcome of the 1981 constitutional conference was, by any standard, a crushing defeat for Quebec, leaving the province constitutionally weaker than ever. Not only had the view of Quebec as a distinct society and the claim to special powers for the province been defeated, but Quebec had now lost its bargaining power and credibility. In effect, it had lost its right of veto, implicitly accepted for years. When Quebec cut short the constitutional reform process by rejecting the Fulton-Favreau formula in 1965 and the Victoria Charter in 1971, nobody suggested going ahead without Quebec. Clearly the new constitution meant that "the provincialist view of coequal provinces had prevailed over the view of a binational Canada" (Simeon and Robinson 1990: 281). The Charter of Rights, for example, comprised language provisions that undercut Quebec's effort to promote "francization" on its territory and assert its cultural distinctiveness (see Chapter 14).

In the following years, Quebec retreated from any attempt to reopen the constitutional question. The province had to deal with the economic downturn of the early 1980s and focus on getting out of a fiscal nightmare. The Conservatives in Ottawa defeated the Liberals in 1984 and came to power with a program of national reconciliation which included bringing Quebec back into the constitutional fold. The PQ was well disposed toward the new federal government and was prepared after three years of isolation to reconsider its constitutional position. In 1985, the Quebec government submitted "Draft Agreement on the Constitution," a document containing 22 conditions for the province's assent to a constitutional accord. In essence, these conditions implied the constitutional recognition of Quebec as a distinct society; the limitation of the applicability of the Canadian Charter of Rights and Freedoms in Quebec to democratic rights; the recognition of Quebec's primary authority over employment and over economic and regional development policies and programs; and the recognition of Quebec's right to veto not only constitutional amendments, but also the creation of new provinces and reform of certain national institutions. Quebec also asked for increased powers in the field of communications; sole jurisdiction over the selection and settlement of immigrants; and a greater role and status in international relations. Finally, Quebec wanted changes that would have limited Ottawa's spending and legislative powers and recognized the province's right to opt out of conditional grant programs with compensation.

The Draft Agreement's reiteration of the basic positions advocated by successive Quebec governments since 1960 divided the PQ. The sovereignty hardliners said the Agreement's apparent intention to maximize the province's powers, resources, roles, status, and autonomy within Confederation was a step backward. They saw the proposal for a provincial veto and the broadening of jurisdictions as tantamount to special status and Quebec's integration into the federal system. An open rift within the party ensued, and several prominent Cabinet members resigned in protest. Lévesque stepped down shortly after. Pierre-Marc Johnson replaced him until the next provincial election, on December 2, 1985, when the Quebec electorate returned Bourassa's Liberal party to power.

Bourassa's Return and National Reconciliation: 1985–

The election, both in Quebec City and in Ottawa, of new governments committed to bringing Quebec back into the Constitution reopened the debate over Quebec's status. In contrast to the highly confrontational attitude of both the Trudeau and the Lévesque government, with Robert Bourassa and Brian Mulroney in power the tone became more conciliatory.

The Quebec Liberal party identified five basic conditions necessary to Quebec's acceptance of any constitutional change:

1. The explicit, constitutional recognition of Quebec as a "distinct society" and homeland of the francophone element of Canada's duality

2. Solid guarantees for Quebec's cultural security by increasing Quebec's constitutional right to a critical role in the recruitment and selection of immigrants to that province

3. A key role for Quebec in the appointment of the three Supreme Court judges who were to have expertise in Quebec civil law

4. A limit to the federal government's spending in areas of provincial jurisdiction

5. A full veto on constitutional reform entrenched in the amending formula

Bourassa came to the June 1987 federal-provincial conference at Meech Lake, north of Ottawa, with these propositions. The other First Ministers all agreed to them, and together they put forth a constitutional amendment to be ratified by June 23, 1990 by all provincial legislatures and the House of Commons. This amendment to the Constitution Act of 1982 was known as the Meech Lake accord. By virtue of the accord, Quebec was finally recognized as a distinct society, to be preserved by the central government, and preserved and promoted by the Quebec government. The accord also required the federal government to select the three Quebec judges for the Supreme Court of Canada and the Quebec representatives to the Senate from among candidates submitted by the Quebec government. In addition, veto over constitutional amendments to all matters outlined in Section 42 of the Constitution Act 1982 was given to Quebec. The accord also permitted Quebec to opt out of national shared-cost programs with compensation in areas of exclusive provincial jurisdiction, provided that the province initiated a comparable program compatible with the national objectives. Finally, Quebec-Ottawa agreements in immigration were to be entrenched in the Constitution. When and where they applied, of course, these prerogatives were also extended to the other provinces.

Opposition to the accord came from many quarters. Quebec nationalists and provincialists criticized it for failing to secure an exclusive veto for Quebec; they also argued that the distinct society clause was insufficient to protect provincial legislation should it conflict with the Canadian Charter of Rights and Freedoms. Federalists and centralists, on the other hand, attacked the accord for leaving too much administrative autonomy to the provinces. They feared it would only promote the balkanization of Canada.

By February 1989, the House of Commons and all but two provincial legislatures, New Brunswick and Manitoba, had ratified the Meech Lake accord. In New Brunswick, a landslide electoral victory of the provincial Liberal party brought to power a government that did not feel as committed as its predecessor to the accord. The new Premier, Frank McKenna, opposed it on the grounds that it ignored women's rights and threatened the position of bilingualism. In Manitoba a politically weak premier faced intense opposition from the provincial Liberals and NDP, who were committed to defeating the accord. Later, the province of Newfoundland elected a new government whose Liberal Premier, Clyde Wells, vehemently opposed the accord and fought it both provincially and nationally, in spite of prior ratification in his province's legislature.

By the spring of 1990, Manitoba and New Brunswick had still not ratified the accord. And though last-minute negotiations in early June of that year finally convinced the premiers of those two provinces, as well as Newfoundland's premier, to support the accord, it was nonetheless defeated. What had happened was that in Manitoba, a motion requiring the unanimous assent of the legislature was repeatedly opposed by the NDP's Elijah Harper. A native Indian, Harper dissented on the grounds that the Meech Lake accord did not sufficiently consider the constitutional situation of native people. By June 23, Manitoba had still not voted on the accord; the deadline for complete ratification having passed, the accord became obsolete.

After Meech Lake

Much to the dismay of Robert Bourassa and his government, Quebec found itself isolated once more from the rest of Canada. More than ever before, the idea of sovereignty appeared to be the only solution. Various polls taken in the aftermath of the Meech Lake debacle consistently showed that close to two-thirds of the Quebec population were prepared to support sovereignty-association. In fact, in the months leading up to the deadline for ratification, momentum in favour of sovereignty was growing. While in the last months of 1989 barely 40% favoured sovereignty-association— the same proportion as those who had voted yes in the 1980 referendum— by the spring of 1990, 60% supported it.

Pressed by the opposition and confronted with unequivocal rejection by Quebec, Bourassa set up, by an act of the legislature in September 1990, a commission of inquiry to study and analyze the political and constitutional status of the province, and to make recommendations. The commission was co-chaired by Michel Bélanger, former president of the Banque nationale, and Jean Campeau, former president of the *Caisse de dépôt et placement*. The so-called Bélanger-Campeau Commission was broader than a parliamentary commission in that half of its 36 members were not MNAs but representatives of various social, cultural, and economic interest groups, including three Quebec members of the House of Commons.

The Commission heard 235 presentations and received more than 600 briefs. Fifty-five experts were consulted, and after three months of public hearings a consensus emerged. According to the final report of the Commission, Quebec needed to make profound changes in its political and constitutional status. The Commission pointed to two courses of action with respect to the redefinition of that status: a final attempt to redefine its status within the federal regime, or the attainment of sovereignty without further delay. In other words, if a final effort to reform the federal model should fail, Quebec's only course of action would be to attain sovereignty.

The Commission also made the following recommendation to the

National Assembly: that legislation be adopted by the spring of 1991 to establish the process whereby Quebec would determine its political and constitutional future.

1. The first part of that legislation was to consist of a preamble that asserted Quebecers' freedom "to assume their own destiny, to determine their political status and to assure their economic, social and cultural development," as well as their "wish to play an active part in defining the political and constitutional future of Québec." That preamble would also recognize that the "Constitution Act, 1982, was proclaimed despite the opposition of the National Assembly," the failure of the Constitutional Agreement of 1987, and the necessity to redefine the political and constitutional status of Quebec.

2. The second part of the legislation was to provide that a referendum on Quebec sovereignty be held either in June 1992 or in October 1992. Should the outcome be positive, Quebec would acquire the status of a sovereign state one year after the date of the referendum. In addition, a special parliamentary commission of the National Assembly would be set up to examine all matters related to Quebec's transition to full sovereignty.

3. The third part of the legislation would provide for the establishment of a special parliamentary commission to assess any offer of a new partnership of a constitutional nature made by the Government of Canada and endorsed by the other provinces.

The members of the Bélanger-Campeau Commission were not unanimous in endorsing their final report. The seven members of the PQ, for example, only signed it subject to dissenting opinions on its conclusions. Rather than choose between renewed federalism or sovereignty, they contended that the deliberations of the Commission proved the constitutional status quo was highly undesirable for Quebec. In their view, any project to overhaul the Canadian constitution was doomed to failure given the history of relations between Quebec and Canada and the nature of their respective constitutional positions. True to their political preference, they stressed sovereignty as a viable alternative to Quebec's aspirations and held it could be achieved in an orderly fashion.

Six other members of the Commission expressed strong reservations about the tenor of the report in spite of their endorsement. They felt that the benefits and advantages Quebec had historically enjoyed had been, in the final analysis, unduly downplayed, and that the report should have been more explicit on the difficulties and costs of sovereignty.

Finally, three members of the Commission did not sign the report at all: two federal MPs and the representative of the Equality Party (an

The Beaudoin-Dobbie Commission on the Renewal of Canada. The Montreal Conference in March 1992 on the Economic Union. [Courtesy Le Devoir and Gilles Paré, Librarian. Photo: Jacques Grenier.]

English-rights political party with four MNAs). Jean-Pierre Hogue, a member of the governing party in Ottawa, abstained so as not to influence the position of his government should negotiations with Quebec take place. André Ouellet, a Liberal party MP, expressed dismay at what he called the one-sidedness of the report, which he said cast the Canadian federation in an unfair light. Sovereignty, he felt, was totally unrealistic and he would rather support renewed federalism. Richard Holden, the Equality Party MNA, refused to endorse the report on the grounds that its conclusions were based on false assumptions: i.e., that Quebec was excluded from the 1982 constitutional deal; that the failure of Meech represented a rejection of Quebec by the rest of Canada; and that the federal system and ethnic minorities threatened the survival of French language and culture in Quebec. Holden also criticized the report for its neglect of the needs and aspirations of Quebec's anglophone and cultural communities.

The Commission's recommendation called for the adoption of a dual strategy. It encouraged the government to remain open to any reasonable proposal of constitutional renewal, while at the same time getting poised for sovereignty.

On June 20, 1991 the National Assembly adopted Bill 150, which legalized the three main recommendations of the Bélanger-Campeau Commission. The Bourassa government thus formally committed itself to holding a referendum on sovereignty before or during the fall of 1992. During the debates on Bill 150 in the National Assembly, Robert Bourassa emphasized the economic costs and the political risks of sovereignty. In spite of his government's adoption of this legislation, Bourassa has always remained reluctant to endorse fully the sovereignty option, and has stated on several occasions his own and his government's preference for renewed federalism. To Bourassa, the Allaire Report was never anything more than a basis for discussion and not a firm policy commitment.

He has said publicly that a referendum would be held only if necessary, i.e., if reasonable proposals are not forthcoming from Ottawa. However, his party has been moving closer and closer to a sovereignty stance. The report of the party's Constitutional Committee (Allaire Report) issued only weeks before the report of the Bélanger-Campeau Commission in March 1991 was unequivocal. It called upon the federal government to propose an in-depth reform of the political and constitutional framework along three axes:

1. The political autonomy of the Quebec state, whereby Quebec would exercise its full sovereignty in its own areas and in shared or residual areas of jurisdiction, leaving only to the central government the administration of customs and tariffs, territorial defence, debt management, currency, and equalization. Powers could be shared in native affairs, taxation, immigration, financial institutions, justice, fisheries, foreign policy, mail and telecommunications, and transportation. An entrenched Charter of Rights and Freedoms would also be adopted by Quebec.

2. The consolidation of the Canadian economic union through the free circulation of goods, people, and capital, a monetary and customs union, and the rebalancing of Canadian public finance through a substantial streamlining of the central state.

3. The restructuring of Canada's political institutions through a new constitution that would include the right of each member of the Canadian federation to withdraw from it; an amending formula based on assent of at least 50% of the Canadian population, including a veto right for Quebec; the abolition of the Senate; the elimination of Ottawa's spending power in Quebec's jurisdictions; the elimination of jurisdictional overlap; the establishment of a tribunal responsible for the enforcement and respect of the Constitution; and a reform of the Bank of Canada that would guarantee regional representation.

The Allaire Report recommended that a referendum be held to ratify the reform proposal by the fall of 1992. Failing successful implementation of the reforms, however, the Report recommended that sovereignty be declared.

Federal proposals would indeed be forthcoming. On September 24, 1991, after consulting with the Canadian public (Citizen's Forum on the Future of Canada—the Spicer Commission) and establishing a joint committee of the Commons and the Senate to study the process of constitutional reform (the Beaudoin-Edwards Committee), the Mulroney government offered Canadians its own constitutional blueprint in a document entitled Shaping Canada's Future Together. Among its 28 proposals was the recognition of Quebec's distinctiveness and Canada's linguistic duality so that the Charter should be interpreted in a manner consistent with "the preservation and promotion of Quebec as a distinct society within Canada; and the preservation of the existence of French-speaking Canadians primarily located in Quebec but also present throughout Canada, and English-speaking Canadians, primarily located outside Quebec but also present in Quebec." Contrary to Meech, however, the distinct society notion was narrowly defined to include essentially the recognition of the existence of a French-speaking majority in Quebec, the uniqueness of its culture, and the practice of a civil law tradition.

Other proposals bore on political and administrative institutions as well as the management of the economy and the sharing of jurisdictions. Although the federal proposals allowed for the devolution of some powers to the provinces, greater limitations on the federal power to spend in provincial jurisdictions, and consultation of the provinces in matters of economic policy, Ottawa was to keep exclusive authority in making laws related to the management of the economic union of the country. The federal proposals were still miles away from the objectives of the Allaire Report and retained only three of the five basic conditions set by the Quebec government in the Meech Lake accord. The role demanded by Quebec in the appointment of Supreme Court judges and its will to exercise full veto in constitutional amendments were to be considered only if there was unanimous consent.

After setting up a special joint committee of the Commons and the Senate to study reaction to its proposals (the Beaudoin-Dobbie Commission), the federal government invited provincial leaders, native leaders, and representatives of the Territories to discuss new constitutional arrangements acceptable to both Quebec and the rest of Canada. In line with its post-Meech declaration, the Bourassa government declined to take part in this particular round of multilateral discussions, which went on during the spring and part of the summer of 1992. On July 7, 1992 the nine English-speaking provinces, the federal government, and native leaders agreed on a new, tentative deal, which, among other things, recognized Quebec as a distinct society on the basis of its dominant language, culture, and civil laws; called for the creation of a triple-E Senate (elected, equal, and efficient); forced the federal government to negotiate legally binding deals with the provinces on matters pertaining to immigration; envisaged the creation of mechanisms of mutual delegation of powers between the provinces and the federal government; modified the amending formula; specified the nomination process of Supreme Court justices; allowed for the creation of a third order of government for native peoples; and clarified provincial powers and the extent of federal intervention.

As Robert Bourassa's strategy rested on English Canada making Quebec a constitutional proposition, and as his reluctance to hold a referendum on sovereignty became unequivocally clear, he had little choice but to respond to the July 7 deal and go back to the constitutional negotiating table after a two-year absence. From August 18 to 22, Bourassa joined the other premiers, the Prime Minister, and native leaders to discuss the project for a new accord, and they finally struck a deal, which as ratified six days later in Charlottetown.

Bourassa's acceptance of the July 7 deal (only slightly altered in Charlottetown agreement) confirmed his government's intention to operate within the parameters of Canadian federalism rather than opt for sovereignty or demands for extensive powers for the Quebec government. Opposition to the new deal from the youth wing of the Quebec Liberal party and from Jean Allaire himself was quickly cast aside on August 29 at a Liberal convention. It did not deter the government and the party from endorsing the agreement; Bourassa acknowledged that the agreement was imperfect, but said it was preferable to sovereignty.

The Bourassa government has hailed the agreement as a victory for Quebec because distinct society was recognized (a fact that many English Canadians are reluctant to acknowledge) and, most importantly, Quebec was given the right of veto over eventual modifications to federal institutions. Of course, from Quebec's point of view this is not negligible, for it means that the province cannot be forced to accept any policy or institution with which it disagrees. The fact remains, however, that the Charlottetown agreement is far from the Liberal party's official constitutional position. Bourassa has chosen political stability over the risks of sovereignty. His view may not be shared by his compatriots.

KEY TERMS

Centralism	**Disavow Independence**
Confederation	**Distribution or division of power**
Constitutional amendment	**Equalization payments**

Federalism

Fiscal federalism

Independentist

Jurisdiction

National interest

Sovereignty-association

Tax fields

Tax-rental agreements

REFERENCES AND FURTHER READING

Adie, Robert and Paul Thomas. 1987. *Canadian Public Administration*. 2nd ed. Toronto: Prentice Hall.

Fitzmaurice, John. 1985. *Quebec and Canada: Past, Present and Future*. New York: St. Martin's Press.

Gagnon, Alain. 1990. "Quebec-Canada relations: the engineering of constitutional arrangements." In Michael Burgess (ed.), *Canadian Federalism: Past, Present and Future*. Leicester: Leicester University Press.

Gagnon, Alain and Mary Beth Montcalm. 1990. *Quebec: Beyond the Quiet Revolution*. Toronto: Nelson.

Gibbins, Roger. 1985. *Conflict and Unity*. Toronto: Methuen.

Morin, Claude. 1976. *Quebec Versus Ottawa: The Struggle for Self-Government, 1960–1972*. Toronto: University of Toronto Press.

Morin, Claude. 1988. *Lendemains piégés*. Montreal: Boréal.

Rocher, François. 1982. "Essai pour une problématique d'interprétation des conflits entre paliers gouvernementaux au Canada depuis 1960." M.A. thesis (Political Science, Université de Montréal).

Roy, Jean-Louis. 1976. *Le Choix d'un pays*. Montreal: Leméac.

Simeon, Richard and Ian Robinson. 1990. *State, Society and the Development of Canadian Federalism*. Toronto: University of Toronto Press.

Smiley, Donald V. 1980. *Canada in Question: Federalism in the Eighties*. 3rd ed., Toronto: McGraw-Hill Ryerson.

Stevenson, Garth. 1984. "Federalism and intergovernmental relations." In M. Whittington and G.S. Williams (eds.), *Canadian Politics in the 1980s*. 2nd ed. Toronto: Methuen.

Stevenson, Garth. 1982. *Unfulfilled Union*. 2nd ed. Toronto: Macmillan.

CHAPTER 3

POLITICAL
CULTURE AND
IDEOLOGICAL
DEVELOPMENT

As far as public opinion is concerned, how we perceive and interact with others and our social environment is influenced by patterns from a wider political culture, that is, from the dominant values, norms, and beliefs in the society. Quebec's political culture has always been rooted in a deeply-felt desire to either defend, promote, or assert its national identity, depending on sociohistorical circumstances. This is not to say that every aspect of Quebec public opinion and policymaking can be explained in terms of the will to nationhood; but national identity has been at the core of public opinion and the making of public policy.

This chapter deals with the recent evolution of the Quebec political culture and its impact in shaping the province's public policy agenda over the past few decades.

3.1 FROM INSULARITY TO MODERNITY

The Church and *La survivance*

The preservation of the cultural integrity of French-speaking Quebecers has always been a key component of Quebec's political dynamic. Quebec first faced the challenge of how to preserve its culture when its links with France were severed and the province was subjected to the assimilative emphasis of various British governors. The first vehicle used to fight assimilation was the House of Assembly, which came into being in 1791.

However, the defeat of the Patriotes[1] in the rebellions of 1837–1838, and the demise of their reformist, secular, state-oriented nationalism paved the way for extended Church control of Quebec society. Ideological coherence, bureaucratic capacity, and the absence of a viable counterelite enabled the Catholic Church to extend its influence well into the 1950s (Gingras and Nevitte 1984: 4).

The Church fostered the ideology of *la survivance* (survival) to protect French Canadians within and outside Quebec from threats posed by other provincial and federal governments. *La survivance* expressed itself in a religiously oriented, non-materialistic cultural isolationism that, to justify itself, took refuge in the idea of "autonomy." Any progressive ideas such as those of the Patriotes, including liberation, fell by the wayside. Rather than striving to build a nation and a democratic state, emphasis was given to using the French and Catholic provincial government to preserve faith, language, and traditional institutions. In effect, Quebec was driven by a conservative ideology known as *ultramontanism*—the integration of Church and State, and, concomitantly, the worship of agriculture, the rejection of industrialization and its underlying modernist values, and belief in French Canada as the vessel for moral and spiritual conversion of North America (Monière 1981: 288).

In contrast to the English Canadians, who thought of themselves not only in terms of their religious identity, but also in terms of their economic, social, political, and familial identity (each assuming a greater or lesser importance at different times), the French Canadians tended to define themselves in accordance with the precepts which flowed from their religious identity. Furthermore, the ultramontanism of the Quebec hierarchy meant that it could not recognize the State as a legitimate instrument in secular affairs. Consequently, placed in a continental milieu in which life was dominated by materialistic impulses and the protestant ethic, and in which changes tended to devaluate and undermine religion, the most a Church-oriented society could hope for was preservation of the status quo (Kwavnick 1965: 514–515). A convenient accommodation was established with the province's anglophone elite: the English were left formal political control and major economic activity—"the dream of opening up a transcontinental economy"—and the Catholic clergy controlled "cultural" matters, such as religion and education (Whitaker 1984: 72).

The State and *Rattrapage*

Until the Second World War, Quebec lived under highly paradoxical conditions. The process of industrialization had introduced it to modernity,

---

1. The Patriotes were a social movement led by representatives of shopkeepers, intellectuals, and radical members of the *Patriote* party, founded in 1827.

but it continued to maintain a conservative outlook on the world, as traditional and clerical elites strove hard to keep the new values implicit in industrialization at bay. The gap between the modernist and capitalistic thrust of society and the sociopolitical norms and values that had so far been dominant widened as the 20th century unfolded.

In the city, the onslaught of monopoly capitalism meant the virtual disintegration of small industrial and commercial concerns, while the French Canadian elite was finding it increasingly difficult to maintain ideological control and political influence in an industrial world dominated by the English language and materialist values (Monière 1984: 166–168).

Pierre Vallières in 1984. The Quebec lower-class resentment during the 1940s and 1950s is portrayed in his autobiography, Nègres blancs d'Amérique, *published in 1967. [Courtesy Le Devoir and Gilles Paré, Librarian. Photo: Jacques Grenier.]*

The election of the Liberals in 1960 and the ensuing "Quiet Revolution" brought about a new outlook, more in tune with the requirements of capitalist modernity—an end to the influence of the prevailing *survivance* mentality.

The 1960s marked the beginning of a period of great cultural effervescence that led to the building of a new Quebec identity. It was tantamount to a thorough mutation that occurred on several planes:

1. It was first apparent in a secularization of attitudes. Not only did the practice of religion drop considerably, but religion ceased to be the intellectual and social point of reference for most French-speaking Quebecers. The Catholic Church, as a major sociopolitical force in Quebec society, was in retreat. It was no longer the main source of inspiration or guidelines for acceptable behaviour in families, social movements, and associations.

2. There was a passage to a "culture of change" in all spheres of society —an emphasis on social, political, and institutional experimentation. Change was no longer perceived as suspect.

3. The economic dominance of the United States over Quebec and the rest of Canada made Quebec even more susceptible to its cultural influence. Quebecers came out of their self-imposed ideological and cultural isolation to adopt lifestyles, consumption preferences, rhythm of life, attitudes, and norms that were originally American. The progress of mass communication and transportation made it increasingly difficult for the proponents of tradition to counteract the outerworldly reach of American culture.

4. Social and political protest, and resistance to authority, became hallmarks of the new era. One of the major facets of French Canadian culture had been its respect for all forms of authority. The 1950s saw

Gilles Vigneault personified the social involvement of the cultural class in Quebec political life in the 1960s and 1970s. This picture was taken in June 1990 during his show. [Courtesy Le Devoir and Gilles Paré, Librarian. Photo: Jacques Nadeau.]

the beginnings of anti-authoritarianism (under the leadership of *Cité libre*, a Montreal monthly, and the labour movement), an emphasis on emancipation which culminated in the 1960s and 1970s.

5. With the arrival of waves of immigrants, Quebec became an increasingly heterogeneous and pluralist society. Quebecers were forced to challenge their own values.

A consensus emerged among progressive forces that the time had come to replace the Church as the dominant institution in society with the State. Growing up in the prosperous times of the post-war era and exposed to a vast array of new ideas conveyed by the mass media of mass communications, the younger generation of French Canadians rejected many of the ideas of their ancestors and unabashedly adopted a more materialistic view of the world. They soon realized the dysfunctional nature of *la survivance*, which doomed them to servitude and low economic status compared to cultures that embraced acquisitiveness and economic prosperity. The new ideological orientation of *rattrapage* ("catching up") quickly rose to prominence; there was a realization that precious time had been lost for social and economic development.

Since other cultures (American and English Canadian) already occupied the positions of economic influence within Quebec's private sector, the State seemed the logical instrument both for the employment of francophones newly trained in the ways of modern economic production and rational organizational structures and for design and support of the educational apparatus that could provide such training. It was perceived as the instrument "to acquire the good things of this earth." Young French Canadians accepted this vision with all the fervour with which it had been rejected by their ancestors (Guindon 1988).

In the Quiet Revolution various Quebec governments nationalized hydroelectric power, democratized political institutions, modernized the public sector, created numerous state-owned enterprises, reformed the educational system and secularized educational, health, and welfare institutions. This, of course, had required more power for the Quebec government, which led to confrontations with the federal government and demands for a new division of powers. It was this confrontation, in part, that spawned awareness of the possibility of a sovereign state and an independent Quebec. Seen in this light, the rivalry between Quebec and Ottawa since the 1960s seems largely to have been a bureaucratic squabble between two levels of government: Quebec's new generation of civil servants were dissatisfied with their limited administrative domain and were seeking to extend their power base. It would be incorrect to say that nationalism in Quebec was *only* bureaucratically driven; though it was partly a political response to the centralistic tendencies of the federal government, it also reached deeply into the collective conscience of Quebecers. However, it must be acknowledged that public servants did become the spearhead of Quebec's will to nationhood in the 1960s and 1970s (Balthazar 1986: 139ff.).

Nationalist Movements

A string of independentist and various other nationalist organizations flourished in the 1960s. On the right end of the spectrum were movements such as the *Alliance laurentienne* and the *Ralliement national*. However, these tended to advocate independence only as a way to protect the cultural integrity of Quebec's French-speaking population; in an era of social progress and forward-looking political culture, this essentially conservative, nostalgic, and at times openly anti-modernist thrust disqualified them almost from the start as plausible political alternatives. They were short-lived and quickly faded into irrelevance and political oblivion (Gingras and Nevitte 1984: 6).

On the center and left of the spectrum, the *Rassemblement pour l'indépendance nationale* (RIN) and later the *Parti québécois* (PQ) embodied a nationalism that was far more favourably received. The PQ response to the challenges of modernity differed substantially from that of the more conservative independentists in that its nationalism was not defensive in its orientation, but assertive. They embraced *rattrapage*, reflecting a new confidence in Quebec's economic potential (Gingras and Nevitte 1984: 8). Both the RIN and the PQ argued that Quebec had been dominated and deprived of the powers that would enable it to take charge and be responsible for itself. The RIN openly called for the separation of Quebec from Canada and for adoption of a series of social and economic objectives that included economic planning, general governmental intervention in the economy, egalitarian distribution of revenues, secularization of society, and nationalization of natural resources and monopoly sectors. However, conflicts within the RIN destroyed the party in 1968, and the torch of mainstream nationalism passed almost immediately to the PQ, led by René Lévesque (see Chapter 5). The PQ insisted on the construction of a semi-socialist provincial state, controlled economically by a francophone managerial elite. In this model, Confederation figured merely as a convenience whose utility was assessed according to how well French civilization could flourish as a province within it. If it could not do so, then separation would become a necessity.

3.2   THE CHANGING FACE OF QUEBEC POLITICAL CULTURE

Until the 1980 referendum, the nationalist stance was essentially founded on a deep-seated sense of the "Québécois" community. The extreme reliance on the Quebec state in the 1960s and 1970s was in a way the triumphant expression of this community. The sociopolitical projects of those eventful decades aimed to create a more generous, more democratic society. To be nationalist was also to be on the side of social change and social development. The whole political culture of those years was rooted in the belief, shared by large segments of the population, that the will to nationhood was a positive and rightful objective. It was a culture of emancipation and national affirmation. In the whirlwind of modernization, nationalism allowed Quebecers to keep alive the sense of identity and community upon which Quebec's distinctiveness was built (Balthazar 1986: 145).

Today, however, support for Quebec sovereignty is driven by sociopolitical motivations that bear increasingly little resemblance to the emancipatory nationalism of the Quiet Revolution, which in a way has been a victim of its own success. In the process of their self-assertion, Quebecers borrowed from modernity its social and economic tools. They embraced the norms and values of market society that their ancestors had resisted for so long. Besides their humanistic and welfarist objectives, the aspiration of the Quebec state elite was to stimulate and enhance the economic competence and competitiveness of Quebecers.

Perhaps the best recent example of this was Quebec's overwhelming support for the Free Trade Agreement (FTA). This development was a far cry from the spirit of the contemplative, religious, insular society that had fostered *la survivance*, with its distaste for commerce, the work ethic, and material comforts, and contempt for the values embodied in American society. In a symbolic way, the massive endorsement of the FTA meant that Québecers had come of age. They felt confident that they had the competence, ability, and expertise to meet successfully the challenges of a highly competitive international environment. While the FTA was a bilateral commercial agreement, for Quebecers it was replete with visions of a local market that would no longer be dependent on Canada for expansion.

In sum, a new spirit has characterized Quebec nationalism since the referendum of 1980. In the past decade, French-speaking Quebecers seem to have gravitated to a different kind of political culture. Disenchantment with the state and the social-democratic ideals of the 1960s and 1970s has allowed a new breed of entrepreneurs to gain prominence in public discourse and the definition of the political and economic agenda. Contrary to their predecessors, whose faith in the virtues of federalism was uncompromising, these entrepreneurs feed on Quebec nationalism and a renewed sense of nationhood, which the recent defeat of the Meech Lake constitutional accord has reinforced. The national conscience of Quebecers is now markedly influenced by this group's vision of the world, which celebrates individual initiative and private enterprise (Létourneau 1991; Balthazar 1991: 41).

Quebecers have realized the limitations of efforts to satisfy their individual material wants through the use of the State and cultural affirmation. To be master in your own home is not especially satisfying if your house is a small one. The international market was far bigger and far more attractive than what the domestic market had to offer. As well as providing even greater space for French-speaking Quebecers to enhance their own material interests, an international outlook would enhance their own culture. Quebec's nationalism is now more than ever rooted in a deepseated will to economic success.

In his analysis of Quebec nationalism, Reginald Whitaker (1984: 91) proposes that the integration of Quebec into the North American economy is the challenge of the future, and although political response in English Canada plays a role in determining the nature of the relationship, Quebec nationalism is partly a product of forces deeper than politics. Whitaker emphasizes the economic aspects of nationalism, and argues that after the death of Duplessis many different forms of nationalism came to prominence. He notes that with the acceleration of industrialization and urbanization in the 1960s, corporate capital began to require white-collar workers and slowly Quebec's educational system began to respond. In the early 1970s, the Bourassa regime emphasized economic development and private investment—a strategy that worked until charges of corruption strengthened the PQ, who hit on the strategy of a referendum and honest government.

In a way Quebec nationalism has always had a calculating, functionalist dimension (Whitaker 1984: 87). Even with the PQ in power, American trade and private investment were considered extremely desirable, as was the strengthening of indigenous, private capitalists—especially when this strengthening was at the expense of English Canada. The PQ used numerous approaches in their attempt to achieve the maximum possible autonomy within the framework of the relations of capitalist production: they aimed at opening up a market to Quebec capitalist interests; they sought and received the support of the masses without granting important concessions; and they attempted to win over the middle class and the bourgeoisie by making its independentist project less dangerous for the capitalist social order by, among other things, abandoning various nationalization projects called for in their early platforms. Even more ambitiously, the PQ sought to boost Quebec's economy at the expense of Canadian capital while seeking to remain or become its partner, and it also attempted to convince American capital that it was the only possible alternative to the Canadian problem (Bourque 1984: 141).

Whatever one's ideological leanings, one has to recognize that the prevailing neoconservative forces in all industrialized societies, which aim to cut growth in the public sector and decrease its size, are also at work in Quebec. In recent years, giving in to the pressures of public finance, the Quebec government has looked for ways to halt the growth of governmental power and provision of services, even though its development functions are generally directed toward maintaining the cultural and economic health of Quebec society. Quebec nationalism, it seems, has had to incorporate in its quest this reversal in the political realities (Roy 1987: 304).

The private sector is now largely perceived as the logical solution to the budgetary predicament of the modern state. Statism is in desrespute, paradoxically, the main source of opposition has come from those entrepreneurial groups who greatly benefitted from state support in the 1960s and 1970s. In 1985, three governmental reports on privatization, deregulation, and the streamlining of the bureaucracy all had indicated unequivocally the road they thought Quebec ought to take: it would be better for the state to withdraw from, or reduce its involvement in, all those fields of socioeconomic activity that had led Quebec society on a modernizing course. In the current political climate there seems to be an emerging consensus to allow entrepreneurs to pursue their objectives unfettered by either level of government. It is hardly surprising that a task force invested with the mission of mapping out Quebec's constitutional future (the Bélanger-Campeau Commission) was co-chaired by two bankers and involved endless discussions on the economic viability of a sovereign Quebec.

It would seem that Quebec has irreversibly adopted the materialistic values and work ethic of homogenizing liberalism. This ideological and cultural stance explains Quebec's rational side, its cost-benefit analysis of Confederation, its use of separatism to augment the interests of its indigenous private capital, and its overwhelming support of free trade.

3.3   THE END OF TWO SOLITUDES?

Quebec nationalism, in its current form, is rooted in soil far different from that which nurtured earlier nationalist and separatist movements. As the "two solitudes" (French and English) continue to compete in the same world and share increasingly similar values, real cultural differences diminish. As

Ethnic minorities represent the new face of Quebec in the 1990s. Young children in a Montreal secondary school. [Courtesy Le Devoir and Gilles Paré, Librarian.]

attested to by its support of free trade and relatively harmonious absorption of immigrant communities, Quebec is quite open to the outside world and prepared to integrate external influences.

As early as 1965, political scientist David Kwavnick warned that the consequences attributed to differences of language really resulted from far more deeply seated differences, ones related to value systems, outlook, and orientation and argued even then that the value system, outlook, and orientation that had traditionally differentiated French Canada were rapidly disintegrating. "Henceforth," he argued, "the points of differentiation between English and French Canadians will only be the differences of language and the immediate implications of this difference" (1965: 522–523).

Contemporary scholars have made similar observations emphasizing the decline in influence of the institutions that affect these value systems. William Coleman points out that by the late 1960s, with the "reform" of educational and social welfare institutions and the withdrawal of the Church into more-strictly-spiritual realms, the most evident distinguishing characteristic of the French-speaking community became its language; the struggle to preserve a distinctive culture became largely a struggle to preserve French. "Whereas language had earlier been one of several foundations of French-Canadian civilization, by the late 1960s it often appeared to be the only visible foundation left" (Coleman 1984: 19).

The Montreal Chinese district. Hydro-Québec's head office in the background.
[Courtesy Le Devoir and Gilles Paré, Librarian. Photo: Jacques Grenier.]

With a confidence perhaps left over from the heady days of *rattrapage*, francophones argue that all is possible because of the power of language and its potential role in cultural preservation. In a recent interview, former federal Liberal cabinet minister Serge Joyal was quoted as saying: "It's not possible to overestimate the attachment Quebecers have for their language. It's stronger than ever before, and it cuts across all political boundaries. It's the common denominator that binds and protects Quebecers" (Maser 1989). Joyal's statement reflects the contemporary logic which holds that as long as the French language is protected, so also is the French culture, and Quebecers can safely enter the world market as individuals or as corporations without state support. Coleman argues that, in fact, although language once acted as a barrier, its recent adaptation to economic life has enabled it to perform as a vehicle for the integration of the French Canadian community into the dominant culture of North America. Hence, the rise of French Canadian entrepreneurship and support for free trade, and the tremendous rise in concern for the protection of the French language.

Many francophones sincerely believe language to be the only means left of ensuring the survival of their culture and any of its unique or distinguishing qualities (Morin 1987: xvii). Of course, they have been exposed to the argument that language will not, in fact, protect their culture, but they choose to ignore such a possibility, using language legislation to justify the continued pursuit of the benefits of progress.

And yet...political scientist Pierre Fournier, argues that most of Quebec's current economic difficulties stem from the fact that it was never prepared for such a sudden and thorough initiation into the North American mainstream (Maser 1989). He observes that, in the past, isolation, church, and family served as the guardians of language and culture. "Now those are gone and Quebec is awash with English radio, television, music and rock videos. And it's worried." Perhaps deep-seated concerns over the risks inherent in Quebec's present stage of development are manifesting themselves in defensive reactions, particularly with respect to language.

Whatever motivations are involved, there is no other direction for Quebec to choose at this point, given its history of struggle merely to survive. If a nation builds a wall around itself against modernity and does not ensure an adequate level of technological sophistication, it quickly falls prey to backwardness and dependency in an aggressive world. Indeed, there is much to be said for optimism, self-fulfilling prophecies and the power of positive thinking, all of which seem very much in evidence in contemporary Quebec.

St. Jean Baptiste day on June 24, 1990, the day after the rejection of the Meech Lake accord. [Courtesy Le Devoir and Gilles Paré, Librarian. Photo: Jacques Grenier.]

3.4 CONCLUSION

Socialists and social democrats who, for a long time, were in the vanguard of Québécois nationalism, have watched perplexed as their society became increasingly consumed by the long-resisted capitalist forces that historically had held sway within English-speaking North America.

But nationalism is a force that does not disappear; it merely takes on different forms. The real challenge is to understand what forces structure each form it adopts. Nationalism does not entail extremist or pathological behaviour, and political parties are not its only vehicles of expression (Gingras and Nevitte, 1984: 2, 18). In Quebec, too, nationalism has been dynamic, and the changes have been intimately connected with social change. Its evolution began with the Church, moved to the State, and now is expressed by individual francophones in the market economy. Nationalism is a permanent fixture of Quebec political culture.

To understand ideological development in Quebec one must appreciate the dominant role played by concerns for cultural and political affirmation. These concerns, combined with the events and realities of each era, inspired the various forms of nationalism that influenced public opinion. In the past, the belief that increased interaction with other, more pervasive cultures would lead to almost certain cultural dilution was common to each form of nationalism.

Gradually, nationalism evolved from this insular, collectivist perspective—rooted in a deep-seated conservatism—to a confident, functional, statist orientation, to, finally, an entrepreneurial, materialistic individualism rooted in economic liberalism. Having achieved all that it could through the State, nationalism began to be expressed through individual entrepreneurs. Francophones believe they can further the cause of their culture through their own, individual activities and progress.

In this context, supporting free trade makes sense to Quebecers, as does the belief that it is the French language that will prevent individual francophones who engage in free exchange with Americans from the fate of assimilation.

KEY TERMS

Cultural isolationism	**Political socialization**
Ideology	**Public opinion**
Liberals	**Secularization**
Nationalism	**Separatism**
Political culture	**Ultramontanism**

REFERENCES AND FURTHER READING

Balthazar, Louis. 1986. *Bilan du nationalisme au Québec*. Montreal: L'Hexagone.

Balthazar, Louis. 1991. "Conscience nationale et contexte international." In L. Balthazar, G. Laforest, and V. Lemieux (eds.), *Le Québec et la restructuration du Canada, 1980–1992*. Sillery: Septentrion. Pp. 33–48.

Bourque, Gilles. 1984. "Class, nation, and the Parti Québécois." In Alain G. Gagnon, *Québec State and Society*. Toronto: Methuen Publications. Pp. 124–147.

Coleman, William D. 1984. *The Independence Movement in Quebec, 1945–1984*. Toronto: University of Toronto Press.

Gingras, Francois-Pierre, and Neil Nevitte. 1984. "The evolution of Québec nationalism." In A. G. Gagnon, *Québec State and Society*. Toronto: Methuen Publications.

Grant, George. 1965. *Lament for a Nation*. Toronto: McClelland and Stewart Ltd.

Kwavnick, David. 1965. "The roots of French-Canadian discontent." *Canadian Journal of Economics and Political Science*, XXXI (4) (November): 514–515.

Létourneau, Jocelyn. 1991. "La nouvelle figure identitaire du Québécois: Essai sur la dimension symbolique d'un consensus social en voie d'émergence." *British Journal of Canadian Studies*, 6 (1): 17–38.

Maser, Peter. 1989. "Season of discontent," *Montréal Gazette*, June 23.

Monière, Denis. 1981. *Ideologies in Quebec*. Toronto: University of Toronto Press.

Monière, Denis. 1984. "Currents of nationalism in Quebec." In Stephen Brooks, *Political Thought in Canada*. Toronto: Irwin Publishing Inc.

Morin, Jacques-Yvan. 1987. "Preface." In George Grant, *Est-ce la fin du Canada?* Tr. Gaston Laurion LaSalle: Éditions Hurtubise HMH Ltd.

Roy, Jean-Louis. 1987. "Nationalism in the 1980s: after failure, the challenge of relevance." In Michael D. Behiels (ed.), *Quebec Since 1945*. Toronto: Copp Clark Pitman Ltd.

Whitaker, Reginald. 1984. "The Quebec cauldron." In A. G. Gagnon (ed.), *Quebec State and Society*. Toronto: Methuen Publications.

CHAPTER 4

STATE-BUILDING
AND CONSOLIDATION
FROM
1960 ON

There have been more changes in Quebec since 1960 than at any previous time in Quebec history. This period of accelerated transformation, often called the Quiet Revolution, has been the dominant political event of the last 30 years, along with the rise of the Parti québécois (PQ).

The period was triggered by the death of Premier Maurice Duplessis in September 1959, whose successor, Paul Sauvé, implemented the first reforms. Under Jean Lesage, elected in 1960, the pace of transformation accelerated. Successive governments continued to make incremental reforms until the referendum results, the recession, and a dominant ideological movement toward liberalism in the 1980s put an end to the Quiet Revolution.

To understand what has happened in Quebec requires an understanding of the eclectic forces involved. It is difficult to single out one key factor from the many variables: urbanization, secularization, statism, spread of mass education, growth of mass communication networks, industrialization, changes in the social structure, greater political participation. Kenneth McRoberts (1988) has suggested that we look at modernization, dependency, cultural division of labour, class relations, national consciousness, and Canadian federalism. All these different elements—and more—have reshaped Quebec society.

In this chapter, we focus on the role of the Quebec state. A *state* can be defined as a collection of institutions, rules of behaviour, norms, roles, buildings, and archives with its own organizational culture and its own operating procedures. In the 1950s, though Quebec's society was evolving in a fashion similar to that of other parts of Canada or North America (Salée 1990), the development of its political structures and of the state was lagging behind. This chapter attempts to explain the transformation of the Quebec state after 1960, its attempts to catch up with a changing social reality, and the attendant reorientation of its economic development.

A state can be relatively autonomous in society, formulating policies not necessarily supported by particular interest groups, institutions, or social forces. In fact, the reformist state had to battle the dominant institutions of the period: the Catholic Church over health and education matters, the English bourgeoisie based in Montreal and Toronto over the economic domain, and the federal government over political affairs. In each of these domains, the provincial state brought about the major reforms: changes in education, the rise of a network of public enterprises, and the still-unfinished quest for more constitutional autonomy.

In addition to burgeoning nationalism discussed in previous chapters, the 1960s were characterized by a vast process of institutionalization. As well as new administrative agencies, whole new departments were created. Then came a major reshuffling as departments were merged or renamed in the 1970s. Throughout the first half of the 1980s, structural changes continued, but were tempered with a strong dose of improvisation. Eventually there was a reduction in the number of departments providing services to the central administration; for example, the Department of Public Works and Supply and the Civil Service Department were abolished (Ambroise 1987).

The evolution of political parties and the creation of powerful interest groups are discussed in other chapters. In this chapter we will focus on the modernization of the Quebec state, and its aftermath, in terms of an ideological revolution that has seen a new nationalism and transfer of power and authority to the state and the subsequent confrontation with the power elites that had traditionally controlled Quebec society. The chapter concludes with a discussion of the readjustment that occurred over the 1980s.

4.1 IDEOLOGY AND TRANSFER OF POWER TO THE STATE

As we have seen, the Quiet Revolution was first an ideological revolution. This neglected provincial state would, it was hoped, become the instrument of "liberation" for the French Canadian nation. Nationalism, which until then had sought the preservation of an idyllic past—the contemplation of a rural life, a Catholic providential mission in North America—became less conservative (Balthazar 1980). Everything now had to change.

The buzzword was *rattrapage*. Duplessis' successor, Paul Sauvé, summed it up in one word, *désormais*, which means "from now on."

During the 1960 election, in Jean Lesage's words, the mood was, *"C'est le temps que ça change"* (It is time for change); during the 1962 election, it was *"L'ère du colonialisme économique est finie dans le Québec. Maintenant ou jamais, maîtres chez nous"* (Economic colonialism is over in Quebec. It's now or never—masters in our own house).

But how was *rattrapage* to be achieved? In 1960, the State was seen by many people as the solution. Of all the societal institutions, only the State could be entirely controlled by Quebecers. In the next two decades, the Quebec government emerged as a mature and complex institution. Young, Faucher, and Blais (1984) have summarized what happened in Quebec in six propositions:

1. The attitude of the province toward the central government has changed: Quebec came to resist federal incursions more staunchly and increased demands pertaining to its own self-interest.

2. The province greatly increased its financial and human resources, both absolutely and relative to the central government.

3. The scope of provincial public policy widened enormously, and state intervention, especially in the economic realm, became deep and pervasive.

4. Provincial policymaking changed profoundly, becoming centralized, planned, and coherent.

5. The province became more strongly linked with the resource sectors.

6. Provincial state-building came into direct conflict with Canadian nation-building: in particular, provincial economic interventions fragmented the common market and caused significant welfare losses.

As Young et al. point out, not all this was true of the other provinces. Since 1960, the Quebec government has been more vocal than the others and has rapidly increased its capacity to govern in the interests of the provincial political economy.

4.2 EXTERNAL AND INTERNAL PRESSURES FOR CHANGE

As has been mentioned, the Quiet Revolution was characterized by the expanded role of the state. State activities became more intensive, and spread to new domains. Though it is true that when the Liberals were elected in 1960 their political platform did not include all of the reformist proposals that would engender the Quiet Revolution. Yet one of the first steps in their agenda, recognizing the importance of the French culture in North America, was the creation of a department of cultural affairs. The department was created the year after; however, it has remained a very modest one (Simard 1989).

What actual powers Quebec inherited in 1867 have proven to be an endless source of debate. The Canadian federal government was given the most significant powers, while provincial governments were given control over local affairs and the imperial government in London retained control over international matters. The real benefit of Confederation for French Canada was the provision of a range of powers, limited but guaranteed, over its own affairs. But until the 1960s, whether due to the presence of a too-conservative ideology or an absence of imaginative leaders, the state of Quebec remained backward, its powers never really exploited. For decades, intervention in the economy was minimal, except for repressive measures toward workers. Policies around such matters as education and welfare were negligible.

Thus, at the time of Duplessis' death, Quebec's political institutions in general, and state intervention in particular, were out of step with the social reality of the time. While Quebec had developed into an urban and industrial society, its political institutions were those of the previous century. Political development lagged far behind socioeconomic transformations.

The ideological revolution in Quebec replaced this conservatism with a combination of nationalism and statism. Rapid modernization occurred, with a transfer of power from private and religious institutions to the state.

However, state-building in Quebec has been shaped by a haphazard vision, the death of three premiers in office, the disproportionate power of a small group of civil servants, and the necessity of reacting to initiatives from the federal government. Reforms were implemented with their own extemporaneous logic, and had to be corrected frequently to compensate for their anarchical beginnings. This is the more true because of the fact that the government of Quebec is traditionally liberal in its orientation, and has been interventionist by necessity. The various attempts made since 1960 to intervene in the economy were to correct market deficiencies rather than because of ideological predispositions.

An important point is that Quebec changed rapidly with very little political violence. There were only about twenty active terrorists during the 1960s (Laurendeau 1990), and only nine people died because of political violence. In fact, two Royal Commissions on the subject have established that several of the terrorist acts were carried out by the Royal Canadian Mounted Police in an effort to undermine the political movement, the *Front de libération du Québec* and the independentist movement in general. This violent movement disappeared entirely with the rise of the PQ in the early 1970s and the real possibility of using the democratic process to achieve the main goal, a more autonomous Quebec.

Indeed, some have questioned whether there was even a "revolution" at all in the usual sense. It should be remembered that the Quiet Revolution had limited political support. It can be argued that the pressure to reform Quebec's society through state-building came from within the state apparatus, from relatively autonomous civil servants who believed in the necessity of the various transformations they had initiated, and also from various social movements that had combatted Duplessis' policies during the 1950s, most notably the labour movement.

This also raises the question of whether the reforms came too fast or too slow. Some observers have argued that Lesage's defeat in 1966 occurred because a significant segment of the population thought that the reforms were coming too quickly. On the other hand, the results of the election indicate that only a small fraction of the population switched parties. Also, there was a third party in the running for the first time.

Quebec Premier Daniel Johnson (in power 1966–1968), and the leader of the Union nationale, *Maurice Bellemare. [Courtesy Archives nationales du Québec.]*

One reason for believing that the reformist policies in Quebec came more from within the state apparatus and less from the society around it, is the fact that cutbacks have been especially difficult to implement in government due to strong opposition from employees, managers, and interest groups. (We shall discuss this aspect later in the chapter.)

What exactly happened during the 1960s has been scrutinized from every angle. One persistent critique posits that the Quiet Revolution has not changed Quebec politics to any great extent (Caldwell and Czarnocki 1977). Daniel Latouche (1974) has argued that changes during the 1960s were not much more extensive than those of the 1940s. He has also noted that budgetary priorities set during the 1950s remained the same during the 1960s. For Latouche, the real shift in budgetary priorities occurred between 1945 and 1950, when natural resources were deemphasized in favour of health and education. There was a marked increase in the overall level of expenditures during the Lesage years, but the distribution of these expenditures over various categories was not significantly different from that of previous years. It might be asked whether budgets are good indicators of government activities, but as René Lévesque pointed out in his memoirs, they are the best indicator of what a government *wishes* to do. McRoberts (1988) suggests, meanwhile, that the Quiet Revolution was not quantitative but qualitative, the essence being transfer of power to the state.

Simard (1977) maintains that to understand what happened we should look at the number of agencies created and who they were confronting, and that state-building in this sense has been innovative in Quebec.

The Quebec state confronted three power elites that, until then, had never been challenged: the Catholic Church, the anglo-Canadian and American bourgeoisie, and the federal government. Usually, challenges to the status quo in the Western world come from conservative institutions that are losing status, power, and privileges due to modernization, and are directed at the state. In Quebec, the reverse happened: modernization spurred the State to challenge the conservative institutions. This modernization ended the practice of locally integrated institutions, like the church or family, taking responsibility for and controlling welfare, health, and education. What has made the role of the state in this sector more important is not only the decline of the Church as a social institution, but also the disintegration of the traditional family unit.

Since the State has replaced the Church and the family, expenditures have increased at one of the fastest rates in the world. For example, if we compare expenditures as a percentage of total expenditures in the health sector for the years 1970–1980 among the members of the Organization for Economic Cooperation and Development (OECD), the greatest increase, in Norway (19%), is followed by that in Quebec (14%, which had been 6%

under the average and is now 2% over). For Canada as a whole, the increase was 5%. In Quebec, 81% of the expenditures are made by the government. In Canada as a whole, 76% of the expenses were made by governments in 1980 (43% in the United States, 96% in Sweden).

4.3   THE PROGRESS OF STATE-BUILDING

We can get some perspective on the growth of the state by looking at a few statistics. Between 1935 and 1957, only five autonomous agencies (as opposed to central) were created in Quebec.[1] Nine were created while Duplessis was in power for the years 1936 to 1939 and 1944 to 1959. Four more had come into being under the 1940–1944 Godbout government. The Quiet Revolution changed these numbers dramatically. Between 1960 and 1965, 12 agencies were added, 22 more between 1966 and 1969, 32 during the first Bourassa government (1970–1976), 32 more during the first mandate of the PQ (1976–1981), 32 more during the second mandate (1981–1985). This is in contrast to only five during the first three years of the return of Bourassa to power.

Simard (1977) lists other organizations that were transformed or created: 23 departments, 55 consultative bodies, 9 administrative tribunals, 63 economic management institutions, the junior colleges (CEGEPs), the state university network, the social services institutions, and the state-owned enterprises. (In such a rapidly growing state apparatus, coordination inevitably becomes more problematic, as we shall see.)

One of the paradoxes of the Quiet Revolution is that it sprang into being under Jean Lesage. Lesage was anything but a reformist, but he did have the political wisdom to accept the reforms put forward by his ministers, Lévesque, Gérin-Lajoie, and Kierans. For six years, Lesage presided over transformations he could never have dreamed of the night he won the election in 1960. Under his premiership, the state of Quebec became active in the economic sector with the nationalization of hydroelectric corporations and the creation of *Hydro-Québec*. The *Caisse de dépôt et placement du Québec* (Quebec Deposit and Investment Fund), was another important state-owned corporation. It was created in 1965 to administer government pension and insurance funds and now owns stock in most major Canadian companies and has a significant international portfolio.

---

1. There is a fundamental difference between central and autonomous agencies. The main purpose of central agencies is to coordinate operations, but because everything cannot be managed from the centre, a certain measure of control (and thus power) must be relinquished to other, autonomous branches of government.

Because it is redefining the nature of ownership in the economy, the Caisse de dépôt might eventually prove to have more impact than Hydro-Québec. With the Caisse, the differences between the public and the private sector almost cease to exist. The legislation creating the Caisse was enacted as a result of the discussions surrounding the creation of the Canada Pension Plan in 1963–1964. In the debates at the Legislative Assembly (now the National Assembly), Lesage, who presented Bill 51, predicted that the Caisse would become the most important and powerful economic instrument ever to exist in Quebec, carefully managing pension money and stimulating Quebec's economic development.

The Caisse eventually emerged as the owner and manager of Canada's single largest stock portfolio. In fact, it became a matter of national interest in 1980. In part, this was due to management's refusal to divulge details about individual shareholdings, a low profile that resulted from a fairly passive investment strategy avoiding visible confrontation with private economic interests in its pursuit of its four primary goals of fiduciary protection of capital, diversity in investments, optimization of yield, and promotion of economic growth (Huffman et al., 1985: 141). But there was also concern about the power of public-sector technocrats vis-à-vis those in the private sector.

In response to these concerns, the Corporate Shareholding Limitation Act, Bill S-31, was introduced in the Senate without consultation or prior notice to the provincial governments. If it had gone through, S-31 would have allowed the federal government to curb province-building through the use of state-owned enterprises (see Tupper 1983: 19). The bill, which finally died on the order paper, was an attempt to stop the Caisse from using direct equity to become involved in significant Canadian enterprises. Managers, accustomed to dealing with powerless shareholders, now had to take into account the economic power of a large provincial state-owned enterprise.[2]

Another important public enterprise was the *Société générale de financement* (SGF). Set up as a mixed enterprise in 1962, the purpose of the SGF was to regroup existing companies and form new ones in a major industrial conglomerate. Today, the SGF is a holding company with investments in pulp and paper, aluminum, petrochemicals, and electrical equipment. The SGF became a public enterprise in 1971 and was restructured in 1978 toward the current areas of investment. In the natural resources sectors, to add to the existing departments, two state-owned enterprises were created: *SOQUEM* for mining operations and *REXFOR* for forest

---

2. As of December 1980, the Caisse had invested about $8,934 million in Canadian stocks and convertible bonds.

Paul-Gérin Lajoie. He was among the key figures in the educational reform of the 1960s that led to the Rapport Parent, *the restructuring of secondary education, and the creation of the CEGEPs. [Courtesy Archives nationales du Québec. Photo: Paul-Gérin Lajoie.]*

products. A third, *SOQUIP*, was formed to handle oil production and distribution.

What was even more dramatic was the nature of the intervention, which embraced not only the economy, but also education, health, and social services. Instead of allocating money to the Church and private institutions for education, for example, the state took charge.

The Liberal political platform had contained several propositions related to education, but there was no mention of a Department of Education, the transformation of the high school system, the creation of the CEGEPs or the network of Université du Québec. These changes came after the *Rapport Parent* (report of the Royal Commission of Inquiry on Education in the Province of Quebec, headed by Monsignor Alphonse-Marie Parent, Vice Rector of the Université Laval). It outlined a complete educational philosophy, stating that everyone should be guaranteed an education consistent with his or her interests, and criticized the existing education system as inadequate, administratively incoherent, elitist, and archaic (Milner 1986: 23).

Since 1964, there has been a major redistribution of responsibilities, with the core of the system, the Department of Education, attempting to maintain a monopoly over the other parts of the system. The results have been impressive. In 1960, of 100 children who entered first grade, 70 went on to high school, 16 attended college, and 7 went as far as university. By 1983, of these 100, almost 100 entered high school, 52 went on to junior college (CEGEP), and 35 attended university.

A similar expansion occurred in health and social services. The *Ministère de la Santé et des services sociaux* (Ministry of Health and Social Services), now an enormous bureaucracy, was set up in 1970 to replace the Church and religious communities in this area. In previous years the Quebec state had played only an indirect role in providing such services.

The biggest innovation in Quebec was the introduction of the principle of universality, by which everyone was entitled to receive the same services. Reforms aimed to achieve universality were made after the application of the recommendations of two task force reports. The first, the Boucher Report of the 1960s, recommended that the State should take over the role of the Church, which was limited in the services it could offer. The second, from the Castonguay-Nepveu Commission, said that the intervention should go further, that services should be expanded so people living on welfare could become productive again.

The PQ and State-Building

On November 15, 1976, René Lévesque and the PQ won the election. Never before had so much emotion—hope on one side, fear on the other—been invested in a newly elected provincial government. Many were counting on a second Quiet Revolution, a second leap forward. In its first mandate the PQ completed reforms started in 1960 in areas such as agricultural zoning, automobile insurance, and electoral and party financing reform.

The inauguration of a new Montreal subway line in November 1984. **Left to right:** *Michel Clair, Minister of Transport; Pierre Desmarais II, president of the Montreal Urban Community; Jean Drapeau, mayor of Montreal; René Lévesque, Premier of Quebec. [Courtesy Le Devoir and Gilles Paré, Librarian. Photo: Jacques Grenier.]*

The most important reform was the completion of legislation concerning the language of work in Quebec: in 1977, Bill 101 was passed as a followup to Bill 22 of 1974. Basically, these laws stipulated that the language of work in Quebec must be French, and required children of immigrants to attend French-language rather than English-language schools.

Aside from the language bill, however, there were few other major changes after 1976. The Lévesque government had its hands full contending with a depressed economy, and because the PQ and its policies were already so securely in power with widespread popular support, the issue of Quebec independence became less pressing (Fraser 1984). It was partly due to this attitude and the gains made within the federal framework that the PQ lost the constitutional referendum in 1980. Despite the referendum, or perhaps because of the lesson learned thereby, the party's policymakers enjoyed a decisive victory in the 1981 election. But that was their last great success of the period.

Although a large part of the business community was at the time opposed to Quebec independence, especially those members closely tied to the Canadian market, the state-owned enterprises initiated during the Quiet Revolution came of age in the 1980s. Hydro-Québec, the institution René Lévesque pushed so hard to get started thirty years ago, is responsible for considerable investment made each year in Quebec. The Caisse de dépôt has helped start up a number of Quebec-owned companies, which in turn have successfully challenged the power of the Montreal English-speaking bourgeoisie, many of whom have since moved to Toronto. Even Sidbec, the government-owned steel mill, after 15 years of losses, is now making money.

4.4 PROBLEMS AND RATIONALIZATION EFFORTS

The more the responsibilities of a government increase, the more difficult it is to coordinate and control its various activities. Before 1960, while the Quebec state was still very small, Duplessis had a tight grip on every aspect of government operations. But today's premier, whose state is far more powerful and able to intervene in more sectors and activities than Duplessis could have imagined, has less control.

Even during the Quiet Revolution, some problems were evident. But once started, the reforms proved impossible to stop. And new programs were added endlessly to the previous ones, causing costs to spiral out of control. In fact, because of federal-provincial competition, programs were frequently expanded.

Institution-building is always complex. Because government is about crisis management, and because different policies simultaneously require constant attention, governments cannot always coordinate the activities of various agencies the way a rational, decision-making body might be expected to. Moreover, priorities are not always clearly defined for government agencies, which means they must engage in a process of soul-search-ing just to understand what is expected of them. For example, Radio-Québec, the educational television service, has only recently decided it should ori-ent itself toward a broader public (see Cabatoff 1978); and Soquia, created in 1975 to provide financial support to medium-sized businesses in the food industry, from production units to retail outlets, had to wait until January 1977 to receive the ministerial directives specifying its mission.

These two examples illustrate that a clear rationale does not always precede the creation of a governmental agency. To generalize further, it takes time before reformist policies can be translated into coherent results. Sabatier (1986) has written that it takes between ten and twenty years to properly evaluate the implementation of any policy. This is also true for the evaluation of institution-building. Many of the state agencies created in the 1960s took several years to achieve their full potential; others fell victim to the cutbacks of the 1980s before they had a chance to fulfill their mission.

The differing levels of involvement of the Quebec state in education, health, and cultural affairs illustrates that the reforms initiated during the 1960s to centralize power in the hands of the provincial government have not been universally successful. In the health sector, it is true that govern-ment provides services directly to the population through Medicare, which was introduced in 1970–1971 and is considered an efficient system. How-ever, there is a well-publicized crisis in cost control. In education, school boards are protected from central control by the constitution. Efforts have been made to reduce their powers and to get rid of their sectarian aspects, but though the boards accommodate religious diversity, they have used the religious element to maintain their autonomy. In cultural affairs, cen-tralization has failed because the Department has attracted relatively inef-ficient civil servants and too many autonomous agencies—16 other departments and 17 agencies or governmental bodies—are involved.

The problem of duplication of departments and services between the federal and provincial government has yet to be solved. It is difficult for governments simply to eliminate programs or agencies. Governments around the world are caught in what has been called "the fiscal crisis of the State": the impossibility of placing any further taxes on the populace. The perception of government has changed: it was once seen as the solu-tion to problems; now, it is seen as the source of problems. The reaction has been to push for reduction of the deficit, privatization, deregulation, more access to information, reduction of union rights, and increased accountability for civil servants.

What happened in Quebec during the 1980s can be explained in terms of normalization and fiscal austerity. Efforts to control expenditures started with a more centralized Treasury Board: procurement expenditures are now tightly controlled from the core; also, budgetary operations are organized according to the programs of the government. When civil servants had their salaries reduced in 1982, it openly signalled the end of state-building.

One reason for the population's growing dissatisfaction with the State was that, in Quebec—as in the Western world in general—the government's inability to control economic cycles had resulted in a severe recession in the early 1980s. (There has been another in the 1990s.) And despite increased spending, social inequalities persisted while services did not improve.

After returning to power in 1985, the Liberal party published three reports: the Gobeil Report recommended a restructuring of government organization and programs; the Fortier Report recommended the privatization of certain state-owned enterprises; and the Scowen Report recommended some deregulation. Although the three reports did not result in a significant transformation of the Quebec state, they had a symbolic importance. Together they signalled the end of the Quiet Revolution and served notice that the State could no longer serve as the engine of change. Instead, the reports asserted the primacy of the private sector. The hegemony of the Quebec state was over after 25 years.

The premise of the Gobeil Report was that government organizations created in a different era had to be reevaluated. With this report, the Liberal party announced their intention to eliminate some of the programs that had been at the core of the reform movement. They concluded that the Quebec state had grown as much as it could, and now lacked the resources to go any further with statism. Former technocrats and business persons who had benefitted from the growth of the state were now deciding that it had grown sufficiently.

The general feeling was that, after 25 years of growth—and as further growth no longer seemed possible—it was time to take stock of existing government organizations and programs. Not all of the Report's recommendations were followed, but the government did reclaim some control over the state apparatus. The recommendations pointed out that a small State is a beautiful State—that it would be more efficient if it restricted itself to fewer areas of involvement. The options considered were, first, to do nothing; second, to abolish some government organizations; third, to reorganize by integrating organizations into regular departments or by merging them or transferring certain functions to municipal governments or the private sector; and fourth, to decrease the resources allotted to the organizations.

Three possible scenarios for rationalization have been promoted in recent years:

1. **A state that produces more**   A state that offers more services for less money is the goal in this model. Besides slashing budgets and cutting programs, there would also be continual reevaluation of existing programs.

2. **A smaller state**   There would be a reduction of the role of the state in the economy via the privatization of public enterprises, and a minimum of regulation in the private sector.

3. **Representative democracy**   As members of parliament have become increasingly aware that bureaucratic influence limits their power, they want civil servants to be accountable to the National Assembly.

Over the years, expenses in the provincial state have been decreased through three different means. The first has been to increase control over procurement expenditures, starting with a parliamentary commission to investigate and approve procurements, and later through the use of the ROSALIE system, a computer program essentially involving a list of companies the government may buy from. Under the previous system, ministers and civil servants had had the power to spend well beyond the budgets of their departments.

The second approach has been to coordinate the preparation of the budgets of the various departments, to plan expenses rather than being told by the departments how much they are likely to spend. Now, the treasury board in charge of the expenses sets a very low ceiling on expenditures, after which the departments have to ask the board for permission to spend further.

The third method has been to organize budgetary operations according to government programs. Instead of making incremental modifications to departmental budgets, departments receive money according to the programs they are in charge of implementing. As a result, program managers who want increased budgets must sell the social value of the programs they are implementing rather than simply request more employees or computers. In this system, high-priority programs get more funding. Ultimately, the entire system is transformed.

It is unclear how much the productivity of the public sector is affected by cutbacks. According to one scenario, it may even improve. To limit cutbacks, government employees need to cultivate support from the people they serve. Coalitions with clients to preserve services might lead to a more productive, client-oriented public service in the future.

Symbol of a modern city: the Olympic Stadium in Montreal. [Courtesy Le Devoir and Gilles Paré, Librarian. Photo: Jacques Nadeau.]

4.5   QUEBEC'S PRESENT STATUS AND THE PREMIER'S ROLE

A major feature of the past thirty years has been the extensive political realignment of Quebec. The nationalist line divided the two main parties, the Union nationale and the Liberal party, into more- and less-nationalist wings; then the PQ replaced the UN as one of the two dominant parties, and deepened the nationalist line between parties.

Another legacy is the economic power the state has cultivated. The rise of the local bourgeoisie during the last decade would not have been possible without this cultivation.

The language policies of the 1970s can be seen as the legislated continuation in the private sector of changes that could not be achieved through the state structures. From the toothlessness of Bill 63 and the vagueness of Bill 22 to the restrictions of Bill 101 and the adjustments of Bill 178, language policy has become an integral, and very sensitive, part of political life. (See Chapter 14.)

Over the 1980s, after the referendum on constitutional matters and the recession, the Quebec state was consolidated and normalized. The government indicated its intention to rationalize state-owned enterprises, adapt language policy to guidelines set out by the Supreme Court, and limit the growth of regulation and the state apparatus. Control of the social and education systems has been centralized, and the emergence of a local bourgeoisie has partly alleviated the economic control problem. Only the constitutional issue remains to be resolved.

The definition of the role of Quebec internationally was a particularly controversial issue during the Trudeau era, especially after Expo 67 in Montreal, at which French President Charles de Gaulle made his controversial speech ending with *"Vive le Québec libre!"* Since the election of Brian Mulroney's Conservative government in 1984, however, several issues have been resolved. One of these is the longstanding debate over Quebec's representation at the Francophone Summit. At the end of the 1950s, the idea of a French Commonwealth was contemplated by leaders of several African states, in particular Leopold Senghor of Sengal. The French government believed that Quebec should play a key role in these summits; however, the federal government consistently refused to recognize the Premier of Quebec as the voice of a unique francophone culture and society, and denied a separate seat to Quebec at these conferences.

Then in March 1970, at Niamey in Niger, the Quebec state became a member of the newly created *Agence de coopération culturelle et technique des pays francophones* (Cultural and Technological Agency of the Francophone Countries), which was an immediate source of conflict with federal bureaucracies and politicians. Giving a seat to Quebec, argued the federal government, would grant it special status as a sovereign state. Finally, in 1984, René Lévesque and Brian Mulroney worked out an arrangement for the first summit of the francophone countries in Paris. At the second summit, which took place in Quebec City in 1988, Premier Robert Bourassa gained credibility not only in Canada but also in the international community.

The Quebec government also initiated an annual meeting of first ministers with the French government. In the first year the two premiers met in Paris, and in the following year Quebec City. When Laurent Fabius became French premier in 1983, his first international trip was to Quebec City, and Premier Lévesque went to Paris in the spring of 1984.[3] For the Quebec Premier, the link with France is important in maintaining economic and cultural relationships, gaining access to the European market, and emphasizing the Premier's status as the leader of a state.

The continental and international role of the Quebec premier, especially in comparison to the period before the Quiet Revolution, has evolved to the point where the Premier's economic and political influence is more powerful and extensive than that of some nations with a seat at the United Nations. As leader of the largest francophone group in North America, the Premier of Quebec is an important political figure.

---

3. In recent years these meetings have been less frequent, and were sometimes cancelled due to unforeseen events (such as the Oka crisis, which superseded Michel Rocard's trip to Quebec).

The beginning of Quebec international relations: a meeting between French President Charles De Gaulle and Quebec Premier Jean Lesage in the mid-1960s. [Courtesy Bibliothèque du Québec.]

Among the institutions inherited from the 1960s is the Department of International Affairs. Its objectives were, first, to achieve a measure of international status (made possible with the help of France) and, second, to develop both export markets and external capital markets to finance modernization. Now, having undergone a few organizational transformations, the Department has come to represent Quebec's interests internationally.

One thing that the Quiet Revolution changed irrevocably is the role of the Premier's office in shaping public policy. Over the years, the Premier's Cabinet has evolved into a core institution in the initiation of legislation. It is the Department of the Executive Council that focusses on promoting the Premier as the representative of the largest francophone group in North America, with an important role to play in Quebec, in Canada, and internationally.

The First Ministers Conference is an important gathering at which provincial premiers from across Canada discuss a wide range of issues. It is an excellent opportunity to discuss various matters of concern, establish friendly relationships with the other premiers, attend seminars, and work on public relations.[4]

The Premier is also invited to the annual Conference of the New England Governors and North-eastern Canadian Premiers, the North England States Conference, and conferences called by the provinces and U.S. states along the Great Lakes and St. Lawrence Seaway. All these are forums for discussion of a variety of topics that concern the governments involved. In recent times local boundaries have become less and less important from an economic perspective; the challenge is to relinquish a strictly isolationist perspective and find an acceptable level of trade and cultural exchange between nations.

Today, Quebec is at a crossroads. A more nationalist government could rejuvenate the large state apparatus, which has the all the necessary expertise and skills to formulate and implement policy. On the other hand, the state apparatus could be reduced to fulfill the more modest functions of another provincial state, for at this point, the monitoring, implementation, and modification of policies started during the Quiet Revolution no longer require the current number of civil servants. The ambiguity of the constitutional situation, however, makes it difficult for state institutions to function smoothly.

---

4. René Lévesque has written of one of these sessions, his last, during the summer of 1984 in St. John's, Newfoundland: "One in particular, on free trade, a subject we were discussing together for the first time, became so heated we forgot to break for lunch. Based on several different assessments of the markets involved, we came up with a view of Canadian regionalism in a nutshell, stated with a brute frankness that was a lot more stimulating than all those maybe-yes, maybe-no attitudes that have been multiplying ever since. Put simply, our talks lined western free-traders up against Ontario protectionists, with Québec somewhere in the middle...." (Lévesque 1986: 41–42)

KEY TERMS

Deregulation

Nation-building

Nationalization

Privatization

Province-building

State-owned enterprises

REFERENCES AND FURTHER READING

Averyt, William F. 1989. "Quebec's economic development policies, 1960–1987: between *Étatisme* and Privatization." *American Review of Canadian Studies*, 19: 159–175.

Balthazar, Louis. 1980. "La Dynamique du nationalisme au Québec." In Gérard Bergeron and Réjean Pelletier (eds.), *L'État du Québec en devenir*. Montreal: Boréal. Pp.37–58.

Cabatoff, Kenneth. 1978. "Radio-Québec: a case study of institution-building." *Canadian Journal of Political Science*, 11: 125–138.

Caldwell, Gary and B. Dan Czarnocki. 1977. "Un Rattrapage raté—le changement social dans le Québec d'après-guerre, 1950–1974: une comparason Québec/Ontario." *Recherches sociographiques*, 18: 9–58.

Gingras, Francois-Pierre and Neil Nevitte. 1983. "La Révolution en plan et le paradigme en cause." *Canadian Journal of Political Science*, 16: 691–716.

Gouvernement du Québec, Assemblée nationale. "Notes du discours de l'honorable Jean Lesage prononcé en chambre le 9 juin 1965 lors de la présentation, en deuxième lecture, de la loi de la Caisse de dépôt et placement du Québec" (Bill 51).

Gouvernement du Québec, Ministère du Développement économique. 1979. *Challenges for Quebec*. Quebec: Éditeur officiel. 1979.

Gouvernement du Québec, Ministère du Développement économique. 1982. *Technology Conversion*. Quebec: Éditeur officiel.

Gouvernement du Québec, Ministère des Finances, Ministre délégué à la Privatisation. February 1986. *Privatisation de sociétés d'état: orientations et perspectives*.

Gouvernement du Québec. June 1986. *Rapport du comité sur la privatisation des sociétés d'Etat, De la Révolution tranquille ... à l'an deux mille*.

Gouvernement du Québec. June 1986. "Réglementer moins et mieux," *Rapport final du groupe de travail sur la déréglementation*.

Huffman, K. J. et al. 1985. "Public enterprise and federalism in Canada." In Richard Simeon (ed.), *Intergovernmental Relations*. Toronto: University of Toronto Press. Pp. 131–178.

Latouche, Daniel. 1974. "La Vraie Nature de la Révolution tranquille." *Canadian Journal of Political Science*, 7: 525–536.

Laurendeau, Marc. 1990. *Les Québécois violents*. Montreal: Boréal.

McRoberts, Kenneth. 1988. *Quebec: Social Change and Political Crisis*. 3rd ed. Toronto: McClelland and Stewart.

Milner, Henry. 1986. *The Long Road to Reform: Restructuring Public Education in Quebec*. Montreal: McGill-Queen's.

Sabatier, Paul A. 1986. "Top-down and bottom-up approaches to implementation research: a critical analysis and suggested synthesis." *Journal of Public Policy*, 6: 21–48.

Salée, Daniel. 1990. "Reposer la question du Québec? Notes critiques sur l'imagination sociologique." *Revue québécoise de science politique*, 18: 83–106.

Simard, Carolle. 1989. "L'Administration de la culture au Gouvernement du Québec" In Yves Bélanger and Laurent Lepage (eds.), *L'Administration publique québécoise: évolutions sectorielles 1960–1985*. Sillery: Presses de l'Université du Québec. Pp. 173–199.

Simard, Jean-Jacques. 1977. "La Longue Marche des technocrates," *Recherches sociographiques*, 18: 93–132.

Trudeau, Pierre Elliott. 1974. *The Asbestos Strike*. Toronto: James Lorimer.

Young, R. A., Philippe Faucher, and André Blais. 1984. "The concept of province-building: a critique." *Canadian Journal of Political Science*, 17: 783–818.

PART

II

People

and

Politics

CHAPTER 5

POLITICAL
PARTIES,
CAMPAIGNS, AND
ELECTIONS

5.1 POLITICAL PARTIES

Dominant Parties in Quebec History

Through most of its history Quebec has been mainly a two-party system. Minor parties have always been present, but they have seldom succeeded in electing a candidate. Between 1867 and 1935, two parties contended in the political arena: the Liberals and the Conservatives. In 1935, the Conservatives joined forces with *Action libérale nationale*, a splinter group from the Liberal party, to form the *Union nationale*. This party, led by Maurice Duplessis from 1935 to 1959, was in power until 1960, except for the period 1939–1944.

When the nationalist movement emerged in the early 1960s, Quebec gained a multi-party system that lasted until the Parti québécois' election in 1976. At times during the 1960s and early 1970s there were as many as three separatist parties. The major development regarding Quebec's political parties since the mid-1970s has been the return to a two-party system, with the Union nationale being replaced as the second party by the Parti québécois.

Throughout its existence, the Union nationale has been identified with the nationalist cause in Quebec. Many would argue, though, that its brand of nationalism was sterile and defensive. The party's stated objective was to defend Quebec's "autonomy"; but it never went so far as to propose sovereignty or independence. Some would say that the Union nationale's attempt to increase provincial autonomy was a smokescreen for its real

A political meeting in 1951. Camilien Houde on the platform saying to Maurice Duplessis, sitting: "L'affaire est dans le sac" ("It's in the bag"). [Courtesy Archives nationales du Québec. Photo: Richard Arless.]

agenda of delaying the advent of the welfare state and protecting laissez-faire economics. Since most social programs between the 1930s and 1950s were initiated by the federal government—even though social policy is constitutionally recognized as being a provincial prerogative—the autonomy stance taken by Maurice Duplessis provided a good excuse not to implement these programs.

By the mid-1950s many intellectuals, union leaders, journalists, and university professors were denouncing Duplessis' brand of nationalism not only with regard to the welfare state and Keynesian economics, but also with reference to the economic, political, and social reforms so urgently needed to bring Quebec into the 20th century.

Parties and Ideologies Since the 1960s

In the 1960 election campaign, the Liberal party promoted itself as the party of much-needed change in all fields of policy and practices of government. It also tried to convey a more positive image of Quebec and Quebecers, declaring that things could be changed and that Quebecers were competent to take the necessary economic initiatives. Having won that election, the Liberals stepped up their nationalist discourse. The 1962 election was in fact a quasi-referendum on the nationalization of several power companies under the aegis of Hydro-Québec, which had already been controlling electric power distribution in the Montreal area since the 1940s.

There had been clashes with the federal government since 1960, and more were to come. Quebec needed to bolster its financial resources if it was to create all the programs it wanted and take over some administered by the federal government. Directly and indirectly, only the Liberals raised Quebec's nationalism to new heights. It was a different, more positive brand of nationalism than the one espoused by the Union nationale. In the Liberals' vision, Quebec and Quebecers had great potential which only needed to be developed. This revived sense of identity was first expressed on the cultural scene with an outburst of "Québécois" affirmation in song-writing, the performing arts, and film-making. The Liberals chose a brilliant slogan for the 1962 campaign: *Maîtres chez nous* (Masters in our own house). They won the election handily and proceeded to nationalize the power companies.

As a result of the mounting nationalism, the Liberal Party began to experience profound tensions and divisions, especially among Cabinet members, during the second half of the 1960s. The party was defeated in the general election of 1966. Thanks to the particularities of the electoral map, the Union nationale won a majority of seats even though it trailed almost seven percentage points behind in the popular vote. However, some observers attributed this defeat in part to the conduct of Premier Jean Lesage during the 1966 campaign. Apparently offended that some of his ministers, among them René Lévesque, shared the limelight during the period 1960–1966, he decided that the party strategy should be focussed on him, his Cabinet members playing secondary roles. The strategy back-fired, and to everyone's surprise the Union nationale was back in power.

Thereafter, tensions within the Liberal party only increased. At its 1967 convention, the party split into two factions: one favouring a redefinition of powers between the federal and provincial levels of government within the Canadian political system, and the other, headed by René Lévesque, then Minister of Social Affairs, proposing that Quebec seek political sovereignty while maintaining economic ties with the rest of Canada.

When put to a vote on what had become a bitter and nasty convention floor, Lévesque's proposal was soundly trounced, and he and his followers walked out. Later on in the fall of 1967, more than eight hundred people gathered around René Lévesque to create the *Mouvement souveraineté-association* (MSA). The main objective of the MSA—which was first thought of as a political movement rather than a party—was to propagate the notion that Quebec, both for its own and Canada's good, should become a sovereign political entity while maintaining close economic ties with the rest of Canada through some form of association which remained to be defined (e.g., customs union, common market, free trade zone).

Mouvement souveraineté-association *(MSA) convention in October 1968, when the* Parti québécois *was founded. A delegate reading a document: "A party to create, a nation to build." [Courtesy Archives nationales du Québec. Photo: Michel Giroux.]*

There were already two active separatist parties on Quebec's electoral scene. The most important was the *Rassemblement pour l'indépendance nationale* (RIN). The RIN, created in 1963, was considered a somewhat leftist party by some, and on the radical left by others. Fielding 73 candidates in the 1966 general election, it did rather poorly, receiving 5.4% of the popular vote without gaining a single seat in what was then called the Legislative Assembly. The other separatist party, the *Ralliement national* (RN), was an outgrowth of the RIN in that it comprised the party's right wing, which had seceded over what it saw as the RIN's excessively radical stands on socioeconomic issues. Actually the RN was the result of two political mergers. In 1964, the right wing had walked out on the RIN to form the *Regroupement national*. In 1966, it merged again, with *Le*

At the MSA congress on the weekend of October 11–14, 1968 in Quebec City, the Parti québécois was founded, and delegates debated hundreds of resolutions to modify the draft program drawn up at the April MSA convention. [Courtesy Archives nationales du Québec. Photo: Michel Giroux.]

Ralliement créditiste—the Quebec branch of the Social Credit Party, which had had considerable success in Quebec in the 1962 federal general election—taking on the name *Ralliement national*. It too ran candidates, 90 of them, in the 1966 election. It gained 3.1% of the vote and did not elect any candidates.

It quickly became apparent to René Lévesque and the MSA that it was pure folly to have two parties and one political movement working separately toward the same end. Talks got under way with the other two parties. In the fall of 1968, the RN agreed to fuse with the MSA to form a new party, the Parti québécois. Negotiations with the RIN, however, were not so productive. There was a clash of personalities between René Lévesque and the RIN leader, Pierre Bourgault. Also, members of the RIN thought they should be absorbing the PQ rather than the other way around, since the RIN had been in existence longer. Other members refused to subscribe to any formula that had Quebec maintain ties with the rest of Canada. Eventually, rather than merge, the RIN officially dissolved itself a few weeks after the PQ's creation. Those members who had not already joined the party were advised to do so.

Quebec now had three major parties, committed to varying degrees of nationalism: all or nothing in the case of the PQ, moderate within the UN and the Liberal party. During its tenure from 1966 to 1970 under the leadership of Daniel Johnson and Jean-Jacques Bertrand, the UN in its dealings with Ottawa had assumed the nationalist stance defined by the Liberals at the beginning of the decade. Daniel Johnson had gone so far as to use the slogan—also used as the title of Johnson's book—*Égalité ou indépendance* ("Equality or Independence"). At that time, both the Liberal party and the UN were seeking special status for Quebec within the Canadian federation. Some spoke of "associated States" or requested that Quebec be recognized as having a "particular status"—the antecedent of the "distinct society" concept.

The 1970 election would decide whether this three-party system was viable, or whether one of them would disappear. To some it seemed that the most likely candidate for elimination was the UN. It had been kept alive by a rural clientele in an era when the existing electoral districts did not reflect the increasingly urban and industrialized character of Quebec society; the 1970 election would be held under a new electoral map— almost every electoral division had been redrawn. Furthermore, electoral statistics showed the UN had been undergoing a steady decline in its share of the popular vote since 1948—with an acceleration in the 1960s— even though it had won four of the six general elections held between 1948 and 1966.

Pierre Bourgault, leader (1964–1968) of the Rassemblement pour l'indépendence nationale *(RIN) until its dissolution in 1968, with René Lévesque in 1970. [Courtesy Archives nationales du Québec.]*

As expected in some quarters, the UN made a poor showing, receiving only 19.6% of the popular vote and electing 17 of its candidates. By the 1973 election, support had eroded even further: the party received only 4.9% of the popular vote and failed to elect a single candidate. For all intents and purposes, it was a dead party, effectively replaced as the official opposition party by the PQ.

The UN did get some measure of support in the 1976 general election, but this was merely a protest vote by anglophones who wanted to "punish" the Liberal party for adopting Bill 22, which made French the official language of the province. In fact, splitting their vote between the UN and the Liberals, Quebec anglophones enabled the PQ to squeeze through and win the election, to the astonishment of political observers, and most of all to that of the PQ leadership. Though the UN was able to gain 11 seats with 18.2% of the popular vote, it was to be its last stand. Most of those seats were won in electoral divisions where anglophones were well represented, namely the western part of the Montreal metropolitan area and in the Eastern Townships bordering the states of Maine and Vermont. From 1970 to the early 1980s, various attempts were made to revive the UN, but with little or no success except for the 1976 election (Quinn 1979: 238–280).

It might be argued that the UN was identified too closely with the persona of Maurice Duplessis, who led the party from 1935 until his sudden death in September 1959. He had created a formidable political machine, which he ran like an autocrat. Corruption, patronage, and discretionary subsidies all became normal government practice. In intellectual circles, the Duplessis years became known as the era of "The Great Darkness." This stigma never really left the party despite efforts to modernize and democratize its structures.

Thus, since the early 1980s, Quebec has reverted to a two-party system, which best accommodates the British parliamentary form of government in that it avoids the political instability brought about by coalition governments.

The Liberal party and the PQ of the 1990s are quite different from their earlier incarnations. The turnaround for the PQ came about during the economic crisis of the early 1980s. Then in power, the party took radical measures with regard to the public sector. In addition to redefining the role of the State in Quebec's economy, public servants and employees of the para-public sector were subjected to pay cutbacks, and then their salaries were frozen at the 1980 level for few a years. These policies alienated this sector from the PQ, which had relied heavily on their support. The disaffection was acutely felt in the 1985 election, which was won by the Liberals.

The Liberal party had also changed since the mid-1970s. For one thing, Robert Bourassa, who had led the party from 1969 to 1976, was back again as its leader in time for the 1985 general election. In the interim, the leadership of the party had been entrusted to Claude Ryan, a prominent intellectual who, for a number of years, had been publisher of the influential daily *Le Devoir*. Ryan never quite lost his journalistic world view and was never able to comfortably make the transition from observer to leader.

Ideologically the parties also made some important changes. For the PQ, the main debate focussed on how to achieve political sovereignty. There had been interminable squabbles within party ranks since the lost referendum of 1980 over which path to choose to independence. Two factions emerged, one moderate and one radical. For the moderates, sovereignty was still the raison d'être of the party, but the referendum had made it clear that Québécois were not yet ready to follow the party down this path, and that therefore the independence question should be put on hold for a while. The radicals, on the other hand, felt the party had failed to sufficiently discuss and explain the whole independence issue. Furthermore, it favoured separating the concepts of sovereignty and association, which had been a single, hyphenated concept since the creation of the MSA in 1967. Their recommended plan of action was as follows: If the party won an election, it would hold a simple, "yes or no" referendum on the question of Quebec's accession to political sovereignty, without mention of an economic association with the rest of Canada. Talks on this question could be initiated, but if they proved fruitless, it would in no way dissuade Quebec from its push for independence. This in fact became the official party position.

René Lévesque stepped down as leader of the party in June 1984. He was replaced by one of his moderate ministers, Pierre-Marc Johnson, who lost the 1985 election. A leadership convention put the radical faction in control of the party, and it selected Jacques Parizeau as leader. Parizeau had been one of the grandmasters of Quebec's Quiet Revolution of the early 1960s in his capacity as a senior civil servant specializing in economic policy issues. He had been a prominent player in the creation of the *Caisse de dépôt et placement du Québec* and the nationalization of the electrical power companies in 1962.

Since its creation in 1968, the PQ has remained a party whose members play an important role in shaping the platform, and in which the platform is of utmost importance. In this sense, it could be called a programmatic party. Its program is spelled out in a 132-page document which details every action that should be taken in every field of activity. The realization of part of the program assumes the achievement of political independence, while the realization of other measures does not. The PQ remains active between elections, unlike the Liberal party, which tends to rouse itself mainly at election time.

The Liberal party is more elitist, though changes made in party-financing laws in the mid-1970s have forced it to be more open and active. The platform provides one example. Though the Liberal platform document is not as substantive and as detailed as that of the PQ—it is only 68 pages long—it is not just something thrown together on the eve of an election as in the old days, but the product of discussions and debates at the party's biennial conventions among party members under the guidance of the party's Political Commission.

After the failure of the Meech Lake accord in June of 1990, the Liberals had to redefine their constitutional position. In the not-so-distant past, this kind of policymaking might have been done in cabinet or in parliamentary caucus; in 1990, all party members were drawn into the process. The Constitutional Committee headed by Mr. Jean Allaire went to work in the fall of 1990 and was instructed to report to the party convention to be held in February 1991. At that convention the report, titled *A Quebec Free to Choose*, was unanimously adopted by party members. The report became the official party line on constitutional affairs. Giving its members a role in party proceedings was a new feature for a party that traditionally had had few dues-paying members and relied on the business community for its financing.

Each of the two major parties maintains permanent headquarters in Montreal. These are staffed by paid personnel. Thus the importance of the annual fundraising campaign, as it enables parties to maintain research services and promote various activities between election campaigns. There is a biannual convention in both cases. Members of other party structures meet on a regular or statutory basis. There are permanent commissions in both parties (see Figures 5.1 and 5.2), although, overall, the PQ's structures are more numerous and complex than those of the Liberal party. Furthermore, the PQ has stronger and more-active regional structures, a phenomenon reflected at other structural levels, and more particularly at the biannual convention.

Figure 5.1
Liberal Party Organizational Chart

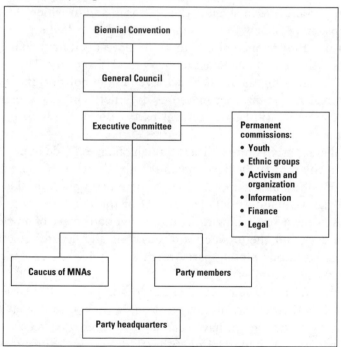

Source: Information provided by Liberal Party of Quebec. February 1991.

As of the 1989 general election, a third party, the Equality Party, had gained four seats in the National Assembly. Just as in the 1976 election, there was deep resentment in the anglophone community regarding the language policy of the Liberals. The National Assembly had recently passed Bill 178, forcing the use of French on any billing or posting of written

Figure 5.2

Parti québécois Organizational Chart

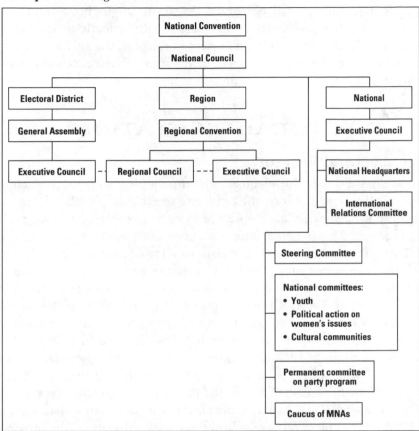

Source: Information provided by Parti québécois. 1992.

signs outside a business location. To achieve this goal, the Liberal government had invoked the "notwithstanding clause" of the 1982 Canadian
Constitution, which allows for the possibility of waiving some of the
Canadian Charter of Rights. Though Quebec's anglophone community is,
traditionally, an almost unconditional backer of the Liberal party, further
affirmation of the French fact in Quebec caused the anglophone community to create two political parties as a way of expressing their discontent.
The Unity Party and the Equality Party received a combined total of 4.7%
of the valid vote in the 1989 general election. Moreover, the Equality Party
elected four of its candidates, all of them in the western part of the island
of Montreal where the concentration of English-speaking people is the
greatest in Quebec. As a matter of fact, the Unity and Equality parties
respectively got 8.1% and 24% of the valid vote in those electoral districts

where they fielded candidates, which translates into massive support from the English community.

In matters other than perceived threats to anglophone rights, the Equality Party's representatives are ideologically eclectic; it is a single-issue party. Under similar circumstances in the past, the anglophone community has gone back to the Liberal party after registering its discontent during the course of one legislature.

5.2 ELECTORAL LEGISLATION[1]

The Electoral System

Quebec has a one-ballot electoral system coupled with single-member electoral divisions in which the candidate receiving a plurality of votes—though not necessarily an absolute majority—is declared the winner. It might be called a *one-ballot, single-member plurality system*.

This system, along with the deviations allowed in drawing up electoral divisions, can sometimes produce distorted results. First, it can bring to power a party that has obtained a majority of seats with a minority of the popular vote (see Tables 5.1 and 5.2 for the 1944 and 1966 results). Second, there can be large gaps between a party's share of the popular vote and the number of its candidates who get elected. The elections of 1970 and 1973 are cases in point. In 1970, the PQ received 23.1% of the popular vote but won only 7 seats (or 6.5%), whereas the Ralliement créditiste got 12 seats (or 11.1%) with a mere 11.2% of the popular vote. In this instance, the Ralliement's vote was heavily concentrated in two semi-urban regions, while the PQ made a relatively strong showing throughout the province, but with no specific strongholds. The PQ met with an even worse fate in the 1973 election, when it increased its share of the popular vote to 30.2%, yet won one less seat than in the previous election (6 instead of 7).

In the face of these anomalies, several commissions and committees have been created since the 1960s to investigate electoral systems in use throughout the world, evaluate them, anticipate their operation if transposed to Quebec, and make recommendations. All these reports have met the same fate. The recommendations—each of which mentioned some form of proportional representation and election of members-at-large—were never implemented. In every case the party in power was content to maintain the system that had put it in power, whatever injustices may have been involved. It seems that, once in power, parties forget how difficult it

---

1. Parts of this section are extracted from Directeur général des élections du Québec, *Election Act: Election Regulations* (Quebec: 1989).

Table 5.1

Seats Held by Each Party and Strength in National Assembly

Election Year	Liberal Party	Conservative Party/Union nationale[1]	Ralliement créditiste	Parti québécois	Others	Electoral Districts
1867	14 (21.9)	50 (78.1)	—	—	—	65 (64)[2]
1871	20 (30.8)	45 (69.2)	—	—	—	65
1875	19 (29.2)	43 (66.2)	—	—	3 (4.6)	65
1878	31 (47.7)	32 (49.2)	—	—	2 (3.1)	65
1881	15 (23.1)	49 (75.4)	—	—	1 (1.5)	65
1886	31 (47.7)	28 (43.1)	—	—	6 (9.2)	65
1890	42 (57.5)	24 (32.9)	—	—	7 (9.5)	73
1892	21 (28.8)	51 (69.9)	—	—	1 (1.4)	73
1897	51 (68.9)	23 (31.1)	—	—	—	74
1900	67 (90.5)	7 (9.5)	—	—	—	74
1904	68 (91.9)	6 (8.1)	—	—	—	74
1908	58 (78.4)	13 (17.6)	—	—	3 (4.0)	74
1912	64 (79.0)	15 (18.5)	—	—	2 (2.5)	81
1916	75 (92.6)	6 (7.4)	—	—	—	81
1919	74 (91.3)	5 (6.2)	—	—	2 (2.5)	81
1923	64 (75.3)	19 (22.4)	—	—	2 (2.3)	85
1927	75 (88.2)	9 (10.6)	—	—	1 (1.2)	85
1931	79 (87.8)	11 (12.2)	—	—	—	90
1935	48 (53.3)	42 (46.7)	—	—	—	90
1936	14 (15.6)	76 (84.4)	—	—	—	90
1939	70 (81.4)	15 (17.4)	—	—	1 (1.2)	86
1944	37 (40.7)	48 (52.7)	—	—	6 (6.6)	91
1948	8 (8.7)	82 (89.1)	—	—	2 (2.2)	92
1952	23 (25.0)	68 (73.9)	—	—	1 (1.1)	92
1956	20 (21.5)	72 (77.4)	—	—	1 (1.1)	93
1960	52 (54.7)	42 (44.2)	—	—	1 (1.1)	95
1962	63 (66.3)	31 (32.6)	—	—	1 (1.1)	95
1966	50 (46.3)	56 (51.9)	—	—	2 (1.8)	108
1970	72 (66.7)	17 (15.7)	12 (11.1)	7 (6.5)	—	108
1973	102 (92.7)	0 —	2 (1.8)	6 (5.5)	—	110
1976	26 (23.5)	11 (10.0)	1 (1.0)	71 (64.5)	1 (1.0)	110
1980	42 (34.4)	0 —	—	80 (65.6)	—	122
1985	99 (81.1)	0 —	—	23 (18.8)	—	122
1989	92 (73.6)	0 —	—	29 (23.2)	4 (3.2)	125

1. Conservative party before 1936.

2. No election in the Kamouraska District.

Sources: *Annuaire du Québec, 1979–1980*; Directeur général des élections, *Rapport des résultats officiel du scrutin du 2 décembre 1985 et du septembre 1989.*

Table 5.2
Percentage of Popular Vote Received by Each Political Party,
1867–1989

Election Year	Liberal Party	Conservative Party/Union nationale[1]	Ralliement créditiste	Parti québécois	Others
1867	45.0	55.0			
1871	35.0	65.0			
1875	44.0	56.0			
1878	49.0	51.0			
1881	42.0	56.0			
1886	51.0	49.0			
1890	53.0	47.0			
1892	45.0	55.0			
1897	54.3	45.7			
1900	56.3	43.8			
1904	67.7	25.4			
1908	55.3	39.9			
1912	54.3	45.1			
1916	64.6	35.1			
1919	70.0	23.7			
1923	55.3	44.4			
1927	62.7	36.6			
1931	55.6	44.2			
1935	50.2	48.7			
1936	41.8	57.5			
1939	54.2	39.2			
1944	39.5	35.8			
1948	38.3	51.0			
1952	46.0	51.5			
1956	44.5	52.0			
1960	51.3	46.6			
1962	56.4	42.1			
1966	47.2	40.9			
1970	45.4	19.6	11.2	23.1	0.7
1973	54.5	4.9	9.9	30.2	0.3
1976	33.8	18.2	4.6	41.4	2.0
1981	46.1	4.0	6.0	49.2	—
1985	56.0	0.2	—	38.7	5.1
1989	49.9	—	—	40.2	9.9

1. Conservative party before 1936.

Sources: *Annuaire du Québec, 1979–1980;* Directeur général des élections du Québec, *Rapport des résultats officiel du scrutin du 2 décembre 1985 et du septembre 1989.*

has been to get there, and are reluctant to change a formula which, in the end, has worked in their favour.

Each political party must select its own candidate to run in an election. In the Liberal party, the party leader calls for a convention at the level of each electoral district association. Only party members of each association are allowed to vote. In exceptional circumstances, the party leader can designate the candidate.

The PQ has a slightly different procedure, which prevents latecomers from joining the party in order to pack the convention hall on convention night and install a last-minute candidate instead of a long-time adherent, as has occurred in the Liberal party. The PQ's National Executive Council calls for a convention at the electoral district level, just as in the Liberal party. However, only members who have joined the party at least 90 days prior to convention day and who reside in the electoral district are allowed to vote on candidates. Also, the National Executive Council can, by a vote of two-thirds of its members, oppose or veto the selected candidate in any given electoral district, in cases where this seems justified.

Election Dates and Electoral Districts

Choice of the date for a general election is the prerogative of the incumbent premier. Most of the time this is done in close consultation with Cabinet colleagues, party pollsters, party organizers, and political insiders, but some Premiers have been known to make the decision to call an election in the greatest of secrecy.

There are 125 seats in Quebec's National Assembly, each linked to an electoral division or district. The boundaries of districts are set immediately after a general election by a three member commission on representation, which is an independent body made up of the chief electoral officer, who acts as chairperson, and two other individuals chosen from among qualified voters. Members of this commission are nominated for a five-year term on a two-thirds majority vote of the National Assembly, following a motion put forward by the Premier.

The general guideline in drawing up boundaries or remapping existent electoral divisions stipulates that the number of voters in each division must not deviate by more than 25% from the quotient obtained by dividing the total number of eligible voters by the number of electoral divisions. For example, if there are five million eligible voters and 125 electoral divisions, the quotient is 40,000 voters per division. Deviations of 10,000 voters more or less per division would be tolerated. However, a division with only 30,000 voters would be acceptable if it covered a very large territory, as is often the case in northern Quebec. Conversely, in densely populated urban divisions, such as Montreal, an electoral division may have as many as 50,000 voters within its boundaries.

Voter Registration

Until the 1966 election, *electors* (eligible voters) had to be 21 years old; now, the minimum age is 18. Additionally, voters must be Canadian citizens and must have resided in Quebec for at least six months prior to the election date. Of course, this includes women. However, Quebec women were the last in Canada to be enfranchised; it was not until 1940 that the Catholic Church's doctrinal reservations and male resistance finally succumbed to the women's suffrage movement.[2]

Various measures have been implemented to facilitate voter registration—or *enumeration*, as it is officially called—and participation in general elections. The most important of these is the stipulation that registration take place at potential voters' places of residence, for purposes of convenience. Once an election date has been set, the registration process is set in motion: From Monday to Thursday of the fifth week preceding election day, every home is called on by two enumerators appointed by the Returning Officer of the electoral division. The two enumerators are representatives of the two parties (or of independent candidates) that ranked first and second in the previous election in that particular division. The Election Act states that, together, they:

> visit every dwelling located in the polling subdivision assigned to them. At each dwelling where the enumerators receive no answer on their first visit, they must leave a card in the prescribed form indicating the date and time of their second visit. (Article 156)

In their house-to-house visits, the enumerators record the surname, given name, address, profession or occupation, and age of each person who will be a qualified voter on election day. Each voter is left with a certificate of registration bearing the signatures of the enumerators. As soon as the enumeration is completed, a list of voters for each polling subdivision is printed up, and, no later than 22 days before election day, a copy is forwarded to every dwelling in the subdivision.

At this point the revision process, an elaborate procedure conducted under the auspices of an official known as the Returning Officer, begins. Voters overlooked during the registration visits may file an application to have their names added to the list. Also, a voter, upon reviewing the regis-

---

2. At the federal level, women who were relatives of members of the armed forces, or who themselves worked for the forces, were "given" the right to vote in 1917, and in 1918 this right was extended to all women over 21. By 1922, women in every province but Quebec were enfranchised for elections held at the provincial level.

Table 5.3
Electoral Results and Participation Rates, 1867–1989

Election Year	Registered Voters	Valid Votes	Rejected Ballots	Electoral Districts	Participation Rate* (%)
1867	161,642†	75,715	—	65	46.8
1871	172,369†	60,266	—	65	35.0
1875	185,783	87,487	1,149	65	47.7
1878	217,825	134,475	1,755	65	63.9
1881	223,221	97,559	1,854	65	44.5
1886	234,844	147,525	2,699	65	64.0
1890	276,641	158,932	2,034	73	58.2
1892	294,335	174,751	1,771	73	60.0
1897	338,800	225,779	2,393	74	67.4
1900	350,517	103,402	980	74	29.8
1904	381,933	113,453	1,013	74	30.0
1908	415,801	244,839	3,222	74	59.7
1912	479,521	291,292	3,378	81	61.5
1916	485,936	208,462	2,767	81	43.5
1919	480,120	129,636	1,448	81	27.3
1923	513,224	290,649	3,768	85	57.4
1927	569,018	318,012	2,843	85	56.4
1931	641,323	489,695	4,190	90	77.0
1935	726,551	536,361	15,232	90	75.9
1936	734,025	569,325	4,930	90	78.2
1939	753,310	563,297	7,334	86	75.8
1944	1,865,396‡	1,329,959	15,591	91	72.1
1948	2,036,576§	1,513,825	17,928	92	75.2
1952	2,246,998	1,679,119	25,648	92	75.9
1956	2,393,360	1,845,729	28,781	93	78.3
1960	2,608,439	2,096,586	33,521	95	81.7
1962	2,721,783	2,136,966	29,509	95	79.6
1966	3,222,302	2,324,829	45,681	108	73.6
1970	3,478,578	2,872,970	57,029	108	84.2
1973	3,764,111	2,970,978	54,760	110	80.4
1976	4,023,743	3,360,506	70,424	110	85.3
1981	4,410,880	3,600,097	38,523	122	82.5
1985	4,579,921	3,411,607	52,625	122	75.6
1989	4,670,690	3,408,909	92,159	125	75.0

* From 1792 to 1834 the participation level was about 60%.

† Ballots were not used.

‡ Increase in number of registered voters due to the fact that women had acquired the right to vote in 1940.

§ Legal voting age brought down from 21 to 18.

Sources: *Annuaire du Québec, 1977–1978;* Directeur général des élections du Québec, *Rapport des résultats officiel du scrutin du 2 décembre 1985 et du septembre 1989.*

tered voters' list, may file a proposal that certain names be struck from the list because they do not qualify, or because they are registered in the wrong polling subdivision. The filing offices are opened from 10:00 a.m. to 10:00 p.m. from Monday to Thursday of the third week preceding the election, again to facilitate and encourage registration. The final list is submitted to a board made up of three persons from every polling subdivision within the division.

Also eligible to register are prison inmates, hospital patients, shut-ins, and those living in retirement homes, who may exercise their right to vote in what are called mobile polling stations. Finally, the Chief Electoral Officer maintains a voters' registry that includes individuals who: (1) expect to be outside Quebec on election day, (2) were qualified voters at the time of leaving Quebec (e.g., students living abroad), (3) have been outside Quebec for less than ten years, or (4) intend to return to Quebec.

To be permitted to vote outside Quebec in a mobile polling station, an individual must apply for registration. For purposes of the vote, the person is sent a ballot indicating the name of his or her electoral division no later than 24 days before the election. Included is a list of candidates for the division. The voter casts a vote by writing the name and surname of the candidate of his or her choice on the ballot paper. He or she then puts the ballot paper in a plain envelope, which is then placed in another envelope bearing his or her signature, name, and former address in Quebec. The completed ballot is returned to the Chief Electoral Officer, who checks that the signature on the envelope matches the one on the file registry. The Officer then sends the ballot to the proper electoral division. Registration in the registry has to be renewed every year.

Besides the procedures reviewed here, there are various other measures to facilitate voter participation, such as: (1) persons who temporarily have to live outside their own electoral division in order to work or study may choose to be registered either in their division or in the one in which they reside; (2) advance polling is possible in every electoral district, and a notice indicating the place, dates, and hours for advance polling are sent to every dwelling in a division; (3) direct participation of citizens in the electoral process as officers or candidates is promoted by requesting employers to grant leave without pay to any employee who wishes to fulfill such a role.

These various measures have had the effect of maintaining electoral participation rates of upwards of 75% since the early 1930s. (See Table 5.3.)

5.3 CAMPAIGNING

Officially accredited political parties and independents receive public funds on an ongoing basis between elections and during an election campaign.

Basically, the amount each party receives is based on its performance in the last general election. According to Article 82 of the Election Act, "The allowance shall be computed by dividing between the authorized parties, proportionately to the percentage of the valid votes obtained by them at the last general election, a sum equal to the product obtained by multiplying the amount of 25 cents by the number of electors entered on the list of electors used at that election."

The allowance is targetted for specific purposes only, such as reimbursement of expenses incurred by the parties for their day-to-day administration, for dissemination of the party platform, or for coordination of party activities.[3]

In order to solicit funds from private sources, claim expenses, or obtain loans, they must first obtain authorization from the Chief Electoral Officer. To be accredited, a political party or independent organization must first designate an official representative with the written approval of the party leader or candidate.

Other rules governing accreditation vary according to whether the request emanates from a political party or an independent candidate. In the instance of a political party, application for authorization or accreditation may be filed if it:

> undertakes to present official candidates in at least ten electoral divisions at any general election. The application must be accompanied with the names, addresses and signatures of one thousand electors declaring that they are members or supporters of the party. (Article 47)

If a party meets these and other, minor requirements, it is granted official recognition by the Chief Electoral Officer. As of December 31, 1990 there were 15 officially recognized parties at the provincial level in Quebec.

As for independent candidates, to be accredited they are required to submit information such as their own name and address, the name of the electoral division in which they are running, and the name and address of their official representative. The chief benefit of early official recognition as an independent candidate is that it entitles the official representative to solicit and collect contributions from the date of accreditation until election day; and after election day, it enables the candidate's representative "to solicit and collect contributions for the sole purpose of paying the debts arising from the candidate's election expenses" (Article 60) or to dispose of the surplus. In the latter instance, "the sums and goods may be used only for political, religious, scientific or charitable purposes" (Article 441).

---

3. For fiscal year 1989–1990, the Chief Electoral Officer distributed $1,136,558 among officially recognized parties.

There are two main circumstances under which official recognition of a party may be withdrawn by the Chief Electoral Officer: (1) it does not field at least ten candidates in a general election or (2) it fails to produce a detailed financial report by April 1 of each year. Of course, a party may also request to cease being recognized as an official party. For independent candidates, recognition automatically expires on December 31 of the year immediately following the election year.

The PQ and Party Financing

Democratization of party finances is now a pillar of Quebec's political system. During its first term (1976–1981) the PQ revolutionized party financing. The main objective achieved was the democratization of party financing through exclusion of contributions by businesses, unions, associations, and other corporate entities; private funding of parties and candidates became strictly regulated by many provisions of the Election Act.

Under the Act, only an individual voter can make a contribution to the official representative of an authorized entity, a political party, or an independent candidate, and the maximum yearly amount is fixed at $3,000. Contributions of over $100 must be made by cheque. Official representatives of political parties and independent candidates must issue receipts for each contribution. Though contributions to a political party are tax-deductible, certain sums of money and services are not deemed to be contributions. These include volunteer work, anonymous donations collected at political rallies, membership dues not exceeding $25 a year, an entrance fee to a political event where the fee is not over $50, free air time on radio or television, and space in a newspaper or periodical.

Only the official representative of an authorized party, or the delegate of this official within a particular electoral district, can collect funds, incur expenses, or contract a loan. Parties must also submit an annual financial report. The Election Act requires very detailed information in terms of income statements and financial reports. Among other things, a monetary value must be assigned to all goods and services, as well as to the various fees and donations not deemed to be political contributions. Article 115 of the Election Act stipulates that the financial report should indicate:

> the financial institutions where the amounts of money collected by the party are deposited and the account numbers used; the total value of services rendered and goods furnished free of charge; for each elector whose total contribution to the party and to each party authority exceeds $100, the elector's name and full residential address and the amount paid; a detailed statement of all amounts borrowed, the date of each loan, the name and full address of the

lender, the rate of interest charged, and the amount of the repayments in principal and of the payments.

The Equality Party, which emerged from the 1989 general election with four seats, has publicly complained that the name-disclosure provision has hindered its fundraising efforts, and reduced the number of potential donors, because publication of the donors' list had led, in some instances, to harassment of the contributors. The party contends that this has meant a loss in revenue as contributors shied away, knowing that their identities would be made public if their contribution was over $100. Yet this provision remains in place under the Liberal party, which returned to power in 1985, even though this party itself—whose greatest contributions used to come from the corporate sector—has had to make major changes in its fund-raising procedures. Apparently there is a tacit agreement between the two major parties not to return to the old days, when secret donations stuffed the war chests of political parties.

Basically the same procedure has to be followed by independent candidates, except that for most of them financial reporting is to be done only within 90 days after a general election, and not every year. If the independent candidate has accumulated debts that have not been acquitted by December 31 of the year following the year of the election, he or she becomes disqualified from running in either the next general election or any byelection.

All documents filed both by parties and by independent candidates are open to inspection by the public.

Campaign Financing

Concerning campaign expenditures, every party and candidate must name an official, exclusive agent to authorize election expenses. Also, an electoral fund must be created and deposited in a Quebec financial institution, and all election expenses must be paid from that fund.

The Election Act does not precisely define what constitutes an election expense, but it is comparatively explicit in its list of goods, services, and costs that do not qualify. One can infer that the main expenses are rent for the candidate's offices, staff salaries, publicity costs, transportation costs, utilities, and so on. Candidates use up to $2,000 of their own money to pay for personal expenses such as meals, housing, and transportation. These expenses are counted as part of the overall expenses up to the amount of $2,000. Advertising expenditures, however, do not qualify.

Parties are limited in their election expenses to the equivalent of 25 cents per eligible voter for all electoral districts in which they field a candidate; candidates are limited to the equivalent of 80 cents per eligible voter in their electoral district. Provisions are made for slightly higher ceilings for large and remote electoral districts, such as those in the northern regions of Quebec.

After the election, authorized candidates, whether members of officially recognized parties or independents, are reimbursed for 50% of their allowable expenses if (1) they were elected, (2) they obtained at least 20% of the valid votes, (3) they had been elected in the previous election, or (4) they were candidates of either of the two parties whose candidates obtained the greatest number of votes in the last election in the electoral district.

But the Election Act also provides that, after the nomination papers have been received by the Chief Electoral Officer, an advance of funds be made to those authorized candidates who will be entitled to reimbursement. The advance is on the order of 35% of the maximum election expenses allowed in a particular electoral district (i.e., 80 cents per registered voter in that district in the case of a general election).

In cases wherein the advance ends up exceeding 50% of the actual spending—a fact that becomes apparent when a candidate files electoral expenses—remittance of the surplus must be made to the Chief Electoral Officer. If the candidate is entitled to a reimbursement greater than the received advance, the Chief Electoral Officer must pay out the difference between the entitled reimbursement and the advance. Independent candidates are often at a disadvantage. Most of them cannot get an advance, since they do not meet criteria for reimbursement. The most likely chance of getting the reimbursement lies in winning at least 20% of the valid votes.

The official agent of an independent candidate must report election expenses to the Chief Electoral Officer within 90 days after election day. Making out this report is a tedious task, as the statement must be accompanied by invoices, receipts, and vouchers, and it must state the source of the sums collected by the election fund. Political parties must go through the same procedure, except that they have 30 more days to do so. Again the official agent is responsible for filing the return. These returns are published in summary form in the major newspapers by the Chief Electoral Officer within 60 days of the filing deadline. Should a winning candidate or a party fail to produce its return of expenses within 10 days after the expiry date "the candidate or party leader, as the case may be, becomes disqualified from sitting or voting in the National Assembly until the return and statement have been filed" (Article 442).

Candidates, Marketing Techniques, and the Election

Candidates   By law, an election must take place on the seventh Monday following the official call for an election if it is issued on a Monday, Tuesday, or Wednesday, or on the eighth Monday if the call is issued on another day. Thus, an election campaign in Quebec has a maximum duration of 53 days.

Candidates must be chosen by their respective parties at conventions held at the level of the electoral divisions. Some parties choose their candidates long in advance, while others nominate most of their candidates only after the election has been called. Nominated candidates (including independent candidates) should:

1. File a nomination paper no later than 2:00 p.m. on the sixteenth day preceding election day. The form used requires the candidate to give basic personal information and must bear the signature of the candidate's official agent.

2. Candidates representing a party must produce a letter from the party leader recognizing him or her as an official candidate of the party.

3. The nomination paper must be accompanied by a document bearing the signatures and addresses of at least 100 electors in the electoral division for which the paper is filed.

This procedure, an attempt to discourage frivolous candidatures—albeit a rather ineffectual one—replaces the former requirement of a $200 deposit.

Marketing Techniques   Since the 1960 election, campaign techniques have become more sophisticated than in the past. Consultants of all sorts, image-makers, pollsters, and media and marketing experts are now staples of every election campaign. Though not much has been written on the subject, one book (Benjamin 1975) describes the ploys and strategies used by the Liberal party and its leader Robert Bourassa during the 1970 and 1973 campaigns.

It seems that the Liberal party and its leaders were terribly impressed by the revelations in Joe McGinnis' *The Selling of the President* (1969), and called on the Chicago firm Social Research Inc. to organize its 1969 leadership convention and then the 1970 election (Benjamin 1976). Social Research was mandated to produce a report on the motivations of the Quebec electorate and the type of leader it would like to have. Robert Bourassa best fitted the profile they came up with, and was elected leader of the Liberal party. During Bourassa's leadership campaign, his advisors made abundant use of the material produced by Social Research, and continued using it during the 1970 election campaign. Heavy use was made of television, and the findings of 1969 study, in which Quebec voters had indicated that they wanted a leader knowledgeable in economics and who could act on that front. Bourassa's election campaign was orchestrated around the slogan "100,000 jobs,"—i.e., the Liberal party was promising to create that many jobs during its term in office. Other parties were less skilled in these new marketing techniques, and the Liberal party enjoyed an easy victory.

In the 1973 election campaign the Liberals relied even more heavily on mass media marketing techniques. By then the other parties had also begun to make good use of these techniques, though still not so extensively as the Liberal party. Each party monitored public opinion through its own polls. In addition to containing messages with universal appeal, publicity was targetted toward specific groups such as the young, the elderly, farmers, and middle-class families.

American campaigning strategies were adapted to Quebec's context; but, as Benjamin (1976: 102) notes, the techniques were not always used to achieve the same objectives from region to region. During the 1970s there were more than two contending parties with, at times, different regional bases. Therefore, because the adversary was not a homogenous group across Quebec, the selling of a candidate or a party had to be done on a regional basis and tailored to various political clienteles.

A campaign technique heavily used in Quebec, namely door-to-door canvassing by candidates (*solliciteurs*), can be traced directly to reforms in electoral and party financing introduced by the PQ in 1977. Limitations on both contributions and expenses have forced traditional parties such as the Liberals and the Union nationale to resort to this more populist approach —which is ironically similar to that which had helped bring the PQ to power in 1976. Ever since, candidates have had to make direct contact with the electorate.

Within these limitations, campaigning styles will, of course, always vary from party to party, and readjustments can always be made along the way. For instance, if public opinion poll findings indicate that a leader is more popular than the party, publicity might suddenly focus almost exclusively on the leader, downplaying the name of the party and its logo. Such was the case during the PQ's tenure (1976–1985), when polls constantly showed Premier Lévesque was more popular than his party. If the reverse is true, party slogans, logo, and platform can be placed at the forefront and local candidates promoted, and the leader made as unobtrusive as possible.

Another important element of campaigning is strategic presentation of the party platform, and the almost daily progression of electoral promises. The opposition party is usually more extravagant in its promises than the party in power, for the simple reason that, once elected, the opposition can always make the excuse that it did not know the exact state of the province's finances.

Televised debates between party leaders have not been characteristic of election campaigns in Quebec, as they have been of other Western democracies. One did take place in 1962, in which Jean Lesage squared off against Daniel Johnson. It was the first, and according to observers it helped Jean Lesage win the election. For various reasons, however, debates have been difficult to organize since then. Parties never seem able to agree on the number of debates, their dates, their format, and other technical issues. The last broadcast debate took place in 1985, but it was aired on radio rather than television, as the parties could not come to a consensus on the conditions put forth by TV networks.

The Election

Election Day   In the 1989 general election, the 125 electoral districts comprised a total of 21,905 polling stations, each representing an average of 213 registered voters. This arrangement was designed to avoid long lineups, which might discourage voter participation. For similar reasons, the Election Act stipulates that polling stations must be conveniently located and accessible to handicapped persons. Provisions must also be made to have a polling station in every hospital and every home for the elderly. Most polling stations are located in public schools, which by law must provide the use of their premises free of charge. Thus, election day is a holiday for public school students. Educational institutions, public or otherwise, must grant leave to students who are eligible voters.

At each polling station there is a Returning Officer—a representative of the Returning Officer of that particular electoral district—who ensures that balloting takes place according to the specifications of the Election Act. Also present are representatives of each of the candidates. These persons, who have been given a list of eligible voters for that polling station, keep count of those who vote and make sure no one attempts to vote more than once.

These electoral officers are entitled by law to a leave of absence without pay from their employer. Throughout this leave, which usually extends to more than one day, the employee is entitled to all the normal benefits except remuneration, and upon expiration of the leave, the employee must be reinstated under the same working conditions as prevailed before the leave. The law is very strict in this matter, giving an employee ample protection to actively participate in the electoral process.

Voting hours are from 10:00 a.m. to 8:00 p.m. To maximize voter participation, the Election Act states that while the polling stations are open, every employer must grant to an employee qualified to vote at least 4 consecutive hours for that purpose, not counting the time normally needed for meals. Also, no deduction of wages or other penalty may be imposed on an employee due to this leave (Article 335).

For all intents and purposes, this means that employees must be discharged from work between 3:00 and 4:00 p.m. on election day. Employers thus bear the costs of enhancing voter participation by paying for one or two hours of unworked time. The measure has few counterparts in the Western world.

Voting is done by hand on paper ballots. There are no voting machines. Formerly, party affiliations were not included on the ballot; only the name, surname, and profession of the candidates would appear. Consequently it was not unusual to find two candidates on the ballot with the same surname, one being the official candidate of one party, and the other a decoy recruited by the other main party to confuse voters. Nowadays, candidates are listed in alphabetical order with their affiliation or status as an independent clearly identified.

The voting procedure is as follows. Voters get to their designated polling subdivision and their name is checked against the voters' list. They are directed to one of the available polling booths. If it is being used, they wait until it is free, and then walk to a table where representatives of the Returning Officer and the candidates are sitting, taking a folded ballot with a

Premier Robert Bourassa casting his vote in his riding on September 25, 1989. [Courtesy Le Devoir and Gilles Paré, Librarian. Photo: Jacques Grenier.]

detachable stub (numbered identically to the ballot). Voters then enter the voting booth, mark the ballot in favour of one candidate, fold the ballot in the same manner as it was originally, return to the table, and in full view of the seated persons remove the numbered stub and hand it to the Deputy Returning Officer, who destroys it. Finally, they enter the ballot into the ballot box.

The ballots are counted by hand by the Deputy Returning Officer, who is assisted by the poll clerk. Any ballot may be rejected by the Deputy Returning Officer, for any one of a number of reasons: if the names of more than one candidate have been checked off; if the name of a non-candidate has been written in; or if there are fanciful or injurious entries. Once the valid votes have been counted, a "statement of votes" is drawn up and the ballots in favour of the different candidates are placed in separate envelopes, the invalid ones being collected into their own envelope. The envelopes are then sealed and all this material is put back into the ballot box along with the electoral list. All ballot boxes of all polling subdivisions are then sealed and delivered to the Returning Officer. A copy of the results is then transmitted to the representative of each candidate and to the Deputy Returning Officer.

Public disclosure of voting results is prohibited until all polls have closed. Thus, the media cannot divulge the results of absentee balloting or advance voting even though the numbers may already be available. Since the whole of Quebec lies within a single time zone, results begin to be aired at 8:00 p.m.

The Official Tally   Official tally of the vote takes place the next day, starting at 9:00 a.m. in the main office of the Returning Officer. Candidates or their representatives, and any voter registered within the particular electoral district, may attend. This official count consists in adding up the statements of votes contained in each ballot box sent to the Returning Officer the previous night. The candidate with the most votes is declared elected in his or her riding.

Any person believing that the duties of the Returning or Deputy Returning Officer have been improperly performed may file for a judicial recount; this is also a prerogative of the candidate who came in second, if the winner's majority was less than one-thousandth of the votes cast. Therefore, the winner is not officially proclaimed until the time prescribed for filing for such a recount has elapsed. A motion for a recount must be presented within four days after the official tally.

On the day appointed for the recount, a judge, in the presence of the Returning Officer, his or her deputy, and candidates or their representatives, examines the ballots and other documents that were sealed into the ballot box. "Upon the conclusion of the recount, the judge shall compile the votes cast in favour of each candidate, verify or rectify any statement of votes and certify the results of the poll" (Article 392). Then the Returning Officer officially declares elected the candidate who received the most votes according to the recount.

Of course, there are costs to be borne for a judicial recount. It is up to the judge to award and fix the amount according to a rate established by the provincial government. An individual who made the request must bear the costs if the results remain unchanged, unless he or she is a candidate who came in second as outlined above, in which case there are no charges.

5.4 MODERN QUEBEC: A SOUND DEMOCRACY SINCE THE 1960s

Since 1960 Quebec has adopted exemplary electoral legislation.

1. *Gerrymandering*—reshuffling of electoral boundaries for political advantage—is no longer possible, as these boundaries are defined by an independent commission. And no longer are elections held year after year under the same, increasingly obsolete electoral map. Remapping of the electoral districts is done after every election so as to keep pace with the electorate's geographical movements. The 25% deviation rule of population difference between electoral ridings has been adopted as the best compromise to achieve the principle of "one person, one vote" or equality of representation while taking into account the demographics of Quebec's population over its vast territory.

2. All told, the rules governing party and campaign spending, the limitations on individual contributions with public naming of the contributors of $100 or more, the introduction of public financing, and the ban on contributions from corporate entities have significantly diminished small- and large-scale *patronage*—i.e., the granting of jobs, contracts, and other favours by the party in power.

3. Governments can no longer award procurement contracts to party friends and financial backers. Governmental contracts in excess of $10,000 may be awarded only to the lowest bidder as a result of a public tendering process.

4. The creation in 1965 of the Public Service Commission has enabled the province to recruit a well-trained, competent public service shielded from the pressures and interventions of the political class. Recruitment is on the basis of competence as judged by entrance examinations. Jobs are clearly defined, there are classification levels, and promotions depend on objective criteria. Firing can no longer be at the whim of any given politician as: once they enter the public

service, civil servants fall under the aegis of the Public Service Commission, an independent body with its own rules. Public servants are unionized, have the right to strike as long as they maintain essential services, and after a probation period acquire job security.

All in all, an individual can pursue a political or public-service career unobstructed by various dishonest practices. This is not to say that favouritism and corruption no longer exist in Quebec. But there is no doubt that the processes of democracy and government have undergone a major facelift since the Duplessis era.

KEY TERMS

Bipartism

Enumeration

General election (in Quebec)

National Assembly

Patronage

Solliciteurs

Valid votes

REFERENCES AND FURTHER READING

Benjamin, Jacques. 1975. *Comment on fabrique un Premier ministre québécois.* Montreal: Éditions de l'Aurore.

Benjamin, Jacques. 1976. "Les Partis politiques québécois et le marketing électoral." In Daniel Latouche et al. (ed.), *Le processus électoral au Québec: les élections provinciales de 1970 et 1973.* Montreal: HMH Hurtubise. Pp. 93–110.

Bernard, André. 1977. *La Politique au Canada et au Québec.* 2nd ed. Montreal: Presses de l'Université du Québec.

Bernier, Robert. 1988. *Le Marketing gouvernemental au Québec: 1929–1985.* Montreal: G. Morin, éditeur.

Black, Conrad. 1977. *Duplessis.* Toronto: McClelland and Stewart.

Boily, Robert. 1982. "Les Partis politiques: perspectives historiques." In Vincent Lemieux (ed.), *Personnel et partis politiques au Québec.* Montreal: Boréal Express.

Boismenu, Gérard. 1981. *Le Duplessisme: politique économique et rapports de force, 1944–1960.* Montreal: Les Presses de l'Université de Montréal.

Bourque, Gilles and Jules Duchastel. 1988. *Restons traditionnels et progressifs— pour une nouvelle analyse du discours politique: le cas du régime Duplessis au Québec.* Montreal: Boréal.

Directeur général des élections du Québec. 1989. *The Election Act: Election Regulations*. Quebec.

Directeur général des élections du Québec. 1990. *Rapport annuel, 1989–1990*. Quebec.

Directeur général des élections du Québec. 1991. *Liste des partis politiques autorisés provinciaux*. Montreal.

Drouilly, Pierre. 1990. "Où va le nationalisme?" In Roch Denis (ed.), *Québec: dix ans de crise constitutionnelle*. Montreal: VLB éditeur.

Laporte, Pierre. 1962. *Le Vrai Visage de Duplessis*. Montreal: Les Éditions de l'homme.

Linteau, Paul-André, René Durocher, and Jean-Claude Robert. 1983. *Quebec. A History, 1867–1929*. Toronto: James Lorimer and Company.

Massicotte, Louis. 1984. "Une Reforme inachevée: les règles du jeu electoral." *Recherches Sociographiques*, 25: 43–81.

Massicotte, Louis and André Bernard. 1985. *Le Scrutin au Québec: un miroir déformant*. Montreal: HMH Hurtubise.

Parti libéral du Québec. 1988. *La Constitution du Parti libéral du Québec*.

Parti libéral du Québec. 1989. *Une Richesse à renouveler: programme politique*. Montreal: Parti libéral du Québec.

Parti québécois. 1989. *Programme du Parti québécois*. Montreal.

Parti québécois. [n.d.] *Les Statuts du Parti québécois*. Mimeograph. Montreal.

Parti québécois. [n.d.] *Règlements*. Mimeograph. Montreal.

Quinn, Herbert. 1979. *The Union Nationale: Quebec Nationalism from Duplessis to Lévesque*. 2nd ed. Toronto: University of Toronto Press.

Roberts, Leslie. 1972. *Le Chef: une biographie politique de Maurice Duplessis*. Montreal: Éditions du jour.

Rumilly, Robert. 1973. *Maurice Duplessis et son temps*. 2 vols. Montreal: Fides.

CHAPTER 6

VOTING
PATTERNS
IN
QUEBEC

Although election and sociological research has become a growing field in Quebec since the first empirical studies of the early 1960s, the amount of research on Quebec election behaviour and party identification has been relatively limited. Nevertheless, various orientations and debates have evolved. Electoral studies of Quebec have followed three patterns: *historical/content analysis*, which concentrates on political party platforms; *ecological analysis* to identify the key factors that influence voting behaviour and correlate each factor with the election results; and election *studies based on opinion polls*. Partisan voting patterns have been studied in an effort to identify which categories of voters are more inclined to support each party. Though the two main categories are urban and rural, many other variables—economics, party leader personality, ethnicity, religious affiliation, age, and education—have also been defined. And several studies have looked at voting patterns from a class perspective.

This chapter focusses on the factors that have affected party politics in Quebec since the early 1960s, on the nature of the electorate, and on the key variables that explain support for political parties. Some issues related to the future of Quebec's political status as a nation-state, changes in voting patterns of Quebec citizens at the federal level, and the impact of electoral campaigns will be examined.

6.1   THE BASES OF PARTY SUPPORT

As we have seen, since the early 1960s Quebec has gone through a period of profound social change. One of the major political demands associated with this change was a certain degree of autonomy from the rest of Canada. Since 1968, this demand has been represented by the Parti québécois, a party that has come to be associated with the separatist elements in the province. What explains the support given the PQ and the decline of other parties, such as the Union nationale?

In the 1960s, the Liberal party had attracted urban dwellers, the well-educated, and the majority of non-francophones. The Quiet Revolution had raised social expectations and created new groups of citizens that made up the vanguard of the major changes that marked Quebec's social development. While the Union nationale captured the support of constituents from rural districts, the "new middle class," i.e., technocrats, public servants, teachers, and cultural leaders, became the hard core of support for the Liberals.

When it was formed in 1968, the PQ was supported mostly by young voters, but it was soon able to attract the "new middle class." By 1973 the party had won over many more segments of Quebec society, in particular the working classes, which led to its victory in 1976. In all, it took the PQ less than nine years, from its founding to the 1976 election, to head the Quebec government. Its political platform was based on social-democratic ideas, but its emphasis on promoting Quebec cultural and economic values also won over a number of voters. Rarely has any North American party been able to secure so quickly the electoral support of the majority.

The Quebec electoral system, sometimes described as the "first past the post" or the "winner takes all" system does not always perfectly reflect the will of the voters, much less reveal how partisan choices are made and identify the key supporters of the Liberal party and the PQ. Several variables must be looked at closely, especially economics, language, age, education, income, and gender, to explain increases and decreases in political support.

Economics

Quebec politicians have come to realize that how they manage the economy, and whether they can present effective and efficient economic programs to the electorate, is a decisive factor in winning elections. According to Anthony Downs, when election time draws near, the incumbent party tends to start throwing around financial incentives to the electorate in order to ensure its reelection. Downs has also noted, "parties in a two-party system deliberately change their platform so that they resemble one another; whereas parties in a multiparty system try to remain as ideologically dis-

The first convention of the Parti québécois, *October 1969. [Courtesy Archives nationales du Québec.]*

tinct from each other as possible" (Downs 1957: 115). According to Monroe and Erikson, however, on the Canadian political scene, when voters cannot distinguish between economic policies and priorities of the two dominant parties, they "will cast their votes on the basis of noneconomic factors, e.g. foreign policy issues" (Monroe and Erikson, 1986: 618–619).

Language

The failure in most studies on Quebec electoral behaviour to consider anglophones and francophones separately, write Hamilton and Pinard:

> gives rise to special problems inasmuch as anglophones on average have higher income and are more educated. Their inclusion [i.e.,

without differentiation] in any analysis, therefore, can only obscure the relationship between those factors and the party choice among the majority of francophones. (1976: 25)

Seeking to identify what kinds of people supported the various political parties in Quebec, they made the anglophone/francophone distinction in their study of the 1973 election, and found that 41.5% of francophones had voted for the PQ. A higher proportion, 53%, of francophone PQ supporters were found in the Montreal area. They were also highly educated, having had 13 or more years of education. The same pattern was observed for the 1976 election, when the support of this group increased to 57%.

In their analysis of electoral support for the PQ in the 1985 Quebec election, André Blais and Jean Crête also found that the key determining factor for the PQ vote was language (Blais and Crête 1986). A little less than half of the francophones, 48%, voted for the PQ, a number comparable to Hamilton and Pinard's findings. In contrast, 8% of anglophones and 17% of "allophones" (persons with some other mother tongue) voted for the PQ. They also found that the PQ obtained 7% more votes among Montreal francophones than citizens living outside Montreal. Support for the PQ is 6% weaker in the region of Quebec City than in the rest of the province excluding Montreal.

In 1989, survey data indicated that francophone support for the PQ had declined in the last two elections (1985 and 1989), falling from 48.8% to 42.1%. This differs from the earlier pattern, which had francophone support steadily increasing from the first time the PQ ran in an election, going from 22.6% (1970), to 29.7% (1973), to 40.5% (1976), to 55.0% (1981). But in 1985 it declined to 48.9% and further down in 1989 to 41.9%. In 1989, the same survey showed that among the non-francophone groups, support ran at 44% for the Liberal party, 30% for the Equality party, and 5% for the PQ. This identifies a key element of the difficulty the PQ has in maintaining support: the Péquiste electoral base is made up essentially of francophones. With this group forming the foundation of its support, it cannot afford to lose them to the Liberals. The role of a third party becomes crucial, as in the 1976 election when the Union nationale helped the PQ win several seats by reaping votes from disaffected Liberal supporters.

Age

After language, age is the most influential factor behind support for the PQ. In the 1973 election, the PQ received most of its support from people between 18 and 25 years of age (Carlos et al. 1976: 213). This finding was later confirmed by Pinard and Hamilton, who stated that the percentage of the vote for the PQ "falls offs with equal sharpness as one moves from the younger to the older age categories" (Pinard and Hamilton 1976: 11). The nucleus of support came originally from the 18-to-28 age group.

In the 1985 election, the probability of a person voting for the PQ was enhanced by 15% when the voter fell into the 40-or-less age category. The strongest support for the PQ came from those born between 1945 and 1959. This group probably accounts for about 80% of the PQ vote. It is a group who were eligible to vote for the first time between 1966 and 1976, the same period that witnessed the birth and growth of the PQ.

The second-largest source of support was those born either between 1940 and 1944 or after 1960. The third-largest comprises those born before 1940 but who are less than 65 years of age; the PQ received support from more than 55% of this group. Lastly, voters born in or before 1915, or who were 65 or more in 1981, make up the smallest proportion of PQ supporters.

The attitudes of the youngest voters, especially those between 18 and 24 years old, is intriguing. This generation developed its own political consciousness and entered political life after Quebec politics had already been transformed by the Quiet Revolution, but before the PQ was elected in 1976. By the time of the referendum of May 15, 1980, it was clear that the main "yes" vote would come from those francophones born between 1945 and 1959. According to Kenneth McRoberts, "as with past support for the PQ itself, the referendum support for the PQ option was rooted in those who had reached adulthood in the 1960s or 1970s (McRoberts 1988: 328).

Furthermore, several findings revealed that the PQ was particularly popular among francophones in their twenties and unpopular among voters 60 years old and over. The opposite was true for the Liberal party. Among francophone voters under 30, support for the PQ peaked at 60.4%. The level of PQ support decreases in the older age group, with its lowest level of support, 22.5%, coming from the 70-and-over age group. Retirement age did not seem to constitute in 1985 a point of rupture as it had done in the past. Findings also revealed that the differences between age groups are not negligible; however, they are less marked than they were in the past.

For the 1989 election, the PQ won support from 40.7% of voters in the 18-to-34 age group, 35.3% of those between 35 and 54, 10.3% between 55 to 64, and 13.7% of those 65 and over. Reviewing the results from the 1989 election, it is evident that support for the PQ seems to decline with age. In 1976, those in the pre-35 age category voted overwhelmingly for the PQ; in 1985, the same people, now of a different age group, did not continue to support it in the same numbers.

Education

In the early 1970s, supporters of the PQ tended to be young, male, highly educated, and to come from professional and skilled occupations. The importance of education as a factor explaining party support for either the PQ or the Liberal party has been disputed, but in general most authors identified education as a key factor explaining party support.

First of all, the analysis of the results of the April 1970 election—the first general election in which the PQ ran candidates—concluded that PQ support came mainly from the more educated francophone Quebecers (Lemieux et al. 1970; Jenson and Regenstrief 1970: 310). Pinard and Hamilton reached the same conclusion, identifying a strong relationship between education and party choice, whereby the highest levels of PQ support came from the better-educated group that resides in the Montreal area and the opposite held true for the Liberal party.

If the 1976 election saw a rejection of the Liberal party by all voters, education not playing a key role in voters' decision, by the 1980s, education became an important determinant. It was noted in the 1981 election that the PQ gains in Montreal came from the more educated group, and that the party had been unsuccessful in its effort to mobilize the less educated voters. Therefore, the majority of highly educated francophone voters support the PQ over any other party, a trend that continued through the 1985 and 1989 elections.

The only study which does not support these claims concerns the results of the 1970 Quebec election. Serge Carlos and Daniel Latouche state that results from a poll conducted prior to the election by the *Centre de sondage de l'Université de Montréal* contradict previous observations that socioeconomic variables in general had a large role in the PQ vote, indicating that the relationship between education and partisan support for the PQ is negligible.

Even though some trend can be observed, further analysis and the development of new methodologies that go beyond simple cross-tabulations are needed to specify the contribution of education to voting behaviour.

Income

With regard to the effect of income level on voting behaviour, again the literature does not indicate a clear pattern. While some studies indicate a relationship between low income levels and support for the PQ, most analyses describe income level as a relatively insignificant variable.

A study conducted in 1970 indicated that those persons with the highest income in the Montreal area provided the lowest support for the PQ, but that this trend disappeared outside the metropolitan area. This fact is hardly surprising in view of the difference in income between French and English in Quebec at the time. The study also showed that voters whose income fell between $7,000 and $10,000 provided the highest support for the PQ. Even if the less privileged tended to give little support. The seven seats won by the PQ in 1970 had been in two of the poorest of Montreal's electoral districts, the east and centre-south. During the 1970 election, support varied directly with income level; even when controlling for age,

René Lévesque and poet-writer-singer Félix Leclerc during the referendum campaign of May 1980. [Courtesy Le Devoir and Gilles Paré, Librarian. Photo: Jacques Nadeau.]

the same pattern occurred within both the younger and the older categories (Pinard and Hamilton 1976: 10). However, a study by Carlos and Latouche in 1970 contradicts this, stating that there is only a negligible relationship between income and voting behaviour. Furthermore, in both the 1973 and the 1976 election, income was not considered to be statistically significant.

In his study of the Montreal area, Daniel Latouche writes that "the Parti Québécois had a particularly strong appeal among the lower income groups. The PQ receives considerable support from the underprivileged segments of the population" (Latouche 1973: 185). Blais and Nadeau also argue that there is more support for the PQ from the underprivileged than from the more privileged. However, another study concludes that "the relationship between income or occupation and support for the PQ party appears to be very weak" (Hamilton and Pinard, 1976: 25). And in fact, the relationship seems to be minimal, the variations between income categories almost disappearing when controls for age and education are taken into consideration. In the 1981 election, the PQ was slightly less popular among higher-income groups than among the lower-income groups. The PQ received most of its support from families whose gross income was between $20,000 and $50,000. Blais and Crête's study of the 1985 election, which took into account the family income variable, found no relation between family income and voting behaviour among francophones. PQ support in the 1989 election seemed to come mainly from families earning between $20,000 and $30,000.

When we take into consideration the general increase in the standard of living, it is fair to conclude that PQ support has remained within the same income group. However, there is no evidence for a *strong* relationship between income and voting behaviour. The results of the 1989 survey confirm this view. Therefore, as in past studies, the message is that income is not a significant factor of voting behaviour.

Gender

Historically, women in Quebec, the rest of Canada, and most industrialized societies, have been less politically active than men and thus less likely to be influenced by political party platforms, especially those concerning economic issues. It has been argued that women in Quebec tended to be alienated or not integrated into political life, and had, overall, very little interest in politics even when their level of information was as high as men's (Dépatie 1971). This is attributed to a perception among women that political affairs were remote from their daily lives, which may have led women to consider themselves politically incompetent. These perceptions were reinforced by the socioeconomic conditions that women faced. For instance, they traditionally occupied positions with little or no responsibility, they were paid less than men, and were socialized to take on most household chores, all of which effectively barred them from political activity.

The study by Serge Carlos and Daniel Latouche of the 1970 election in Quebec revealed that 23.8% of the women had intended to vote for the PQ, 33.6% had intended to vote for the Liberals, and 31.8% were undecided. The PQ's intended support among males was 35.1%; for the Liberals the figure was 39.8%; and 18.5% were undecided. The authors concluded that it was impossible to draw a relationship between gender and voting behaviour, because the number of undecided women voters was too high (Carlos and Latouche 1976: 196).

Analysis of the relationship between party identification and the gender, age, and education variables while controlling for francophones have given mixed results. Concerning the relationship between gender and party identification, it was found that the PQ received 35.9% of the female and 51.5% of the male vote. The Liberals, meanwhile, received 51.5% of the female and 40.8% of the male support in the 1970s. It seems, therefore, that there is a strong relationship between gender and party identification. Results revealed that the PQ was most favoured by respondents born since 1950, who came of age politically in the years after 1970, when the effects of the Quiet Revolution and the PQ organization itself were relatively well established (Bashevkin 1983).

Moreover, data indicates much larger generational disparities in Liberal party support among women and men, with an approximate 50% decrease

Universal suffrage and democratic rights have always been at the forefront of the development of democracy in Quebec since the 1960s. [Courtesy Le Devoir and Gilles Paré, Librarian.]

in Liberal party identification between the oldest and youngest female categories, compared with a decline of about 30% across the five male categories. Men tend to support the PQ in substantially larger numbers than women in all categories, including the youngest ones who represented respondents born between 1950 and 1961. Among the latter, 66.3% of males and 54.0% of females identified with the PQ, for a gender difference of 12.3%. In short, while support for the PQ among both sexes was highest in this category, younger men were clearly more supportive of the party even in this group, in which a generational argument would seem to predict slight or possibly no gender disparities.

Analysis does not suggest that the gender gap in partisan, particularly PQ, support was eliminated among younger respondents. Notably, males in the two youngest age groups reported somewhat higher levels of identification with the PQ than females in the same categories. Thus we cannot conclude that gender disparities disappeared among younger respondents.

6.2 THE ISSUES OF SOVEREIGNTY-ASSOCIATION AND INDEPENDENCE

The rise of the independence issue in Quebec has often been seen as the main reason for the rise of the Parti québécois. It has been theorized that if the PQ dropped its political stance in favour of Quebec independence, it would immediately lose the support of the electorate and disappear (Pinard 1977). This argument is often made to minimize the importance of the social movement represented by this party.

Of course, it must be recognized that the PQ could not have emerged as a new political party without the prior development of many movements that favoured independence. The independence issue provided the PQ at the outset with a core of militants and supporters, and since the early 1970s, that core has grown only in relatively small increments. But the growth of popular support for the PQ, as early as 1970 and 1973 but particularly in 1976, cannot be attributed to its independence stance alone. Another important factor has been the great dissatisfaction of the anglophone community with the language legislation of Bill 22, which polarized the electorate between the PQ and the Liberals and set the stage for the election of 1976.

In one study, Hamilton and Pinard (1973) did find a very strong relationship between the attitude toward separatism and support for the PQ for the 1973 election; findings indicate that among those in favour of separatism 92% supported the PQ.[1] But in a later study, Pinard and Hamilton (1976) found that support for the independence option had been growing much more slowly than support for independentist parties in the 1966, 1970, 1973, and 1976 Quebec elections. The data indicate that support for independence increased by only 18% during the ten-year period before the 1976 election, while support for independentist parties had increased by twice that proportion. The fact that the 1976 data indicate a 17% difference between those supporting independence and those supporting independentist parties suggests that the PQ victory of 1976 was greatly facilitated by an increase in supporters who did not necessarily favour Quebec's independence. This is not to say that the independence option was not central in building the core of PQ's militants and supporters. But by 1976 the pool of independentists had almost all been recruited by the PQ, and the growth of that pool was too small to explain the PQ's rise to power. The findings also indicate that while 39% of all PQ voters were for independence in 1970 and that proportion rose to 72% in 1973, it then dropped

---

1. With respect to education, they state that the PQ/Liberal polarization following the separatist/non-separatist cleavage was particularly strong among the better educated.

to 49% in 1976. One can infer that while there has always been a close association between separatism and PQ support, it was weaker in 1976 than in 1973.

The PQ promised that if elected it would conduct a referendum on Quebec independence. After its election on November 15, 1976, and the month before the referendum of May 20, 1980, the support for independence rose sharply in the polls to a high of 28%. But the actual terms used were always somewhat ambiguous. The Parti québecois advocated *sovereignty-association*, that is, a sovereign Quebec with an economic union with the rest of Canada. This concept had always been more popular than the issue of independence, meaning that the voters wanted independence only if the Quebec government could guarantee some form of economic union that preserved relations with the North American market. In a survey by the *Centre de recherche sur l'opinion publique* (CROP) published a month before the referendum, Quebec voters supported sovereignty-association by 42%. This was very close to the outcome of the referendum, which was 40.2% in favour of sovereignty-association and 59.8% against.

After the referendum, and even after the defeat of the PQ in 1985, the issues of independence and sovereignty-association continued to dominate Quebec politics. The failure of the Meech Lake accord in June 1990, with the rejection of the "distinct society" concept, stimulated renewed expectations, and Quebecers looked to independence or sovereignty-association as increasingly viable solutions. At this point, sovereignty-association received popular support of 62% with outright independence a close second at 55%.

In February 1991, the Liberal party proposed in the Allaire Report a new form of power-sharing with the federal government, requesting full control in certain areas. Some saw this proposal as the last chance for Canada to accommodate Quebec's demands.

In the fall of 1991, polls indicated that though support for independence had decreased by 10%, support for sovereignty-association remained relatively high. Interpretation of the data is difficult, as the questions asked by the polls differ. But one thing remains clear: the idea of sovereignty-association, especially in the aftermath of the rejection by Quebec of the Charlottetown agreement, has become a more viable solution for many Quebec citizens.

6.3   QUEBEC ELECTORAL BEHAVIOUR AT THE FEDERAL LEVEL

Though it is difficult to draw parallels between federal and provincial voting behaviour of Quebecers because different major parties exist at the two levels, a number of political scientists have tried to explain apparent inconsistencies between the two patterns of voting behaviour. The phenomenon was most conspicuous with the election of the independentist PQ, only two years after Quebec voters had supported the federalist Liberals of Pierre Elliott Trudeau. This inconsistency is not unique to Quebec voters. As Howard Scarrow puts it:

> The Canadian Electorate has shown an inclination to put in power at the provincial level parties that stand in opposition to the party which has been entrusted with power at Ottawa. (1960: 82)

Somewhat surprisingly, Quebec supported both the federal and the provincial Liberals in the early 1970s, then elected the PQ in 1976 and 1981. There was a similar discrepancy between 1984 and 1989, when Quebec voted Conservative federally and for the Liberals provincially. Two things can at least partly explain it. First, the one-party dominance at the federal level (the Liberal party has dominated Canadian politics since the Great Depression of the 1930s) has not been reflected at the provincial level. Second, circumstances such as the organizational split between the federal and the provincial Liberals in the mid-1960s, the absence of a strong Quebec conservative party to replace the crumbling Union nationale, and the emergence of the PQ, a strong nationalist party, at the end of the 1960s, made it difficult to compare federal and Quebec outcomes.

Nonetheless, two theories have emerged: the "Balance Theory" and the "Establishment Theory." The Balance Theory was proposed by Frank Underhill, whose hypothesis is that Canadian voters, including Quebec, like to create a balance of power by voting for different parties at the two levels of government (Underhill 1955). Howard A. Scarrow describes this theory as follows:

> By some instinctive sub-conscious mental process, the Canadian people have apparently decided that, since freedom depends upon a balance of power, they will balance one-party dominance at Ottawa with effective opposition in the provincial capitals. (Scarrow 1960)

Typically, therefore, Quebec voters tend to balance federal power by electing strong governments—often of opposite political affiliation—for Quebec (Drouilly 1978). This theory assumes a certain pragmatism and rationalism on the part of voters and does not consider the role of candidate and election issues.

On the other side, the Establishment Theory, suggested by Cunningham, Rubin, and White (1972), posits that voters with a high level of education, income, and professional status tend to vote for the dominant party at the level in question. In this interpretation, the dominant party is the one that promises the highest rewards to that group. This is a very conservative theory about social change, suggesting that the status quo will prevail until major factors mobilize voters' support. The strong support of the Quebec business community until 1976 for the Liberal party would be an example of how it works. But the high-status groups represent only a fragment of the electorate, and it is hard to find evidence to support such a theory.

The empirical evidence for either theory has never been conclusive. Several other factors may explain the apparent inconsistencies. For instance, the decreased participation rate of Quebec voters in federal elections and the high number of spoiled ballots seem to have been the result of a PQ campaign asking supporters to spoil their ballots or abstain from voting during the federal election of July 8, 1974. There was indeed a decrease in the participation rate. However, the success of this campaign was minimized by the fact that many members of the PQ also supported the NDP. It is possible that the strategy actually helped the federal Liberals gain several seats. Another factor is the fact that after 1976, the number of Quebec Liberals who supported the federal Liberals had declined from 80% to 65%, though there were still some PQ voters who supported the federal Liberals. In the 1974 federal election, 6.2% of the PQ supporters voted for the Liberal party.

Supporters of the Balance and Establishment theories distinguish several voter profiles for Quebec: the consistents, the switchers, the migrants, and the vote-splitters or split-identifiers (Nevitte 1984: 246). According to both theories, the *consistents* or partisans always vote for the same party at both the federal and Quebec level, and the *switchers* vote either for a strong Quebec government to counteract federal decisions or for the party supporting their own interests. The Establishment Theory then defines *migrants* as those ready to change party support at either the federal or the Quebec level, the choice depending on which party will maximize their gains. The Balance Theory defines *vote-splitters* as those who choose a strong Quebec government to counteract federal powers, which leads to voting for different parties at the two levels. Francophones seem more inclined to adopt this tactic than anglophones.

There has been cricitism pointing out the inadequacy of these profiles and offering alternative explanations. For example, Quebec voters might have supported the Lévesque-Trudeau tandem only because they both were francophones, or both were charismatic leaders. And in recent years, since the election in 1984 of the federal Conservative party of Brian Mulroney and the Quebec Liberals of Robert Bourassa in 1985, Quebec voters may have chosen these two leaders simply because both their parties favoured a renewed federalism.

6.4   POLITICAL REALIGNMENTS AND ELECTIONS

The difference between a "realignment election" and a normal election is in the movement of partisan choices—that is, modifications in the composition of partisan cleavages. For example, the Quebec election of 1970, when supporters of the Union nationale decreased rapidly in favour of both the Liberal party and the PQ, constituted a major political realignment. A realignment election is thus one in which there is a significant political shift among traditional supporters of a political party in favour of another party, quite often a third or minority party. Fundamental societal and economic changes can often lead to such major transformations in partisan support. A key indicator of such an election is a high political participation rate; the 1970 Quebec election had a participation rate of 84.2%, approximately 10% higher than that of the previous 1966 election. Another characteristic of a realignment election is that it is followed by highly stable support for a political party. The Liberal party won 102 out of 110 seats in the 1973 election.

The 1985 and 1989 elections, which saw the election of the Liberal party and the end of nine years of PQ government, have been described as realignment elections. In 1989, for example, the traditional support of the anglophone community for the Liberals switched to a newly formed political party, the Equality Party, as had happened with the Union nationale in 1976. However, other indicators show that neither can really be called a realignment election. First, we observe a decrease in participation rates after 1981, from 82.5%, to 75.6%, and finally in 1989 to 75.0%. Second, if

Talk show during the 1985 Quebec election. **Left to right:** Claude Charron, former PQ MNA and minister; Robert Bourassa, leader of the opposition; Solange Chaput-Rolland, journalist and political critic. [Courtesy Le Devoir and Gilles Paré, Librarian]

we look at the volatility indicator, that is, the sum of losses and gains of each political party between elections, we observe that between 1981 and 1985 support for the PQ decreased by 11.7% and support for the Liberal party increased by 10.0%. But between 1985 and 1989, the Liberal party, even though it remained in power, saw a decrease of 7.0% in its popular support while the PQ saw a small increase of 1.5%, when the Equality Party was able to get 3.7% of the vote.

6.5 SATISFACTION LEVEL AND THE IMPACT OF ELECTION CAMPAIGNS

Do election campaigns affect voting behaviour? This was one of the key questions raised in the 1989 Quebec election, when strikes by the nurses, union members of the Social Affairs Federation, and public sector employees may have caused a decline in voter satisfaction with the Liberals and influenced the outcome. To evaluate the impact of these events on the 1989 election campaign, three periods might be distinguished: (1) the beginning of the campaign in August to the end of the month when the issue of the shipping of Saint-Basile's toxic waste was making headlines; (2) the illegal nurses' strike; and (3) the end of the nurses' strike and the beginning of the strikes by health workers, teachers, and public employees.[2]

Before the election was called, the Liberal party seemed to be far ahead in terms of popular support. Premier Bourassa was leading in the polls and was expected to receive between 50 and 55% of popular support. In June 1989, the polling institute CROP reported that the Liberal party led the PQ by 21 points (53% vs. 32%). A survey by Sorécom the following month established that the Liberal party was still leading by 18 points over the PQ (53% vs. 35%). With such a gap between the two major parties, the Liberal victory seemed secure.

Throughout the 1989 campaign, the voters' level of satisfaction with the Bourassa government was constantly declining. The day before the nurses' strike, a CROP survey indicated that a majority were dissatisfied with the way the government was handling negotiations with the health and hospital employees (62%) and its public sector employees (52%). Furthermore, 55% of the respondents declared themselves sympathetic to the nurses' strike, and 28% were of the opinion that the negotiation results would determine the outcome of the election.

The satisfaction level with the Quebec government evolved rapidly throughout most of the campaign. Between the first period and the third,

---

2. For these periods there were four, two, and three opinion polls respectively.

Table 6.1

Public Opinion Polls Results and Satisfaction Level Toward the Quebec Government for 1989 Election

	Period I	Period II	Period III	Election Day
Period of interview	Aug. 17–Sept. 4	Sept. 5–13	Sept. 14–20	September 25
Number of polls	4	2	3	
Quebec Liberal Party	48.9[1] (48.7)[2]	48.1 (47.7)	47.6 (46.2)	49.9
Parti québécois	35.8 (37.5)	37.9 (40.2)	37.8 (39.6)	40.2
Others	10.6 (13.8)	9.3 (9.3)	10.9 (14.2)	9.9
Satisfaction level	52.4	51.2	45.6	

1. Redistribution of the undecided respondents according to the "62–38" formula.
2. Proportional redistribution of the non-respondents.

the dissatisfaction toward the government went from 40.7% to 53.7%. It is surprising that this was not translated into voting intention. Even though the satisfaction level declined steadily, popular support for the Liberals

"Our real country is Quebec." The Quebec flag, symbol of patriotism and nation-alism. The 1990 Saint-Jean-Baptist *or* Fête nationale *parade on the day following the failure of the Meech Lake accord. [Courtesy Le Devoir and Gilles Paré, Librarian.]*

remained high. Furthermore, the PQ was unable to win over the electorate, especially by the end of the campaign. The other parties, after a loss of 1.3% during the second period, were able to regain 1.6%.

So it is difficult to assess whether the 1989 election campaign had a major impact on voters. The PCBs saga (when fire broke out in a warehouse containing barrels of used residues from Hydro-Québec transformers in St-Basile-le-Grand), the nurses' strike, and then the public employees' strike did not provoke any major shifts in voting. And in spite of the fact that there was a significant decrease in the satisfaction level towards the Liberal government, especially in the second and third phases of the campaign, this dissatisfaction did not generate more support for either the Parti québécois or third parties.

6.6   CONCLUSION

In this chapter we have looked at the key determinants and issues that affect Quebec voters' behaviour in elections. The seemingly ambiguous behaviour of Quebec voters in electing one political party at the federal level and another one at the provincial level seems largely to be due to the pragmatic behaviour of Quebec voters: by counterbalancing strong federal government with an even stronger Quebec government that would defend the unique character of the province, voters created a system of checks and balances that the electoral system itself did not offer.

The impact of opinion polls and election campaigns, and the correlation, if any, between satisfaction levels and voting behaviour, remain subjects for further investigation. The fact that Quebec voters in 1976 elected a party supporting the independence of Quebec has several possible explanations that deviate from the obvious ones. However, as noted, a certain rationality and pragmatism has been evident.

KEY TERMS

Constituents	Minority party
Discreet respondents	Party identification
Franchise	*Péquiste*
Gender gap	Political participation
General election	Realignment election
Independence	Referendum
Independentist	Sovereignty-association

REFERENCES AND FURTHER READING

Bashevkin, Sylvia. 1983. "Social change and political partisanship: the development of women's attitudes in Quebec, 1965-1979." *Comparative Political Studies*, 16 (2) (July): 147–173.

Blais, André and Richard Nadeau. 1984. "L'Appui au Parti québécois: évolution de la clientèle de 1970 à 1981." In Jean Crête (ed.), *Comportement électoral au Québec*. Chicoutimi: Gaétan Morin éditeur. Pp. 279–334.

Carlos, Serge and Daniel Latouche. 1976. "La Composition de l'électorat péquiste." In Daniel Latouche, Guy Lord, Jean-Guy Vaillancourt, *Le Processus électoral au Québec: les élections provinciales de 1970 et 1973*. Montreal: Editions Hurtubise HMH Ltée. Pp. 187–211.

Carlos, Serge, Edouard Cloutier and Daniel Latouche. 1976. "Le Choix des électeurs en 1973: caractéristiques sociales et orientation nationale." In Daniel Latouche, Guy Lord, Jean-Guy Vaillancourt, *Le Processus électoral au Québec: les élections provinciales de 1970 et 1973*. Montreal: Editions Hurtubise HMH Ltée. Pp. 213–234.

Clarke, Harold D., Jane Jenson, Lawrence LeDuc, and Joan H. Pammet. 1984. *Absent Mandate: The Politics of Discontent in Canada*. Toronto: Gage Publishing Limited.

Cunningham, R., J. Rubas, and G. White. 1972. *Differential Loyalties: Split Identification and Voting at Federal and Provincial Levels*. Paper presented at Annual Meeting of Canadian Political Science Association. Montreal.

Deller, Joanne Elizabeth. 1981. *The Effect of Female Candidatures on Voting Behavior*. M.A. in thesis Political Science. Montreal: McGill University.

Dépatie, Francine. 1979. "La Participation politique des femmes au Québec." In Edouard Cloutier and Daniel Latouche (eds.), *Le système politique québécois*. Montreal: Editions Hurtubise HMH Ltée, Pp. 267–285.

Downs, Anthony. 1957. *An Economic Theory of Democracy*. New York: Harper and Row.

Drouilly, Pierre. 1978. *Le Paradoxe canadien*. Montreal: Parti-Pris.

Hamilton, Richard and Maurice Pinard. 1976. "The bases of the Parti québécois support in recent Quebec elections." *Canadian Journal of Political Science* 9(1): 3–26.

Hudon, Raymond. 1976. "Les Études électorales au Québec: principales orientations et quelques débats." *Recherches sociographiques*, 17(3) (September–December): 283–322.

Kay, Barry J., Ronald D. Lambert, Steven L. Brown, James E. Curtis. 1987. "Gender and political activity in Canada, 1965–1984." *Canadian Journal of Political Science*, 20(4) (December): 851–863.

Jenson, Jane and Peter Regenstrief. 1970. "Some dimensions of partisan choice in Quebec, 1969." *Canadian Journal of Political Science* 3(2): 308–317.

Lachapelle, Guy. 1986. "Les Répondants-discrets et l'élection québécoise de 1985." *Politique* 10: 31–54.

Latouche, Daniel. 1973. "The independence option: ideological and empirical elements." In Dale Thompson (ed.), *Quebec Society and Politics*. Toronto: McClelland and Stewart.

Lemieux, Vincent, André Blais, and Marcel Gilbert. 1970. *Une Élection de réalignement: élection générale du 29 avril 1970 au Québec*. Montreal: Editions du jour.

McRoberts, Kenneth. 1988. *Quebec: Social Change and Political Crisis*. Toronto: McClelland and Stewart.

Monroe, Kristen and Lynda Erickson. 1986. "The economy and political support: the Canadian case." *Journal of Politics*, 48: 616–647.

Nevitte, Neil. 1984. "Le Réalignement fédéral-provincial et l'interaction électorale au Québec, 1962-1979." In Jean Crête (ed.), *Le comportement électoral au Québec*. Montreal: Gaétan Morin. Pp. 243–277.

Pinard, Maurice and Richard Hamilton. 1977. "The independence issue and the polarization of the electorate: the 1973 Quebec election." Canadian Journal of Political Science, 10(2): 215–259.

Scarrow, Howard A. 1960. "Federal-provincial voting patterns in Canada." *Canadian Journal of Economics and Political Science*, 26(2) (May): 289–298.

Underhill, and Frank H. 1955. "Canadian liberal democracy in 1955." In G. V. Ferguson and F. H. Underhill (eds.), *Press and Party in Canada*. Toronto: Ryerson Press.

CHAPTER 7

INTEREST GROUPS

The role and power of interest groups in Quebec has not been widely documented in Quebec. Whether this is because it is unimportant, or because no one has payed attention to it, is not clear. In this chapter, we describe a few of the major interest groups in Quebec and look at how they participate in the political process.

First we note that, for various reasons, the power of political parties in Quebec and the association of indigenous interest groups with other groups based outside Quebec limit the influence of the indigenous groups. Then we try to illustrate how different groups have risen and fallen over the years, from the hegemony of the Catholic Church in the 1950s to the rise of the new francophone bourgeoisie in the 1980s.

Pluralist theory, whereby Quebec is a system of competing interest groups, assumes that every group has the power to influence political decision-making. In this chapter, that assumption is challenged. Many groups are excluded from the process due to certain institutional settings, parliamentary commissions, and corporatist decision-making procedures. As Schattschneider (1960) wrote more than thirty years ago, the flaw in the pluralist heaven is that the heavenly chorus sings with a strong upper-class accent. Furthermore, political institutions often redefine the interests promoted by the groups. And, as discussed in Chapter 11, civil servants often have their own agenda, one that interferes with group demands.

We also illustrate that the centralization of power in the hands of the state that came with political modernization was paralleled by a similar process in the organizations dealing with the state—i.e., the interest groups.

Also, over the years, the government has tried to institutionalize its relations with the interest groups. The laws concerning the establishment of professional corporations and the *concertation* (consultation) attempts of the early 1980s exemplify these trends. In some policy domains, the relative importance of specific groups has varied over time. Groups that barely existed a decade ago are now powerful players.

7.1 POTENTIAL AND LIMITS OF GROUP POWER

How Groups Influence Policymaking

Representation at Parliamentary Commissions Officially, interest groups and the government discuss their respective concerns before parliamentary commissions. At present, after the 1984 reforms, there are eight parliamentary commissions dealing with the various policy issues addressed by the government. They study the bills presented by ministers, the budgets, regulations, and other subjects brought to their attention by the National Assembly. These commissions, initiated to improve the operations of the Assembly, have become a lively public forum. In some cases—when a bill must be sent to more than one commission—a plenary commission can be created.

These commissions can decide to consult any groups affected by the bill under study. Consultation can be either particular or general. *Particular* consultations are limited to a few people or groups selected by the commission for their expertise or involvement in the policy area. For *general* consultations, a public announcement is made inviting groups or individuals to prepare a *mémoire* and eventually present it to the commission. The announcement is made in Quebec's daily newspapers, giving the name of the commission, the purpose of the consultation, the specifications of the requested *mémoires* and the due dates for them. Once the commission has received the documents, it decides whether to hold public hearings. Normally, a bill is studied by a parliamentary commission after its "passage in principle" (first reading). At the end of the hearings, the commission presents a report to the National Assembly so that the debate can move on.

In 1990–1991, the Quebec government decided to allow extra-parliamentary members in parliamentary commissions, creating the *Commission sur l'avenir politique et constitutionnel du Québec* (Commission on the Political and Constitutional Future of Quebec), better known as the Bélanger-Campeau Commission. Its membership is an interesting who's who of Quebec society according to the government. The co-presidents were two former deputy ministers from the Quebec government. After leaving the civil service, Michel Bélanger became the CEO of the National Bank, the largest francophone commercial bank in Canada, and Jean Campeau became the CEO of the Caisse de dépôt et placement du Québec. Like any parliamentary commission, Bélanger-Campeau consisted of 16 MNAs, plus the Premier and the leader of the opposition. Additional members were two city officials, four businessmen, the three presidents of the three main unions in Quebec, the president of the *Union des producteurs agricoles*, the president of the *Mouvement Desjardins*, one person from the school system, the president of the *Union des artistes* and three members of the House of Commons representing Quebec ridings.

Apart from parliamentary commissions, three other traditional strategies for promoting special interests are lobbying, electioneering, and litigation.

Lobbying Lobbying is a communication, by persons not acting on their own behalf, directed to a government decision-maker with the hope of influencing his or her decision (Lineberry 1980). In Quebec, lobbying appears to be a growing phenomenon, though it is still not regulated.

Two examples, involving the issues of auto insurance and the nationalization of asbestos mining, illustrate the use of lobbying as a policy instrument.

The 1977 auto insurance plan in Quebec was a compromise aimed at avoiding the high costs and battles with the insurance industry experienced in Manitoba and British Columbia. The original plan had been bitterly opposed by the bar association (a high proportion of small-town lawyers' incomes came from fighting insurance claims) and by the insurance companies and insurance brokers (who faced losing an important chunk of their business). Due to effective lobbying at the time of preparation of the bill, property damage insurance was left in the hands of private companies, the state controlling a no-fault plan for personal injuries.

In the case of asbestos mining, General Dynamics—which had understood well the lessons of the nationalization of the power companies—launched an impressive lobbying effort when the government announced it was going to nationalize the company's mines in Quebec. It took the government to court, argued over technicalities, and dragged the process out over four years. The effort was not aimed at keeping operations going (at the time the product was faced with marketing difficulties) but at getting better compensation. The government, fearful of appearing too economically radical just before the referendum, agreed to pay a substantial amount to General Dynamics.[1]

Following the American example, Canada has decided to regulate lobbying activities at the federal level; since September 1989, anyone who wants to lobby the federal government has to be registered. But the Quebec

---

1. Asbestos production has declined every year since the deal has been completed.

government has yet to regulate lobby groups in this way, partly because it is not clear who is and is not a real lobbyist; also, since strong lobby groups are so few, it is doubtful whether many of the smaller ones would register. Most of the lobbying being done now in Quebec is carried out by lawyers or public relations firms who have more "respectability" than admitted lobbyists (Boivin 1984).

It is not clear whether lobbyists are effective in Quebec. Dominique Boivin, a self-described lobbyist, cites only one example of effective lobbying, that carried out by the auto insurance industry, which managed to salvage some of its domain. But even here, it may be that the government always wanted a system of mixed public and private insurance, and that lobbyists had simply endorsed the government decision, justifying their honoraria after the fact (Fraser 1984).

Electioneering   Electioneering is the direct involvement of interest groups in the electoral process. Since the Quebec Election Act prohibits political parties from receiving funding from interest groups, such groups are not allowed to contribute money. However, "private" advertising flourishes and is not well controlled, or even well documented: the literature on electoral behaviour in Quebec ignores interest groups (Crête 1984).

Even governments get in on the act. In 1980, during the constitutional referendum campaign, the federal government spent *four times* the total advertising budget allowed to each of the "yes" or "no" umbrella organizations. Provincial governments, too, behave like interest groups vis-à-vis the federal government. In fact, the Quebec government has an official delegate posted in Ottawa for lobbying purposes. In the early 1980s, the *Caisse de dépôt et placement* successfully lobbied the federal government to withdraw Bill S-31, which would have limited its capacity to buy stock in private companies involved in interprovincial transport activities.[2]

Electioneering figured greatly in Quebec during the 1988 federal campaign. A group of 150 companies called the Canadian Alliance for Trade and Job Opportunities published across Canada 800,000 copies of a four-page brochure on free trade, and full-page advertisements in Sunday newspapers, the day before the election—all of which was completely outside the controls and restrictions of the provisions of the Electoral Act. In Quebec, the province most in favor of free trade, individual business persons who had never been involved in politics became very active on that issue. The president of Montreal-based Alcan, for example, became active

---

2. Ostensibly, the bill was intended to protect the federal government's jurisdiction over the transportation sector. But in fact, Bill S-31 had been introduced by the federal government to protect Canadian Pacific Limited from a possible, though unlikely, takeover by the Caisse and related private interests. The only provincial agency that would have been affected was, and still is, the Caisse.

in both the Business Council on National Issues and the Alliance. Today, powerful business groups such as the *Conseil du patronat du Québec* and *Économie et constitution* lobby in favour of the renewal of the federal union. They have the wherewithal to advertise their views. Guy St-Pierre, a provincial minister in the 1970s and currently president of SNC-Lavalin, the huge engineering firm also based in Montreal, belongs to this group. Though their expenditures are not included in the electoral budgets, they greatly help the incumbent Conservative party.

Litigation   Litigation, traditionally the third instrument of interest groups, allows groups that are unable to influence policy-making initially to take their policy goals to court. Groups representing the English-speaking community in Quebec have successfully challenged some aspects of the linguistic policies. Indian groups, Greenpeace, and other environmentalist groups have also used the courts to delay energy projects in Quebec, the rest of Canada, and the United States.

The Importance of Organization and Membership

In order to effectively exert their influence, interest groups must be well organized. Organization allows groups to present their cases knowledgeably, with the necessary persistence, and with enough financial resources to communicate their point of view to both government and the public. Size of membership is also important: masses who join behind a cause can often compensate for lack of organization or poorly defined goals. Aboriginal movements in Quebec have yet to delineate their precise objectives regarding autonomy, but they have been very effective in mobilizing support in Quebec and around the world.

Of course, interest groups can also develop into massive bureaucracies, and inevitably one of the main functions of these organizations becomes self-maintenance. Permanent staff of large, bureaucratic interest groups may also be tempted to pursue their own interests rather than the interests of the membership. It is unlikely this will ever be a widespread problem in Quebec, however, simply because a society of only seven million people cannot support such huge memberships and the resultant bureaucracies. (There do exist large interest groups, such as doctors' associations, that are initially created for nonpolitical purposes, but whose activities involve increased interrelations with government.)

In a political system where organization is so important, business has a competitive advantage over other pressure groups, because it already has the continuity, financial resources, and long-term, articulated goals that other groups have to build. In groups representing a small number of people, the interests to be pursued are often very clear. Other groups have to mobilize support, build organizations, create a system to secure the necessary financial resources, and go through a process of internal mediation of the group's interests. Groups that are well organized can seek to influence government on the quality of the argument they push; others have to resort to public confrontations with the government.

Another factor is whether the organization is a public interest or a constituency group. A public interest group might be defined as a nonprofit organization, which seeks to promote policies in the name of some *general* good. "Public" interests are likely to be perceived as more legitimate than "private" ones. Public groups are usually weakened, however, by financial dependency and difficulties in defining priorities. Consequently, constituency groups, ones that have relatively specific goals and highly committed memberships, might be more efficient than public interest groups in countering the influence of established economic interests.

An example of the difficulty faced by public interest groups is given by the case of the Consumers' Association of Canada (CAC), a public interest group founded in 1947. Like its American counterpart, the CAC presents its viewpoint before regulatory agencies, Royal Commissions, and the courts. This "legal advocacy" has been the CAC's main approach over the 1960s and 1970s, one supported by the Department of Consumer and Corporate Affairs (created by the federal government in 1968). More recently, however, constituency groups such as the *Associations coopératives d'économie familiale* (ACEFs) or the Automobile Protection Association have been more effective because they are able to maintain a strong cohesiveness through commitment to a more limited cause (Goldstein 1979). Also, they operate only in Quebec. In Canada, linguistic and regional divisions limit the usefulness of some books, articles, and conferences despite their great success for people like Ralph Nader in the United States.

Impact of the Parliamentary and Federal Systems on Influence

One reason why the study of groups in Quebec is difficult is that they are not all exclusively oriented toward Quebec politics. The American organization of Greenpeace sees the energy projects of the Quebec government very differently from the way its Quebec cousin does. In late 1991, the Quebec branch was not even consulted by the American one before the latter published an advertisement about the James Bay project in the *New York Times*.

Factions of certain groups at different levels of government can also hold different views. For example, some aboriginal groups in Quebec were very surprised to hear the Canadian leader of the native nations arguing in early 1992 before a parliamentary commission in Quebec City that there is no Quebec nation and that Quebec has no right to constitutional self-determination, since many aboriginal nations in Quebec recognize the right of Quebec to become a sovereign country.

Some interest groups are organized to operate at both the federal and the provincial level. For example, Canada's major labour organization, the Canadian Labour Congress, has a Quebec-based federation, the *Fédération des travailleurs du Québec* (FTQ or Quebec Federation of Labour), that pursues mainly political activities at the provincial level. According to Thorburn (1985), an interest group often relates more to one level of government than to the other: finances and transportation to the federal level, and the resource industries and small business to the provincial.

Policy-making in Quebec is characterized by two separate processes of combined consultation and negotiation: one between interest groups and

Table 7.1

Quebec Union Membership According to Type of Union, 1991

Type of Union	Unions (N)	Locals (N)	Union Membership (N)	Union Membership (%)
International unions:	63	3,186	1,262,077	31.0
AFL–CIO/CLC	39	2,555	859,660	21.2
AFL–CIO/CFL	10	388	205,111	5.0
CLC only	2	29	8,272	0.2
AFL–CIO only	7	111	172,742	4.2
Unaffiliated unions	5	103	16,292	0.4
National unions:	240	13,591	2,618,929	64.3
Canadian Labour Congress	48	6,282	1,496,245	36.8
Confédération des syndicats nationaux	9	2,138	219,362	5.4
Centrale de l'enseignement du Québec	12	404	103,651	2.5
Confédération des syndicats (CSC)	13	88	29,774	0.7
Confédération des syndicats démocratiques	3	176	17,215	0.4
Canadian Federation of Labour	4	42	8,960	0.2
FCNSI	11	11	2,253	0.1
Unaffiliated unions	140	4,450	741,469	18.2
À *charte directe* (direct charter):	330		50,775	1.3
Confédération des syndicats nationaux	307		43,700	1.1
Canadian Labour Congress	21		7,000	0.2
Confédération des syndicats nationaux	2		75	0.0[1]
Independent local organizations	359		136,642	3.4
TOTAL	992	16,777	4,068,423	100.0

1. Less than 0.1%.

individual governments and one between governments themselves. Bargaining between the federal and the provincial government has historically limited the power of interest groups in the political system (Simeon 1972). Whenever an issue enters the intergovernmental arena, the operation of policy-making is designed primarily to accommodate the interests of governments, not groups. Moreover, the absence of formal mechanisms for interest group consultation means that governments can exclude groups from the process. Political leaders, including the senior bureaucracy, have defined "public interest" over the years without much consultation with the public (Thorburn 1985). The process in both Quebec and Canada could be described as closed and elite-driven.[3] It has been said:

> The parliamentary system of cohesive political parties raises barriers to both representation and conflict management that are not encountered in the United States Congress, where both party discipline and the adversarial government-opposition relationship are problematic. (Skogstad 1985:742)

In Quebec, Cabinet solidarity inhibits functional competition between ministers and therefore diminishes pressure groups' access to them. Moreover, the policy-planning process established in Quebec, where ministerial committees supervise policy planning, has limited the capacity of individual ministers to respond to interest groups, since interest groups must convince all members of these committees to accept their proposals.

The Quebec political tradition has not defined a role for interest groups. Government bodies and political parties can claim that, like public interest groups, they too serve the public interest. Political parties, however, generally have a long list of topics on which they take a position; they are generalists. Interest groups, on the other hand, tend to focus on a limited number of issues; they are specialists. Groups in Quebec don't have the power of their American cousins because they compete for attention with political parties which, unlike American parties, have very strong organizations capable of mobilizing support and proposing comprehensive electoral platforms. As we have seen, both the Liberal party and the Party québécois have extensive electoral programs in which they offer different policies to attract interest group support.[4] Consequently, some groups decide that in order to promote their interests they should become political

---

3. After being systematically excluded from this process, Canadian native groups attempted in 1990 to break through using both traditional pressures and political violence.

4. In theory, electoral platforms contain different proposals in which the benefits accrue to specific groups but the costs are spread over the general population. In practice, according to a study done in Quebec for the period 1960–1985, it is possible to calculate who will *benefit* three out of four times but who will *pay* only one out of ten times (Landry and Duchesneau 1987).

parties, as when the PQ was created from the Mouvement souveraineté-association. The first objective of the party—a sovereign Quebec—is the same as the movement's but the party has added different proposals that cover other domains of Quebec society in which the government is active.

It should be noted that though interest groups have always been more powerful in the United States than in Quebec, their influence in Quebec—and in Canada—may have increased over the past few decades due to the declining influence of political parties, the diminished role of Parliament, and the growing power of the Premier. However, the fact that many groups have come to rely on the state for their funding limits their capacity to confront government policies. For example, *Info-Sectes*, a public interest group in Montreal that distributes information about religious sects, had its grant cut by a minister who belonged to a sect criticized by the interest group.

7.2   GROUPS OPERATING IN QUEBEC

Interest groups in Quebec include the various groups that made representations to the Bélanger-Campeau Commission, as well as groups devoted to social problems such as the *Associations coopératives d'économie familiale* (ACEFs), the *Cliniques populaires*, professional corporations, and associations such as the *Société St-Vincent-de-Paul*. These groups have a narrowly defined membership, have alternative ways to finance their activities, and are organized around volunteer work. Unfortunately, it is impossible to cover all of them adequately here. Setting up a typology is also not an easy task. Some groups focus exclusively on Quebec politics, such as the *Centrale des enseignants du Québec* and the *Conseil du patronat du Québec*. Some are sub-groups, such as the Quebec branch of the Canadian Manufacturers' Association. Groups involved in domains of shared jurisdiction, such as the *Union des producteurs agricoles* (UPA), have to deal with both federal and provincial governments. There are groups divided along linguistic lines, as the Montreal Board of Trade and the *Chambre de commerce de Montréal* were until recently. Groups outside Quebec can also have a great influence on the policy process: for example, the decision by New York State not to buy electricity from the *Grande baleine* project was influenced by environmentalist groups based in New York and New England.

The Development of Groups in Quebec

It could be said that Quebec became a pluralist society only in the 1960s, when the government began to take a more active role. Until then, the conservative role of the state and of the dominant ideology (Trudeau 1974) did not allow for much intervention or activism. Accounts of the 1930s describe a monolithic society (Milner and Milner 1973). The remedies for the Great Depression put forward by the different existing groups of the time was a *corporatism* inspired by Salazar or Mussolini. *L'Ecole sociale populaire, L'Action nationale, les Jeunes-Canada* were all right-wing nationalist movements differing only in the degree by which they were promoting corporatism, a "back to the land" policy, and the social teachings of the Catholic Church.

The Church's social doctrine pervaded these movements among francophones. The Church had been an entrenched power in Quebec since 1840, when the interests of the state and of the Church coincided, each reinforcing the power of the other and preventing challenges from the discontented. The Church went further by establishing its own groups in all areas of Quebec society. For example, the *Confédération des travailleurs catholiques du Canada* (CTCC), which saw the rapid growth of international unions in Quebec as a threat to its control over the French-Canadian population, was organized by the Church. The Church also promoted the creation of related movements, the *Jeunesse ouvrière catholique* (JOC) for young workers and the *Jeunesse étudiante catholique* (JEC) for students, to name just a few.

While Duplessis controlled the political system, the only access to government was through the patronage machine of his party, the *Union nationale*. Opposition movements such as Laval's School of Social Sciences were marginal, and *Cité libre* (Pierre Trudeau's magazine), and the daily *Le Devoir* had a limited circulation. The church-sponsored groups in Quebec existing prior to 1960—farmer, labour, youth, caisses populaires, and various cooperatives—were either secularized or eliminated during the 1960s. For example, the church-sponsored CTCC became the *Confédération des syndicats nationaux*, the most militant and radical union in Quebec. Also, the former *Union catholique des cultivateurs* has become the powerful *Union des producteurs agricoles* (UPA). And movements such as the *Jeunesse étudiante catholique* have lost most of their past importance.

Transformation of Quebec's Interest Groups after 1960

During the 1960s, three tendencies characterized the development of groups in Quebec (Meynaud 1970). The first was the *multiplication* of interest groups in certain sectors.

Meynaud observes that during the 1960s, consumers, the elderly, low-income families and people needing medical treatment were not well represented. Then, over the 1970s, the state took care of the health sector and established a comprehensive and universal Medicare system. Senior citizens were not yet organized as an interest group, but their growing number raised concerns in the state apparatus, and the government gradually improved the representation of consumers and low-income families through reforms of the legal aid system.

The second tendency was *specialization*—the breakup of many larger groups. An example is the division of doctors into 22 specialties. Unions in Quebec, which represent more than 30% of all workers, are now divided into four main federations and many smaller groups. And there are now a total of 40 professional corporations in Quebec—for example, lawyers, doctors, architects, chartered accountants, social workers, etc.

The third tendency observed by Meynaud was the *growing use of violence and civil disobedience* in Quebec to promote political interests. Relations between the government and its unionized workers became particularly strained in 1972, when presidents of the three unions were jailed.

It should be pointed out, however, that, despite several violent strikes and the limited violence of the FLQ, violence has been limited in Quebec. The *Front de libération du Québec* (FLQ) is the only political movement in Quebec's recent history that has used violence for political purposes. The FLQ, which started its activities in the early 1960s and was extinguished by the early 1970s, was born of the mingled hope and despair of a handful of young people dedicated to the realization of independence for Quebec. The *felquistes* were a collection of more or less connected groups, whose ideology was a mixture of leftist nationalism and the decolonization ideas of Fanon and Memmi, from whom they borrowed the idea of the usefulness of violence as a political tool. During the Quiet Revolution, some 90 of 176 violent events were bombings, and nine deaths can be linked to the political violence of the period. There were also several bank holdups and thefts of dynamite or military equipment. However, all the violent activities were characterized by amateurism (Fournier 1982; Laurendeau 1974).

Moreover, the FLQ activities were restricted almost exclusively to the Montreal metropolitan area—where the media are concentrated. Rather than being meant to overthrow the government, violence for the FLQ seems to have been designed to attract media attention for the cause of independence. With the rise of the PQ in the early 1970s, this rationale began to disappear, and the FLQ with it. The 1970 October Crisis was the beginning of the end for the FLQ. The federal government declared the War Measures Act after the FLQ's kidnapping of James Richard Cross, a British diplomat, and provincial minister Pierre Laporte. Under the Act, over 450 people were arrested while civil liberties were suspended. The Canadian government's severe measures after Laporte's kidnapping and death succeeded in getting rid of the FLQ.

One of the groups that changed during the 1960s was the *Union des producteurs agricoles* (UPA), which represents all farmers in Quebec. Difficulties in this economic sector over the years prompted the union to radicalize its demands. Traditionally, it has been associated with the labour unions in Quebec, because its membership of farm owners has often worked in cooperatives. The UPA has a dual structure consisting of local and specialized unions. At the base of the organization are 180 local syndicates, which provide province-wide representation, and 150 specialized syndicates to which producers of a specific commodity may belong.

> The UPA is structured to generate policy specific and technical information, to mobilize members and public support for its policy proposals, and to maintain the internal cohesion that is necessary for effective lobbying. Moreover it possesses the organizational requirements needed to participate with the state in [policy] formulation and implementation (Skogstad 1990:73).

The UPA's structure ensures that grassroots concerns and policy positions are known to the daily-decision-making body, an executive committee comprising the president, two vice presidents, and four elected members. Since the 1972 Farm Producers Act—passed after an intense UPA lobbying campaign that allowed the organization an annual budget of over $33 million and helped the movement maintain a staff of about 200 people—the UPA has enjoyed financial security and stability. Modifications in international agreements such as the GATT may create more turmoil in years to come, once more modifying the role of the UPA.

One of the results of modernization in Quebec has been the growth of a powerful labour union movement. An important element was the unionization of the civil service, and the recognition of its right to strike, in 1964–1965. In 1964 a new labour code was adopted defining working conditions, and in 1965 the new law of the civil service completed the reforms. In that year, Quebec's was the only Canadian government to grant union rights, including the right to strike, to some of its employees (Ambroise 1987). By 1970, 40% of unionized labor in Quebec was working in the civil service. This was highly innovative at time.

However, unionization peaked in the early 1970s and has been steadily decreasing since then. The number of unionized workers increased from 29% in 1964 to 42.1% in 1971, but by 1984 the figure was under 35%. As a percentage of the active population, unionization, after moving up to 34.2% in 1974, diminished to 27% in 1984, went up again after the recession of the early 1980s, and stood at 35.6% in 1990. Also, the generous terms granted in the 1960s to government employees have been revised over the past decade. Although the negotiation formula adopted thirty years ago has not been supplanted, since 1982 the government has legislated the terms of agreements.

In Quebec, there are four major unions and a number of independent unions. The largest is the *Fédération des travailleurs du Québec* (FTQ), the

"One day we will have to negotiate." Marcel Pépin, former leader of the Centrale des syndicats nationaux *(CSN)* during a strike of the Montreal Urban Community Transportation Employees in August 1974. [Courtesy Archives nationales du Québec. Photo: Michel Elliott.]

relatively autonomous Quebec branch of the Canadian Labour Congress. Next largest is the *Centrale des syndicats nationaux* (CSN), which resulted from the transformation of the Catholic unions. The third is the *Centrale de l'enseignement du Québec* (CEQ), which represents most of the teachers in Quebec and other employees in the public sector. A smaller union movement, the *Centrale des syndicats démocratiques* (CSD), is a dissatisfied branch of the CSN that broke away after the bitter strikes of 1972.

Since the major confrontation with the government in 1972, and another in 1982 over salary reductions, the unions have become more moderate in the 1990s, with a neo-corporatist structure based on the European model. In different industries, unions and business have reached agreements that guarantee there will be no strikes in exchange for a minimum employment level for periods ranging from two to five years.

The new approach taken by the labour movement in Quebec illustrates the eclipse of the dominant forces that engineered the province's modernization. Along with the middle-class technocrats, salaried professionals, and wordsmiths who formed the nucleus of the nationalist movement, organized labour has retreated from centre stage in Quebec politics. Taking their place is a rising class of dynamic francophone entrepreneurs (Tanguay 1987–1988). This emerging business class is less interested in the constitutional issues that have monopolized national attention for the past three decades. But then this business class relies on the provincial state rather than on the federal government for its expansion.

Lately, the FTQ has created one of the most original and interesting economic organizations in North America. Over the 1980s, this new organization reconciled to a large extent employers' and workers' interests by creating, by act in the National Assembly, the *Fonds de solidarité des travailleurs du Québec*. Financed through individual contributions in the form of retirement savings helped by tax credits, the *Fonds de solidarité* is a risk capital pool for investments. The *Fonds* assets are a highly diversified trust fund and also an economic tool to create and maintain thousands of jobs in Quebec-based companies. This trust is an example of the institutionalized relations between the government and interest groups. The *Fonds* complements the public pension system and fosters economic development the same way some government agencies do.

Another economic movement and powerful interest group is the *Mouvement Desjardins*, a network of caisses populaires or credit unions that has accumulated assets of some $50 billion. At the time of their creation, founder Alphonse Desjardins had sought a federal charter, which he was not able to get; but subsequently, a bill passed by the National Assembly legalized the movement. The caisses populaires were initially organized on a parish basis, designed to teach the virtue of saving and to provide low interest rates to members; in the first half of this century, members had to swear that they were practising Catholics. Being cooperatives, these credit unions are controlled by members at the branch level. Decisions concerning the movement as a whole are made at regional and national meetings. The Mouvement Desjardins has maintained a broad interest in social issues that is rather unique for a financial institution.

The Rise of the New Business Class over the 1980s

Among the major business groups that operate in Quebec are the *Conseil du patronat du Québec* (CPQ), the *Centre des dirigeants d'entreprises*, the various *Chambres de commerce* (Montreal, provincial, Quebec City, etc.), and the Montreal Board of Trade. There are also associations representing the various industrial sectors such as pulp and paper, manufacturing, and exporters.

The CPQ, created in 1968–1969, is a federation of public and private associations that represent employers who control more or less directly 70% of the Quebec workforce. Its members are made up of both individual firms and other employer associations. Overall, the CPQ does not really speak for small business. The Quebec division of the Canadian Manufacturers' Association is a member of the CPQ, as is the small-business federation, the Centre des dirigeants d'entreprise; but the Chambres de commerce, whose membership comes from small business, are not. The Chambre de commerce de Montréal represents 7,000 to 8,000 members, individuals, and enterprises. The Montreal Board of Trade representing the English-speaking business community in Montreal recently merged with the Chambre de commerce de Montréal. The Chambre de commerce du Québec comprises 230 local Chambres de commerce throughout Quebec (7,300 members). There is also the *Fédération canadienne de l'entreprise indépendante (section Québec)*.

Ghislain Dufour, president of the Conseil du patronat du Québec *(CPQ), the large business association.* [Courtesy Le Devoir and Gilles Paré, Librarian. Photo: Jacques Nadeau.]

The idea of sovereignty-association, put forth by the PQ during the 1980 referendum campaign, was bitterly opposed by the business community. In order to win the following 1981 election, the PQ had to court this community, in particular the small-business owners that had traditionally supported the Union nationale. The strategy proved successful: the PQ won or kept virtually every small industrial town from Montreal to Sept-Îles on both sides of the Saint Lawrence River. This shifted the heart of the party away from its sources in the eastern part of Montreal to small-town Quebec (Fraser 1984). In the long run, it established the framework for a more market-oriented economic policy philosophy, one that the Liberal Party pushed further when they returned to power in 1985. The corporatist agreements put forward by Minister of Industry and Trade Gérald Tremblay are a variation on those attempted by the PQ. The government around 1982 favoured *concertation*: government, business, and labour working together to plan economic development, as is done in some European countries such as Austria. One of the results was the creation of *Corvée-Habitation*, a program involving cooperation between business, labour, and government to build new low-cost housing with below-market mortgage rates.

At the same time, the government expanded its intervention in the economy. The state-owned enterprises flexed their muscles: the Caisse de dépôt helped the *Société québécoise d'initiative pétrolière* (SOQUIP) gain control of Gaz Métropolitain and began speeding up the distribution of natural gas in Quebec. This distribution made electric power produced by Hydro-Québec available for export. The Caisse also bought substantial interests in Noranda and Domtar, two major natural resources conglomerates. As more and more francophones entered corporate boardrooms, the Caisse de dépôt helped francophone entrepreneurs expand their businesses. Francophone ownership grew significantly in the pulp and paper and energy industries, mining, the food distribution business, transport equipment, and services such as drugstores, hardware, and engineering. Much of this expansion would not have been possible without the help of the Quebec state and its public corporations. The rise of the new business class in Quebec relied on the provincial state, which set up networks for the movement of business capital. Thus, a decade after the referendum, the business community is not opposed to a significant transformation of Quebec's constitutional status. In fact, the only major sector of Quebec business that does rely on federal cooperation is aeronautics.

In 1982, the recession was worsening and the unions and the government were on a collision course over the renewal of collective agreements. The result was a major defeat for the unions—and only a Pyrrhic victory for the government, whose measures alienated the teachers, government employees, hospital workers, and others who had been the traditional base of support for the PQ. At the end of 1982, the government imposed 109 collective agreements on 300,000 public-sector employees. As Fraser (1984: 336) writes, "the conflict virtually ended the party's hunger to identify with the labour movement; simultaneously, it accelerated its tendency to think in almost corporatist terms of 'concertation.'" The next budget, in 1983, was clearly pro-business: opportunities for small businesses to go public, tax breaks for research and development, and a promise to examine the tax levels for high-income earners. This pro-business drive reached full speed when the Liberal party won the election in 1985 and decided to reduce government services, deregulate business, and privatize some of the state-owned enterprises.

Non-Economic Groups and Institutionalization

The relative power of noneconomic interest groups is illustrated by the development of the Quebec state in education and health.

In education, due to protection granted by the BNA Act, school boards and private schools have been able to resist the attempts by the state to reduce their autonomy, even though most of the expenses of the boards are paid from provincial revenues. For example, government has not been able to transform the religious school boards into linguistic ones. And the process of reform over the past twenty years has been stopped due to opposition by existing interest groups.

In 1982 a white paper was released that proposed a reduction in the power of the boards, and a more important role for parents at the school level. Under the plan, each school was to be a corporation governed by a council made up of teachers and parents, the principal being an administrative advisor. On the Island of Montreal, for example, there were to be eight French and five English school boards, thus ensuring the breakup of the two largest boards in the province, the Montreal Catholic School Commission and the Protestant School Board of Greater Montreal. Overall, the plan was opposed by the education establishment, school boards, teachers' unions, and Protestant parents. Only the provincial committee of parents and school principals were in favour of the plan.

At the core of the issue lie two of the most sensitive questions in Quebec's political history: religion and language. Since Confederation, the school system has been based on religion. Article 93 of the BNA Act guarantees the right of religious minorities in all provinces to maintain their own school boards. In Quebec, the Protestant boards (which actually encourage religious diversity) have used these guarantees to preserve their powers.

On the Catholic side, school boards and Catholic parent groups have been able to dominate school board elections, where the turnout rarely exceeds 15%. Since 1964, these groups have been able to limit reform of the system and attempts to centralize power in the hands of the government. Two groups have lost at this game: the English-speaking Catholic and the French-speaking non-Catholic parents. School boards can refuse to administer schools such as Nôtre-Dame-des-Neiges, where immigrant students come from 32 different religious affiliations. Such complications resulting from immigration patterns can be used as an argument for ending the religious school system, which is at present restricted to the Protestants, Jews, and Catholics.

In the health sector, the Medicare system has been established despite the opposition of physicians whose associations were unable to mount a powerful enough lobby against it. A recent attempt to reform health policy that would have resulted in depriving recently graduated physicians of the right to practise in locations of their choice has been shelved for the time being as a result of pressures from the *Corporation professionnelle des médecins du Québec*; but it appears that the doctors will only be able to slow down the process, not to stop it.

In municipal affairs, cities, and urban communities, and the *Municipalités régionales de comté* (MRCs) (regional municipal councils) have created unions that try, like interest groups, to pressure the Quebec government. MRCs are given the responsibility of seeing to the preparation of land use and proposing plans for economic development of their regions. The creation of these MRCs allowed for the continuing existence of small municipalities (more than 1,600 in Quebec, in contrast to 650 in Ontario) who would share services and costs, justifing their survival. Lately, the government has tried to alleviate its own financial difficulties by transferring to the local governments the obligation to tax citizens for mass transportation, police services, and highway maintenance. After six months of bargaining, cities and towns have obtained only a slight decrease of the tax burden for their electorate.

On the linguistic front, the more than one century old *Société Saint-Jean Baptiste* (SSJB) has been joined by the *Mouvement Québec français* and other, smaller movements. The SSJB is a traditional national group with preponderantly liberal professional and conservative bases. It was created in 1834 and has since engendered the *Société nationale de Fiducie* (a trust) and two insurance companies. The SSJB advocates the promotion of the French language as well as, over the past few years, better relations between the various ethnic communities in Quebec.

In 1982, *Alliance-Québec* was created. This lobby group, funded for $1 million a year by the federal government, quickly emerged as the most visible and sophisticated anglophone organization in Quebec. Alliance-Québec has pursued anglophone interests according to a strategy based chiefly on articulated "minority" language rights (Levine 1990).

Aboriginal groups have become more vocal: the Mohawks around Montreal have taken advantage of the failure of the Meech Lake agreement

The Oka crisis during the summer 1990. Mohawk from Kanesatake. [Courtesy Le Devoir and Gilles Paré, Librarian. Photo: Jacques Nadeau.]

to push land claims in the context of poor management of the issue by the federal government, responsible for this area of policy. The native Cree have also made claims, protesting hydroelectric projects of Hydro-Québec in the James Bay area, and have been able to persuade the New York State government to renege on its energy deal with Hydro-Québec.

Although native Americans and Inuits are supposed to be the responsibility of the federal government, the Quebec government has created the *Secrétariat des activités gouvernementales en milieux Amérindiens et Inuit* (SAGMAI). Current policy, developed between 1978 and 1985, focusses on negotiated agreements and subsequently granted legal protection (Gourdeau 1988). This legal protection has been used by the Cree to stop development of the second phase of the James Bay project.

Another non-economic group are women, though, of course, their problems are partly financial and social. There are 5,350,000 people over 15 years old in Quebec, of whom 2,755,000 are women. Close to 1.5 million of these women work, but only 39.4% full-time. Of part-time jobs, 70.8% are filled by women. For all women the average salary is $24,992, in contrast to $36,863 for men. Of persons working for the minimum wage, 66% are women. Perhaps an indication of change is that 58% of enrollment at the CEGEP level and 57% at the university level are women.

One woman out of ten participates in women's movements in Quebec (Lamont 1984). By 1977, women made up one-third of unionized workers. Feminist groups created six new province-wide organizations between 1957 and 1973, five of them after 1966. These groups and smaller ones have established homes for battered wives and children, rape crisis centres, abortion referral services, and birth control information services, and have organized protests against pornography and sexual harassment (Trofimenkoff 1983). The *Fédération des femmes du Québec* has 75,000 members, the *Cercle des fermières* has 74,400 members, and the *Association féminine d'éducation et d'action sociale* has 35,000 members. The number of women's centres has jumped from 4 in 1979 to 36 in 1983 and the Common Front (which is anti-pornography) includes 300,000 people backed by 70 associations. Women's publications are led by *Châtelaine*, which has a circulation of 295,000—i.e., 40,000 more than the general magazine *L'Actualité*, Quebec's equivalent of *Time* or *Newsweek* (Lamont 1984: 75). There is a Women's Experimental Theatre Group, an information network called *Réseau d'action et d'information pour les femmes*, a research institute at Concordia University (the Simone de Beauvoir Institute), a publisher (*Editions du remue-ménage*), and a literary review (*La Nouvelle barre du jour*). The *Cercle des fermières*, originally for women living on farms, now takes positions on family matters, the school system, and pensions for the benefit of women who no longer work on a farm.

In the field of politics and administration, there is a delegated minister for women's affairs; the *Conseil du statut de la femme*, a government body; and various associations, such as the *Fédération des femmes du Québec* and the *Coalition nationale pour l'avortement libre et gratuit* (National Coalition for Free Abortion). In 1978, the *Conseil du statut* published a document, *Pour les Québécoises: égalité et indépendance* (For Quebecers: Equality and Independence), in which were summarized the demands of various women groups in Quebec—namely, access to education, economic integration, legal equality, and an end to sexism.

The *Fédération des femmes du Québec* helped create the *Conseil du statut* to deal with issues related to education, birth control, abortion, day care, sexual education, contraceptives, maternity leave, health, and labour (pensions, minimum wage). Another important movement is the *Association féminine pour l'éducation et l'action sociale* (AFEAS) (Women's Association for Education and Social Action), which aims at improving the situation of women in more-traditional roles, such as those working at home. In the three major union movements, *Comités de la condition féminine des syndicats* (Committees on Women's Affairs) have been established.

A recent study suggests that the most radical, active, and difficult years for the feminist movement in Quebec were the 1970s. The 1980s have been more individualistic (Clio 1992). The four women who wrote this study suggest that women should not be considered an "interest group," since they constitute half of the population.

7.3 HAS QUEBEC BECOME A CORPORATIST SOCIETY?

The PQ enabled people who cannot afford to pay a lawyer to sue collectively—have *recours collectif*—through a corporation created to organize financing for launching class-action suits. This corporation is headed by three people selected after consulting the Quebec Bar and the *Commission des services juridiques* (Legal Services Commission).

Similarly, the *Office de la protection du consommateur* (Consumer Protection Office), created during the first PQ government, aims to enforce the Consumer Protection Act, register requests from the population, distribute information in this area, make studies, inform business, and so on. The *Office* publishes *Protégez-vous* and *Protect Yourself*, two versions of a monthly magazine that evaluates products and services and deals with consumer-related matters.

The creation of SAGMAI, the provisions of the Farm Producers Act, the existence of a delegated minister for women's affairs, the creation of an *Office des professions* in charge of regulating the forty professions that

Figure 7.1

Network of Business Associations Related to the Quebec Government

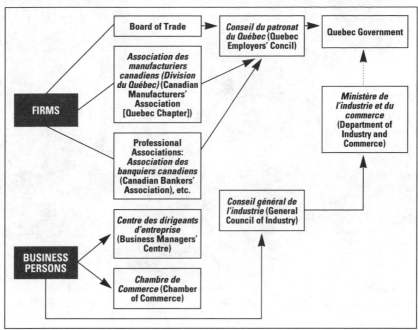

Source: Bernard Pratte, "Le Conseil du patronat du Québec: rôle et idéologie, 1963–1976," M.A. paper, Department of History, Université de Montréal, 1985.

are officially recognized in Quebec, and the law of *recours collectif* are all indications of the *institutionalization* of relations between groups and the government in Quebec, a process which has helped change the confrontational nature of the relations between them that existed during the 1970s.

Committees and commissions facilitate the inclusion of citizens' groups in the policy process. Consultative bodies such as the *Conseil d'orientation économique* or the *Conseil supérieur de l'éducation*, created over the years by the government, are instruments that organize group participation in the process. And, as has been discussed, the number of such government agencies has blossomed since 1960.

Archibald (1973) asks: Have all these efforts made Quebec a "corporatist" society? The most common modern definition of corporatism is Schmitter's (1979):

Corporatism can be defined as a system of interest representation in which the constituent units are organized into a limited number of singular, compulsory, noncompetitive, hierarchically ordered and functionally differentiated categories, recognized or licensed (if

Several interest group leaders had clearly stated their support for Quebec sovereignty. Many of them gathered together in early 1992, on the same day as that on which the Beaudoin-Dobbie commission held a conference on the economic union to discuss with the press all the reports presented to the Bélanger-Campeau commission. **Left to right:** *Sylvain Simard, president of* Mouvement national des Québécois *(MNQ); Serge Demers, president of* Mouvement Québec; *Gérald Larose, president of* Centrale des syndicats nationaux *(CSN); Jacques Parizeau, leader of the* Parti québécois; *Jean Dorion, president of* Société Saint-Jean-Baptiste *(SSJB); Fernand Daoust, president of* Fédération des travailleurs du Québec *(FTQ); Lucien Bouchard, federal leader of the* Bloc québécois. *[Courtesy Le Devoir and Gilles Paré, Librarian. Photo: Jacques Grenier.]*

not created) by the state and granted a deliberate representational monopoly within their respective categories in exchange for observing certain controls on their selection of leaders and articulation of demands and supports.

Corporatism assumes comprehensiveness of membership, which does not seem true for either unions or business associations in Quebec. Exclusion mechanisms exist, as illustrated by the Bélanger-Campeau Commission and the previous socioeconomic conferences—groups have not been included as members, and other mechanisms have limited their presentations in front of the Commission. Although efforts have been made to improve tripartite cooperation, and state agencies, trade unions, and private businesses do cooperate in Quebec, there are still confrontations between the state and its employees over collective agreements and between business and the government over environment policy implementation. Thus, although steps may have been taken in that direction, Quebec hardly qualifies as a corporate state in Schmitter's terms.

7.4 CONCLUSION

In the past, interest groups in Quebec have been less influential than those in the United States, but that situation may be changing. Also, group definitions are changing rapidly. During the 1950s, the dominant groups in Quebec were sponsored by the Church; now, they are business-oriented. Over the 1960s and 1970s, the union movement rose, to decline in the early 1980s. In recent years, the unions have worked hard to redefine themselves, to get rid of passé ideological stands and become more business-oriented. The rise of the *Fonds de solidarité du Québec* is an example. The recent "social contracts" between employees and business are another: these contracts, in summary, guarantee that there will be no strikes for five years as long as there are no layoffs for the same period. It appears that traditional lines of conflict no longer apply. Using the Canadian Charter of Rights and Freedoms, a group of aboriginal women recently asked for the protection of the courts in the event that aboriginal nations are granted governmental autonomy. Other groups may use the Charter to obtain political recognition.

It is quite possible that in Canada, and particularly in Quebec, the power of interest groups has been underestimated. Thorburn (1985), in summarizing the evolution of economic policy since Confederation, speaks of a cozy relationship between business and the state. Similarly, in present-day Quebec, businesspeople are likely to have a political influence that epitomizes the power of interest groups.

Interest groups articulate the aggregate opinions of some part of the population. How representative they are is arguable; experience shows that they might not even represent their own members if their own staff become more powerful than the people they are supposed to represent. Interest groups are the lesser-known part of the Quebec and Canadian political scene. Their relative importance in Quebec as well as in Canada is a question on the research agenda for the future.

KEY TERMS

Class conflict

Consultant

Corporatism

Direct lobbying

Elite theory

Grassroots lobbying

Hyperpluralism

Interest groups

Lobbying

Lobbyist

Pluralist theory

REFERENCES AND FURTHER READINGS

Archibald, Clinton. 1983. *Un Québec corporatiste?* Hull: Editions Asticou.

Banting, Keith (ed.). 1985. *The State and Economic Interests.* Toronto: University of Toronto Press.

Bélanger, Yves and Pierre Fournier. 1987. *L'Entreprise québécoise: développement historique et dynamique contemporaine.* Montreal: Hurtubise HMH.

Berry, Jeffrey M. 1984. *The Interest Group Society.* Boston: Little, Brown.

Boivin, Dominique. 1984. *Le Lobbying ou le pouvoir des groupes de pression.* Montreal: Editions du méridien.

Coleman, William D. and Grace Skogstad (eds.). 1990. *Policy Communities and Public Policy in Canada: A Structural Approach.* Mississauga: Copp Clark Pitman.

Collectif Clio. 1992. *L'Histoire des femmes au Québec.* Montreal: Editions du jour.

Crête, Jean. 1984. *Le Comportement électoral au Québec.* Montreal: Gaétan Morin.

Fraser, Graham. 1984. *PQ: René Lévesque and the Parti Québéois in Power.* Rev. ed. Toronto: Macmillan.

Goldstein, Jonah. 1979. "Public interest groups and public policy: the case of the Consumers' Association of Canada." *Canadian Journal of Political Science,* 12: 137–155.

Gourdeau, Eric. 1988. "Quebec and aboriginal peoples." In J. Anthony Long and Menno Boldt (eds.) *Governments in Conflict? Provinces and Indian Nations in Canada.* Toronto: University of Toronto Press.

Lamont, Michèle. 1984. "Les Rapports politiques au sein du mouvement des femmes du Québec." *Politique,* 5: 75–107.

Landry, Réjean and Paule Duchesneau. 1987. "L'Offre d'intervention gouvernementale aux groupes: une théorie et une application." *Canadian Journal of Political Science,* 20: 525–552.

Levine, Marc V. 1990. *The Reconquest of Montreal: Language Policy and Social Change in a Bilingual City.* Philadelphia: Temple University Press.

Lineberry, Robert L. 1980. *Government in America.* Boston: Little, Brown.

Long, J. Anthony and Menno Boldt (eds.). 1988. *Governments in Conflict? Provinces and Indian Nations in Canada.* Toronto: University of Toronto Press.

Meynaud, Jean. 1970. "Groupes de pression et politique gouvernementale au Québec." In Jean-Charles Bonenfant et al., *Réflexions sur la politique au Québec.* Montreal: PUQ. Pp. 65–92.

Milner, Henry and S. H. Milner. 1973. *The Decolonization of Quebec.* Toronto: McClelland and Stewart.

Milner, Henry. 1986. *The Long Road to Reform: Restructuring Public Education in Quebec.* Kingston: McGill-Queen's University Press.

Pross, A. Paul. 1986. *Group Politics and Public Policy.* Toronto: Oxford University Press.

Ripley, Randall B. and Grace A. Franklin. 1991. *Congress, the Bureaucracy and Public Policy.* 5th ed. Pacific Grove, CA: Brooks/Cole.

Schattschneider, E. E. 1960. *The Semisovereign People.* New York: Holt, Rinehart and Winston.

Schmitter, Philip. 1974. "Still the century of corporatism?" *Review of Politics,* 36: 85–131.

Simeon, Richard. 1972. *Federal-Provincial Diplomacy.* Toronto: University of Toronto Press.

Skogstad, Grace. 1985. "Interest groups, representation and conflict management in the standing committees of the House of Commons." *Canadian Journal of Political Science,* 18: 739–772.

Skogstad, Grace. 1990. "The farm policy community and public policy in Ontario and Quebec." In William D. Coleman and Grace Skogstad (eds.), *Policy Communities and Public Policy in Canada.* Mississauga: Copp Clark Pitman. Pp. 59–90.

Tanguay, Brian A. 1987–1988. "Business, labor, and the state in the 'New Quebec.'" *American Review of Canadian Studies,* 17: 395–408.

Thorburn, Hugh G. 1985. *Interest Groups in the Canadian Federal System.* Toronto: University of Toronto Press.

Trofimenkoff, Susan Mann. 1983. *The Dream of Nation: A Social and Intellectual History of Quebec.* Toronto: Gage.

Trudeau, Pierre Elliott. 1974. *The Asbestos Strike.* Toronto: James Lorimer.

CHAPTER 8

MASS MEDIA
AND THE
PUBLIC
AGENDA

Quebec has played a key role in the development of Canadian mass media. In 1929, under the Taschereau government, it became the first province to adopt legislation regulating radio broadcasting. The authority of the Quebec government in this matter was subsequently contested by the federal government right up to the Supreme Court, an oft-repeated scenario over the next fifty years, especially at the end of the 1970s when the main issue was control over cable television. Quebec was also the first province to create a Department of Communications, and one of the first to have TV service.

Over the years, conflict over communications issues has been a constant theme of Quebec's relations with the federal government; it also led to the failure of the 1971 Victoria constitutional conference, where Robert Bourassa launched the idea of cultural sovereignty for Quebec. Communications, and who controls them, are vitally important to the preservation and development of the French character of Quebec society. Every Quebec government, regardless of party, has pursued control of this field through legislation, policy documents, and regulations. As Minister Gil Rémillard puts it:

> Communications are, in our modern society, a powerful tool in cultural development and they are having more and more influence over economic and social development as well. From this viewpoint, communications and the mass media are at the heart of the Canadian federalist controversy—essential for the development of Quebec nationalism, as well as vital to Canadian nationalism. This

is why the communications file has been among the most discussed issue of the federal-provincial relationships. (1983: 438)

There are five key functions of the media in Quebec and North America: to inform citizens, to form public opinion, to express opinions, to influence decision-makers, and to entertain. Over the years, and especially since the beginning of the 1960s, the Quebec media have become more and more politicized, reflecting the overall political changes in Quebec society.

8.1 THE PRESS

The history of the Quebec press differs from the history of television in that it has always been more subject to political intervention than to administrative or legislative action. The relationship between state, government, and the print media has always been close. As a result, the press was rarely independent right from the start; editors and journalists who tried to retain that independence were prosecuted or strongly condemned by the government, occasionally ending up in jail.

The importance of journalism and the press in Quebec from a sociological perspective is that many of the best intellectuals, writers, and political

Henri Bourassa, founder on January 10, 1910 of the Montreal newspaper Le Devoir. *[Courtesy* Le Devoir *and Gilles Paré, Librarian.]*

leaders have been closely associated with the media. As W. S. Wallace puts it:

> The history of journalism is of peculiar importance in Canada, not only because of the profound influence newspapers have exerted on political and social life, but also because, in Canada, literature has been an offshoot of journalism. In England the pamphlet gave birth to the newsletter or newspaper; but in Canada the process was reversed, and the newspaper gave birth to the pamphlet and the book. (Wallace 1948: 310)

This is particularly true of Quebec, where indigenous literature remains a relatively recent phenomenon. Among the best thinkers in Quebec's history who were also active journalists were Henri Bourassa, the founder of *Le Devoir* (1910); André Laurendeau, a writer for that paper; and René Lévesque, who started out as a broadcast journalist for the Canadian Broadcasting Corporation (CBC/Radio-Canada). Also worthy of mention are Jean-Louis Gagnon, Gérard Pelletier, and T. D. Bouchard. Such individuals greatly influenced the social and political history of Quebec. Their careers also serve to illustrate how the Quebec press evolved, from being closely tied to developing political parties, to becoming more and more independent, and then to nurturing their own journalistic organizations, which marked the rise of professionalism.

One notable fact about Quebec's and Canada's press history is that the first journalists were not British or French, but American:

> The Canadian Press is the daughter of the American Press. In Quebec and Montreal, as well as in Halifax, our first journalists were Americans. Even when they were from another ethnic origin, they had lived in the United States before crossing the border. (Fauteux 1934: 55)

According to Kesterton, the first printing press had arrived in Halifax by August 1751. Bartholomew Green, Jr., grandson of the founder of the *Boston News Letter*, moved to Halifax and probably brought a printing press with him. His goal was to start a newspaper, but he died before the end of the year. Green's partner, John Bushell of Boston, succeeded him and published the first issue of the *Halifax Gazette* on March 23, 1752 (Kesterton 1967: 23-24).

However, the role of the state was all-pervasive during this period:

> The earliest newspapers took their quality from the conditions surrounding their production. Government patronage was essential to their existence, so that revenue-producing government announcements, proclamations, orders, and enactments made up a large part of their content. The first editor to establish himself in each province

was usually the King's Printer, even though he did not always wear the official title of his position. (Kesterton 1967: 6–7)

During the French regime and until the fall of Montreal in September 1760, there were no newspapers and not even a printing press in New France. All orders, governmental decrees, and other official messages were proclaimed by a "sounding of the drum" in Montreal, Quebec City, Trois-Rivières, and other towns and villages, and publicized in rural areas with the help of parish priests (Fauteux 1940: 54, 68).

With the Treaty of Paris on February 10, 1763, the French government signed over Acadia, Canada, Newfoundland, and Cape Breton to England. A few months later, on October 7, 1763, a civil government was proclaimed by the King of England, George III. The following spring, printers William Brown and Thomas Gilmore, from Philadelphia, published the first issue of the *Quebec Gazette*, on June 21, 1764; 143 copies were sold. That first newspaper was published in both official languages.

In 1774, the British parliament passed the Quebec Act, which defined Quebec's boundaries and reestablished French civil law. This coincided with the growing insurrection in the American colonies, and the occupation of Montreal by the Americans Arnold and Montgomery until the spring of 1776. That same year, on May 6, Fleury Mesplet, one of the founders of a free press in Quebec, and his family, arrived in Montreal. Mesplet was born near Lyon in France, but was commissioned by the American Congress to push the idea of a republic to the French-speaking population in Quebec. It was not an easy mission. After the American troops fled, Mesplet was charged with espionage and put in jail for a month. Once American independence was proclaimed on July 4, 1776, any French in Quebec who were suspected of supporting the Americans were punished by the religious authorities.

In the end, however, Mesplet came out with a publication that marked the beginning of a free press in Quebec. On June 3, 1778, he published the first copy of the *Gazette du commerce et littéraire* with the help of Montreal lawyer Valentin Jautard. The paper was published only in French, had four pages, and measured about eight by ten inches. As Mason Wade wrote:

> Mesplet has the distinction of establishing the first purely French press in Canada, since the bilingual *Quebec Gazette* established in 1764 was published by Britishers and was a government organ.... Two years later, however, his press gave birth to the *Gazette littéraire de Montréal*, the French forerunner of French-Canadian journalism. (Wade 1955: 72)

Soon, however, relations with the British governor, Frederic Haldimand, turned stormy. After Jautard criticized Haldimand's administration, an order came down to stop publication of the newspaper and the editors were asked to leave the country. Pressure from Montreal citizens persuaded Haldimand to keep the newspaper open, but since then all articles had to be approved before publication. As soon as the censor turned his back Jautard published an article entitled *Tant pis, tant mieux* ("So much the worse, so much the better"), which again displeased the authorities, and Jautard and Mesplet both landed in jail for three years in Quebec City. After his release in 1785, Mesplet founded another newspaper, the bilingual *Gazette de Montréal*, the ancestor of what is now the only anglophone daily newspaper in that city.

After proclamation of the 1791 Constitution, which divided Canada into Upper and Lower Canada (Ontario and Quebec) and marked the beginning of the parliamentary system, several newspapers quickly adopted a political stance favouring protection of the French-speaking population from assimilation by the English. Among them was *Le Canadien*, founded on November 23, 1806 by members of the Lower Canada Assembly: Pierre Bédard, Jean-Thomas Taschereau, Joseph-Louis Borgia, and François Blanchet. Their newspaper often clashed with *The Mercury*, which promoted anglicization and assimilation of the French population. In 1810, editor Lefrançois of *Le Canadien* and Bédard, Taschereau, and Blanchet were arrested, and the paper's printing house was seized. In 1832, the editors of *La Minerve* and *The Vindicator* were sentenced to one month in jail after having written remarks about the Legislative Council that, in the eyes of British colonial authorities, were derogatory.

Similar troubles befell the Montreal *patriote* newspaper *La Minerve*, founded in 1826 by Augustin Norbert Morin, with the support the following year of Ludger Duvernay, founding father of the Société Saint-Jean-Baptiste. *La Minerve* played a key role in events leading up to the 1837–1838 insurrections, supporting requests made in the Legislative Assembly by the *Parti patriote* and its leader Louis-Joseph Papineau. The newspaper closed at the beginning of the insurrection, when Duvernay fled to the United States. After the beginning of the new regime under *L'Acte d'union* on February 10, 1841, Duvernay returned from exile, and *La Minerve* began to publish once again in 1842.

This period also produced the first daily newspaper in Canada, the *Daily Advertiser*, launched in 1833 in Montreal by H. S. Chapman. Between 1840 and 1867, there was a new literary movement with the establishment of several newspapers that published only the works of *écrivains du terroir* (soil writers): *L'Encyclopédie canadienne*, *L'Abeille canadienne*, *Le Répertoire national*, *La Ruche littéraire et politique* (1853–1859), *Le Journal de l'instruction publique* (founded by Pierre-Joseph-Olivier Chauveau, who later became Premier of Quebec), *Soirées canadiennes* (1861–1865), and

Revue canadienne (1861). The primary goal of all these newspapers was the advancement of French-Canadian culture and literature.

After Confederation in 1867, several francophone and anglophone newspapers sprang up: in 1869, Hugh Graham founded the *Montreal Star*; in 1870, Joseph-Alfred Mousseau became the editor of *L'Opinion publique*; in 1876, Honoré Beaugrand founded *La Patrie*. The end of the 19th century saw the founding of two important daily newspapers that still exist today. The oldest Quebec francophone daily newspaper, Montreal's *La Presse*, was founded in 1884 by Trefflé Berthiaume in collaboration with Joseph-Alfred-Norbert Provencher and Clément-Arthur Dansereau, both from *La Minerve* (1863–1876). On December 28, 1896, *Le Soleil*, the largest daily newspaper in Quebec City, was founded. In 1900, *La Presse* had a circulation of 66,000, the largest in Canada. By the end of the 19th century,

Mrs. Pamphile Du Tremblay and the first issue in 1961 of Le Nouveau Journal *after Mrs. Du Tremblay and Jean-Louis Gagnon left the Montreal daily* La Presse. *Unfortunately, this newspaper, which has been admired by journalists for its outstanding quality, disappeared in 1962 amid financial and administrative difficulties. [Courtesy Archives nationales du Québec.]*

The Montreal daily La Presse *on rue St-Jacques at the time of the lockout on July 20, 1971. [Courtesy Archives nationales du Québec.]*

newspapers were part of daily life throughout Quebec society, and they were highly political, in the European tradition.

The Canadian Press Association was created in Kingston in September 1859, and in 1876 the anglophone Province of Quebec Press Association was born. (In the same year, Alexander Graham Bell made the first long-distance call between Paris and Brantford, Ontario). In 1879 its French counterpart, *Presse associée de la Province de Québec*, was created. But it was not until December 1910 that the Canadian Press Limited (CP), the first coast-to-coast press agency affiliated with Associated Press (AP), was founded. In 1922, the second press agency in Canada, United Press International of Canada (UPI) was established.

Other Quebec daily newspapers began to publish at the beginning of the century. The Montreal daily *Le Devoir* was founded on January 10, 1910 by Henri Bourassa. Senator Jacob Nicol launched *La Tribune* in Sherbrooke the same year. In 1920, J. H. Fortier purchased the weekly *Le Trifluvien* and created a new weekly newspaper, *Le Nouvelliste de Trois-Rivières*. In 1935, the weekly newspaper *La Voix de l'Est* of Granby, was founded. Ten years later, it became a daily. Finally, the largest Quebec daily newspaper, *Le Journal de Montréal*, was founded at the time of the Quiet Revolution, in 1964, by Pierre Péladeau and Serge Roy when the employees of *La Presse* went on a seven-month strike. Later on, during the strike of *Le Soleil*, Pierre

Pierre Péladeau, president of Québécor and owner of the Montreal daily Le Journal de Montréal *and the Quebec City daily newspaper* Le Journal de Québec. *[Courtesy* Le Devoir *and Gilles Paré, Librarian. Photo: Jacques Grenier.]*

Péladeau launched the *Journal de Québec*. For the record, the oldest francophone daily newspaper outside Quebec is *Le Droit* of Ottawa, founded in 1913 by Charles Charlebois, an oblate priest.

Today, there are some 559 newspapers in the province. Twelve are dailies, and ten are published in French and two in English. There are five daily newspapers in the Montreal market. The most important French daily newspapers are *La Presse*, *Le Journal de Montréal*, *Le Devoir*, and *Le Soleil*. The main organ of the English community is the Montreal newspaper the *Gazette*, which, as mentioned, was originally a French newspaper.

There are 196 regional weekly newspapers, of which nearly half are published in the Montreal region, followed by the Quebec region with 29. General-interest (102 in number) and special-interest periodicals (also 102) also occupy an important segment of the market. Among the rest of the print media, there are community newspapers published in several languages. At the beginning of the 1980s, 55 newspapers were being published in 17 different languages, with a total distribution of 369,455 and a readership of about 500,000; of these, eight were published in Italian, five in Arabic languages, five in Greek, and three in Polish (Schwartz 1980). The proliferation of community newspapers serving the recent waves of immigration are a good indicator of the changing social character of Quebec, and especially of Montreal.

8.2 RADIO AND TELEVISION

In the winter of 1919 the Marconi company established in Montreal the first permanent broadcasting station in Canada, and possibly the world: station XWA, later changed to CFCF, which still exists today. On September 26, 1922, CKAC, owned by *La Presse*, was founded in Montreal to become the world's first French radio station. On June 1, 1923, the founding president of Canadian National Railways (CNR) created a radio broadcasting service; the following year, on February 27, 1924, the first radio station of the CN, CNRO, was inaugurated in Ottawa. Other stations soon followed: CNRA-Moncton and CNRV-Vancouver. By 1926, there was already a professional organization: the Canadian Broadcasters' Association. With the growing importance of radio broadcasting services in Canada, the Mackenzie King government created the Royal Commission on Broadcasting on December 6, 1928 to explore the realities and possibilities of radio broadcasting, and to make recommendations concerning the administration, control, direction and financial needs of such a service. These recommendations appeared in the Sir John Aird Report of 1929.

One month later, the Quebec government indicated its intention to serve Quebec with legislation regulating radio broadcasting. On January 8,

1929, the Lieutenant Governor, Narcisse Pérodeau, in his inaugural speech in the Quebec parliament, stated:

Radio has become one of the greatest information and teaching instruments. My government intends to create a broadcasting station which will deliver to our homes instructive and pleasant programs, inspired by Quebecois and Canadian subjects.

Two days later, the Liberal Premier Alexandre Taschereau declared to the Legislative Assembly: "We believe that if the Quebec government has its own broadcasting station, leaders and educators will be able to speak to families grouped around the fireplace at regular times." On April 4, 1929, the Lieutenant Governor ratified the law concerning radio broadcasting in Quebec. According to this legislation, the Quebec government would (1) buy CKAC in Montreal for $200,000 or less, (2) reach an agreement with the other broadcasters to cover all of Quebec, and (3) operate this station at an annual production cost of no more than $15,000. The project was never realized.

That year, on September 11, the Aird Report was made public. Its key recommendations were that a publicly funded broadcasting corporation be created; that the provinces be given full responsibility for its content; and that the board of directors be made up of twelve members, three named by the federal government and nine by the provinces. However, after the defeat of the Liberal party in the federal election of 1930, the implementation of these recommendations was delayed. On January 27, 1931, Quebec Premier Alexandre Taschereau wrote in a letter to federal minister Alfred Duranleau, "The control of radio-broadcasting in the province and emission of broadcasting licenses is the responsibility of the provincial government." Quebec and three other provinces challenged the authority of the federal government in this matter. On February 18, the federal government asked the Supreme Court to decide who had constitutional responsibility for broadcasting; on June 30, the Supreme Court gave full control to the federal government. Quebec subsequently appealed the decision—it was the only province to do so—taking the matter to the Privy Council in London. On February 9, 1932, the Privy Council confirmed the opinion of the Supreme Court, stating, "The Parliament of Canada has exclusive legislative power to regulate and control radio communications in Canada."

Soon after this decision, on May 26, 1932, the federal parliament adopted its first broadcasting act, creating the Canadian Radio Broadcasting Commission (CRC). Its mandate was to regulate and control the broadcasting industry in Canada, to issue licences, to assign radio frequencies, and to monitor the time allotted to advertising. The CRC was also commissioned to broadcast across Canada, but was unable to do so for financial and political reasons. Many Westerners were opposed to using the national network to broadcast French programs. In 1936, the Mackenzie King government, back in power, passed a second law creating the Canadian Broadcasting Corporation (CBC).

In 1939, the Quebec government established the *Régie des services publics* (Public Services Commission) to replace the *Commission des services d'utilité publique* (Public Utility Services Commission). But the most important legislation of this period was the adoption, on April 20, 1945, of legislation authorizing the creation of a provincial broadcasting service. Nothing came of it, however, until February 22, 1968, when the Quebec government created its own Broadcasting Corporation, Radio-Québec, to counterbalance and compete with both the public CBC (Radio-Canada) and private broadcasters.

Television came to Quebec in the year 1952. During the summer of that year, the first cable programming company, Rediffusion Inc., opened its doors. Based in Montreal, the company offered viewers two TV channels and six sound channels. Later, this British firm was sold to an American company, the CBS network, and became National Cablevision Ltd. In 1971, National Cablevision was acquired by the Caisse de dépôt, the Mouvement Desjardins, and private Quebec insurance companies.

On September 6, 1952, the first TV station in Canada opened in Montreal: CBFT (Channel 2) of the CBC. At first, it was bilingual and aired only a few hours each day. At the time, Maurice Duplessis was Premier and the dominant ideology was that of Catholic Church. With the introduction of television, the Québécois were exposed to world events, different ideas, and new interpretations of Quebec's sociopolitical reality for virtually the first time. This inevitably gave rise to ideological clashes that divided the elites.

An important event at the end of the 1950s that symbolized the incursion of new ideas preceding the Quiet Revolution, was the strike of Radio-Canada producers from December 1958 to March 1959. Jean Marchand, a union leader, who later joined Pierre Trudeau at the federal level, was put in jail. It was also a seminal experience for an influential journalist at the French network, René Lévesque, involved in the strike by virtue of having his own TV show, *Point de Mire*. As Lévesque remembered it, the strike lasted longer than anybody expected:

> The couple of days stretched out to weeks, and we had to put water in our wine. The strike turned nasty, as they inevitably do when questions of principle are involved. The producers had dared to set up their own union. But the fact that they had to direct others, no matter how small the groups were, made them management, that is, part of the administration, and the right to bargain had never been accepted or even seriously envisaged on that level. The airwaves

were under federal jurisdiction, and the poor devils of strikers ran into another legalism, a typically Anglo-Saxon one this time: Where is the precedent? There wasn't any. (Lévesque 1986: 151)

This strike turned out to be just a taste of all the tensions and conflict that was to follow between the federal government and the provinces over the control of communication.

On February 19, 1961 the first private TV network, CFTM-TV (Channel 10), was launched. In 1968, the Quebec government passed legislation creating an educational TV network, *Radio-Québec*. The following year the federal government floated a proposal to regulate educational television but strong provincial protest forced Ottawa to withdraw its proposal. On October 17, 1969, the Quebec government created the *Office de radiotélédiffusion du Québec* (Quebec Radio-Television Office), and on December 12, the Department of Communications was created.

According to its CRTC licence, Radio-Québec was to broadcast educational programs, and could not rely on commercials to finance its operating costs. On November 5, 1972, Radio-Québec aired its first program on cable television. For several years, Radio-Québec broadcast for only two hours in the evening, from 7:30 to 9:30 p.m. In Montreal, the channel was available from National Cablevision Ltd. and Cable TV Ltd (Channel 9), and in Quebec City from Télé-Câble (Channel 13). The legislation was modified on December 12, 1972, to give the Quebec Radio-Television Office the right to produce television programs under the name of Radio-Québec. Concurrent legislation modified the Department of Communications and the Public Service Commission, expanding the latter's powers to:

the broadcast, transmission or reception of sound, images, signs, signals, data or messages by wires, cable, waves or any other electrical, electronic, magnetic, electromagnetic or optical means.

Since then the role of Radio-Québec as a reflection of the Quebec culture has continued to grow, and people across Quebec can watch Radio-Québec's programs and TV series daily on the regular airwaves.

Today there are seventy AM and forty-six FM radio stations in Quebec. Almost all of them (104) broadcast in French. Only 12 broadcast in English or other languages; of those 12, 10 English radio stations broadcast in Montreal. But even though most radio stations have been licensed by the CRTC, the issue of French content remains central. As we will see in more detail, state intervention has been necessary due to the peculiar situation of Quebec in North America. In view of the invasion of British and American music, for example, the CRTC has imposed quotas (such as the requirement that 60% of the popular music be French) in order to protect Quebec culture by helping artists survive in a small market.

Table 8.1

Sociopolitical Chronology of Broadcasting Development in Quebec

Year	Events	Legislation
1919	• First Canadian AM radio broadcast by XWA (CFCF)	
1922	• First francophone radio station in the world, CKAC of Montreal	
1929		• First legislation regulating radio broadcasting; federal government plans to ask Supreme Court to determine who has full control in this field
1932	• Privy Council in London, England recognizes Canadian federal jurisdiction in radio bradcasting	
1937	• Opening of francophone radio station CBF-Montreal controlled by the CBC	
1939	• Establishment by Quebec government of Public Services Board	
1945		• Legislation authorizing creation of a Quebec radio station: Radio-Québec
1952	• Beginning of television in Quebec; opening of Radio-Canada (CBFT) in Montreal	
1959	• Producers' strike at Radio-Canada	
1961	• Opening of two private TV stations: one French, CFTM (Télé-Métropole Channel 10) and one English, CFCF (Channel 12) in Montreal	
1968		• Legislation creating Quebec Radio-Television Board
1969		• Legislation creating Quebec Ministry of Communications
1971		• Publication of document *For a Quebec Communication Policy*
1972	• Opening of Radio-Québec	• Public Services Board begins to regulate cable television
1978		• Regulations concerning pay television in Quebec
1979		• The Quebec Radio-Television legislation modified to create Société Radio-Québec; legislation regarding educational television; policy concerning community media
1982		• Publication of document *Building the Future* (Bâtir l'avenir)
1986	• Opening of *Télévision quatre saisons* (TQS)	

While most of the radio stations (72%) are private (though still under the authority of the federal government through the CRTC regulations), 18 of 35 TV stations are public. There are 32 francophone stations and three anglophone networks, two in Montreal (CBC Channel 6 and CFCF (CTV) Channel 12), and one in Quebec City (CBC Channel 5); 13 of the francophone stations are affiliated with Radio-Quebec, 10 with the private network TVA, and 9 with the CBC. However, these figures do not include the new francophone private station, Télévision Quatre Saisons (TVQ Channel 35 in Montreal), which began broadcasting in 1986. Nor do these figures reveal the penetration of the American TV station on the cable system. Stations such as PBS-Vermont ETV, ABC-Burlington-New York, NBC-Plattsburg, CBS-Burlington, and several others are accessible to Quebec viewers. This poses a serious challenge to the Quebec government. To counterbalance the enormous power of the English/American media, the Quebec state must find new and effective ways to encourage and support Quebec culture through television.

8.3 THE *CONSEIL DE PRESSE DU QUÉBEC*: OWNERSHIP AND ETHICAL ISSUES

Since the early 1960s, the Quebec media, like the media in the rest of Canada, have been jeopardized by concentration of ownership. Many daily and weekly newspapers have been shut down, and the survivors, such as Montreal's *Le Devoir*, must continually launch subscription campaigns to stay afloat. Many solutions have been suggested over the years: state intervention and subsidies to the press, the establishment of a preventive committee, stipulations that collective agreements include clauses forbidding the concentration of ownership, and publicity regulation. One solution— adopted by every Canadian province but Saskatchewan—has been to create press councils.[1]

Even in the 1950s, the idea of having a press council like those in Britain (1953) had been discussed in Quebec. Many journalists were lobbying to have newspaper standards upgraded and the *Union canadienne des journalistes de langue française* (UCJLF) (Canadian Union of French-Language Journalists), created in 1954, was the first to ask for the creation of a press council in 1957. But press owners were opposed to the idea, mainly because the proposed council's seats were all foreseen to be occupied by journalists. Another proposal was made by the UCJLF in the spring of 1959, but it was rejected by regional newspapers afraid of being overwhelmed by the Montreal media.

---

1. At the end of 1990, in the United States, only the state of Minnesota boasted a full-fledged press council, while in Canada every province but Saskatchewan had its own press council. (Pritchard 1990: 5)

In 1962, the local journalists' unions, who contributed the most financially to the UCJLF, quit this association to form the *Alliance canadienne des syndicats de journalistes*, all of whose members were also union members. With the decrease of its membership and the creation in February 1969 of a new association, the *Fédération professionnelle des journalistes du Québec* (FPJQ) (Professional Federation of Quebec Journalists), which also represented anglophone journalists, the idea of a Quebec Press Council continued to grow. Finally, in the late 1960s, under Union nationale Premier Jean-Jacques Bertrand, a special legislative committee that was formed to investigate the impact of concentration of ownership on freedom of the press strongly recommended the creation of a press council (Pritchard 1990; Clift 1981). In 1971, an agreement was signed between newspaper owners, broadcasters, and the FPJQ. The *Conseil de presse du Québec* (Quebec Press Council) was created in 1973, establishing a forum for journalists, publishers, and the public to debate problems and difficulties emerging in the media. In 1981 the *Gazette* created a position of ombudsman.

The *Conseil* is a nonprofit, private, nongovernmental, autonomous organization. Its mandate is to protect the public's right to be informed and to protect the freedom of the press. It also provides ethical guidelines for news publication and broadcasting. Since its creation, the Council has investigated over eight hundred complaints. It publishes an annual report. The survival and effectiveness of the *Conseil* depends on the stability of its financing, which is based on contributions from each member association. As its former president, Marc Thibault, has stated, the *Conseil* had been underfunded since it began, and it has to rely more on its own trust. (Thibault 1991)

8.4   REGULATION: THE CENTRAL PUBLIC ORGANIZATIONS

Besides the Department of Cultural Affairs, there are three public organizations that work together in creating cultural and educational policy for Quebec: the Department of Communications (1969), the Public Service Agency (1979), and the Motion Picture Board (1985). Aside from the efforts of the Taschereau government, whose 1929 legislation regulated broadcasting in Quebec, and Maurice Duplessis, who created Radio-Québec, there was no real effort by the Quebec government to develop a coherent communications policy until the end of the 1960s. In December 1969, the Jean-Jacques Bertrand government became the first provincial government in Canada to establish a Department of Communications. Under the umbrella of this department are three agencies: the *Commission d'accès* à *l'information*, the Public Service Commission, and the Quebec Radio-Television Society.

But it wasn't until May 1971, following the first election of the Liberal party of Robert Bourassa in 1970, that the first policy proposal came out of the Quebec government in the field of communications. The head of the new department, Jean-Paul L'Allier, tabled to the Cabinet a document entitled *A Policy of Communications for Quebec/Pour une politique québécoise des communications* (1971). This was followed in November 1973 by another key document, *Le Québec: maître d'oeuvre de la politique des communications sur son territoire* (Quebec: Master of Communication Policy on Its Own Territory), which was tabled during the first federal-provincial conference on communications policy. This document explicitly proclaimed responsibility for the Quebec government to develop, regulate, and implement its own communications policies.

In the aftermath of the 1973 decision of the Quebec government to control communications, the Public Service Agency Act was modified. The Public Service Agency, created in 1909 under the name *Commission des services d'utilité publique du Québec* (Quebec Utility Services Commission), assumed its current name in 1940 and is the oldest administrative tribunal of Canada. In 1972, its mandate was modified to include "the emission, transmission or reception of sounds, images, signs, signals, data or messages by wires, cables, waves or any other electrical, electronic, magnetic, electromagnetic or optical means." According to this amendment to the Act, the Agency was supposed to regulate cable television concurrently with the CRTC.

Quebec was not the only province that believed it should have control over cable television; other provincial communications ministers also held the view that each province should be responsible for broadcasters acting on their territory. But the federal government refused to move on the issue. The Public Service Agency then passed a regulation requiring all cable TV companies to obtain a permit. This decision led to a major conflict with the federal government, which refused to recognize the jurisdiction of the Quebec government to issue permits. According to Ottawa, previous legislation cited the CRTC as the only board qualified to issue broadcasting licences. The situation became particularly contentious when the Quebec government wanted to give an exploitation permit for the city of Rimouski to the company of Raymond D'Auteuil, Quebec Eastern Cable Distribution. Instead, the CRTC awarded the area to another company, owned by one Frank Dionne. This debate ended in 1977 when the Supreme Court awarded sole authority to the federal government in this matter.

After the ruling of the Supreme Court, the Quebec government and the other provinces had few options; all Quebec could do was to modify the mandate of the Public Service Agency. Since 1979, in accordance with the Educational Programming Act, it has been responsible for the educational content of Radio-Québec. Today, this agency comprises nine members, including a president and two vice presidents named for a period of ten years by the Executive Council. The president and vice presidents must be lawyers and have no interest in any public communications firms.

The third central public agency is the Motion Picture Board, created in 1985. Its role is to supervise the distribution and use of films. The origin of the board goes back to 1913 when the Film Censorship Bureau was responsible for the moral content of each new film release. It was not until 1975, when the Bourassa government passed its first act regulating the film industry, that the first film policy emerged. In 1981, a commission was created to examine issues and problems related to the film industry and to propose recommendations for a film policy in Quebec. The commission's findings led to legislation in 1985 creating the Motion Picture Board to protect the cultural and linguistic identity of Quebec society. The issues of dubbing or adding subtitles and the simultaneous release in French and English of American movies were raised and led to several agreements between the producers and distributors of foreign-language films in Quebec. Three persons named by the government assume all the responsibilities of this board and the supervision of film activities in Quebec.

8.5 THE ROLE AND MISSION OF RADIO-QUÉBEC

One idea behind the 1929 legislation passed by the Taschereau government was that the Quebec government could own and finance any communications enterprise for the sole purpose of promoting the Quebec culture and identity. On April 20, 1945, the Quebec government passed a law creating the Quebec Radio Office. When an educational broadcasting system was proposed in 1968, the federal government tried to intervene with its 1969 proposal to regulate educational television. But since education is clearly identified in the Constitutional Act as a provincial jurisdiction, every Canadian province strongly opposed this move and the project was withdrawn.

Several meetings between the federal government and the provinces finally led to an agreement, signed in 1972, that recognized provincial authority on the programming of educational radio and TV stations.

Many provinces, including Ontario and Quebec, have created their own public TV networks. Though Quebec legislation creating Radio-Québec as a state-owned enterprise was passed in 1969, it was not until 1975 that the first two stations, CIVM Montreal and CIVQ Quebec City, began operations.

In 1979, the Quebec government, following several recommendations made by the Permanent Cultural Development Ministerial Committee, established nine regional offices of Radio-Québec. The Quebec government also passed the Educational Programming Act, which, as mentioned earlier, defined the cultural and educational mission of Radio-Québec and charged the Public Service Agency with determining whether the programming of Radio-Québec has an educational character.

In 1985, Radio-Québec received authorization from the CRTC to broadcast advertising. However, by 1986—like the other major Canadian broadcaster, the CBC—it had to close four regional offices and reduce its personnel for budgetary reasons.

The involvement of the Quebec government in TV broadcasting has led to joint productions with other francophone countries. These productions have aimed to supply shows to TV5, the worldwide francophone cable network which was set up to broadcast programs made by the world's francophone TV stations (such as those in Belgium, France, Luxembourg, and Switzerland). (TV5 has been particularly popular in Quebec and has disseminated Quebec culture throughout the world.) But the financing of this project has been threatened in recent years, and the issue of who has full responsibility over the TV5 network has concerned some members, especially France. Another source of conflict has been the question of who should have access to the network.

8.6 THE RISE OF COMMUNITY MEDIA

One interesting development over the past ten years has been a growing recognition in Quebec of the importance of the *médias communautaires* (community media). In 1979, the Quebec government passed legislation recognizing this importance. In fact, since 1973 a governmental program—*Programme d'aide aux médias communautaires* (PAMEC)—has existed to help the community media, which makes Quebec the only province subsidizing this sector. The aim has been to encourage active participation of citizens in the educational, political, cultural, and economic development of their community.

In 1985, there were 26 community radio stations broadcasting 120 hours per week and 37 community TV stations producing 16 hours of programming per week. These stations offer several types of programs: services to the community, information on municipal politics, and the environment, regional and local history, and programs for specific groups such as the young, the elderly, members of religious groups, and local associations. The focus on this sector attests to governmental efforts to support media that reflect and serve the needs of the citizens.

The number of community media has been growing in Quebec since the beginning of the 1980s. This is CIBL-FM in Montreal, one of the best known. [Courtesy Le Devoir and Gilles Paré, Librarian. Photo: Jacques Grenier.]

8.7 THE MEDIA AS POLITICAL ACTORS

The power structure that exists in society is never so clearly revealed as in moments of crisis, when the power and legitimacy of the state are challenged by civilians or the military. At such moments, governments often attempt to assert their authority through the medium of journalism, hoping that the journalists will affirm the legitimacy of governmental decisions and actions. In the past twenty years, these events, the October Crisis of 1970, the PQ referendum of 1980, and the 1992 referendum, have illuminated the relationship between the Quebec government and the media.

The independence of a free press and the journalists' social responsibility were at stake. But, as Arthur Siegel argues, in comments that can also apply to the print media:

the role of the broadcast journalist in French Canada appears to have an enhanced political component, with the journalist seeing himself as an important political actor, compared with the role of the journalist in the English broadcast media. (1983: 227)

This is certainly true, despite the rise of professional journalism, because Quebec journalists also feel obliged to preserve the French cultural and political heritage of Quebec. In a survey conducted in 1979, 79% of Quebec journalists said that they voted for the PQ in 1976, and 66% declared themselves in favour of independence. (Godin 1979: 32) These statistics certainly help explain why so many journalists got involved in politics.

The role of the media, and especially radio and the press, was crucial during the October Crisis, because the *Front de libération du Québec* (FLQ) used radio station journalists almost as "couriers." Journalists were routinely phoned by communications cells of the FLQ, who were told where to find press communiqués. The strategy totally disrupted the government's strategy during this extremely tense period. This episode was also momentous for the Quebec media and the journalism community, forcing it to evaluate its role and stance vis-à-vis Quebec's future.

During the crisis, *Le Devoir* once again became a prime force against the political establishment, for two reasons according to Daniel Latouche:

> The Montreal daily *Le Devoir* soon became a key protagonist in the crisis as well, when it was the only daily newspaper to suggest that the governments should negotiate "in good faith" with the FLQ in order to ensure the safe release of the hostages. In addition, because of its unique position as a link between the various segments of the Quebec intellectual community, *Le Devoir* also became a focal point for the generation and distribution of information among Quebec intellectuals, technocrats and public figures both in and out the government. (Latouche 1975: 380)

When the politicians saw an apparent erosion in public support, they believed that intellectuals were plotting to overthrow the political establishment and that Claude Ryan and his friends were somehow linked to the plot. Marcel Rioux (1977: 207–230) and Denis Smith (1971: 5) went so far as to suggest that the attitude of *Le Devoir* represented a further justification for intervention of the army to crush the *felquistes*, as well as all members of the Quebec intelligentsia who were aligned with the paper.

Le Devoir soon found itself in an uncomfortable position. Though the newspaper considered the crisis essentially a "Quebec crisis," it could not deny the authority of the federal government. In Ottawa, the fact that *Le Devoir* favoured negotiations with the FLQ stood in direct opposition to the more hardline stance of the Trudeau government. The dominant power structure attempted to put *Le Devoir* in its place. So it was that the events of October precipitated an even wider crisis within Quebec society: the actions of the FLQ, although unanimously condemned, forced Quebec intellectuals and journalists to ponder existing societal relations.

The 1980 referendum, in which the PQ asked Quebecers for a mandate to negotiate sovereignty-association, was another key event that forced the media to reexamine its role. Journalists were solicited to take a stance, and did so, publicly saying Yes or No to sovereignty-association. The Yes proponents found it difficult to defend their choice through the print and electronic media, since most of these were owned by people who were opposed. Many journalists were put in an extremely difficult position, torn between their sympathy for the PQ and the exigencies of their job.

An analysis of the editorial endorsements of each daily newspaper during the two months of the campaign, from April 16 to May 20, illustrates the evolution of opinion in the media (Lachapelle and Noiseux 1980). From a total of 158 editorials published during this period in the eight Quebec daily newspapers (*Journal de Montréal* had no editorial page), we can observe major changes during the period.

In the beginning, editorial positions in general were closer to the No side, even though no extreme views were adopted. Then came a change. Though in April four daily newspapers favoured the Yes side, three favoured the No side, and one was neutral, in May six became favourable to the No side, leaving only two (Trois-Rivières' *Le Nouvelliste* and Montreal's *Le Devoir*) on the Yes side. Most surprising were Sherbrooke's *La Tribune* and Ottawa's *Le Droit*, which completely reversed their positions, both switching from Yes to No. Overall, it was clearly demonstrated that the press, and the media in general, could not be considered neutral.

Although as we go to press similar data are not available on the 1992 constitutional referendum, obviously the media played an important role during the campaign. Francophone Quebecers and their journalists debated the future of Quebec in the light of both the federalist and the sovereigntist course. Though several events, such as the Wilhemny-Tremblay affair, occupied most of the media and it was difficult for the Yes side to filter its arguments, and the No campaign was more visible overall, it would appear that Quebec journalists were not biased in favour of one option or the other.

8.8 CONCLUSION

The history and development of the Quebec media, and recent events such as the October Crisis and the referendum, clearly demonstrate the difficult position of Quebec media and journalists. Whatever the future of Quebec in the Canadian federation, the press will continue to serve as an essential instrument in the development of Quebec's ideological and political culture.

By promoting Quebec's identity through public ownership of educational programs, the Quebec government has come into direct conflict with the federal government. However, as Canadian culture overall is increasingly threatened by American culture, the control of mass communications becomes absolutely essential. A major priority for Quebec is development and protection of its cultural identity. The leadership of the Quebec government since the 1960s has certainly helped to create a better understanding of this identity, and its regional programs are another step toward nurturing the economic and cultural identity of different regions of the province. The creation of Radio-Québec and the expansion of community media clearly demonstrate the will of the government to assume full responsibility for cultural and social development.

Of course, the Quebec media are also part of a global network of communications, and the rise of new technology has inevitably had an effect on the policy positions of the government. Fundamentally, Quebec media are not very different from other North American mass media, and reflect many similar consumer and commercial values. But the central role played by Quebec's government and the notion of social responsibility as defined by journalists have given birth to a media structure that, overall, does reflect the specific cultural character of Quebec.

KEY TERMS

Conseil de presse du Québec
  (Quebec Press Council)

Cultural sovereignty

Mass media

Médias communautaires
  (community media)

Radio-Québec

REFERENCES AND FURTHER READING

Beaulieu, André and Jean Hamelin. 1973. *La Presse québécoise des origines à nos jours*. Quebec: Presses de l'Université Laval.

Bonville, Jean de. 1988. *La Presse québéquoise de 1884 à 1914: génèse d'un média de masse*. Quebec: Presses de l'Université Laval.

Clift, Dominique. 1981. "Press councils and ombudsmen." In *The Journalists*. Ottawa: Minister of Supply and Services Canada. Pp. 137–161.

Fauteaux, J. -Noel. 1934. "Le Journalisme français dans le Québec des origines à nos jours." In *Les Journées de Presse Française à Québec*. Quebec: Henri Gagnon, Le Soleil. Pp. 53–73.

Godin, Pierre. 1979. "Qui nous informe." *L'Actualité*, 4(5) (May).

Kesterton, W. H. 1967. *A History of Journalism in Canada*. Toronto: McClelland and Stewart.

Lachapelle, Guy and Jean Noiseux. 1980. "La Presse quotidienne." In *En collaboration; Québec un pays incertain: réflexions sur le Québec post-référendaire*. Montreal: Québec-Amérique. Pp. 135–155.

Lachapelle, Guy. 1990. "The editorial position of *Le Devoir* during the Quebec October Crisis of 1970." *Quebec Studies*, 11: 1–15.

Latouche, Daniel. 1975. "Mass media and communication in a Canadian political crisis." In Benjamin D. Singer (ed.), *Communications in Canadian Society*. Montreal: Copp Clark. Pp. 374–385.

Lévesque, René. 1986. *Memoirs*. Toronto: McClelland and Stewart.

Ministre des communications. 1971. "Pour une politique québécoise des communications." Working paper. May. Quebec: Éditeur officiel du Québec.

Prichard, David. 1990. "The role of press councils in a system of media accountability: the case of Quebec." Paper presented at annual meeting of the American Council for Quebec Studies. Chicago.

Raboy, Marc and Peter A. Bruck (eds.). 1989. *Communication: For and Against Democracy*. Montreal: Black Rose Books.

Rémillard, Gil. 1983. *Le Fédéralisme canadien*. Montreal: Quebec/Amérique.

Rioux, Marcel. 1977. *La Question du Québec*. Montreal: Partipris.

Schwartz, Georges. 1980. "La Presse ethnique entre l'intégration et la 'troisième solitude.'" *Antenne*, 17(1st semester): 49–53.

Siegel, Arthur. 1983. *Politics and the Media in Canada*. Toronto: McGraw-Hill Ryerson.

Smith, Denis. 1971. *Bleeding Hearts...Bleeding Country: Canada and the Quebec Crisis*. Edmonton: M. G. Hurtig.

Thibault, Marc. 1991. "Pour que vive le Conseil de presse." *Le Devoir*, July 13. P. B–12.

Wade, Masson. 1955. *The French-Canadians, 1760–1945*. Toronto: MacMillan Company of Canada Limited.

Wallace, W. S. 1948. "Journalism." In *The Encyclopedia of Canada*. Vol. 3. Toronto: University Associates of Canada Limited.

PART III

Politics and Policy

in Quebec:

The

Policymakers

THE
NATIONAL ASSEMBLY
AND ITS
MEMBERS

9.1 QUEBEC'S EARLY EXPERIENCE WITH PARLIAMENTARISM

Any discussion of Quebec's legislative branch first requires a slight detour into history. For some, the establishment of parliamentarism in Quebec in the late 18th century (through the implementation of the 1791 Constitutional Act) is an inconsequential historical footnote; for others, it has informed every significant aspect of contemporary political culture in Quebec. The important early history is generally ignored in the literature on Quebec's political development. Yet parliamentarism, and its effect on the early development of political parties, has proved to be of analytical importance.

The 1791 Constitutional Act imposed by the British imperial government granted the province of Quebec—then called Lower Canada—a Legislative Assembly elected by the people. According to one author (Brun 1970) suffrage was almost universal, as the right to vote depended on only minimal requirements of property ownership. City dwellers could also participate, their right to vote being based on the amount of rent paid. Thus it appears that at the beginning—though it was to be restricted in the following decades—suffrage was almost universal for male heads of families (Brun 1970: 90-91; Laforte and Bernard 1969).[1]

---

1. At first women were not excluded, as long as they met the spelled-out criteria, but this had changed by 1834. Children over 21 years of age, particularly sons of farmers and city dwellers, were excluded if they resided with their parents.

The 1791 Constitutional Act also had an impact on the shaping of political parties as we now know them (Bernier 1982). The *Parti patriote*, which led the Rebellions of 1837–1838 in Lower Canada, had evolved from a parliamentary group to a full-fledged political party in 1827 and by the early 1830s met most modern criteria of a political party: membership, sophisticated structures from the local to the national level, party-controlled newspapers, a youth branch, a well-articulated platform, organization by electoral districts, an elaborate executive structure, and so on.

Quebec's parliament house, built between 1877 and 1886. The building was origi-nally intended to accomodate the Assembly and all government departments. Other buildings were later added as the civil service expanded. [Courtesy Le Devoir and Gilles Paré, Librarian. Photo: Jacques Nadeau.]

Yet in the first stage of its existence—until its dissolution in 1836 by then-governor Gosford—the Legislative Assembly had only a facade of democracy. Its legislative powers were limited, and, more importantly, all of its legislative activity was controlled by another part of the legislative branch called the Legislative Council, made up of members appointed by the Governor and the Executive Council of which the Legislative Council was the legislative arm. In order to become law, a bill had to be passed by both Houses, signed by the Governor, and then transmitted to the British government, which reserved for itself a two-year period for final approval. As it turned out, most significant bills emanating from the Legislative Assembly were vetoed by the Legislative Council—or were not taken up for study by it, which amounted to a veto.

Thus, even though Quebec was introduced early on to its institutions, democracy did not really take root until 1848, when the colony was granted ministerial responsibility. This meant that, from then on, Cabinet ministers were held accountable for their actions before the elected representatives of the people sitting in the Legislative Assembly. Cabinets could be defeated if a motion of non-confidence gained a majority of the votes in the Assembly.

Quebec's legislative institutions as we know them today were put in place by the Constitution of 1867, which established the federal form of government in Canada. Each of the federated entities known as "provinces" was given a set of legislative institutions with which to govern the fields of jurisdiction inherited through the division of powers set forth in the Constitution. At first provinces were clearly at a disadvantage, since the division of fiscal powers in 1867 heavily favoured the central government. However, in time the provincial governments and their legislative branches saw some increase of their powers through decisions of the Judicial Committee of the British Government's Privy Council (which acted as Canada's highest court until 1949 when the Canadian Supreme Court became the court of final appeal).

Thus, with the evolution of Canadian federalism, provincial legislatures came to acquire a status not foreseen by the Fathers of Confederation. Because Quebec was generally the instigator of constitutional battles over the recognition or confirmation of its prerogatives in particular fields of jurisdiction, it was usually at the centre of every major power play between federal and provincial governments. This demand for full recognition of its constitutional rights and responsibilities has characterized Quebec's legislature throughout the 20th century, with varying levels of intensity depending on the government of the day.

9.2   ROLE AND FUNCTIONS OF MNAs IN 1940s AND 1950s

During the 1940s and 1950s, members of the Legislative Assembly—whom we shall call MNAs, since the body was renamed the National Assembly in 1968—had a very limited legislative role. The parliamentary system, and the strict party discipline it imposed, reduced the government's own MNAs to little more than rubber-stamping the government's agenda. Opposition

MNAs, meanwhile, were locked into their own rigid code of behaviour, systematically opposing every piece of legislation put forward by the government, regardless of its merits. Also, MNAs had little opportunity to participate in the legislative process due to the absence of procedures or institutions (for example, standing parliamentary committees) through which they could take action.

Up to the 1960s, the MNA's primary role was that of go-between between (1) his[2] constituents and (2) the bureaucracy and members of the Cabinet. Patronage and patron-client relationships characterized the interactions between a governmental MNA and his constituents. An opposition MNA, for his part, had almost no room to manoeuver in this capacity.

In the absence of universal social security programs and public tendering for government contracts and purchases, it was an MNA's role to convince a bureaucrat or Cabinet minister that a particular individual should get a scholarship to pursue graduate studies abroad, that a given road-builder should get a paving contract, or that the school boards in the MNA's electoral district should buy their stationery from a certain supplier.

Since then, the role of MNAs has changed significantly. As in most other sectors of Quebec's public life, reforms have been brought to bear on the conduct of the legislative process. Moreover, there has been, during the past thirty years or so, a movement toward "professionalization" of the political representation function. Amateurs have withdrawn, and local elites recruited from the ranks of the liberal professions have seen their proportion of total representation in the National Assembly diminish. A host of new, more technical professions are now represented. The creation of a competent public service and its insulation from partisan politics has contributed to this changing role for MNAs. So has the adoption of universal social programs, the democratization of access to education, and the adoption of a public tendering code for governmental contracts and purchases. These legislated changes are all governed by rules and regulations that have largely eliminated the arbitrary and discretionary aspects that allowed previous legislators to intervene in favour of certain constituents.

Quebec MNAs' transition from the role of go-between clouded by overtones of patronage and corruption to that of modern-day legislator has not been easy. Overall, they are still searching for a definition of their proper role within the context of an institutional system that has evolved in favour of a strengthened executive branch.

---

2. In those days, of course, members of the Assembly were certain to be male.

9.3   THE PARLIAMENTARY SYSTEM SINCE 1960: THE NATIONAL ASSEMBLY AT WORK[3]

Each member of the National Assembly represents a certain *comté* (electoral district or riding) and is elected by those riding inhabitants who are 18 years old and over. Currently, 125 such electoral districts are represented. MNAs are expected to represent the interests of the *comté* and its constituents. They enjoy parliamentary immunity, which means that they cannot be prosecuted for anything said or written in a document tabled by them within the confines of the Assembly or, a committee or subcommittee thereof. Members are also immune from court proceedings while the Assembly is in session. As in the British parliamentary system, the Premier, members of the Cabinet, the leaders of the opposition parties, and other parliamentary officials are chosen from the ranks of elected MNAs.

The National Assembly is headed by a President, the equivalent of the Speaker in other British-inspired parliamentary systems. Elected at the beginning of a new legislature by the MNAs, the president chairs debates in the Assembly and the Committee on the National Assembly, acts as the general manager of the Assembly (which has a staff of up to 800 employees), and represents the Assembly at international parliamentary conferences. Upon his or her election, the President ceases to be a member of the majority parliamentary group and assumes a nonpartisan role.

There are two Vice Presidents who assist the President and tend to administrative tasks—for example, they might be put in charge of a particular dossier. Unlike the President, they remain active members of the parliamentary group to which they belong and thus preserve their voting rights in the Assembly.

By tradition, the Premier is the leader of the majority party that forms the government and the Cabinet. At the start of each session, the Premier delivers the opening speech outlining the legislative agenda for the coming months. He or she is the main spokesperson for the party, the government, and the Cabinet vis-à-vis the opposition parties.

If several parties are represented, the head of the party that won the second-highest number of seats after the governmental party is declared Official Leader of the Opposition, and is the first among opposition leaders entitled to intervene during debates—though all other party leaders enjoy equal speaking time.

---

3. This portion of the text borrows from the publications Deschênes (1982) and Assemblée nationale (1985). Also, throughout the chapter some phrasing is inspired by Assemblée nationale (1987).

The ministers are chosen by the Premier from the elected members of his or her party. Each is assigned a ministry (department). While the Assembly is in session, they are spokespersons for their ministry, responding to MNAs' questions and supervising the development and study of bills that concern their ministry. In keeping with British parliamentary tradition, ministers must respect the fundamental principles of responsibility and Cabinet solidarity. A minister is ultimately responsible for whatever happens in his or her department, including any administrative blunders. Irrespective of personal views on a question, a minister must defend the line adopted by the Cabinet, or resign.

The Parliamentary Leaders are chosen by their party's caucus. Their role focusses on the daily workings of the National Assembly: jointly, they set the general agenda, organize daily activities, and see to it that the rules of procedure are followed by the President.

The role of Whips, who are chosen by their party leader or elected by members of the party caucus, mainly concerns matters of party discipline and organization. Party whips seek to ensure cohesion and team spirit in their respective parties, see to it that the requisite number of members can be rounded up quickly when a vote is about to be taken in the Assembly, and determine the order in which party members address the Assembly. Outside the Assembly, they preside over party meetings, summon members of the various committees to convene, and are responsible for support services (e.g., research staff, documentation, etc.) provided by the Assembly to all its members.

The Premier may appoint party members as parliamentary assistants to help a minister in the fulfillment of his or her duties. As such, parliamentary assistants may fill in for a minister in the Assembly or at certain outside functions, particularly those of a social nature; they may answer questions addressed to the minister or take note of them on the minister's behalf; and they may supervise matters and files pertaining to the ministry to which they are linked.

The Assembly's eight standing committees are presided over by MNAs. Five presidents belong to the ministerial parliamentary party and three to the opposition parties. They are elected for two years by members of their committee. The president of each committee organizes and plans its working sessions. In doing so, he or she is assisted by a vice president recruited from some party other than that of the president.

In order to be recognized as a parliamentary group and enjoy the associated benefits, a party must have had at least 12 of its members elected, or have received no less than 20% of the popular vote regardless of the number of members elected in the previous general election.

Parliamentary groups are provided with, among other things, a small research staff paid for by the National Assembly. The House Leader and Whip are consulted by the President on matters specified in the rules of procedure; the House Leader is automatically given limited speaking time on occasions such as the Opening Speech and the Budget Speech, or following ministerial statements.

9.4 RULES AND PROCEDURES

In the National Assembly, special rules and procedures govern not only a variety of specific events, such as the Opening Speech, the presentation of financial estimates, and the Budget Speech, but also day-to-day affairs, which are divided between "routine business" and "orders of the day" (daily business). *Routine business* covers a wide range of parliamentary activities. It may include:

- Ministerial statements
- Introduction of bills, public and private
- Tabling or presentation of documents and papers
- Reports from standing committees
- Presentation of petitions
- Oral questions and answers (during the daily 45-minute Question Period)
- Deferred votes
- Motions without notice
- Notices concerning committee proceedings
- Information on Assembly proceedings

Orders of the day are events that occur at different times during the parliamentary calendar, and have different degrees of importance. They include such legislative events as the Opening Speech and its debate, the Budget Speech and the ensuing replies and debate, debate on reports from the committees that have examined the estimates for the upcoming fiscal year, nonconfidence motions, the holding of an urgent debate, and so on.

During a session of the Assembly, except for the months of June and December, Wednesday is set aside as "MNAs' day." On this day, ministers respond to written questions put to them by MNAs. On this day also, motions from members of the Opposition or independent members— referred to as private members' bills—are taken up for study and debate.

Orders of the day can be so time-consuming that the Assembly adjourns, after having dealt with routine business, in order to allow for sittings of the standing committees. Such is the case at budget time, when credits allocated to each ministry are studied in detail by the standing committee responsible for that ministry; at the same time, the Budget is debated in the Assembly.

Every session begins with the Lieutenant Governor's Address. Then the Opening Speech is given by the Premier, in which the government's legislative agenda is announced. The Premier may not speak longer than two hours.[4]

The Opening Speech is debated in the sitting, which follows the Speech. The sitting begins with the speech of the Leader of the Official Opposition, also limited to two hours. The whole process, including the speeches by the Premier and the opposition leader, must last no longer than 25 hours. The leaders of other parliamentary groups may speak for one hour each. Every member may make one speech, on any subject. In this speech, a motion of nonconfidence may be proposed. Such a motion does not require notice, and is not amendable. Motions of nonconfidence brought by the opposition parties after the Opening Speech have become standard practice.

9.5 THE BUDGET SPEECH AND BUDGETARY ESTIMATES

The Minister of Finance delivers the Budget Speech. The speech may last two hours, as may the response from the spokesperson for the Opposition. The ensuing debate must not exceed 25 hours.

Immediately after the Budget Speech has been read, each parliamentary group is allowed ten minutes for comments. This brief, spontaneous reaction precedes the formal debate that is initiated at the next sitting. Again, every member is allowed to make one speech, on any subject. These speeches may conclude with the moving of a nonconfidence motion. After 13½ hours of debate, or when there are no further members wishing to speak, debate is suspended in the Assembly but continued in the standing committee which handles Budget and Administration. There the debate can last for a maximum of ten hours and the Finance Minister sits in on the committee throughout. Upon conclusion of the debate in committee, the chairperson reports to the Assembly, whereupon debate resumes. A spokesperson for the Opposition is allowed to speak for no more than one half-hour. The Finance Minister concludes the debate with a speech lasting no more than an hour. Then a vote takes place on the motions of non-

---

4. Prior to 1969, it was the Lieutenant Governor, as representative of Her Majesty Queen Elizabeth II, who, in the name of the Government, used to deliver what was then known as the Speech from the Throne. This practice came to an end in 1969 under the Union nationale.

confidence, followed by a vote on the motion of the Finance Minister to adopt the Budget.

During the course of the year, the Finance Minister may make a supplementary statement on the Budget. The rules under which this supplementary statement is studied by the Assembly are quite similar to those relating to the Budget per se.

Concerning the *estimates*—the sums of money which the Government plans to appropriate for each ministry and other governmental organizations—Article 279 of the Rules of Procedure states, "the Assembly shall examine the estimates annually laid before it by the Government for its approval." This is a complex process.

To enable the Government to pay its bills at the end of its fiscal year (March 31) and before the Budget for the following year has been adopted, the Assembly may, before April 1, give general approval to one-quarter of the estimates (subject to certain rules). Consideration of the estimates in general, except those for the Assembly, is referred to the standing committees.

Each committee deals with those estimates that apply to areas within its jurisdiction. This means that most committees consider the estimates of several ministries. Overall, 200 hours may be devoted to consideration of the estimates, but no more than 20 hours may be spent on a given ministry. When all the estimates have been voted on in committee, or when the time limits have expired, all the reports from the committees are laid on the table at one sitting. At the next sitting, a limited debate is held, after which the reports, and the supply bill accompanying the reports, are put to a vote.

As with the Budget, supplementary estimates may be laid before the Assembly during the course of the year. Disposition of these estimates largely follows the same procedures as those for the regular estimates.

9.6 MOTIONS OF NONCONFIDENCE AND CALLS FOR URGENT DEBATE

Two other procedural acts are likely to be encountered during the course of a session: motions of nonconfidence and calls for urgent debate.

The Opening Speech and the Budget Speech rarely escape unscathed. They almost always provoke *motions of nonconfidence*. In addition, members of the opposition are allowed to call for six such motions during a session. Debate on a motion of nonconfidence takes precedence over all other business, is not amendable, and must be held in the course of a single sitting. Should a motion of nonconfidence receive a majority of votes from MNAs, the Premier, and the government, must resign. While, in theory, the Lieutenant Governor could then ask the Opposition parties to form a new government, more likely a general election will be called.

Any member who feels that the Government has not or will not address a specific subject of special importance that comes under the jurisdiction of the Assembly, may move to hold an *urgent debate*. After having been notified in writing at least one hour before the period for routine business, the President decides, without any discussion, whether the motion is in order. If it is, every member may speak for ten minutes. The member who requested the debate and the spokesperson for the Government are allowed to address the Assembly for 20 minutes each. The debate must end no later than 6:00 p.m. and without any questions being put to the Assembly.

9.7 OTHER PRACTICES

Brief mention should be made of other routine practices of the National Assembly relating to: (1) Question Period; (2) prorogation of the Assembly; (3) televised debates; (4) quorum; (5) length of speeches; and (6) "pairing off."

1. **Question Period** Every day, 45 minutes are set aside for oral questioning of ministers by MNAs. Certain rules define the types of questions that can be asked. They must relate to public matters of an urgent or topical nature. Questions cannot be hypothetical, nor can they contain an expression of opinion. Supplementary questions may be asked, provided they are brief, specific, and without any preamble. Answers are subject to the same rules.

   Questions which do not meet the specified criteria may, however, be put in writing for written reply. In fact, questions originally put orally may eventually have to be put in writing because they cannot be answered without a certain amount of research on the part of the ministry involved. In such cases answers are tabled at a later sitting.

2. **Prorogation** What happens to pending business when the Assembly is *prorogued*—i.e., adjourned. Normally, unless the Assembly decides otherwise, the prorogation of the session terminates any committee appointed by the Assembly, cancels all orders not fully executed, quashes all proceedings pending, and causes all bills that have not received final passage to lapse. However, contrary to the practice of many other legislatures, consideration of any bill introduced before prorogation of a session may—under certain conditions and on a motion by the Government House Leader—be resumed at the stage at which it was interrupted.

3. **Televised debates**   Since 1978, the proceedings of the National Assembly have been televised, along with, occasionally, the sittings of special and standing committees. At first the debates were aired by affiliate stations of the Radio-Québec network. Nowadays, they are televised by a channel reserved for that purpose on the cable system. Production and retransmission costs are borne by the National Assembly.

   Certain provisions apply to this process. First, the camera must always be trained on the member who is addressing the Assembly; it cannot pan across the hall—for fear it will reveal a lot of empty seats, or members reading the newspaper or personal mail, catching up on their sleep, acting in derision of or applauding the speaker, or engaged in shouting matches. The object is to show the nation's business being conducted in a serious manner. Even if the absent members are actually hard at work, many constituents—not familiar with the modus operandi of the Assembly—may expect their member to be present in the Assembly hall at all times.

4. **Quorum**   Since standing committees may be at work while the Assembly is sitting, quorum (i.e., the lowest number of members required to be present to transact business) is set relatively low. There are 125 members. The quorum of the Assembly, or of a committee of the whole House, is one-sixth of these, including the President (who is always present); however, when a committee of the Assembly is sitting, the quorum drops to one-seventh of the members.

   Following the daily Question Period, as members run off to perform other tasks, the Assembly hall almost empties, often leaving just enough members to meet the quorum. However, the members will return to their seats if a vote is about to be taken, or if a debate reaches a crucial stage and they want to contribute. As mentioned, poor attendance is one of the reasons TV cameras never give a panoramic view of the Assembly.

5. **Length of speeches**   Unless otherwise stipulated (as may be done in the case of special debates following the Opening Speech or the Budget Speech), a member may speak to a formal motion for 10 minutes and to any other matter for 20 minutes, but may speak only once. "However, the mover, the Premier and the other Leaders of parliamentary groups, or their spokespersons, may speak one hour to substantive motions and one half hour to formal motions" (Article 209). "Substantive motions are motions to bring business before the Assembly. Formal motions have to do with the manner of deciding a substantive motion or with the procedure of the Assembly" (Article 187).

6. **Pairing off**   When representation in the National Assembly is split almost evenly between the two main parties, the practice of "pairing off" occurs. This is a custom whereby, if a vote is to be taken and the ministerial party member is absent from the Assembly, the opposition member with whom he or she is "paired" diplomatically finds an excuse not to be present in the Assembly at that time. This prevents the Government from being defeated for mere lack of numbers over a trivial matter.

9.8 STANDING COMMITTEES, COMMITTEE REFORM, AND ROLE OF MNAs: INSTRUMENTS OF CONSENSUS-BUILDING[5]

In 1984, a parliamentary reform took effect which had a dramatic impact on the form and function of the standing committees. Besides significantly reducing their number, from 27 to 9 (Assemblée nationale 1990: 2), this reform sought to give them more autonomy and more powers, both in the legislative process and in administrative oversight. In part, it was an institutional response to the growing malaise felt by legislators over their limited effectiveness.

There are now eight sectoral committees—plus the Committee on the National Assembly, which appoints the committee members, oversees the proceedings of the Assembly, and is a forum for ongoing suggestions through its subcommittee on parliamentary reform. Each of these eight has a minimum of 10 members, including a chairperson and vice chairperson. Members of a sectoral committee are nominated for a two-year term, and no member may be named to more than one committee.

The Committee on the National Assembly also decides who will preside over each of the committees. Five of the eight committees are presided over by representatives of the governing party; the other three are chaired by members of the opposition parties. Within each committee, smaller parliamentary groups and independent members are represented proportionally.

At the beginning of the first session of each legislature, each committee elects its chairperson and vice chairperson for a two-year term by majority vote of the committee members belonging to each parliamentary group. All committee sittings, other than *working sittings*, are open to the public, but provision is made for committees to sometimes sit behind closed doors. Committee deliberations are recorded in the *Journal des débats* (the equivalent of *Hansard* at the federal level).

---

5. This section draws on Secrétariat des commissions parlimentaires (1986).

Under certain conditions, a committee can invite individuals and organizations to submit briefs. After examining the briefs in a working sitting, the committee may decide to hold public hearings. From among those who have submitted briefs, it invites further presentations and determines the amount of time allotted for each presentation and discussion of each brief. A committee can also extend special invitations those with expertise, experience, and knowledge in the field under consideration. This disposition compensates somewhat for the fact that committees do not have at their disposal specialized staff, special counsel, or researchers except for a clerk.

Finally, the report of a committee—consisting of the minutes of its proceedings and its comments, conclusions, and recommendations, if any —is tabled before the Assembly.

The Committee on the National Assembly comprises the President (formally known as the Speaker), the two Vice Presidents, the House Leaders and Whips of the parliamentary groups, and the chairpersons of the standing committees. This Committee's functions are many, but one of its main jobs is to draw up the standing orders and operating rules of the Assembly and its standing committees, subject to the vote of the Assembly. It also coordinates the proceedings of the other committees by drawing up their operating rules; determines to which committee any public body (such as state-owned enterprises, like Hydro-Québec) is answerable, and if need be determines the scope of powers of each committee; gives an annual hearing to the Director General of Elections, the Auditor General, and the Public Protector (Ombudsman); and is responsible for examining questions of parliamentary reform. This last task is done by means of a standing subcommittee which takes up any matter relating to the powers and functioning of the Assembly or its committees. The standing subcommittee reports to the Committee on the National Assembly at least once a year (Assemblée nationale 1987: Articles 115–117).

The Assembly also has eight other standing committees, each with a wide range of responsibilities. Their names, fields of jurisdiction, and the ministries or administrative bodies they oversee are as follows:

1. **Committee on Institutions**   Presidency of the Executive Council, Justice, Intergovernmental Affairs, Constitution, and Consumer Protection

2. **Committee on the Budget and Administration**   Finance, Budget, Public Accounts, Government Administration, Public Service, Privatization, and Supply and Services

3. **Committee on Social Affairs**   Family, Health, Social and Community Services, Status of Women, Relations with Citizens, Manpower, and Income Security

4. **Committee on Labour and the Economy**   Industry, Commerce, Tourism, Labour, Technology, Energy and Resources

5. **Committee on Agriculture, Fisheries, and Food**

6. **Committee on Planning and Infrastructures**   Local Communities, Planning, Transport, Public Works, Environment, Recreation, Fish and Game, and Housing

7. **Committee on Education**   Education, Science, and Vocational Training

8. **Committee on Culture**   Culture, Communications, Cultural Communities, and Immigration

The committees have both statutory and discretionary duties. On a motion of the Assembly, the committees are required to examine bills, estimates, and any other matter referred to them. Also, on their own initiative, the committees may examine draft regulations and regulations; the guidelines, activities, and management of public bodies; financial commitments; and any other matter of public interest. However, the annual reports on the committees' activities show that in fact they rarely take the initiative, and when they do, it is to examine financial commitments. Hence the bulk of their activities is laid out in mandates received from the National Assembly, and the committees have less autonomy than one might think. A mandate from the National Assembly essentially means a mandate from the reigning government, which controls a majority in the Assembly.

For fiscal years 1988–1989 and 1989–1990, of 326 mandates taken on by the eight committees, only 4 were initiated by the committees themselves. Over a four-year period (i.e., 1986–1987 to 1989–1990), the committees took on a total of 557 mandates. Of these, only 8 stemmed from the committees. In terms of hours, over the two-year period 1988–1990, the committees spent 31 3/4 hours studying their self-imposed mandates out of a total of 2,488 hours spent in committee sessions (Assemblée nationale 1989: 23-24; Assemblée nationale 1990: 27).

Yet, back in 1984, committee initiatives that included supervision of public bodies (state-owned enterprises, administrative commissions, state boards, and so on) were hailed as the main achievement of the parliamentary reforms introduced that year. No explanations have yet been offered to account for the limited use legislators make of the tools put at their disposal to participate more directly in the legislative process and to exercise greater control over the bureaucracy and the government.

One reason may be that committees lack sufficient autonomy from the executive branch. The Government is very much present in various phases of committee work; in fact, it is often represented on a committee.

Article 125 of The Rules of Procedure states, "The Minister or Member introducing a bill is ipso facto a member of the committee that examines it." Furthermore, whatever the topic at hand, "a committee must hear a Minister who requests to speak to a matter being considered" (Article 163). Yet, "where a committee wishes to hear a Minister, it shall give him written notice of at least fifteen days unless he waives his right to it" (Article 164).

Likewise, there is an unequal balance of expertise between the committees and the Executive. The former are lacking in personnel, especially compared to their counterparts in the American Congress. Committee staff is limited to the services of a clerk. No permanent expertise is employed. Members must conduct their own background research, or rely on reports provided by the modest research staff allotted to each party and paid for by the Assembly. Obviously, these four or five staff persons cannot meet the needs and demands of all the members sitting on the eight committees. In an era wherein expertise and information constitute perhaps the most precious political resources, one must conclude that the legislative and executive branches are competing on unequal terms. The Executive has access to a vast range of expertise from the public service and private consultants, whereas the legislature lacks the necessary expertise to seriously scrutinize pending legislation.

As the Head of the Research Division of the National Assembly Library, certainly an informed observer, puts it:

> Consequently, only Ministers have had "complete" dossiers at their disposal to efficiently work in commission. It is not exaggerated to say that parliamentary committees have become useful tools at the hands of the Executive. (Deschênes 1984: 319)

Consensus-building seems to be an outstanding feature in the rules and procedures governing the work of the standing committees. The committees and the rules by which they abide seem designed to soothe conflicts, dissipate partisan frontiers between political parties, and institute a spirit of cooperation. Also, the fact that three commissions are headed by members of the opposition parties, and that in every standing committee the chairperson and vice chairperson are elected by the members of the committee, strengthens the consensus-building aspect of standing committees. This is a rather puzzling development. In the British parliamentary system, for example, if the ministerial party has a majority of seats in the Assembly, it is almost sure to win every vote because of the strong party discipline needed for this system to work. There is no special need to establish any kind of coalition, or greater cooperation between the parties.

At any time, the Assembly may appoint special committees or *special enquiry commissions*. Their "terms of reference" (mandate) are specified by the Assembly, which also appoints its members. These committees are different from committees created and appointed by the Government, being rarely made up of parliamentarians. Recruitment is done from among experts in the field to be studied; in addition, there are always representatives of business and labour as well as prominent citizens who represent the general public. The followup on a report of a special committee can range from shelving of the report (i.e., ignoring it completely) to full implementation of its recommendations by way of legislation.

Finally, upon a non-debatable motion from the Government House Leader, the Assembly as a whole may resolve itself into a committee called the Committee of the Whole House. Recourse to this procedure is usually for reasons of convenience, flexibility, or expediency, since it is the less stringent committee rules rather than Assembly rules that apply to the proceedings. A Committee of the Whole House might be formed before a bill is sent to committee for detailed consideration so that the Government House Leader can take the pulse of the Assembly. A motion for a Committee of the Whole House enables all members to participate in the debate instead of only the members of the standing committee to which the bill will eventually be referred.

9.9 HOW A BILL BECOMES LAW

In British parliamentary terminology a law or Act (of Parliament) is so called only when it has been passed by Parliament. At the various preliminary stages, the potential law is termed a bill. In Quebec's National Assembly a bill must go through several stages before it becomes law: (1) introduction or tabling; (2) passage in principle; (3) detailed consideration in committee; (4) consideration of the report from the committee; (5) passage; (6) assent by the Lieutenant Governor.

1. Introduction or Tabling

Public bills are those tabled by the Government—usually through the minister responsible for the area covered by the bill. However, any member of the National Assembly can table a "public bill"—paradoxically referred to as a "private members' bill"—as long as it takes into account the general interest of the people.

Private bills, which also may be introduced by any member, are those regarded as in the particular interest of some person, organization, or locality. Such bills are introduced by special request. For example, when individuals want to change their names, or when a city wants to amend its charter, private bills are tabled.

Public and private bills take slightly different routes in the enactment

Figure 9.1

How a Bill Becomes an Act (Law)

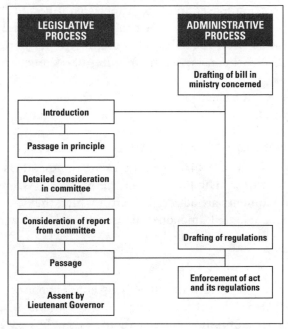

Source: Adapted from Gaston Deschênes, *Organisation et fonctionnement de l'Assemblée nationale* (Quebec: Assemblée nationale, Collection Vie parlementaire, 1982), p. 38.

process. Because private bills are less important on the legislative menu, the rest of this section will concentrate on procedure for public bills.

2. Passage in Principle

In this stage, members agree that the bill is worth taking a look at, a process that used to be called "First Reading." Usually there is no provision for debate at the "passage in principle" stage, except for procedural considerations.

3. Detailed Consideration in Committee

This step, and the next one, correspond to what used to be called "Second Reading." It is at this stage that most of the debate on a bill takes place.

After passage in principle, the Government House Leader moves that the bill be referred to the appropriate committee for in-depth study. This is the most important step in passage of a law. (There is also the possibility, as mentioned above, that referral could be made to a Committee of the Whole House.)

Before starting its detailed consideration, a committee may decide to hold private hearings. Then study of the bill takes place; the committee goes through it section by section. Attention is confined to the details of the bill, for its principle cannot now be challenged, and amendments must be relevant to the object of the bill and not contrary to its spirit or purpose. The committee's report consists of the minutes of its proceedings and the text of the bill as passed.

The amount of time spent in committee with reference to a particular bill is agreed upon by the House Leaders of the various parties.

4. Consideration of Report from Committee

This is the stage at which MNAs may intervene to amend the bill as proposed by the committee. The President of the National Assembly decides whether the amendments are admissible, after which they are debated and put to a vote. The adopted amendments are incorporated with the committee's report, which is then voted on.

5. Passage

Formerly known as the "Third Reading," this phase consists in the actual passage of a bill. Debate must be confined to the contents of the bill, and no amendments are admissible. In fact, there is usually very little debate at this stage.

6. Assent by Lieutenant Governor

Finally, for any bill to become law, it must be signed by the Lieutenant Governor, who acts as the representative in the province of Quebec of Her Majesty Queen Elizabeth II, who is the formal Head of State of the Canadian federation. Though a purely symbolic gesture, this is an essential requirement.

The lawmaking procedure has evolved to keep step with an increasingly complex society that has required more and more legislation. For Parliament to be able to pass more laws during a session, it has had to streamline the process. Thus it has become accepted practice to omit from the text of a proposed law anything requiring periodic adjustment or that concerns practical matters only. Such omitted elements are treated by way of *delegated legislation*. That is, the Assembly delegates to the Cabinet, or to the appropriate minister, the power to work out regulations concerning the application of the law and other matters pertaining to it. In effect, the National Assembly votes on the outer shell and leaves a large part of the contents to the Executive, even though everything that is eventually added will have the force of law. In this sense, the National Assembly delegates some of its legislative powers to the Executive. Most laws thus contain regulations drafted by civil servants of the ministry responsible for their administration long after a law's adoption by the National Assembly.

The reform of 1984 creating the eight standing committees assigned to them control over delegated legislation. This power, however, has not yet been exercised. One document states that "the nature, the scope and the modalities of this control have yet to be specified" (Secrétariat des commissions parlementaires 1986: 8). Noting that parliamentary committees have had this power since 1969 but have not made use of it, Deschênes (1984) has proposed a procedure that might lead to more committee supervision:

> Would it not have been possible each time a law granted a regulatory power to introduce an amendment making it mandatory for the government to submit the regulations to the competent standing committee for approval? (Deschênes 1984: 321)

It should be mentioned here that the increasing amounts of delegated legislation have been worrying legislators since the late 1960s. Numerous special committees have studied the situation without finding feasible ways for the legislative branch to adequately oversee and control delegated legislation. The problem continues to the present, without a solution in sight.

9.10 THE ROLE OF MNAs

In a parliamentary system in which the government has a solid majority, the role of members of parliament can be very limited indeed. Backbenchers from the majority party are expected to vote indiscriminately in favour of every piece of legislation put forth by the government, while members of the opposition are expected, in similar fashion, to consistently oppose the government's legislative agenda.

Party discipline is a necessity for the operation and stability of a parliamentary system and precludes any departure from these rather static modes of behaviour. Recent research shows that between the 19th (1935–1936) and the 33rd Legislatures (1985–1989), average voting cohesion among the ministerial party has never fallen below 98.9%. Without presenting figures, the author goes on to suggest that this cohesion is present on both sides of the Assembly and is not limited to members of the party in power (Massicotte 1989: 509–510).

Both ministerial and opposition members have felt excluded from the political process. This is borne out by periodic studies of parliamentarians' perception of their role and their overall degree of satisfaction (Gélinas 1969; Ducasse 1979; Rioux 1990). The most remarkable feature of these studies is their consistency over a thirty-year span. MNAs see themselves as primarily representatives of their constituents, acting on their behalf in dealings with the administration and the government. In this respect, ministerial MNAs have a slight edge over opposition members in that they have greater access to Cabinet ministers via caucus meetings and other party functions. However, they also see their second most important role as that of legislator, playing some sort of active part in the legislative process. MNAs continue to desire a more important function than merely rubber-stamping, or rejecting out-of-hand, legislation emanating from the Executive. MNAs have repeatedly expressed dissatisfaction at not possessing the necessary tools and information to perform their legislative tasks with competence and impact.

As for MNAs' assessments of their other perceived roles, from the studies it is difficult to come to any useful conclusions because questionnaires submitted over the years to MNAs have not been standardized. Two features do stand out, however. First, members resent being characterized as partisan. Second, unable to play the role of legislator in its true sense, members feel they have a great responsibility in administrative roles.

Given this state of affairs, it is not surprising that Quebec's MNAs have, since the early 1960s, set up numerous committees with a specific mandate to come up with recommendations that would enhance their legislative role.

9.11 PARLIAMENTARY REFORMS SINCE THE 1960s

Parliamentary reform has been a recurring item on the National Assembly's agenda since the early 1960s. As one former MNA, Yves Michaud, wrote with some irony:

> Parliamentary reform is an inexhaustible and restful topic. Inexhaustible because MNAs never get tired of speaking about it. Restful because their interventions hardly risk sabotaging the eternal order of things. (Quoted in Deschênes 1984: 289)

The most recent and most exhaustive reform in 1984, which continues to shape the destiny of the National Assembly, was the culmination of an introspective process begun in the 1960s and 1970s through various committees. Sometimes these committees were composed strictly of MNAs; sometimes they were "blue ribbon" committees made up of MNAs plus various specialists in the fields of constitutional law and parliamentarism. The incremental reforms that ensued set the stage for the major reform in 1984. According to Gaston Deschênes, "this new parliamentary reform did not emerge spontaneously. It is tied to prior reforms and most likely is a result of their lack of efficiency" (Deschênes 1984: 290). He adds that while preparing background reports for the subcommittee on parliamentary reform, "it was found that there were no evaluations of previous reforms and not even a simple narration of their linking together" (Deschênes 1984: 290).

Deschênes set out to retrace and piece together the various elements of reform that had taken place since the early 1960s. The salient features of his analysis are presented below.

Over the years, reforms have addressed three issues: (1) parliamentary procedure, (2) institutional change, and (3) changes in the working conditions of parliamentarians.

The first steps were taken between 1963 and 1966, the most important of which was the creation of the *Journal des débats*, a verbatim transcript of all proceedings in the National Assembly. Until 1964, no such official transcripts had existed; one had to rely on newspaper reports.[6] In early 1965, verbatim transcripts of the debates in the various standing committees also began to be published.

In the second phase, between 1967 and 1973, reformers sought to make the sittings of the Assembly more efficient. Standing committees were restructured and received broader mandates. Their number was increased to 22, and by 1978 it had reached 27. Each committee was to monitor one ministry. The Rules of Procedure were simplified, and the number of articles reduced from 812 to 179. Working conditions also received some attention. Salaries and allowances were upgraded, as were the pension plan and the collective life insurance policy. Members' staff was increased to two secretaries per member, one in Quebec City and the other one in the riding.

Emphasis was also placed on improving members' access to information that would enable them more effectively to pursue their activities. To this end, parties were allocated funds for research purposes and clerks and researchers were appointed to the Secretariat of the Standing Committees.

The third phase, from 1973 to 1976, was a period of consolidation in which various special committees sought to fine-tune the previous reforms. Measures to increase the input of members of the ministerial party into the policymaking process were implemented. Rules for recognition of opposition parties enabling them and their leaders to intervene more frequently, and at greater length, were adopted.

The fourth phase, from 1976 to 1981, was very productive and laid the groundwork for the major reform of 1984. The Parti québécois, which had

---

6. The National Assembly (then named the Legislative Assembly) had kept a journal and had done so since 1792, but only the text of the motions and the votes of members were recorded.

come to power in 1976, made substantial reforms in the Cabinet; some ministries were abolished or restructured and new ones created—among them a State Ministry on Electoral and Parliamentary Reform, which was given the following mandate:

1. To enhance the role played by MNAs through (a) better filing and research services and (b) a more frequent use of, and strengthening of, the powers delegated to the standing committees and allocation of statutory resources for them to hire more professional staff

2. To make the National Assembly more accessible to the people by means of an access-to-information policy and by televising its debates

3. To improve the internal functioning of the Assembly by (a) fully recognizing the role to be played by the opposition and (b) developing a more or less fixed parliamentary calendar of the various tasks to be performed during a session (Deschênes 1984: 305–306)

Some amendments to the Rules of Procedure were implemented in 1978 and 1979 and renewed by the 1984 reform. Most notably, the televising of the Assembly's debates, which began in 1978, met with great approval by both members and the general public. That same year, the Assembly

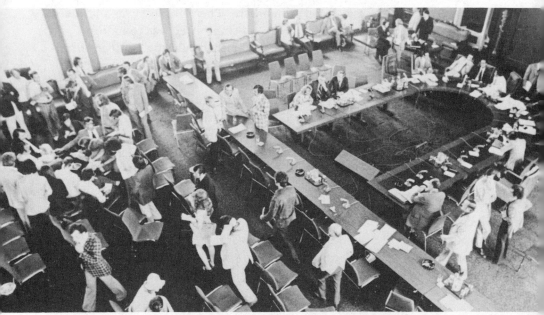

Parliamentary committee on the referendum legislation in 1979. It was in this room that the parliamentary committee on the political and constitutional future of Quebec, co-chaired by Michel Bélanger and Jean Campeau, was held.
[Courtesy Archives nationales du Québec. Photo: Jean Fiset.]

started working on the basis of a semi-permanent calendar, fixing dates for the winter and summer recesses.

Still, much was left to be done. Numerous state-owned enterprises, public agencies, and regulatory bodies were not fully under the supervision of the Assembly, for the Assembly had negligible control over the delegated legislation.

Also, the recommendations made in 1979 by the Michaud committee, and which went much further in expanding the role of the legislative branch, were almost completely ignored until the 1984 reform (Deschênes 1984: 308–310).

Phase five, from 1981 to 1984, took place during the Parti québécois' second term (1981–1985). In May of 1981, the government asked a parliamentary assistant to prepare a document outlining solutions that would make the parliamentarians' work more efficient, as well as giving them a sense of true participation in the legislative process. By now, the deep-seated feeling of uselessness expressed since the 1960s was resulting in fairly high personnel turnover rates from one election to another.

The final report, tabled in February of 1982, led to a bill on parliamentary reform being put forward by the government in the fall. This bill—fought by the opposition, who read into it a reduction of its own role—was referred for detailed study to a subcommittee, which recommended pursuit of the same objectives by different and more radical means. Finally, out of this subcommittee came the major proposals enacted in the 1984 reform, as well as a complete revision of the Rules of Procedure of the Assembly.

These reforms (described in greater detail earlier in this chapter) led to restructuring and reorganization of the National Assembly, changes in the lawmaking process, the creation of the eight standing committees, and new Rules of Procedure of the Assembly.

9.12 SOCIOECONOMIC PROFILE, PROFESSIONALIZATION, AND WORKING CONDITIONS OF MNAs

There has been an evolution in Quebec politicians in terms of professional occupation, education, origin (rural vs. urban), and so on. The most important influence in this evolution seems to have been electoral reform, specifically the geographical limits of each electoral district. During the 1940s, 1950s, and early 1960s, a majority of electoral ridings were located in rural areas, even though a majority of Quebec's total population had been urban since the 1921 census. When these discrepancies were rectified, and new ridings reflected the realities of a new Quebec, and especially its urban nature, new social forces found representation in Quebec's political élite. One way of measuring these changes is to track the evolution of MNAs' social background, particularly with reference to professional occupation. Table 9.1 conveys this evolution somewhat.

Table 9.1

Members of National Assembly by Occupational Status and Legislature, 1944–1985[1]

Occupation	1944	1948	1952	1956	1960	1962	1966	1970	1973	1976[2]	1981	1985
Liberal professions and financiers	49.5	41.3	49.5	40.5	50.0	52.2	61.6	46.3	40.0	66.0	58.5	47.0
Industrialists and upper management	11.0	10.8	7.9	13.5	12.8	8.8	7.7	9.2	21.8	16.0	13.0	24.0
Semi-professionals	1.1	—	—	—	3.2	4.4	9.7	16.1	25.5	8.0	20.0	11.0
Merchants, lower management, and employees	21.9	30.4	28.0	32.6	24.5	25.9	15.4	18.4	10.0	6.0	4.0	12.0
Workers	5.5	4.4	3.4	2.2	2.1	2.2	—	2.0	—	1.0	—	—
Farmers	11.0	12.0	10.1	10.1	6.4	5.4	4.8	5.5	2.7	4.0	3.0	1.0
Unknown	—	1.1	1.1	1.1	1.0	1.1	0.8	2.5	—	—	2.0	5.0
TOTAL	100.0	100.0	100.0	100.0	100.0	100.0	100.0	100.0	100.0	100.0	100.0	100.0

1. A new legislature begins after a general election. Thus, a general election took place on each year of the years indicated in this table.

2. Categories used by Deschênes for the period 1976–1985 are slightly different from previous ones. For the sake of uniformity we have kept the older categories and entered Deschênes' data under those headings.

Sources: Gérald Bernier and Robert Boily, *Le Québec en chiffres de 1850 à nos jours* (Montreal: ACFAS, 1986), pp. 281–282; Gaston Deschênes, *Portrait socio-politique de l'Assemblée nationale* (Quebec: Bibliothèque de l'Assemblée nationale, Service de la recherche et de la documentation, 1986).

Though since the 1940s the largest contingent of MNAs has come from the ranks of the liberal professions and finance, there have been qualitative changes that are not evident in the raw figures in the table, but that can be gathered from the biographies of MNAs in Quebec's *Parliamentary Guide* and, since the 1976 election, from biographical notes on MNAs produced by the research service of the National Assembly. For instance, the small-town or rural lawyers of the early days have, for the most part, given way to corporate lawyers. Financiers, who used to be bank or credit union managers, now are more likely to be associated with a holding company, an insurance company, or a brokerage firm.

In terms of political personnel, there are two distinct periods to be considered. The first extends from 1944 to the election of 1966, thus covering the Duplessis era and the early years of the Quiet Revolution. The second extends from 1970 to the present. Though it may seem odd to associate the Duplessis years with the Quiet Revolution, the fact is that the three elections of the 1960s took place before the various measures of electoral reform had been enacted. Those reforms were put into effect during the late 1960s and early 1970s. Essentially, they sought to reflect the realities of an urban Quebec and the principle of "representation by population." Previously, a rural riding might have 8,000 eligible voters while an urban riding had 135,000. To remedy those discrepancies, an average number of voters per electoral district was determined and the electoral map redrawn. In consideration of such phenomena as large but sparsely populated districts or densely populated areas in urban settings, allowance was made for a spread of plus or minus 25% from the average. (See Chapter 5.)

There are no standardized data for the whole period 1944–1985. However, the various occupational categories reported in both sets of data (i.e., 1944 to 1973 and 1976 to 1985) are close enough not to cause major distortions. More important are the qualitative changes within each occupational category, which, as stated earlier, are not reflected in the data. For instance, the range of professions included in the category "liberal professions and financiers" became much broader in the early 1960s. Besides the traditional presence of lawyers, solicitors, and doctors, other professionals such as engineers, architects, university professors, and so on started getting elected. Primary- and secondary-level teachers, journalists, and technicians also became much more prominent in Quebec politics. They are included in the "semi-professionals" category. Workers have never been well represented, even under the PQ government (1976–1985), a self-proclaimed social-democratic party. Farmers, on the other hand, have had a fair share of representation and the recently declining percentages merely reflect the situation within the general population. (In the 1981 census, farmers accounted for 2.9% of the general population.)

Women have only been represented since 1961, when Claire Kirkland-Casgrain won a byelection. She was reelected in the 1962 general election and entered the Cabinet as Minister Without Portfolio on December 5, 1962, a post she held until November 23, 1964. On November 25, 1964 she was named Minister of Transportation and Communications, a portfolio she held until the defeat of the Liberal party in the 1966 general elections.

Note that Quebec was the last Canadian province to enfranchise women. Though women have had the right to vote in federal elections since 1918, they only acquired this right at the provincial level in 1940. The first woman candidate in Quebec ran in a byelection in 1947; the first woman to run in

Marie-Claire Kirkland-Casgrain was the first woman elected to the National Assembly, after a byelection held in 1961 in the electoral district of Jacques-Cartier. She succeeded her father. In 1962, she became the first female minister ever. Here, she is seen shaking hands with Robert Bourassa after the 1970 election. Women are far from having achieved equal representation in politics, and political parties will have to give them more prominence in their structure. [Courtesy Archives nationales du Québec.]

a general election did so in 1952. To this day the proportion of women candidates tends to be larger in fringe parties than mainstream parties. Though some progress has been made since the 1960s in terms of number of candidates, number of elected candidates, and representation within the Cabinet, there is still much room for improvement.

Since the 1960s there has also been a professionalization of politics and of the MNA function. This is reflected both in the duration of sessions (which have become much longer) and in terms of remuneration, allowances, and reimbursement for certain expenses. Politics has become a full-time occupation. The number of days in session is more than double what it was in the 1930s to 1950s.

Since the 1984 parliamentary reform, the National Assembly operates under a partially fixed calendar. There are normally two sittings per calendar year: (1) from the second Tuesday in March to no later than June 23 and (2) from the third Tuesday in October to no later than December 21.

To avoid the temptation to pass an avalanche of bills without serious consideration at the last minute (i.e., within 48 hours of adjournment), a rule has been made which states, "No bill introduced in the period from

Table 9.2

Women Candidates in General Provincial Elections in Quebec, 1960–1989

Election Year	Number of Women Candidates	Total Number of Candidates	Women as % of Total Number of Candidates	Total Number of Elected Candidates	Total Number of Women Elected	Elected Women as % of Total Number of Elected Candidates
1960	1	253	—	95	0	—
1962	3	224	1.3	95	1	1.1
1966	11	418	2.6	108	1	0.9
1970	9	466	1.9	108	1	0.9
1973	25	479	5.2	110	1	0.9
1976	47	556	8.5	110	5	4.5
1981	83	525	15.8	122	8	6.6
1985	132	666	19.8	122	18	14.8
1989	121	557	21.7	125	23	18.4

Sources: Pierre Drouilly and Jocelyne Dorion, *Candidats, députées et ministres: les femmes et les élections* (Quebec: Bibliothèque de l'Assemblée nationale 1988), p. 44; Directeur général des élections du Québec, *Rapport des résultats officiels du scrutin du 25 septembre 1989* (Quebec).

Table 9.3

Women Ministers in the Original Cabinet After the Quebec General Election, 1960–1989

Election Year	Party Forming the Government	Head of Ministry	Minister of State	Minister Without Portfolio	Total Number of Women Nominated as Ministers During Government's Tenure[1]
1960	Liberal	0	0	0	0
1962	Liberal	0	0	0	1
1966	Union nationale	0	0	0	0
1970	Liberal	1	0	0	1
1973	Liberal	0	0	0	1
1976	Parti québécois	1	0	0	2
1981	Parti québécois	2	0	1	6
1985	Liberal	4	0	0	5
1989	Liberal	5	0	0	5

1. Cabinets are frequently reshuffled during a government's term in office and new members named to the Cabinet. Results reflect this fact, and include all women named to the Cabinet during the government's tenure. If a given woman was named to more than one portfolio, she is only counted once.

Sources: Assemblée nationale, *Guide parlementaire québécois* (Quebec: Bibliothèque de l'Assemblée nationale, Division de la recherche, 1990).

November 15 to December 21 or from May 15 to June 23 may be passed in the same period" (Article 22).

During most of the year, the Assembly sits on Tuesdays, Wednesdays, and Thursdays, Monday and Friday being reserved for work in committee or attention to the needs of constituents in the member's riding. Each member has an office in his or her riding. (For ridings spread over a large territory, more than one office is sometimes necessary.)

From June 1 to 23 and December 1 to 21, the Assembly may meet five days a week if it needs to. "Ad hoc" sittings may be held at any time during the year. In the event of a major crisis, the National Assembly, at the request of the Premier, may be recalled during its winter or summer recess.

Since being an MNA has become a full-time job, salaries and allocations have been increased. As of January 1, 1990, an MNA's basic salary was $57,260 plus an expense allowance of $10,070 to defray the cost of maintaining a second home, and of the frequent travel necessary between Quebec City and the constituency. Members also get a substantial allowance for maintaining a staffed office in their electoral district and to cover their travel costs, as well as those of their staff, within the riding. The amount of this allowance varies according to various considerations, such as size of the electoral district, its distance from Quebec City, and whether it is urban or rural. (Despite all this, it is safe to assume that most professionals and business people who become MNAs make less money than they did in their previous jobs.)

The Premier gets a basic MNA's salary plus 105% of that figure, for a total of $117,383. Ministers and the House Leader of the government get the basic MNA salary plus 75%, for a total of $100,205.

Holders of such functions as President and vice presidents of the Assembly, parliamentary assistants, Leader of the Official Opposition, parliamentary leaders and whips, presidents and vice presidents of standing committees, and so on, all receive an income supplement that varies according to function.

Salaries and allowances are now adjusted annually according to a formula based on the annual increase in the cost of living. This is a welcome change from the not-so-distant past, when, during the rush of the last days of a session, members would vote themselves a pay raise without any set criteria.

9.12 UNFINISHED AGENDA AND OUTSTANDING PROBLEMS

Assessing the various reforms introduced since the early 1960s, Deschênes proposes that the major problem is in the establishment of a balance between efficiency and greater control exercised by the National Assembly. When the previously established equilibrium disappears, calls for parliamentary reform are heard anew, which explains, according to Deschênes, why every four to five years committees emerge and again try to find new ways to promote the Assembly and its members (Deschênes 1984: 316–317).

Deschênes is quite cynical in his conclusion, stating, "parliamentary reforms require a great amount of effort and...the results seem to be very relative, if not totally useless" (Deschênes 1984: 316). He notes that over the past 30 years "the parliamentary function has not gained any ground vis-à-vis the Executive function" (Deschênes 1984: 325). One might add, however, that this is the lot of every legislature in parliamentary systems worldwide. And a close look at presidential systems would probably reveal the same tendencies.

Expressing a view contrary to that maintained at the outset of this chapter, Deschênes goes on to say: "Be they from the Ministerial party or from the Opposition, members do not have as much legislative initiative as they used to; quite the contrary, they have less" (Deschênes 1984: 325). To a great extent, adds Deschênes, Parliament has contributed to its own demise by passing laws that have brought it to the rank of an administrative institution. In the eyes of some civil servants, the National Assembly is but another ministry (Deschênes 1984: 328).

There is no doubt that legislators are less visible and socially prominent than they were in the 1940s and 1950s, when, for lack of welfare-state institutions, they exercised discretionary power in allocating state funds to individuals, be it to pay a hospital bill or someone's university tuition. It would be foolish to pine for those "good old days."

In a world where problems become more complex every day, Quebec legislators are presently ill equipped to make any significant input into the law-making process. Reforms of the 1960s and 1970s, and more particularly the 1984 reforms, have failed to adequately address the fundamental problem of the National Assembly's lack of professional staff, and consequently the lack of well-informed members. Standing committees, who could make a difference and be the locus of MNAs' legislative input, are staffed with only one clerk. Obviously, professional support should be vastly increased, somewhat along the lines of American congressional committees.

But beyond this problem, one wonders how much of a legislative role MNAs really want to play. As stated earlier, standing committees have been given the power to investigate and oversee the administration, to query members of the Cabinet, to examine financial commitments, and so on, yet they have rarely used it. Perhaps lament ought to give way to resolve.

KEY TERMS

Bill	Parliamentary system
Caucus	Private bills
Consensus-building	Private members' bills
Filibuster	Responsible government
Law	Standing committees
Majority leader	Standing orders
MNAs	Universal suffrage
National Assembly	Whips
Parliamentary group	

REFERENCES AND FURTHER READINGS

1992. "Marking the bicentennial of parliamentary institutions of Quebec: reflections on democracy." *Forces*, 96 (Winter 1991–1992) (Special issue).

Assemblée nationale. (Various years). *Journal des débats*. Quebec: Editeur officiel du Québec.

Assemblée nationale. 1985. *L'Assemblée nationale et les femmes*. Quebec: Editeur officiel du Québec.

Assemblée nationale. 1987. *Rules of Procedure and Related Statutory Provisions*. Quebec: Editeur officiel du Québec.

Assemblée nationale. 1989. *Rapport statistique sur les travaux et les dépenses des commissions parlementaires pour l'année financière 1988–1989*. Quebec: Secrétariat des commissions.

Assemblée nationale. 1990. *Rapport statistique sur les travaux et les dépenses des commissions parlementaires pour l'année 1989–1990*. Quebec: Secrétariat des commissions.

Assemblée nationale. 1990. *Guide parlementaire québécois*. Quebec: Bibliothèque de l'Assemblée nationale, Division de la recherche.

Bernier, Gérald. 1982. "Le Parti patriote, 1827–1838." In Vincent Lemieux, ed., *Personnel et partis politiques au Québec*. Montreal: Boréal express. Pp. 207–228.

Brun, Henri. 1970. *La Formation des institutions parlementaires québécoises, 1791–1838*. Quebec: Presses de l'Université Laval.

Chevrette, Guy. 1981. "Le Député ministériel: ses relations avec le caucus et le cabinet." *Revue parlementaire canadienne*, 4(1)(Spring): 2–6.

Deschênes, Gaston. 1979. *Le Député québécois. Vie parlementaire* series. Quebec: Assemblée nationale.

Deschênes, Gaston. 1982. *Organisation et fonctionnement de l'Assemblée nationale. Vie parlementaire* series. Quebec: Assemblée nationale.

Deschênes, Gaston. 1984. "Les Réformes parlementaires ou le mythe de Sisyphe." In Centre d'études politiques et administratives du Québec (ed.), *Contrôle de l'administration et la réforme parlementaire.* Sainte-Foy: E.N.A.P. Pp. 290–333.

Deschênes, Gaston. 1986. *Portrait socio-politique de l'Assemblée nationale.* Quebec: Bibliothèque de l'Assemblée nationale, Service de la recherche et de la documentation.

Drouilly, Pierre and Jocelyne Dorion. 1988. *Candidates, députées et ministres: les femmes et les élections.* Quebec: Bibliothèque de l'Assemblée nationale.

Ducasse, Russel. 1979. "Les Députés et la fonction parlementaire: éléments d'une enquête à l'Assemblée nationale du Québec." *Journal of Canadian Studies/Revue d'études canadiennes,* 14(2)(Summer): 109–116.

Gélinas, André. 1969. *Les Parlementaires et l'administration au Québec.* Quebec: Presses de l'Université Laval.

Guay, Richard. 1984. "La Réforme parlementaire au Québec." In Centre d'études politiques et administratives du Québec (ed.), *Contrôle de l'administration et la réforme parlementaire.* Sainte-Foy: E.N.A.P. Pp. 9–23.

Laforte, Denis and André Bernard. 1969. *La Législation électorale au Québec, 1760–1967.* Montreal: Cahiers de Sainte-Marie.

Le Directeur général des élections du Québec. 1989. *Rapport des résultats officiels du scrutin du 25 septembre 1989.* Quebec: Bibliothèque nationale du Québec.

Massicotte, Louis. 1987. "Quebec: the successful combination of French culture and British institutions. In G. Levy (ed.), *Provincial and Territorial Legislatures in Canada.* Toronto: University of Toronto Press. Pp. 68–89.

Massicotte, Louis. 1989. "Cohésion et dissidence à l'Assemblée nationale du Québec depuis 1867." *Canadian Journal of Political Science/Revue canadienne de science politique,* 22(3)(September): 505–521.

Pelletier, Réjean. 1978a. "Peut-on revaloriser le rôle du député?" *Le Devoir,* February 17. P. 5.

Pelletier, Réjean. 1978b. "Urgente et nécessaire: la revalorisation du rôle du député présente de nombreux obstacles." *Le Devoir,* March 28. P. 5.

Pelletier, Réjean. 1979. "Le Député: un législateur défaillant?" *Journal of Canadian Studies/Revue d'études canadiennes,* 14(2)(Summer): 48–56.

Pelletier, Réjean. 1984. "Les Fonctions du député: bilan des réformes parlementaires à Québec." *Politique,* 6(Fall): 145–164.

Richer, Jocelyne. 1991. "Femmes de pouvoir: dossier." *La Gazette des femmes,* 12(5) (January–February): 12–20.

Rioux, Danielle. 1990. "Les Parlementaires québécois et leurs rôles." Paper presented at annual conference, La Société québécoise de science politique, May 16, at l'Université Laval, Quebec.

Ryerson, Stanley B. 1968. *Unequal Union: Confederation and the Roots of Conflict in the Canadas, 1815–1873*. Toronto: Progress Books.

Secrétariat des commissions parlementaires. 1986. *Organisation et fonctionnement des commissions parlementaires*. Quebec: Assemblée nationale.

Vaugeois, Denis. 1982. *Pour un meilleur équilibre de nos institutions: L'Assemblée nationale en devenir*. Quebec: Assemblée nationale.

CHAPTER 10

THE PREMIER
OF QUEBEC:
LEADERSHIP AND THE
POLICYMAKING PROCESS

> The heads of the Quebec government have always had to fight, much
> more than the leaders of the other Canadian governments. Being 5
> million against 250 million, I think we are born to fight.
> —Robert Bourassa (St-Pierre 1977: 64)

The office held by the Premier of Quebec is defined in various ways, depending on how one perceives the role of the leader. Those who consider the
office to be invested with the same political power as that held by the
Premiers of the other Canadian provinces use the term "Quebec Premier."
However, provincial premiers occasionally call themselves "First Ministers"
—e.g., at the annual First Ministers Conference, which is never held in
Ottawa—to demonstrate that they consider themselves to wield as much
political power as, if not more than, the federal government. In the mind
of the Quebec people, ultimately, there is no doubt that their Premier is
Premier ministre du Québec. Furthermore, the constitutional history of
Canada has given premiers of Quebec an important symbolic role: protec-
tors of the French heritage in North America. This fact gives the Premier
of Quebec a political position different from that of the other Canadian
premiers in historical, symbolic, economic, and political scope.

Quebec has had 24 premiers since 1867. Overall, they fall into three
periods in the evolution of the Quebec Premier's role since Confederation.
From 1867 to 1905, with the exception of Honoré Mercier, the premiers of
Quebec were basically puppets of the federal government. From 1905 to
1960, the role and function of the office expanded, with greater involvement of the state in the economy, mostly due to the charismatic leaders

Table 10.1

Quebec Premiers, 1867–1905

Premier	Tenure	Party Affiliation	Father's Profession	Own Profession/ Highest Degree	Age Office Assumed (Birthdate)
Pierre-Joseph-Olivier Chauveau	1867–1873	Conservative	Merchant	Lawyer Ph.D.	46 (Sept. 22, 1840)
Gédéon Ouimet	1873–1874	Conservative	Farmer	Lawyer Ph.D.	49 (June 2, 1823)
Charles-Eugène Boucher de Boucherville	1874–1878 1891–1892	Conservative	Seigneur	Physician	52 (May 4, 1822)
Henri Joly de Lotbinière	1878–1879	National Party Liberal	Seigneur	Lawyer	48 (Dec. 5, 1829)
Joseph-Adolphe Chapleau	1879–1882	Conservative	Mason	Lawyer Ph.D.	39 (Nov. 9, 1840)
Joseph-Alfred Mousseau	1882–1884	Conservative	Farmer	Lawyer	45 (July 17, 1837)
John Jones Ross	1884–1887	Conservative	Captain; woodmonger	Physician	50 (Aug. 16, 1833)
Louis-Olivier Taillon	1887 1892–1896	Conservative	Farmer	Lawyer	46 (Sept. 26, 1840)
Honoré Mercier	1887–1891	Liberal	Farmer	Lawyer	46 (Oct. 15, 1840)
Edmund Gabriel Flynn	1886–1897	Conservative	Fisherman	Lawyer	48 (Nov. 16, 1847)
Félix-Gabriel Marchand	1897–1900	Liberal	Landowner; trader; militia field officer	Lawyer	55 (Jan. 9, 1832)
Simon-Napoléon Parent	1900–1905	Liberal	Farmer and trader	Lawyer	45 (Sept. 12, 1855)
Lomer Gouin	1905–1920	Liberal	Physician	Lawyer	43 (Mar. 19, 1861)
Louis-Alexandre Taschereau	1920–1936	Liberal	Lawyer and judge	Lawyer	53 (Mar. 5, 1867)
Joseph-Adélard Godbout	1936 1939–1944	Liberal	Farmer	Agronomist	43 (Sept. 24, 1892)
Maurice Le Noblet Duplessis	1936–1939 1944–1959	Union nationale	Lawyer and judge	Lawyer	46 (April 20, 1890)
Paul Sauvé	1959	Union nationale	Journalist	Lawyer	52 (Mar. 24, 1907)
Antonio Barette	1960	Union nationale	Civil servant	Mechanical engineer (blue-collar)	60 (May 26, 1899)
Jean Lesage	1960–1966	Liberal	Teacher and civil servant	Lawyer	48 (June 10, 1912)
Daniel Johnson	1966–1968	Union nationale	Journeyman	Lawyer	51 (April 9, 1915)
Jean-Jacques Bertrand	1968–1970	Union nationale	Stationmaster; telegraphist	Lawyer	52 (June 20, 1916)

Robert Bourassa	1970–1976 1985–	Liberal	Civil servant	Lawyer	37 (July 14, 1933)
René Lévesque	1976–1985	Parti-québécois	Lawyer	Journalist	54 (Aug. 24, 1922)
Pierre-Marc Johnson	1985	Parti-Québécois	Lawyer	Lawyer and physician	39 (1946)

Source: Assemblée nationale, *Les Premiers Ministres du Québec* (Quebec: Éditeur officiel, 1984).

Quebec had over this period. Finally, from 1960 to the present, the Premier has become more and more a national and international figure, a development that has coincided with the Quiet Revolution and the rise of the Parti québécois.

This chapter examines the day-to-day duties of the Quebec Premier, and how he or she influences and exercises power over the decision-making process. The office of the Premier can be analyzed by four different approaches. The *sociopsychological approach* looks at the life and personality of the Premier in search of character traits that might explain behaviour and attitudes. The *institutional approach* examines the Premier's roles and functions in a formal organization built around committees and subcommittees, and how some decisions are made with little input from, or even awareness by, the Premier's office. The *legislative process approach* attempts to explain why the Quebec legislature might respond differently to environmental changes than other provinces. Finally, the *behavioural approach* tries to delineate the mechanisms by which groups or individuals—through community elites, establishment, power structures, or social relationships—can influence the Premier, the legislators, and their activities. Each approach has its merits. In characterizing the office of the Premier, we will also try to assess whether it has really come to resemble the American presidency as much as some authors have suggested (Louis Bernard, 1987).[1]

10.1 THE OFFICE OF THE PREMIER, THE *CONSEIL EXÉCUTIF*, AND THE *MINISTÈRE DU CONSEIL EXÉCUTIF*

Decisions in a parliamentary system like Quebec's are rarely made solely by the Premier; premiers do not enjoy the blanket authority of, say, the American president. Three important bodies participate in the decision-

---

1. In the following sections, French titles have been used for important positions and bodies.

making process: the Office of the Premier; the *Conseil exécutif* or *Conseil des ministres* (Executive Council) or Cabinet; and the *Ministère du Conseil exécutif* (Department of the Executive Council). Though the *Conseil* is part of the *Ministère*, and both are under the responsibility of the Premier, we shall consider them separately here. Figure 10.1 presents the administrative structure and the Premier's circle of influence.

The Office of the Premier or Cabinet is made up of a *Directeur de cabinet* (Chief of Staff) and an *Adjoint au directeur de cabinet* (Deputy Chief of Staff). The Premier also makes use of a number of advisors, directors, and secretaries.

The *Directeur de cabinet*, with an assistant and services clerk, has a number of functions: to organize the Premier's agenda, to respond to citizens' letters, and to monitor the Premier's relationship with his or her

Figure 10.1
Administrative Structure Under and Circle of Influence of Premier

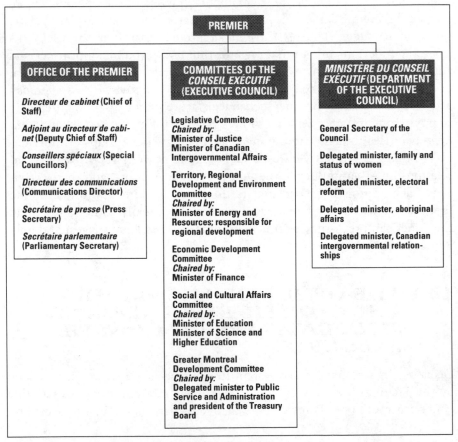

Source: Various governmental publications.

Figure 10.2

The Office of the Premier and Cabinet*

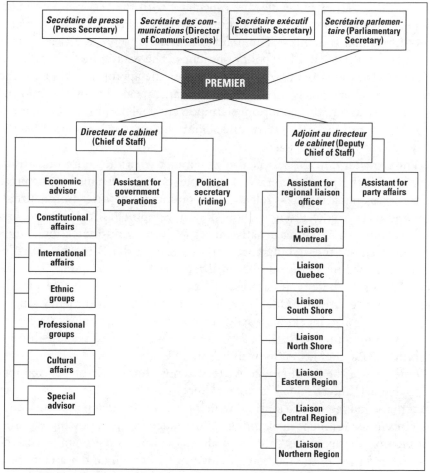

* The structure varies from premier to premier. This chart gives the structure under
  René Lévesque in 1980, which is a good example of how responsibility is generally
  distributed.

Source: Daniel Latouche, "The organizational culture of government: myths,
symbols and rituals in a Québécois setting," *International Social Science
Journal*, 35(2): 257–278.

administration, the MNAs, and the media. The Premier is badgered by an
endless stream of individuals and organizations requesting speeches and
appearances at various social and political events. The role of the *Directeur*
in the policymaking process is therefore central, as was the case with Louis
Bernard (1976–1977) and Jean-Roch Boivin (1977–1985), under the premiership of René Lévesque, or Mario Bertrand (1985–1990) under Robert

Bourassa; all were key players in the dynamic between the Premier's office and the administration. To organize the agenda, the *Directeur de cabinet* liaises with a variety of people, and especially with the *Secrétaire exécutif*, who is responsible for the relationship between the Premier and the members of National Assembly. The main task here is to prepare the Premier for Question Period and key policy speeches. The *Secrétaire exécutif* then talks with the parliamentary leader to discuss the appropriate time for the Premier to attend the National Assembly and speak. He or she informs the Premier about the adoption of important legislation, about who is responsible for presenting bills, and about the strategies adopted by the party and the opposition party.

The *Directeur de cabinet* is also in contact with the communications director and the press secretary. These persons are responsible for press conferences, preparing press releases, responding to inquiries from journalists, and briefing the Premier about key developments in the news and public affairs. The Premier usually meets with the communications director and attends a press conference daily. Assisting the *Directeur de cabinet* is an assistant and a number of directors. Under the premiership of René Lévesque, there were two assistants: one responsible for keeping in touch with the different Quebec regions and one to monitor party affairs. The *Directeur* also meets with special advisors called *conseillers spéciaux* about relationships with the party. The *conseillers* are responsible for keeping the Premier generally well informed.[1]

One duty of the Premier is to write (often with the help of a parliamentary secretary) the *Discours inaugural* (Opening Speech) for each new parliamentary and legislative session, which presents the key policy measures the current government is planning to introduce in the following months. The text of this speech is submitted ahead of time to the members of the Cabinet and then to the Lieutenant Governor, after which not a word may be changed. The *Discours inaugural* is usually followed by speeches from Cabinet ministers.

The Premier and the Government are not bound to deliver all the legislation promised in the speech; often, they are merely trying to reshape the agenda (and, especially in recent years, to revive a crippled economy). In his memoirs René Lévesque argues:

> The Speech from the Throne at the beginning of the session is scarcely more than a sketchy itinerary, inevitably incomplete, sometimes stuffed with illusions and, very luckily, as malleable as you please. (Lévesque 1986: 34)

---

1. Under the PQ government, these duties were carried out by political scientist Daniel Latouche (1978–1980) before the referendum of 1980, and by economist Pierre Fortin during the economic crisis of the early 1980s.

To some, the *Discours* is a bit like Christmas, with a gift for everyone; to others, it is a list of serious legislative and political proposals designed to announce economic and social changes and raise expectations.

The key speech, however, for any Quebec government remains the Budget Speech, in which citizens are, more often than not, notified of the inevitable tax increase, and a clear message is sent to the business community, bankers, and citizens about the government's immediate priorities and coming guidelines. Even though the Quebec government has relatively little control over the monetary policy of Canada as a whole, especially in the matter of interest rates, it can present programs to stimulate the economy.

Among such programs was Corvée-Habitation, started in the early 1980s in collaboration with the housing industry and bankers, to increase the number of housing projects and offer lower interest rates to families buying a first home. Another example of typical Budget Speech fare was Robert Bourassa's second James Bay project, whose aim was to increase electricity production and create new jobs. Aside from the Opening Speech, René Lévesque argues:

Jean Lesage, Liberal party leader and Premier from 1960 to 1966. [Courtesy Le Devoir and Gilles Paré, Librarian. Photo: Jerry Donati.]

nothing is more important than the budget.... [It] is a finished product, a carefully documented picture of the economic and financial situation and of perspectives for the future. A well-made budget, as long as one knows how to read it, is the most exact annual photograph that you can possibly have of a society, with all its bread and butter plainly visible. (Lévesque 1986: 34)

According to André Bernard (1982), in a normal day the Premier spends one to two hours with staff getting briefed about his or her agenda, political events in Quebec, legislative activities, and any other pertinent matters, sits in the National Assembly for one or two hours, and spends two or three hours meeting with ministers or MNAs. At least once a week, ideally, the Premier holds private discussions with key ministers. And at various times he or she meets with members of the party, voters, the leaders of various interest groups, and journalists.

10.2 THE *CONSEIL EXÉCUTIF* OR *CONSEIL DES MINISTRES*

The *Conseil exécutif* or *Conseil des ministres* is the central decision-making institution, defining the orientation of governmental activities and supervising the implementation of its legislative and administrative decisions. It is the central body of the Quebec state administration. In fact, together, the *Conseil* and the Lieutenant Governor are the Government.

The *Conseils exécutifs* of Quebec and of Ontario were created by Article 63 of the BNA Act,[2] where the "Executive Council" is described in the following terms:

The Executive Council of...Quebec shall be composed of such Persons as the Lieutenant Governor from Time to Time thinks fit, and in the first instance of the following officers, namely,—the Attorney General, the Secretary and Registrar of the Province, the Treasurer of the Province, the Commissioner of Crown Lands, and the Commissioner of Agriculture and Public Works, with in Quebec, the Speaker of the Legislative Council and the Solicitor General.

The members of the *Conseil* are chosen by the Premier. All are ministers or assistant ministers.

But who appoints the Premier? According to the Constitution of Canada, the Premier is "chosen" by the Lieutenant Governor. Because the Premier depends on support from the National Assembly, that is, the support of

---

2. This article has been amended more than fifty times since Confederation, sometimes just after election of the PQ, by the Executive Power Act, R.S.Q. 1978, c. E-18.

MNAs, the Lieutenant Governor is obliged to choose a Premier capable of such a leadership role. If the party in office has a majority of seats in the National Assembly, its leader is the person who usually becomes Premier. However, if another party wins more seats—due to the resignation of MNAs, electoral defeat, a scandal that leads to a minority government, etc.—the Premier and Cabinet resign and the Lieutenant Governor appoints as Premier the leader of that party which has the new majority. In a case where the party in power is defeated on an important policy issue, the Premier can either resign or ask the Lieutenant Governor to call an election; if the Premier resigns, the Lieutenant Governor normally appoints the leader of the opposition Premier. If the Premier is forced to resign while still holding a majority, protocol dictates that the Lieutenant Governor be informed. (This happened with Premier Lévesque in 1984—since his party still held the majority, a new leader was elected at a party convention.) In the meantime, the Lieutenant Governor consults with members of the party holding the majority and designates a provisional Premier.

If the leader of the party loses in his or her riding, while the party wins overall, he or she may still attain office. Robert Bourassa, for example, was defeated in his electoral district of Bertrand in the election of December 2, 1985. So even though his party was elected to form the next Quebec government, Bourassa at first could not sit in the National Assembly as Leader; as Premier, he could perform all the functions of that office, but he would have to listen to the Opening Speech from a balcony (la galerie). The solution to this embarrassing situation was to have one of his MNAs resign so that Bourassa could try to win back the vacated seat in a byelection. (He did win in the district of Saint-Laurent on January 20, 1986.)

The first task of a newly elected Premier is to choose a Cabinet from among his elected party members. In an editorial in *Le Devoir*, Claude Ryan wrote in 1976: "The Creation of a Cabinet is essentially an act of equilibrium: the interests to be reconciled are so numerous and so varied that the Premier must demonstrate an abundance of flexibility" (Ryan 1976: 4).[3] In Ryan's view, the Premier's cabinet should project competence, moderation, and responsibility; it is the key to success for any new government. But, as Lévesque put it after his election on November 15, 1976: "There is nothing easier to begin with than to put together a cabinet. The first names drop into place all by themselves. But who does what? And who's left over to do the rest? That's the rough part" (Lévesque 1986: 278). Today the Premier must take into account regional representation in the Cabinet, as well as adequate representation of minorities and women (Hamelin and Beaudoin 1967). There has been a tradition in Quebec of including at least one or

---

3. Translation ours.

two anglophones in each Cabinet; however, the first government of the PQ in 1976 had no anglophones.

In 1976, Louis Bernard, the *Directeur de cabinet* of the newly elected PQ, created the new position of state minister (*Ministre d'état*), i.e., minister without portfolio. The role of state ministers was to plan and coordinate governmental activities concerning social, economic, cultural, and regional policies. (Quebec was not the first province to have such a position; Ontario had preceded it.) However, by 1982, having no administrative or political powers, the state ministers had become ineffective and frustrated. They felt they had been demoted to administrative staff—in effect, mere advisors to the government. At the end of the 1970s, for example, Daniel Latouche had criticized the way the Cabinet was structured and called for a return to three basic organizing principles: a formal structure, a clear division of the authority, and a clear understanding of the responsibility of each member (Latouche 1988: 299). In 1982 the old structure was reintroduced.

While in office, the Premier performs from time to time what is called a "cabinet shuffle" (*remaniement ministériel*), a change-around of certain ministers or the switching of portfolios. Usually, the Premier chooses ministers from the party's MNAs—hence, a "shuffle." However, virtually anyone can be named to the Cabinet, even individuals who have not been elected to public office. Since 1960 in Quebec there have been several such appointments: Eric Kierans was named labour minister under Lesage, Jean-

Daniel Johnson, Union nationale leader and Premier from 1966 until his sudden death in 1968. [Courtesy Archives nationales du Québec.]

Guy Cardinal education minister under Jean-Jacques Bertrand, Claude Castonguay health and welfare minister and Jean Cournoyer labour minister under Bourassa, Francine Lalonde status of women minister under Lévesque. Under the premiership of Pierre-Marc Johnson four non-elected ministers were chosen: Louise Beaudoin (international relations), Jean-Guy Parent (external trade), Lise Denis (status of women), Rolande Cloutier (citizen relationships and Handicapped Persons Office). With the exception of Louise Beaudoin, all the members were elected only after being appointed Cabinet ministers. The case of Jean Cournoyer is unique, since he was an MNA under the Union nationale government and after quitting his party to join the Liberals was asked by Bourassa to become labour minister.[4]

The Premier in Quebec traditionally does not hold a portfolio, but chairs all Cabinet meetings. The *Conseil des ministres* (Executive Council) usually meets once a week, usually on Wednesday morning, and in times of crisis on an ad hoc basis. During the fiscal year 1989–1990, the *Conseil* held 53 meetings. On the Friday of the preceding week, the Premier usually goes over the agenda with the *Secrétaire général du Conseil exécutif*, plans the upcoming meeting, and devises a strategy to follow. Only five members are required for a quorum, but all ministers are expected to understand how important it is to attend every session. All the meetings are held *in camera*. Each minister in turn outlines points of legislation and delivers other information crucial to the workings of the government. If the Premier feels there is a consensus in the Cabinet, he or she signs all the documents, such as nominations or modifications to decrees. If there appears to be no consensus, the Premier may prefer to adjourn the debate. In some cases, the Premier may take sole responsibility for an issue and leave it off the *Conseil*'s agenda. This was the case with the legislation concerning language policy in Quebec: i.e., Bill 63, adopted under the premiership of Jean-Jacques Bertrand, and Bill 22, adopted in 1973 under that of Robert Bourassa.

10.3 THE COMMITTEES OF THE *CONSEIL EXÉCUTIF*

The Premier can create two types of committees to facilitate the decision-making process: ad hoc or special committees and permanent committees. The *special committees*, which are created to deal with matters related to specific issues, have three functions: (1) to document important matters

---

4. Changing Cabinet members was especially difficult for Lévesque in the fall of 1984 after the resignation of several key ministers, including minister of finance Jacques Parizeau and Camille Laurin. In them he lost a number of his closest allies, some who had been with him since the founding of the PQ.

for the *Conseil*, (2) to discuss salient policy issues with key ministers before they are presented to the *Conseil*, and (3) to facilitate discussion during Cabinet meetings by providing relevant facts and figures to all members. Special committees do not make decisions on their own, since all decisions must be approved by the Cabinet, in accordance with the principle of "ministerial solidarity;" however, this committee structure, and the ministers responsible, are sometimes referred to as the "Inner Cabinet." In Quebec, special committees have traditionally exerted less power and influence than their British counterparts.

During the first Bourassa reign (1970–1976), there were three *permanent committees*: the Treasury Board Council, the Priority and Planning Committee, and the Legislative Committee. These committees were created by decree, with the exception of the Treasury Board, which was created by financial administrative law and was the most important committee during this period. In September 1975, four new permanent committees were created to replace the then-largely-inactive Priority and Planning Committee: their mandates were related to human resources, citizen well-being, renewable resources and industrial development, and regional development. Their creation marks the point at which the *Conseil*'s department started to play a key role in governmental decision-making. After the PQ's election in November 1976, the committee structure was again modified; Priority and Planning was restored and the four other committees received new mandates: social development, cultural development, economic development, and regional/territory development. Today the *Conseil* is made up of several committees: the Legislative Committee and four permanent ministerial committees handling territory and regional development and the environment (COMPADRE), economic development, (CMPDE), social and cultural affairs, (COMPACS), and the development of greater Montreal. Basically, the goal of each of these committees was to identify and establish, on an ongoing basis, the government's priorities, and to coordinate government activities in all these different sectors.

After the election of the Liberal party in 1985, the structure remained fundamentally the same. However, the mandate of the Legislative Committee was again modified on September 24, 1986, and Priority and Planning disappeared again. The task of the Legislative Committee was to present the *Conseil* with opinions on the legislative or regulatory impact of memoranda submitted by the *Conseil*, the *Secrétaire général*, or the parliamentary leader of the government. Altogether, the Committee now has five mandates: to harmonize new legislation with [Quebec legislation overall], to ensure that the legislative approach will resolve a problem, to evaluate the nature and size of a piece of legislation and its implications for the daily life of citizens, and to ensure that legislative texts are clearly and carefully written.

In March 1990 the Legislative Committee included the delegated minister for Canadian intergovernmental affairs, who chaired the committee; the justice minister; the food, fisheries and agricultural minister; the minister for international affairs; the delegated minister for aboriginal affairs; the delegated minister to the Public Service and Administration; the revenue minister; the labour minister; the minister of technology, commerce and industry; and the delegated minister for regional development and mines. During the 1989–1990 fiscal year, this committee met 27 times and made 122 decisions.

The mandate of the Cabinet Committee on Territory and Regional Development and the Environment (COMPADRE) is to ensure the coherence of government policy in these sectors, and to advise the *Conseil* on priority issues: territorial development and urbanization, regional development and regionalization, environment and sustainable development, aboriginal affairs, agriculture, mines, forests, wildlife and energy resources, municipal functions and structures, housing, transport, common equipment, cultural heritage and infrastructures, land ownership, administration

Jean-Jacques Bertrand, who succeeded Daniel Johnson as leader of the Union nationale *and Premier from 1968 to 1970. [Courtesy Archives nationales du Québec.]*

of public lands and Quebec territorial integrity, development of the nation's capital, the city of Quebec, and information coordination. COMPADRE is chaired by the minister of natural resources and energy. Between April 1989 and March 1990, it held 30 working sessions and four special meetings, and studied and made recommendations on 141 files, 27 legislative projects, and 375 decrees.

The Committee on Permanent Economic Development (CMPDE), chaired by the finance minister, has as its mandate to ensure that everybody in the *Conseil* has a clear idea of the economic repercussions of their decisions. CMPDE also prepares documents explaining the government's position on the development of natural resources, agricultural production, the development of the processing industry, the promotion of exports, innovation, and technological development. Recently the environment minister also became a member of CMPDE. During 1989 and 1990, this committee studied 145 dossiers submitted to the *Conseil*.

Two other permanent committees presently assist the Premier and *Conseil* in their legislative roles: the Committee on Social and Cultural Affairs (COMPACS) and the (relatively new) Committee on Greater Montreal. The mandate of COMPACS is to advise the Cabinet on such issues as the status of women, education, higher education, scientific research, housing, language, cultural communities, demography, family, immigration, social services, security at work, and professional training. This committee held 31 meetings in 1989–1990 and studied 111 memoranda. The objective of the Committee on Greater Montreal is to improve the economic growth of this city and the surrounding region through a strategic coordination of all its economic activities.

10.4 THE *MINISTÈRE DU CONSEIL EXÉCUTIF*

It was not until the early 1970s that the Quebec government decided to establish a department for the *Conseil*. The *Secrétaire général* is also clerk of the *Conseil* and, with a team, keeps all the ministers informed. This *Ministère du Conseil exécutif*, similar to the Privy Council at the federal level, was proposed to respond to the new role of the Quebec government in the wake of the Quiet Revolution. Before 1960, and very often between 1960 and 1970, meetings of the *Conseil des ministres* were characterized by long discussions, a lack of coordination, and contradictory decisions. According to the law that created the *Secrétariat général*, which later became the *Ministère du Conseil exécutif*, it falls under the leadership of the Premier and has nine functions.

The *Secrétariat général* was incorporated as part of the ministry of the *Ministère du Conseil exécutif* when the *Ministère* was created in 1977 under the PQ to supervise all legislative and administrative work of the Premier; since 1978–1979, the Premier has been responsible for this ministry and has produced an annual report of its activities. According to the last annual report, the department assists the Premier. Louis Bernard was the *Directeur de cabinet* before he became *Secrétaire général* of the government (1978–1985).

At the beginning of the 1980s, the *Ministère* had a budget of $70 million and a staff of 500; of those, 200 were *political appointees*. Today, it is made up of the general *Secrétaire* and the clerk of the *Conseil*, the associate general secretaries, the committee secretaries, the directors of the different administrative units, and the assistant clerk. The total number of people working for the Office of the Premier and the *Ministère du Conseil exécutif* has remained relatively stable over recent years; for 1989–1990, the ministry had 244 permanent employees. During this period, 368 memoranda were received and studied by the *Conseil* and 1,923 decrees adopted.

To facilitate discussion during Cabinet meetings, the *Secrétaire général* has four functions: (1) to distill information down to the key elements, (2) to present facts, (3) to present different policy alternatives, and (4) to formulate recommendations for future action. Thus, each document or memorandum submitted to the *Conseil* is sent first to the *Ministère du Conseil exécutif*; there, the information about the situation is summarized and legislation affecting the issue is included, along with policy alternatives, the pros and cons of each possible course of action, ministers' recommendations, policy impact, consultation reports, general information, and federal-Quebec implications. This document is restricted to a maximum of eight pages or 1,000 words.

10.5 THE DELEGATED MINISTERS AND THEIR CABINETS

Delegated ministers (*ministres d'état* or state ministers) are a relatively new addition to the governmental structure. These ministers have legislative, administrative, and political roles to play in advising the Premier in special areas. Currently, four delegated ministers cover the following areas: the family and the status of women, aboriginal affairs, electoral reform, and Canadian intergovernmental relationships. Delegated ministers enjoy a special status, since they respond directly to the Premier and the *Conseil*. They also rely on the support of the *Ministère*.

The delegated minister for the status of women is responsible for the implementation of an affirmative action program for Québécoises. This

René Lévesque, leader of the Parti québécois *and Premier from 1976 to 1985. Picture taken at Montreal International Airport on June 25, 1985 a few days after his resignation. [Courtesy Le Devoir and Gilles Paré, Librarian. Photo: Louise Lemieux.]*

minister also ensures that all policies and actions taken by the government in this matter are consistent. The minister promotes women's issues during *Conseil* meetings and is responsible for the implementation of the law creating the *Conseil du statut de la femme* and the implementation of legislation concerning day-care services. Since February 1986, this Minister has been working on a governmental plan to facilitate and implement an employment equity program everywhere. In December 1986, current minister Monique Gagnon-Tremblay received a mandate to revise day-care policy. Since October 1989 her assignment has also been to expand policies concerning the family.

The head of the delegated ministry for aboriginal affairs is in charge of developing and implementing policies concerning Quebec's aboriginal and Inuit peoples. This minister's duties include meeting with representatives of the aboriginal and Inuit communities and investigating how different government projects and programs are responding to their needs. In the fall of 1989, delegated minister John Ciaccia had several meetings with the coordinators of about twenty ministries involved directly or indirectly in native affairs. During the Oka crisis in the summer of 1990, Ciaccia played a key role as a representative of the government in negotiating a settlement.

The delegated minister for electoral reform is in charge of ensuring that democratic voting rights are respected. This ministry is responsible in particular for the electoral law passed by the Quebec government in March 1989. It is up to this minister to propose mechanisms that will ensure fair representation of all groups in society and preservation of the democratic rights of citizens. Other areas of responsibility are the size and boundaries of electoral districts and party financing.

Finally, the delegated minister for Canadian intergovernmental relationships has played a key role in shaping Quebec relations with the federal government and the other provinces. Since the election of Robert Bourassa in 1985, and the Quebec proposal to rejoin the Canadian federation, this office has been particularly active in making proposals to the other governments to accomodate Quebec's historical and constitutional demands. The Quebec proposal that led to the Meech-Langevin accord and its rejection by two provinces in June 1990 made this department more visible. The minister responsible for this department quickly became a national figure who works closely with the Premier in elaborating constitutional strategy. This department was highly instrumental in Quebec's constitutional agreement of August 1992.

Overall, these four ministers are commissioned to advise the Premier and Executive Council on matters judged to be priorities for the Government.

10.6 THE PROGRAMS OF THE *MINISTÈRE DU CONSEIL EXÉCUTIF*

By March 31, 1990, the *Ministère du Conseil exécutif* was responsible for five institutions relating to:

1. The Office of the Lieutenant Governor
2. Support services to the Premier and the *Conseil*
3. Promotion of women's rights
4. Canadian intergovernmental affairs
5. The technological development fund.

The first, the Office of the Lieutenant Governor, is set up to help the Lieutenant Governor carry out duties as spelled out by law. However, the

Lieutenant Governor is not a member of the *Ministère* even though the budget is part of that department. The Lieutenant Governor, as representative of Queen Elizabeth II, remains Quebec's head of state. The Lieutenant Governor gives royal sanction to all legislative documents passed by the National Assembly. In certain cases he or she may refuse to pass, or ask the Governor General of Canada to sign, legislation; however, recent constitutional conventions and traditions have precluded the possibility of such actions. The Lieutenant Governor officially names the Premier to office and technically approves the members of the *Conseil.*

The support services program for the Premier and Cabinet assists the Premier and the *Conseil* and its committees in their tasks. The institution in charge of the program has five areas of responsibility: (1) the Office of the Premier, (2) the *Secrétariat général* and clerk office of the *Conseil*, (3) the secretariat for aboriginal affairs, (4) internal management and administrative support, and (5) *Conseil* salaries. In the exercise of power, the Premier is assisted by the *Conseil*, which is a different administrative component than the Department of the *Conseil*. The *Conseil*, as we have seen, operates under the aegis of the *Secrétaire général*, who holds the status of a *sous-ministre* (deputy minister) under the Public Service Act. One of his or her tasks, besides preparing documentation for meetings of the *Conseil*, is to act as the main councillor of the Premier on all matters raised by the Premier.

The institution handling women's rights has as its main objective the implementation of coherent policy concerning conditions, equality, and respect for women's rights. The two main components of this institution are the Cabinet of the State Minister for Women's Issues and the Secretariat for Women's Issues.

The institution in charge of intergovernmental relationships with the federal government and other Canadian provinces was set up to assist the Cabinet of the State Minister for Intergovernmental Affairs.

The fifth institution, which covers technological development, is intended to help and promote technological research and innovation.

10.7 THE SELECTION OF PARTY LEADERS

The Premier is the leader of the majority party in office. In a parliamentary system the Premier maintains important relationships with the members of his or her party, who help set the agenda or clarify the position of the party on various issues. A distinction should be made between the elected *party* and the elected *government*, which are two separate entities. The

Premier is the leader of the political party in office and all Cabinet members belong to that party. But as an elected official, the Premier is obliged to speak not only for party followers but for all citizens.

The selection of leaders at a party's leadership convention is a relatively recent phenomenon in Quebec. Before the 1960s, there were very few leadership conventions. Some countries, such as Britain, still do not hold leadership conventions where the rank and file can democratically vote a leader in. For example, after the resignation of Margaret Thatcher, John Major was elected leader of the British Conservatives by the MPs of that party. Since the beginning of this century, the evolution of the selection process in Quebec has gone from the imposition of political favourites by Ottawa to the election of the premier by a very small group, to a leadership convention, and finally to a general vote among party members, with all citizens who registered as members for a memberhip card eligible to cast a ballot. Throughout this period, changes in the process have usually been implemented by the party in opposition.

By 1919, conventions were used to select party leaders in all provinces except Quebec. The first party to hold a leadership convention in Quebec was the Conservative party, which later became the Union nationale (UN). The first conventions were held in 1922, 1929, and 1933. The Conservative convention of July 9–10, 1929, at the Château Frontenac in Quebec City, came after the resignation of Arthur Sauvé as leader of the opposition. In a letter dated August 15, 1928, Sauvé wrote that it was impossible for him

Robert Bourassa, leader of the Liberal party and Premier from 1970 to 1976 and from 1985 to the present. [Courtesy Le Devoir and Gilles Paré, Librarian. Photo: Normand Blouin.]

to stay on as leader with such little support from his colleagues: "The opposition must regain solidarity, vigour, mobility.... It would not be just to leave me alone responsible for the party, for its miseries and its problems" (Black 1977: 31). Camilien Houde was subsequently elected leader of the Conservatives. Maurice Duplessis became leader of the Quebec Conservatives in 1933, after the resignation of Houde. After the sudden death of Duplessis in September 1959, Paul Sauvé became Premier of Quebec. Only three months after Sauvé took the job, the UN again lost its leader, in January 1960. Antonio Barette emerged as leader and Premier, but was forced out after losing the election of 1960. In September 1961, Daniel Johnson became leader of the UN and in 1966 he was elected Premier. Johnson died of a heart attack in September 1968 and his successor, Jean-Jacques Bertrand, acted as interim Premier until the UN party convention in June 1969 made it official.

It took longer for the Liberals to decide to elect their leader by convention. In 1920, Alexandre Taschereau was named leader by a very small group of people. He was forced to resign in 1936 when it was revealed that 45 of his relatives were on the government payroll. Adélard Godbout succeeded him; however, as in 1920, Godbout was selected leader by a small group, which consisted of Taschereau himself and a few of his advisors. There is no indication that ordinary MNAs or any extra-parliamentary members of the party were consulted beforehand. After the disastrous election of 1948, Godbout resigned in favour of Georges Lapalme, who became leader in May 1950. Up to this point, Lapalme had been an MP in Ottawa. In 1958, Jean Lesage became Liberal leader following the resignation of Lapalme. When Lesage retired in 1969, Robert Bourassa, the current Premier, was the first leader of the Liberal party to be elected at a convention, on January 17, 1970, at which all members were eligible to vote. The other two candidates were Claude Wagner and Pierre Laporte. Bourassa won the leadership after the first ballot with 843 votes (53%), followed by Claude Wagner with 455 votes and Pierre Laporte with 288. Three months later, at age 37, Bourassa became Premier.[5]

---

5. Bourassa's career started when he was elected to the National Assembly in 1966; he had some contact with René Lévesque when he was member of the Liberal party, but he remained relatively close to Premier Jean Lesage. After losing the 1976 election, Bourassa resigned effective January 1, 1977, when he was succeeded by Claude Ryan as leader. However, in the 1981 election, even though most of the polls indicated that the Liberals would form the next government, Lévesque's PQ held on. In August 1982, Claude Ryan resigned and Gérard D. Lévesque became temporary leader for the second time. This was the signal for Robert Bourassa to reenter politics. He was able to score a second victory at the Liberal leadership convention on October 15, 1983, defeating Daniel Johnson Jr. and Pierre Paradis.

The Case of the PQ

The relationship between the Premier and his or her party can be difficult and complex. The most famous case in recent history involved the resignation of Lévesque on June 20, 1985 as leader of the PQ. The founding father of the PQ stepped down 17 years after its creation and after nine years in office. Earlier that year, on April 26, members of the party's national executive had met secretly to discuss the leadership question. Members of the PQ were not invited, nor was Lévesque in attendance. The majority expressed the wish that Lévesque resign in the best interests of the party and Quebec. However, after a meeting between the members of the national executive and Lévesque in Quebec City on May 14, the following motion was adopted:

> The Executive National Council judges that it remains to the leader of the Party, René Lévesque himself, to take the decision concerning his political future. On this matter, the Executive Council asks that all members of the party respect the decision of their leader.

One month later, on June 18, the ministerial caucus, during its weekly meeting, adopted the motion. Two days later, on the evening of June 20, Lévesque resigned as president of the PQ and as Premier.

Of course, the resignation immediately sparked a leadership race, since the PQ was still in power and the newly elected leader would also become the next Premier. On June 23, 1989, the members of the national council of the PQ met to set rules for the campaign. The national council is made up of about 350 individuals: the members of the executive, presidents of each region and electoral districts, and 200 delegates, one for each region and one for each electoral district plus all MNAs. The election of a new leader is a momentous political event that attracts huge media attention. It is an opportunity for candidates to explain why they should be the next Premier, as well as a time for political parties to renew their platforms and demonstrate party unity.

It was decided that the total budget for the 1985 leadership convention should not exceed $500,000 and that the money would come primarily from membership fees. Individuals could become party members for a minimum fee of $5. Between June 22 and October 1, all the money collected would be sent to the party executive, 65% of any new subscriptions going to party headquarters and 35% to the local organization. With this money, the party funded ten regional assemblies where candidates could debate issues and ideas in most of the regions of Quebec, the leadership convention, information packages for the media, mailings to the rank and file, space rentals, equipment, telephone, services, etc.

The president of the 1985 PQ leadership convention was Francine Jutras; her basic duties were to control candidates' spending and ensure the fairness of all procedings in all electoral districts where voters were casting their votes. For example, candidates who were already ministers had the advantage of a staff, free long-distance calls, and transportation facilities that came with the job. Should these benefits be counted as campaign expenditures? Candidates were therefore required to distinguish between campaign and governmental activities.

The six candidates for leadership were Pierre Marc-Johnson, Pauline Marois, Jean Garon, Guy Bertrand, Francine Lalonde, and Luc Gagnon. The outcome surprised nobody. Of the 160,000 members, some 48% voted, close to 75,000. Pierre-Marc Johnson received 60% of the vote on the first ballot, thereby becoming the second PQ leader and the 24th Premier of Quebec.

The PQ had also planned a leadership convention for the spring of 1988, after the resignation of Pierre-Marc Johnson on November 10, 1987. However, there was only one candidate, Jacques Parizeau, on the ballot. A plebiscite was held and he became the new PQ leader on March 17, 1987.

10.8 UNDERSTANDING THE PREMIER'S ROLE

Is the Office of the Premier moving toward a more presidential decision-making process? Since the beginning of this century, there has been an erosion of the Lieutenant Governor's power in relation to that of the Premier. One important factor is that over the years, the administrative and political structures surrounding the Premier have become more and more complex. If nothing else, it is ample evidence of the greater policy role played by the Premier and the growth of the Quebec state. In the 1950s, Maurice Duplessis was *"le chef"* ("the boss") and at that time it was possible for one person to make all the decisions. Today, the Premier needs administrative support. The development of the Department of the *Conseil*, and also the role of the Premier as *Conseil* president, demonstrates that the power is now shared by several ministers. Ministerial responsibility remains a key principle, and all decisions are made by Cabinet. As the number of people around the Premier has increased over the years, many tasks have been delegated to support staff. Some observers might argue that the collegiality and involvement of many people in the decision-making process has reached the point where the Premier's role is primarily political.

The relationship between the head of the government and his or her party can be difficult. René Lévesque and more recently Robert Bourassa

During the Sommet de la francophonie *in 1987 the Quebec Premier played a key role in the francophone commonwealth to promote democratic rights and economic aid for development of poorer members.* **Left to right:** *Jean Doré, mayor of Montreal; Robert Bourassa, Premier of Quebec; Jacques Chirac, mayor of Paris. [Courtesy Le Devoir and Gilles Paré, Librarian. Photo: Jacques Grenier.]*

after the failure of the Meech Lake accord, ended up in a different position than that endorsed by his party in the Allaire Report. Lévesque was always popular with the people, more so even than his party, but Bourassa has frequently had to deal with a public that more often sided with his party than with him. Between his first election in 1970 and the events of 1976, most notably Bill 22, he became the most hated man in Canadian politics (Vastel 1991). Yet in September 1989, when the people of Quebec were asked to choose between Robert Bourassa and Jacques Parizeau, they finally chose Bourassa. With the support of 43% of the electorate, the supposedly-despised leader of the Liberals was apparently twice as popular as the PQ leader with 21%.

However, it should be noted that 36% were undecided. And the fact remains that Robert Bourassa was unable to win a seat in the 1985 election. This raises serious concerns as to whether the leader of the elected party should also be a regional candidate. Some have suggested moving toward a presidential system.

Finally, in the past thirty years or so we have witnessed increasing involvement of the Premier in constitutional and international matters.

The Quebec Premier's role is by no means an easy one; it brings with it great responsibility and requires the support of many people.

KEY TERMS

Cabinet

Conseil exécutif/des ministres (Executive Council)

Directeur de cabinet (Chief of Staff)

Discours inaugural (Opening Speech)

Leadership convention

Lieutenant Governor

Ministère du Conseil exécutif (Department of the Executive Council)

Office of the Premier

Secrétaire exécutif (Executive Secretary)

Secrétaire général (General Secretary)

State ministers/Delegated ministers/Ministers without portfolio

REFERENCES AND FURTHER READING

Assemblée nationale. 1984. *Les Premiers Ministres du Québec*. Quebec.

Bernard, André. 1965. "The parliamentary control of public finance in the province of Quebec." Master thesis (McGill University). Montreal.

Bernard, André. 1982. *La Politique au Canada et au Québec*. Quebec: Presses de l'Université du Québec.

Bernard, Louis. 1987. *Réflexions sur l'art de se gouverner: essai d'un praticien*. Montreal: Québec/Amérique.

Black, Conrad. 1973. "Career of Maurice Duplessis as viewed through his correspondence, 1927–1939." Master thesis (History Department, McGill University.)

Black, Conrad. 1977. *Duplessis*. Toronto: McClelland and Stewart.

Elazar, D.J. 1978. "Federalism" In *International Encyclopedia of the Social Sciences*. New York: Macmillan. Pp. 553–567.

Garneau, Raymond. 1973. "La Réforme de l'administration financière au Québec." *Canadian Public Administration*, 16(2): 182–206.

Hamelin, Jean and Louise Beaudoin. 1967. "Les Cabinets provinciaux, 1867–1967." *Recherches sociographiques*, 8(3): 299–319.

Hockin, Thomas A. (ed.). 1971. *The Apex of Power: The Premier and Political Leadership*. Scarborough, Ont.: Prentice-Hall.

Hopkins, P. D. 1977. "Daniel Johnson and the Quiet Revolution." Master thesis (Political Science Department, Simon Fraser University). Burnaby, B.C.

Jackson, Robert J. and Doreen Jackson. 1990. *Politics in Canada: Culture, Institutions, Behavior and Public Policy*. 2nd ed. Scarborough, Ont.: Prentice-Hall.

Latouche, Daniel. 1983. "The organizational culture of government: myths, symbols and rituals in a Québécois setting." *International Social Science Journal*, 35(2): 257–278.

Latouche, Daniel. 1988. "From Premier to Prime Minister: an essay on leadership, state and society in Quebec." In Leslie A. Pal and David Tarras (eds.), *Prime Ministers & Premiers: Political Leadership and Public Policy in Canada*. Scarborough, Ont.: Prentice-Hall: 137–157.

Lévesque, René. 1986. *Memoirs*. Tr. Philip Stratford. Toronto: McClelland and Stewart.

Nish, Cameron. 1969. *Quebec in the Duplessis Era, 1935–1959: Dictatorship or Democracy?* Toronto: Copp Clark.

Pigeon, Louis-Philippe. 1943. *Canadian Bar Review* (December).

Ryan, Claude. 1976. "Le Premier Cabinet de René Lévesque." *Le Devoir*, November 19. P. 4.

Silverson, R. W. 1979. *Robert Bourassa's Ideas on Canadian Federalism: His Concept and Rationale*. Master thesis (Queen's University). Kingston, Ont.

St-Pierre, Raymond. 1977. *Les Années Bourassa*. Montreal: Héritage.

Stark, Frank. 1973. "The Premier as symbol: unifier or optimizer?" *Canadian Journal of Political Science*, 6(3): 514–515.

Thompson, Dale C. 1984. *Jean Lesage et la Révolution tranquille*. St-Laurent, Que.: Éditions du Trécarré.

Vigod, B. L. 1986. *Quebec Before Duplessis: The Political Career of Louis-Alexandre Taschereau*. Montreal: Queen's University Press, McGill University.

Wearing, Joseph. 1971. "President or Premier." In Thomas D. Hockin (ed.), *Apex of Power*. Scarborough, Ont.: Prentice-Hall. Pp. 224–260.

BUREAUCRACY
AND
ADMINISTRATIVE
MACHINERY

A rational method of public administration is founded on specialization and efficiency. Trained civil servants should be assigned fixed responsibilities, and not participate directly in politics—or at least not in a partisan manner. Ideally, bureaucracy is a complex organization characterized by consistent application of abstract rules, employment based on merit, protection from arbitrary dismissal, and impartial behaviour toward subordinates and clients.

With the growing influence of the public bureaucracy—or the *civil service*, as it is often called—over policymaking, there have been concerns that its technical expertise has afforded it too much power. Civil servants, it is thought, may be tempted to use this power to their own advantage, or even to change the shape and intent of public policies with little respect for the democratic process, the more so because of a proliferation of departments and agencies.

In this chapter we discuss these points in the light of the historical evolution of the Quebec state. We will see that before 1960 and the Quiet Revolution the power of the civil service was very limited. The Quiet Revolution propelled the civil service to the forefront of political life and the policy agenda in the 1960s and 1970s. But since the early 1980s, the state's role was being questioned, and the bureaucracy has gradually become somewhat less prominent.

11.1 HISTORICAL PERSPECTIVE

In the early years of Confederation, the civil service in Quebec had a very limited policy role in what was a very small state. In 1870–1871, the state of Quebec employed only 94 full-time civil servants. By 1899–1900, that number had increased to 212, and most of these were hired through patronage. Nevertheless, the civil service was quite competent and lacked the resources to shape and generate policy. The dominant ideology of the time prevented a more imaginative use of the state. In the Duplessis era, nepotism was somewhat reduced, and at the end of Duplessis' regime the bureaucracy in Quebec was still small and poorly trained (Gow 1979).

However, nepotism and patronage remained rampant and the long tenure of the dominant party in office had led to a tight party-bureaucracy connection. Recruitment by the Civil Service Commission was discretionary. At the time of Duplessis' death, it was obvious that there was a pressing need for change.

Conditions were also unsatisfactory from the civil servants' viewpoint, for the job classifications dated from 1925; reforms had been under way since 1943 but were not yet complete. As a result, the classification of personnel with respect to rank and salaries was disorganized and inconsistent.

Jacques Parizeau, current leader of the Parti québécois, *has been one of the symbols of the growing bureaucracy and the administration of the Quebec state since the beginning of the 1960s. [Courtesy Le Devoir and Gilles Paré, Librarian. Photo: Jacques Nadeau.]*

Salaries were so low that many needed a second job to survive. Finally, there were no union rights and no right to strike (Ambroise 1987).

At the beginning of the 1960s, qualified personnel were difficult to find. The nature and practices of the Duplessis government had no doubt repelled the most qualified university graduates. A first step in the much-needed revitalization was a reclassification of posts and increase in salaries. As Coleman (1984) has discussed, the power basis for a new middle class in 1960, which would eventually use the state to establish its predominance over Quebec's society, was very weak.

The main reform of the 1960s, and the basis of the modern civil service, was the 1965 Civil Service Act. The features of the Act were: (1) a definition of the civil service, (2) adoption of a civil service system, (3) establishment of general staff regulations, (4) effective recognition of the merit system, and (5) participation of administrators in the management of the civil service through unionization (Ambroise 1987).

Finally, late in the second half of the 1960s, a large number of graduates qualified to work in a modern state apparatus came out of Quebec universities to fill the ranks of the rapidly growing civil service. Entire classes of university graduates came to work for the Quebec government when the doors of the English-speaking private sector proved to be closed to them.

With the growth of the bureaucracy in the 1960s there was a need for new administrative buildings. The "Édifice H" on Grande-Allée street in Quebec City, on the right side of the Parliament building, is the symbol of this new bureaucratic state. Several departments, such as the Conseil exécutif and International Affairs, have their offices in this building.

The number of permanent employees in the Quebec civil service grew from 29,298 in 1960–1961 to 53,791 in 1969–1970 to 62,542 in 1979–1980 (Ambroise 1987). The slower pace of growth during the 1970s partly indicates the consolidation of the departments after the accelerated evolution. However, these numbers are a bit misleading, because they deal only with the departments. When state enterprises are included, the total number of government employees increases steadily until 1984. Only in the 1980s did social transformations and the state's financial inability to hire additional employees begin to change this trend.

In 1969, the government set up the Civil Service Department to devise measures to enhance the efficiency of civil servants, to advise government on employment contracts, and to act as coordinator in labour relations. Nominations previously authorized by the *Conseil de la trésorerie* (Treasury Council) were to be controlled by this new department. In 1970, this *Conseil* became the *Conseil du trésor* (Treasury Board) and was given additional powers over civil service management.

The entrance to the Treasury Board building in Quebec City.

In 1979, the new civil service law reinforced the merit system for both recruitment and promotions through an evaluation system that compared, planned and achieved performance over the year. Over the 1980s, amendments to the law have attempted to increase minority hirings and guarantee more equality in the treatment of employees. However, since the government has done very little hiring over the decade, these amendments

Following its reelection in 1981, the Lévesque government had reduced substantially public sector employee salaries. A union meeting in 1983. [Courtesy Le Devoir and Gilles Paré, Librarian. Photo: Réjean Meloche.]

have not had a significant effect. Attempts were also made during the 1980s to make the civil service employees more accountable for their actions (Conseil du trésor November 1985).

11.2 THE THREE LEVELS OF BUREAUCRATIC ORGANIZATION

In Quebec three levels or types of state organizations can be distinguished. First, there are the *central agencies* that perform those functions thought to be crucial to the state. Second, there are the *departments* in charge of carrying out the normal activities of government. Finally, there are the *autonomous agencies*, which are given specific missions over which political control is deemed unnecessary.

1. **Central agencies** Central agencies coordinate the interdepartmental development of policy. They also frequently develop policies that other departments must follow, and monitor the performance of the traditional departments or ministries (Campbell and Szablowsky 1979). Civil servants in central agencies work very closely with the Premier and the cabinet. In Quebec, the central agencies are the *Conseil exécutif* and the Treasury Board.

2. **Departments** Some departments (e.g., International Affairs, Municipal Affairs, Finance, Justice) also coordinate activities in other departments, and thus might be called "horizontal." "Vertical" departments, on the other hand, are in charge of providing services directly

to the population or special segments thereof. Of course, "horizontal" departments have their own "vertical" activities (e.g., International Affairs helps Quebec-based companies export their goods and services to the U.S. market). The distinction between these two types of departments is not clear-cut, however (Gélinas 1975).

3. **Autonomous agencies**   At the other end of the administrative system are the various agencies, offices, and state enterprises. Over the past thirty years, a number of autonomous agencies have been created in which employees are not always subject to the rules of the Civil Service Act the way civil servants in regular departments are. In state enterprises, civil servants are insulated from political pressures. Day-to-day operations, as well as hiring and salaries, are not controlled by the Treasury Board as is the case for regular departments. State enterprises gain autonomy by generating their own revenues.

The position of a civil servant in the administrative system determines his or her power over the making of policy. There is a balance between administrative autonomy and the scope of the decisions. In central agencies, civil servants have less autonomy vis-à-vis elected politicians, but participate in decisions that influence the entire state apparatus. In state enterprises, political control is less frequent, but decisions do not involve all government agencies and departments.

11.3 BRITISH, FRENCH, AND AMERICAN INFLUENCES

Though there are difficulties in adapting a political and administrative system from another culture, the civil service in Quebec has been influenced by three other systems: the French, the British, and the American. From the British tradition comes the idea of a neutral and tenured civil service. Institutions such as the *Caisse de dépôt et placement* or the *Office de planification et de développement du Québec* have adopted the French model. Management and budgetary systems have been imported from the United States.

Louis Bernard (1987) has commented that, with a few adjustments in the implementation but not in the principles, the British parliamentary system has worked well in Quebec. Civil servants have continued the reforms started during the Quiet Revolution under three different premiers: Jean Lesage, Daniel Johnson, and Jean-Jacques Bertrand. Later in the 1970s, policies initiated under one government, such as the no-fault auto insurance scheme, have been completed under the next. And even during the 1980s, important policies, such as the privatization of state enterprises initiated under the Parti Quebecois, came to full strength under the Liberal government. In other words, civil servants have been able to continue policies while the elected politicians have come and gone.

In the British parliamentary tradition, a minister is responsible for the decisions and activities of the civil servants in his or her department; similarly, in Quebec, ministers have to answer questions about the activities of their department and even about the activities of the autonomous agencies related to their department.

Following the French model, attempts at economic planning were made during the 1960s with the creation of the *Office de planification et développement du Québec* and the *Bureau d'aménagement de l'est du Québec*. These planning efforts did not work very well, mainly because powerful decision-makers based in Toronto, New York, and Chicago remained beyond the control of these offices. Quebec's economy relies too heavily on continental markets for local planning to work. The *Caisse de dépôt* is one of the few institutions that have entered the economic world sucessfully in order to develop the Quebec economy.

Jean Mercier (1985), in a comparative study of two similar public organizations in Quebec and in Ontario, focusses on the different cultural elements that come into play in organizations based in Quebec. Though overall he finds that organizations in Ontario and Quebec are very similar, differences do exist, in that the Quebec organizations tend to be more centralized and more formal.

Nevertheless, in Quebec organizations, immediate superiors have less power than in Ontario, a difference reflected in the stronger union movement in Quebec within the public sector. The weakness of the immediate superior, Mercier argues, justifies the need to centralize decision-making even more. He concludes that the French influence has hampered the functioning of Quebec organizations.

One Quebec state institution derives from the French influence, namely the *Ecole nationale d'administration publique* (ENAP). One of the institutional reforms of the 1960s, ENAP was created in 1969 as a joint experiment of the Quebec government and Université du Québec networks. Modelled on the French *École nationale d'administration*, ENAP is a graduate school of public administration that trains civil servants in Quebec. The school was initially set up for professionals already working for the government or its autonomous agencies. In 1991, a new program began for students with a bachelor degree who want to join the civil service after completing a master's degree at ENAP.

Finally, the American influence can be felt in the application of methods to control expenses. For example, management systems such as PPBS and Zero Base Budgeting have been adopted. Lately, hiring of some deputy

The École nationale d'administration publique *in Montreal. This school, where many bureaucrats and civil servants were trained, was one result of government growth in the 1960s and the need for specialized employees.*

ministers has been done on a short-term basis only, much like political appointees in the American system.

11.4 NEUTRALITY AND TENURE

In Quebec, as in other parliamentary democracies, civil servants are supposed to be politically neutral. Constitutionally, it is the elected executive of the provincial government who is responsible for formulating policies; civil servants are merely in charge of the implementation of policy. In the modern state, however, the division between politics and administration has become blurred. In fact, fears have been expressed by governments the world over that bureaucracies have become too involved in the political process. The scope and complexity of policymaking has led to the increased involvement of the administrative apparatus that has to create and implement these policies. Also, civil servants and unionized workers in the para-public sector and in state-owned enterprises constitute a sizeable chunk of voters, which has to be taken into consideration.

When governments change, civil servants, with only a few exceptions, remain at their posts. In Quebec, in contrast to the United States, the upper ranks of the civil servants do not change every time a new government is elected. Since 1960, no political party has stayed in power for more than two consecutive mandates, but the civil service, including the technocrats closest to the premiers, have kept their positions. For example, Claude Morin, before becoming a PQ minister, worked closely as a civil servant with premiers Jean Lesage, Daniel Johnson, and Jean-Jacques Bertrand until the early days of Robert Bourassa's reign in 1970.

It is true that because of their technical expertise the importance of civil servants in terms of policy-making has increased. Yet in Quebec they are now less directly involved in politics than they were during the 1960s. In the small state apparatus of that period, decisions were often made in interministerial committees, where ministers and civil servants worked together. It was not unusual during those years for ministers and civil servants whose association dated back to their college years to find themselves drafting policies together. In recent years, with the growth of government operations, the increased number of people working around ministers, and the increased specialization of departments, those kinds of interpersonal relationships do not have the same import on the policy process.

The political influence of civil servants can be seen as cyclical (Bourgault 1988). The upper-level bureaucrats are the ones most likely to have influence over policy-making. Shortly after an election the immediate political staff around a new minister does wield great influence. But this influence decreases rapidly as ministers come to rely more on deputy ministers and upper-level bureaucrats. Deputy ministers, who receive larger salaries than their ministers, are depended upon to provide expert advice, be loyal, work from dawn until midnight if necessary, let the minister be the public figure, and present all relevant information while the minister makes the decisions (Bourgault and Dion 1990).

Studying the higher civil service in Quebec, Jacques Bourgault (1988) has concluded that the legal statutes defining its work have changed very little since the 1960s. Deputy ministers are selected by the Premier with or without consultation with the minister. Some of them are drawn from the civil service and therefore have tenure, but others are hired strictly on a contractual basis. Most deputy ministers consider themselves politically neutral.

The highest civil servant in the hierarchy of Quebec is the *Secrétaire général du Conseil exécutif*, a deputy minister of the Premier. The role of the top civil servant comes more from British parliamentary traditions than from a clear definition of the responsibilities attached to the job. His or her influence over policymaking comes from whatever political skills and influence are developed working with the Premier. The *Secrétaire général* also presides over the other deputy ministers and has a great influence over their careers.

On average, in Western governments, ministers' and deputy ministers' length of service has decreased since the early 1960s. Although different measures have been considered to increase the accountability of deputy ministers toward the Treasury Board or the *Conseil exécutif*, ministers prefer to retain ministerial responsibility and control over the work of their deputies. The relation between ministers and deputy ministers is complex. Ministers expect deputy ministers to be experts in their field, outstanding managers and policy advisors who can also sell the programs and policies to the staff of the department. Although this might seem an impossible task, most ministers (81%) are satisfied with the accomplishments of the deputy ministers they have worked with (Bourgault and Dion 1990).

The absence of a legal status and the selection process have left upper-level civil servants in Quebec in a limbo of uncertainty. They can become policy entrepreneurs, though without the public image, or they can hide behind their ministers. The lack of a clear job description also means that these civil servants can attain more political power than they might otherwise. On the other hand, the absence of a legal framework prevents them from developing a "mandarin" class such as exists in Ottawa or in the French model.

Though the legal status of the upper level has not changed much, its social and economic advantages have evolved greatly. The diversity of the origins of upper-level civil servants has increased greatly over the years, and these people are better trained than their counterparts in the earlier stages of the Quiet Revolution. They come from all sectors of the French-speaking population, and from every university in Quebec (Bourgault 1988). Ethnic minorities are still poorly represented.

Upper-level civil servants have very little contact with the private sector, possibly because their salaries are extremely low compared with upper-level salaries in the private sector and so consequently movement is only from the public to the private sector. The majority of the deputy ministers do not leave for jobs in the private sector; most are laterally transferred to similar positions elsewhere in the government. This mode of transfer gives them the opportunity to develop an overview of the government and certainly helps the coordination of the whole.

In a study done in 1978, Alain Baccigalupo concluded that the upper-level civil servants (deputy ministers and associate and assistant deputy ministers) were almost exclusively men; 97% had university degrees (30% a master's and 9% a Ph.D.). They were between 40 and 55 years old. 58% were previously civil servants, 21% came from the private sector, 9% were from universities, and 6% were political appointees. Bourgault (1988) arrived at similar results.

The people interviewed by Baccigalupo considered themselves to be well paid, though not as well as they would be in the private sector. But they believed they were doing more interesting work and had more power than they would in the private sector. Though overworked, they felt it was worth it because of the mission of the state, and the feeling of being part of a technocratic elite, close to power and to politicians.

The State Versus the Francophone Private Sector

Governments around the world operate through bureaucrats. Due to the increasing number of organizations created by governments and the complexity of modern policymaking, more and more technical or scientific expertise is required to make policies workable. From this perspective, the growth of the public bureaucracy is an indication of growing "technocratic" power.

"Technocrats" achieve their elite status through their knowledge of science and their position in the bureaucracy. In the pejorative sense, technocrats are people who try to justify their existence, income, power by "scientific" rationales, using arguments based on statistics, expert opinion, definition of specific functions, etc. They claim that their rise to power will benefit society as a whole, and that they are not pursuing success and power in their own interests. The focus is on rational analysis of reality, the need to develop, the requirements of modern technology, and so on.

Simard (1977) and Guindon (1978) have argued that in Quebec a new religion has replaced the old one: science. Science is worshipped as the source of progress, enabling the State to produce more public goods. This idea of science leads to a greater respect for the symbols surrounding science, expertise, specialization.

It is unlikely that the importance of technocrats will vanish. For example, the procurement of technologically advanced equipment, such as sophisticated equipment for hospitals or desktop computers, requires the expertise of civil servants who have an understanding of these technologies. Those who handle purchasing, too, must know where the components are produced and be able to judge whether regional development will be stimulated by the acquisition, whether old equipment should be maintained or replaced, and where to find the best technology available.

At the same time, the resources needed to recruit and pay such highly trained people are in short supply. Also, morale may be a problem, for the simple reason that Quebec civil servants feel a lack of purpose after the 1982 and 1991 cuts, the 1986 Gobeil, Fortier, and Scowen reports, and a general aging problem. Downsizing and cutbacks are not as exciting as state-building. Moreover, maintaining high-quality services with less money has proven to be difficult. Tanguay (1987–1988) argues that the 1980s marked

Table 11.1

Evolution of the Civil Service in Quebec, 1961–1987

Year	Number of Public Employees	Rate per 100,000 persons	Index (1961=100)
1961	60,980*	1160	100
1962	65,467*	1219	105
1963	69,870*	1275	110
1964	74,191*	1329	115
1965	78,206	1376	119
1966	83,382	1442	124
1967	91,484	1560	135
1968	92,623	1562	135
1969	98,886	1652	142
1970	93,648	1557	134
1971	99,279	1647	142
1972	100,742	1664	144
1973	107,788	1773	153
1974	110,182	1800	155
1975	112,383	1819	157
1976	114,295	1833	158
1977	126,036	2006	173
1978	135,406	2148	185
1979	132,800	2095	181
1980	135,754	2126	183
1981	129,670	2014	174
1982	134,971	2083	180
1983	131,153	2011	173
1984	155,206	2370	204
1985	153,996	2340	202
1986	149,863	2291	198
1987	141,468	2146	185

* Estimated values.

Source: Simon Langlois, *La Société québécoise en tendances*, 1960–1990 (Quebec: Institut québécois de recherche sur la culture [IQRC], 1990).

the eclipse of the social forces that engineered the province's modernization in the 1960s. The "techno-bureaucracy" has retreated from centre stage in Quebec politics, its place having been taken by a rising class of francophone entrepreneurs in the private sector.

At the end of the 1960s, the civil servants and the business class, after agreeing with each other in the previous decade on the necessity of mod-

The 1983 Front commun *(Common Front) is one of several movements formed since the early 1970s combining members of different public and para-public unions. [Courtesy Le Devoir and Gilles Paré, Librarian. Photo: Jacques Grenier.]*

ernization, were fighting over what the next step should be. In the public sector, the technocrats confronted with the constitutional limits of the provincial state pushed for an independent state. Businesspeople were more in favour of the status quo. Although in recent years there has been a new relationship between the business class and the upper levels of the civil service, a new bourgeoisie benefitting from alliances with the Caisse de dépôt, contracts with Hydro-Québec, etc., sees the state as limiting rather than helping their rise.

Over the 1980s, several technocrats have left to work in the private sector. For example, Michel Bélanger started out as a deputy minister in the 1960s before moving on to become president of the Montreal Stock Exchange, CEO of the National Bank of Canada, and, in 1990, co-chairman of the Bélanger-Campeau Commission. Another example is Guy Coulombe, who after holding several top-level positions in Quebec City and then becoming CEO of the two state enterprises SGF and Hydro-Québec moved to the private sector.

Another reason why technocrats have not been able to maintain their power in society is that they have not developed efficient channels of communication with the population. Civil servants need sources of feedback with regard to the implementation of policies besides traditional political channels such as elections. To meet this need, various consultative bodies have been created, but the public's participation has been weak.

Support can be found, however, in that part of the population which has benefitted from various measures seeking socioeconomic transformations. But even this support has not been cultivated. In fact, a 1985 governmental report on the administrative organization of the Quebec state—the Gobeil Report—suggested that 20 of the aforementioned consultative bodies be abolished because in practice they give civil servants greater input in the decision-making process than the general population in terms of advice to the ministers. Also, the idea, widely accepted in the West after 1945 until the 1980s, that capitalism works better when regulated and when the state takes care of some expensive but necessary activities such as research and development, technical education, etc. has been more contested over the past decade than it has ever been in the previous four.

11.5 CONTROLLING THE BUREAUCRACY

In western Europe and in the United States, how to control the bureaucracy has been amply discussed. But the issue has remained unsolved, and the situation is no different in Quebec (Aberbach et al. 1981).

The main instrument of control in the Quebec government is the Treasury Board, a central agency that assumes the principal responsibilities of the Cabinet in matters of revenues, finance, expenditures, and commitments. The period of rationalization in the 1970s was characterized by growing unionization. Ultimately, this led to the centralization of management in major agencies. In encouragement of fiscal restraint, the Treasury Board has out-distanced its rivals, the Civil Service Department and the Civil Service Commission (replaced in 1978 by the Public Service Commission), becoming over the years the dominant agency. This status was reinforced in 1983 by the abolition of the department of the Civil Service, a reform intended to improve management of the civil service and balance the requirements of the technocratic, economic, and political spheres (Gow 1984).

The National Assembly also had some control over the civil service. In an empirical study done at the end of the 1960s, André Gélinas (1969) found that for the members of the National Assembly the most important functions of the civil service were to give advice to the government, to deliver goods and services to the population, and to implement laws and regulations. Gélinas concluded that MNAs saw the civil service as a subordinate entity, loyal to the government, and that it was the government that throughout the Quiet Revolution had gained power vis-à-vis the National Assembly, not the civil servants. The primacy of expertise and technique, the existence of large organizational networks, and the research and planning branches were only beginning to grow. Only later, during the 1970s, would the power of the civil service become a cause for concern.

In the early 1980s, the Special Commission of the National Assembly on the Civil Service (1982) suggested that civil servants should be held accountable in order to improve the services delivered to the population. While Gélinas stated that until the 1960s, Quebec had been too much governed and not enough administered, the Commission concluded the opposite: that ministers had difficulty assuming their responsibilities. It suggested that too much autonomy was given to civil servants and that the presumption of ministerial non-responsibility was detrimental to the public.

11.6 THE BUREAUCRACY IN THE 1990s

The 1980s brought back a laissez-faire ideology, allowing the state to act only as a complement to the private market. Governments, formerly seen as the solution to social and economic problems, were now perceived as the source of them. According to this "neoconservative" ideology, the size and activities of public bureaucracies should be reduced, and what is left of them more efficiently managed.

After the 1980 referendum and 1981–1982 recession, the Quebec state underwent severe constraints. For a number of years, it had managed its affairs not only as a provincial state, but also with an eye to the possibility that it might eventually become a national state. The referendum result eliminated this possibility, and so an important element of the organizational culture of the state apparatus fell apart.

Two years later, caught in the worst recession since the Great Depression of the 1930s, the government came to the conclusion that it could not afford to uphold the agreements signed with its public and para-public unions during the 1970s. It unilaterally went back on its promise and imposed severe salary cuts on the civil service.

In 1984 the Treasury Board released *Pour une rénovation de l'administration publique*, a document that advocates greater accountability for the civil service. A survey of civil service managers had indicated too much centralization, too many conflicts between the different ministries, and difficulties in adaptation to the economic realities of the early 1980s. On the positive side, these same managers believed the civil service had never been more competent. Asked to list the strong points of the current public administration, they cited the resources available and the competence of individual bureaucrats; but they also believed motivation was low.

The equivalent of many lifetimes of expertise and experience cannot be replaced by massive hiring of recent graduates of various schools of public administration. On-the-job training is an essential component of competence and proficient management.

It is difficult to motivate employees who have a slim chance of being promoted to managerial jobs occupied by people of about the same age. Because the seniority system in the Quebec civil service limits upward mobility, horizontal mobility might have to be increased.

A factor that will have to be dealt with in coming years is the aging of the Quebec civil service. Ideally, an aging workforce means increased experience and managerial skills. But there are problems in the long run: because hiring has been frozen for almost a decade, most of the civil service consists of staff who started working for the government in the late 1960s or early 1970s, and who will likely retire en masse in the second half of this decade. Their replacement in the short time that will be available will be a major challenge.

With fewer resources and growing public demand for benefits, the efficiency of the entire state apparatus will have to be improved. How to do so is the management challenge of the coming decade.

KEY TERMS

Administrative regions   Collective bargaining

Affirmative action   Merit system

REFERENCES AND FURTHER READING

Aberbach, Joel D., Robert D. Putnam, and Bert A. Rockman. 1981. *Bureaucrats and Politicians in Western Democracies*. Cambridge, Mass.: Harvard University Press.

Ambroise, Antoine. 1987. "Political and administrative modernization in Quebec (1960–1985)." *International Review of Administrative Sciences*, 53: 147–170.

Assemblée nationale, Commission spéciale sur la fonction publique. 1982. *Rapport pour une fonction publique sensible aux besoins des citoyens, moderne, efficace et responsable*. Quebec: Gouvernement du Québec.

Baccigalupo, Alain. 1978. *Les Grands Rouages de la machine administrative québécoise*. Montreal: Agence d'Arc.

Bernard, Louis. 1987. *Réflexions sur l'art de se gouverner*. Montreal: Québec/Amérique.

Bourgault, Jacques. 1988. "Evolution de la haute fonction publique des ministères du gouvernement du Québec." In Yves Bélanger and Laurent Lepage, *L'Administration publique québécoise: évolutions sectorielles 1960–1985*. Sillery: Presses de l'Université du Québec. Pp.13–34.

Bourgault, Jacques and Stéphane Dion. 1991. "Haute Fonction publique et changement de gouvernement au Québec: le cas des sous-ministres en titre (1976–1989)." *Revue québécoise de science politique*, 19: 81–106.

Bourgault, Jacques and Stéphane Dion. 1990. "La Satisfaction des ministres envers leurs hauts fonctionnaires: le cas du gouvernement du Québec, 1976–1985." *Canadian Public Administration*, 33: 414–437.

Campbell, Colin and George J. Szablowski. 1979. *The Super-Bureaucrats: Structure and Behaviour in Central Agencies.* Toronto: Macmillan.

Coleman, William D. 1984. *The Independence Movement in Quebec, 1945–1980.* Toronto: University of Toronto Press.

Conseil du trésor. November 1985. *Pour une rénovation de l'administration publique—l'administration publique sous le regard de ses gestionnaires: résultats d'un sondage.* Quebec: Gouvernement du Québec.

Gélinas, André. 1969. *Les Parlementaires et l'administration au Québec.* Quebec: Presses de l'Université Laval.

Gélinas, André. 1975. *Organismes autonomes et centraux.* Montreal: Presses de l'Université du Québec.

Gow, James Iain. 1979. "L'Administration québécoise de 1867 à 1900: un état en formation."*Canadian Journal of Political Science*, 12: 555–620.

Gow, James Iain. 1984. "La Réforme institutionnelle de la fonction publique de 1983." *Revue québécoise de science politique*, No. 6: 51–101.

Gow, James Iain. 1990. "L'Administration publique dans le discours politique au Québec, de Lord Durham à nos jours." *Canadian Journal of Political Science*, 23: 685–711.

Guindon, Hubert. 1978. "The modernization of Quebec and the legitimacy of the Canadian state." In Daniel Glenday, Hubert Guindon, and Allan Torowetz (eds.), *Modernization and the Canadian State.* Toronto: Macmillan. Pp. 212–246.

Mercier, Jean. 1985. "Le Phénomène bureaucratique et le Canada français: quelques données empiriques et leur interprétation." *Canadian Journal of Political Science*, 18: 31–55.

Simard, Jean-Jacques. 1977. "La Longue Marche des technocrates." *Recherches sociographiques*, 18: 93–132.

Tanguay, A. Brian. 1987–1988. "Business, labor, and the state in the 'new' Quebec." *American Review of Canadian Studies*, 17: 395–408.

THE
COURTS

All too often, textbooks on Canadian politics and government neglect to consider judicial institutions, as if they operated outside the realm of politics. Yet the judiciary is an integral part of the state and the political process; as the supreme arbiter of the socioeconomic relations of individuals in a society, the judiciary is eminently and unavoidably political. Like the bureaucracy, judges and courts and the administrators of justice are the natural extension of the legislator in society. Any account of political and administrative institutions would be incomplete without the judicial institutions. As we will see, given the historical nature of parliamentary institutions and constitutional powers in Canada, the judiciary in Quebec plays a central role in carrying out policy.

Typically, the law is divided into two broad areas: private and public. The realm of private law deals with the rules governing social and economic interrelations of citizens. In Quebec, these rules are embodied in the Civil Code and comprise everything that pertains to interpersonal relationships, property, contracts, and commerce. Public law is generally understood to include the rules governing the relationship between the state and the citizens, and between individual citizens in matters that stem directly from the public domain. Constitutional law and administrative law—and criminal law, to the extent that criminal prosecution is a state responsibility—are branches of public law.

12.1 FRAMEWORK OF LAW AND ADMINISTRATION OF JUSTICE: CONSTITUTIONAL SOURCES

The character and nature of both public and private law in Quebec derive essentially from Canada's constitutional arrangement and history. In fact, Quebec's judicial system, and its evolution, is a direct product of the Canadian constitution and cannot be defined or evaluated separately on its own. It has always been part of a larger legal system and encompassing legal principles. Not only does Quebec law integrate legal and judicial influences inherited from its bicultural colonial past—first French and then British—it also has existed for the past 125 years within a constitutional regime outside the province's control.

The old Quebec City law courts close to the Château Frontenac.

Quebec's judicial system is largely based on the British parliamentary model, imposed in Quebec at the time of the British Conquest of 1760. While parliamentary sovereignty is paramount in the British tradition, its concomitant principle of legislative supremacy has always been substantially curtailed in Quebec. The main reason for this is that the Canadian constitution has supra-legislative power. In Canada, all the laws, legislations, and rules of the provincial and federal government must be enacted in conformity with the tenets of the Canadian constitution regarding administrative jurisdictions and fundamental rights. Only in exceptional cases is any recourse allowed to the "notwithstanding clause"—Article 33 of the Charter of Rights—and provinces may use this clause only in regard to certain articles in the Charter and not to the overall Constitution.

In a sense, then, it can be said that the judiciary branch is the ultimate site of power in Canadian, and by extension in Quebec society, for it is incumbent on the courts to interpret and apply the Constitution when it contravenes the laws of the federal and provincial legislatures.

The Quebec legal and judicial system is based on a hierarchy of bodies of law, of which the Constitution is firmly located at the top. The formal laws adopted by the federal and Quebec legislatures are next; in third place is the jurisprudence of judiciary tribunals. Finally, at the bottom of the hierarchy are administrative and governmental decisions. This hierarchy is stable and informs the whole judicial logic. It flows from top to bottom and dictates legal reasoning; that is, the legal principles of a law or rule must stem from or abide by some higher source. Thus, for example, it is illegal for legislators to make laws that contravene articles of the Constitution; similarly, judiciary decisions cannot rest solely on jurisprudence.

Another factor that shapes the functioning of Quebec's judicial institutions is the jurisdictional division between federal and provincial law. As we saw in the chapter on constitutional history, the Constitution Act of 1867 determined the legislative domains of the provincial and federal legislatures. Some jurisdictions are clear-cut and belong unequivocally and exclusively to one or the other levels of government; others overlap in shared domains. As a result, Quebec is subject to the logic of two different legal systems, as federal and provincial law exist as two parallel legal structures. In the case of fundamental rights, for example, the Constitution was supplemented by a "Charter of Rights and Freedoms" in 1982 that is applicable to both levels of government. But other charters of rights in Canada have been enacted by both Parliament and provincial legislatures. Although Quebec has its own "Charter of Rights and Freedoms," its charter cannot be invoked in matters of federal jurisdiction; similarly, the Canadian law on human rights (1977) cannot be invoked in provincial matters.

In Quebec, this dual legal logic is further complicated by the fact that each stems from a different conception of law. Indeed, a chief peculiarity of Quebec law is that it is based on the French legal system, but operates with reference to federal law founded on English public law, the so-called common law. The result is an assortment of judicial institutions that are intertwined into a kind of hybrid system.

Until 1760, as a French colony, Quebec was governed by the French civil law introduced in 1663 by Louis XIV. The colony was provided with an organized legal system and an initial body of written law known as the

Coutume de Paris. It was adapted to local conditions and supplemented by royal edicts and ordinances. After the Conquest, English public law was introduced in Quebec, but French private law was maintained. In fact, the nature of the legal system remained ambiguous for over a decade, marked by such directives as the 1763 ordinance from Governor James Murray (the first British governor of Quebec) stating that common law would be in force "as much as possible." Wary of growing political discontent in the American colonies, British authorities agreed to maintain French private law in the colony, in hopes of securing the loyalty of their North American French subjects. The Quebec Act of 1774 provided that French civil law would prevail in matters concerning property and civil rights. However, the more enlightened aspects of English law (such as *habeas corpus*, trial by jury, and an elected assembly) were accepted as common law principles to govern public and criminal law.

In the years following the American Revolution, an influx of loyalists to Canadian territory helped to revive the dispute over the introduction of English law, especially in commercial matters. The problem was eventually resolved with the 1791 Constitution, which divided the former colony into Lower Canada (later, Quebec) and Upper Canada (later, Ontario). In Lower Canada, French civil law continued to prevail, while Upper Canada became an exclusively common law jurisdiction. This division of legal systems and philosophies remained in force when the two provinces were administratively reunited by the Union Act of 1840, and later at Confederation in 1867. Throughout the history of Quebec, French civil law has been maintained, but its influence stops at the borders of the province. Francophones outside Quebec are ruled by English law (Lemieux 1989: 17).

By the 1850s, Quebec civil law consisted of the Coutume de Paris plus a hodge-podge of pre-1664 ordinances; ordinances adopted by New France's *Conseil souverain* until 1759; various regulations by the intendants; case law; and acts of the new colonial institutions set up after 1763. It had become increasingly apparent that this complex and changeable body of law needed to be codified. Work on the code was commissioned by the Quebec legislature and began in 1859. The final report was submitted in 1866 as the Civil Code of Lower Canada. It was divided into four books. Book One covered the law of persons, Book Two the law of property, Book Three contracts and torts, and Book Four commercial law. Extremely flexible, the Code is, with few major alterations, still in use today, more than one hundred years after its adoption. However, in view of the economic and social changes in the past century, a comprehensive revision of the Civil Code has been necessary. This task was started in 1962 under the leadership of P. A. Crépeau, a law professor at McGill University, and 15 years later the Civil Code Revision office submitted a revised version, which it took another 10 years to fine-tune. Of the new Quebec Civil Code, only Book Two, dealing with family law, has been implemented. Book One, dealing with persons and property has merely been adopted and the other Books are still being discussed.

In the Canadian context, this Civil Code has certain political connotations. In a common law world, it operates as a kind of bulwark for Quebec's so-called distinctiveness. The fundamental difference between the two is that the civil law approach works from an accepted set of principles included in the civil code, and each case is decided according to these basic principles; in the common law approach, judgements in previous cases determine the principles to be applied to problems as they emerge. That is, the basic feature of the common law approach is that it attaches greater importance to precedent than civil law systems.

The McGill law school, where both civil and common law are taught, exemplifies the division of legal systems and philosophies in force both inside and outside Quebec. Throughout Quebec's history, French civil law has been maintained, while francophones outside Quebec are ruled by common law.

Understandably, Quebec's civil law has been unable to operate in isolation from the common law system; over the years, common law has had a pervasive influence on civil law and its underlying legal philosophy. But through it all, Quebec's civil law has retained its own coherence and logic. In fact, when Quebec courts operate within a civil law approach, they normally refuse to apply common law principles. Even the Supreme Court, an essentially common law institution, applies civil law principles in matters that pertain essentially to the Civil Code of Quebec.

12.2 STRUCTURE OF THE JUDICIARY

Tasks of the Judiciary

The judiciary in Quebec basically performs two kinds of tasks: judicial and administrative. To most citizens, it is the judicial function that is the most obvious: courts hear disputes between parties, evaluate and punish delinquent behaviour, adjudicate, and issue injunctions. But beyond these eminently visible activities, there is a whole administrative dimension to the courts that makes up a sizeable chunk of their responsibilities. It is incumbent on the judiciary in Quebec to collect fines, unpaid alimonies, and voluntary deposits toward the payment of debt; issue distraints and summonses; register corporate names; keep the records of dead notaries; and to register judicial deeds such as marriages and name changes.

All of these tasks are assigned to the different courts according to the responsibilities set out in the Constitution and the various provincial and federal legislations. To each court corresponds particular areas of jurisdiction and functions, performed with the assistance of a complete administrative apparatus. Both the courts and their administrative arms make up a complex judiciary structure whose aim is to bring justice and enforce the rule of law as diligently as possible.

Organization of the Judiciary[1]

The judiciary system and the administration of justice in Quebec are defined by clear constitutional parameters that divide responsibility for the administration of justice between the federal and provincial territorial governments. Section 92(14) of the Constitution Act of 1867 states that provincial legislatures can make laws bearing upon "the Administration of Justice in the Province, including the Constitution, Maintenance and Organization of Provincial Courts, both of Civil and of Criminal jurisdiction and including Procedure in Civil Matters in those Courts." Section 91(27) gives the federal government the power to make laws pertaining to "the Criminal Law, except the Constitution of Courts of Criminal jurisdiction,

---

1. This section and that entitled "Federal Courts" borrow from Statistics Canada, Civil Courts in Canada, 1985. Catalogue 85–209.

but including the Procedure in Criminal Matters." Section 101 allows Parliament to "provide for the Constitution, maintenance and organization of a general court of appeal for Canada, and for the establishment of any additional courts for the better administration of the laws of Canada. It is under the authority of Section 101 that the Supreme Court of Canada, the Federal Court of Canada and the Tax Court of Canada have been established. Finally, Section 96 states: "the Governor General shall appoint the Judges of the Superior, District and County Courts in each Province...."

In other words, the organization of courts in Quebec falls within the jurisdiction of the Quebec legislature. However, the nomination of judges of superior courts—for example, of the Court of Appeal or the Superior Court—is a federal responsibility. The organization of Quebec courts is governed by the *Loi sur les tribunaux judiciaires* (Court of Justice Act). This particular piece of legislation establishes civil and criminal courts (the Superior Court, the Court of Quebec, and the municipal courts) and an appellate court (the Court of Appeal). Of course, Quebecers are also subject to the jurisdiction of the Supreme Court of Canada and the Federal Court. While these are not, in the strict sense, part of the Quebec judiciary system, they are nonetheless part of the general judiciary environment of Quebecers as citizens of Canada. Finally, a whole array of administrative tribunals operate parallel to the main courts. These will be discussed in the next section.

First Instance Courts

The Superior Court   The Superior Court consists of 132 judges, including a Chief Justice, a Senior Associate Chief Justice, and an Associate Chief Justice, appointed federally. There are also 20 "supernumerary" (part-time) judges.

In civil matters, the Superior Court sits in 49 permanent locations and goes "on circuit" to six others. In criminal matters, the Court sits in 40 permanent locations and one "circuit" location. The Chief Justice resides in either Montreal or Quebec.

When the Chief Justice resides in Quebec City, the Senior Associate Chief Justice performs the duties of the Chief Justice in the Montreal division and must reside in or near Montreal. When the Chief Justice resides in Montreal, the Senior Associate Chief Justice performs the duties of the Chief Justice in the Quebec City division and must reside in or near Quebec City. Each of the "puisne" (regular) judges is assigned to a specific judicial district, but may sit in other districts when necessary.

The Superior Court is the court of original general jurisdiction for Quebec. It holds supervisory powers over all lower courts in Quebec and hears every case not assigned exclusively to another court by a specific provision of law. It has both civil and criminal jurisdiction. The Superior Court holds all the powers of a court as outlined in Section 96 of the Constitution Act of 1987. Judges of the Superior Court are also justices of the peace and coroners throughout Quebec.

In civil matters, the Superior Court generally hears cases in which the value of the claim exceeds $15,000. It also has jurisdiction in non-contentious matters such as class-action suits, rectification of the vital statistics registers, probate, and matters falling under the Divorce Act or the Bankruptcy Act (both federal statutes).

In criminal matters, the Court sits both as a "court of first instance" and as an appeal court. It hears appeals allowed under Section XXIV of the Criminal Code. When sitting as a criminal court of first instance, the Superior Court is required to hold at least three terms per year in each district.

The Court of Quebec   The Court of Quebec was established by an act of the Quebec legislature on June 17, 1988. The "Act to Amend the Courts of Justice and Other Legislation" came into force on August 31 of that year, merging into a single judicial body the former Provincial Court, the Court of the Sessions of the Peace, and the Youth Court, which formerly had functioned independently of each other with specific jurisdictional responsibilities, as outlined below. The Court of Quebec now performs all the duties for which these three courts were formerly responsible.

The jurisdiction of the Provincial Court, which comprised 155 judges nominated by the Quebec government, was mainly civil matters. It also had jurisdiction over certain criminal matters. Exclusive jurisdiction was assigned to this Court over:

- Claims less than $15,000, except alimony suits and claims under the Federal Court of Canada
- Execution or rescission of contracts when the plaintiff's interest is less than $15,000
- Annulment of commercial leases when the amount claimed for rent and damages is less than $15,000 (*residential* leases being under the exclusive jurisdiction of the Rental Board)
- Recovery of taxes or other sums due a municipal or school corporation under the Municipal Code or any general or special law or bylaw thereunder, and questions regarding the holding or exercise of an office in such a corporation
- Voluntary payments to creditors (except in bankruptcy cases)
- Exemptions of fixed assets which would normally be taxable for municipal or school purposes
- All actions under the Code concerning certain extraordinary remedies

and relating to the usurpation, holding, or unlawful exercise of an office in a municipality or school corporation

The Provincial Court also comprised a Small Claims Division whose jurisdiction included claims not exceeding $3,000 related to a contract, quasi-contract, offence, or quasi-offence, against a debtor either resident or having a place of business in Quebec launched by any private citizen in his/ her own name and on his/her own behalf or by a tutor or curator in his/her official capacity. The jurisdiction of Small Claims also extended to any motion for the dissolution, rescission, or cancellation of a contract where the value of the contract and amount claimed did not exceed $3,000.

In criminal and penal matters, judges of the Provincial Court had the same powers as judges of the Court of the Sessions of the Peace. Provincial Court judges heard certain criminal and penal matters in judicial districts not served by the Court of the Sessions of the Peace. For example, they could preside over summary conviction cases and over hearings for all but the most serious indictable offences. They also had jurisdiction in federal penal matters, generally involving traffic violations and impaired driving charges. The Provincial Court was, however, primarily a court of civil jurisdiction dealing with matters under the exclusive control of the provincial government. Provisions of the Courts of Justice Act relating to the criminal jurisdiction of the Provincial Court must be viewed as supplementary to any similar provisions enacted by Parliament as regards matters within its exclusive control.

A judge of the Provincial Court could also act as member of the Labour Court or as Director General of Elections. In addition, the judge could perform other quasi-judicial duties for the government as set out in the Courts of Justice Act.

The Court of the Sessions of the Peace was composed of 74 provincially appointed judges and, as a court of first instance, heard criminal matters only. Offences referred to in Section 483 of the Criminal Code (e.g., thefts of less than $1,000) were under the exclusive jurisdiction of this Court. It had concurrent jurisdiction in certain cases with the Superior Court.

Criminal acts not the exclusive domain of the Superior Court may be heard either by a judge alone in the Court of the Sessions of the Peace or by a judge and jury in Superior Court. This is the only choice open to anyone accused of a crime. However, with approval from the Crown, a defendant who initially elects trial by judge and jury may, after the preliminary inquiry but before the criminal trial begins in Superior Court, elect to be tried by judge alone in the Court of the Sessions of the Peace. The Court of the Sessions of the Peace may hear, as well, certain breaches of federal and provincial laws.

Sessions Court judges could also hold quasi-judicial positions pursuant to Section 82 of the Courts of Justice Act. A judge could act as president or vice president of a commission, board, bureau, or committee instituted under a Quebec law, or serve as a member of the Public Security Commission of the Montreal Urban Community or the Quebec Police Commission. A Sessions Court judge could in addition act as an arbitrator or carry out any mandate entrusted to him or her by the Governor in Council.

The Youth Court was composed of 45 provincially appointed judges and its jurisdiction covered all cases in which a Quebec law was breached by a person under 18 years of age. It also exercised exclusive jurisdiction in adoption matters.

The Court of Quebec incorporates into one body all the responsibilities of these three courts. The scope of its jurisdiction represents a major reform in Quebec's judicial structures. This reform sought to solve three major problems that had arisen over the years (Belleau 1988):

1. Overlap in the three courts had obscured the division of responsibility. The result was confusion as to which court was supposed to handle a dispute or point of contention. The Court of Quebec was established in hopes of ending the confusion by reducing the number and variety of courts.

2. The specialization and separation of courts prevented judges from performing their duties in the most efficacious manner. A judge attached to the Youth Court, for example, was not allowed to preside, even temporarily, over a case in the Provincial Court. This meant that in remote districts where no resident judges were available, cases could not be heard by a judge from another court who happened to be in the district. Long delays became common. Now, in the Court of Quebec, a judge formerly assigned to the Provincial Court is required to hear cases that would traditionally have been heard in the Youth Court or the Sessions of the Peace and vice versa. The reform increases the mobility of the judges.

3. Finally, the consolidation was intended to standardize management practices and administrative policies that hitherto differed considerably from one court to another, even one region to another, with no apparent justification. The new judicial structure should allow for better and cheaper coordination and planning of human, material, and financial resources.

Municipal Courts   Municipal courts may establish their own municipalities by passing a bylaw, subject to approval by the Minister of Justice and the Minister of Municipal Affairs. The jurisdiction of a Municipal Court is confined to the geographic boundaries of the municipality it serves and governed by a number of statutes. There are 14 full-time judges in Montreal, 2 in Quebec City, and 3 in Laval. Employees of municipal courts are hired by the municipalities involved.

In civil matters, municipal judges hear actions primarily for the recovery of taxes or licence fees owed to municipalities. In penal matters, their jurisdiction extends to breaches of municipal bylaws and certain provincial laws such as the Highway Code. In criminal matters, municipal judges are *ex officio* justices of the peace. As soon as the council of a municipality has established a Municipal Court, no judge of the Court of Quebec or justice of the peace may give consideration to infringements of the Cities and Towns Act, the city charter, or any bylaws of the council.

The territorial jurisdiction of municipal judges is generally limited to the municipality in which they sit. The Municipal Courts Act does provide, however, that the council of any municipality may adopt a bylaw to submit its territory to the jurisdiction of the Municipal Court of another municipality within a radius of ten miles. The province may withhold its approval for such a bylaw.

The final decision of any Municipal Court case can be taken to the Court of Appeal if the amount in dispute exceeds $500 or if the action relates to the interpretation of a contract that has a value of at least $500 to which the municipality is a party.

Whenever the judgement of a municipal judge or Municipal Court affects future rights, a defendant may ask that the case be transmitted to the Superior Court of the same district. The Municipal Courts of Montreal, Quebec City, and Laval are governed by special statutes. While judges of other municipal courts generally sit part-time, these three courts have permanent judges with more extensive powers in penal and criminal matters. Their jurisdiction is similar to that of Sessions Court judges.

Court of Appeal   The Court of Appeal is the general appeal tribunal for Quebec. It hears appeals on any judgement. The Court consists of one Chief Justice and 15 puisne justices. These justices are governed by the Judges Act and are appointed federally by the Governor in Council. In addition, there are four supernumerary justices.

The jurisdiction of the Court of Appeal extends throughout Quebec. Appeals from judgements rendered in certain western judicial districts of the province are heard in Montreal, while all others are heard in Quebec City. Five judges must reside in or near Quebec City and 11 must reside in the Montreal area. Generally, the judges preside over hearings in their own district, although the Chief Justice may vary this arrangement.

In civil matters, an appeal can be forwarded to the Court from any of the following:

- Any final judgement of the Superior Court or the Court of Quebec, except in cases where the amount of the claim is less than $10,000

- Any final judgement of the Court of Quebec in cases where that court has exclusive jurisdiction under any act other than the Code of Civil Procedure

- Any other final judgement of the Superior Court, the Court of Quebec, or a judge of the Court of Appeal, when the dispute is one that ought to be submitted to the Court of Appeal

- Any final judgement rendered in matters of contempt of court for which there is no other recourse

- Any interlocutory judgement of the Superior Court, the Court of Quebec, or, in adoption matters, the Youth Court, when such judgement decides an issue in part, or when it orders the doing of anything that cannot be remedied by the final judgement, or when it needlessly delays proceedings (an interlocutory judgement rendered during a hearing cannot be appealed immediately unless it disallows an objection to evidence)

- Any judgement or order rendered under Book VI of the Code of Civil Procedure (non-contentious matters)

- Any judgement or order rendered in adoption matters

The Court has jurisdiction to hear, on first appeal, any case resulting from a trial held before a court of criminal jurisdiction. This includes appeals from a verdict pronounced by either a judge and jury or judge alone. It also hears, on second appeal, decisions rendered by the Superior Court in summary conviction cases for offences contemplated in Part XXIV of the Criminal Code.

Appeals are heard by three judges, although the Chief Justice may increase this number when deemed necessary. The Court of Appeal also studies various constitutional questions put before it by the Government.

In civil matters, an appeal can be heard by the Supreme Court of Canada from any judgement rendered by the Quebec Court of Appeal when the Supreme Court is of the opinion that, by reason of its public importance or the importance of any issue of law and fact involved, it is a matter that ought to be decided by the Supreme Court.

In criminal matters involving indictable offences, a person whose conviction is affirmed by the Court of Appeal, or whose acquittal is set aside by the Court of Appeal, may further appeal to the Supreme Court on any question of law if either a judge of the Court of Appeal dissents or leave to appeal is granted by the Supreme Court.

Federal Courts

Federal Court   The Federal Court is a superior court whose jurisdiction covers federal administrative law and parts of the federal statutes. It was established in 1970 by an Act of Parliament. It is a travelling court with headquarters in Ottawa.

It is incumbent upon the Government to nominate the 16 judges of this Court. Ten of them sit on the trial division, the other six in the appellate division, but all are members of both divisions. Four of these judges must be from the province of Quebec.

In the first instance, the Federal Court hears disputes between citizens and the federal public administration. It also hears disputes in matters pertaining to maritime law and industrial ownership. Appeals in fiscal and citizenship matters are heard in the first-instance division as well. The appellate division of the Federal Court hears appeals from federal administrative tribunals and against decisions rendered in its first-instance division.

Tax Court of Canada   Created by an Act of Parliament in 1983, the Tax Court of Canada consists of a chief judge, an associate chief judge, and not more than ten other judges. The Court can sit anywhere in Canada and has jurisdiction to hear and determine appeals on matters arising under the Income Tax Act, the Canada Pension Plan, the Petroleum and Gas Revenue Tax Act, Part IV of the Unemployment Insurance Act, 1971, and any other Act of Parliament in respect of which an appeal is filed.

Supreme Court of Canada   The Supreme Court of Canada, located in Ottawa, is the highest court in the country; its decisions supersede those

The Supreme Court of Canada in Ottawa. Three of the nine judges are chosen by the Quebec government.

of all other courts. Its responsibilities and jurisdiction are defined by an Act of Parliament.

This Court is composed of nine judges including one Chief Justice and eight puisne judges. They are nominated and paid by the federal government. At least three of these judges must either come from Quebec's Court of Appeal or Superior Court or be a member of the Quebec Bar.

In addition to being the interpreter of the Canadian constitution, the Supreme Court is an appellate court of last instance in both criminal and civil matters. Appeals in the Supreme Court are made upon permission only; they bear exclusively on any judgement of a court of last resort in a province and they are heard only if deemed by the Supreme Court to be of sufficient legal and public importance. There can be appeal of a guilty verdict in the Supreme Court, provided a Court of Appeal judge has dissented on a question of law.

12.3 JUDGES AND JUDGING

It is incumbent upon judges to dispense justice, i.e., to delineate the rights and obligations of individuals, corporations, and the state in the cases over which they preside. The judge's role is that of an impartial arbiter between two parties: between the state and citizens in criminal trials, between citizens, or between corporations in civil suits. This impartiality is the central element of the judicial process.

The process by which a judgement is reached is threefold:

1. The judge must consider the facts presented by both parties during a trial or the hearing of a case. In keeping with the British legal tradition, gathering evidence is the responsibility of the parties involved in the trial. In a criminal case, the Crown prosecutor must, with the support of material evidence and testimonies, convince the court that the accused is guilty of a criminal offence. In civil cases the plaintiff is responsible for providing all the relevant elements and testimonies that will allow him/her to rest his/her case; the defendant is likewise permitted to submit evidence to prove the plaintiff wrong. The judge's role is to make sure that each side has the opportunity to present the evidence and state its case. Then, the judge's evaluation of the situation must rest solely on the facts presented.

2. The judge must determine what legal rules apply to the facts under consideration. It is his/her duty to locate the law(s) or statute(s) within existing legislation that applies to the case. In the interests of equality for all, the judge must apply the same treatment to all identical cases. The judge is bound by the law. This said, however, he/she has

considerable leeway in applying the law, for the law is never totally clear or perfectly defined. In Quebec civil law, the judge has to produce a judgement on every case brought before him/her, even if no clear law or legal guideline is available. Jurisprudence doctrine, custom, or even ideas of natural justice may often be his/her only recourse. Quebec judges thus have far-reaching powers of interpretation and have often been called makers of law.

3. Finally, the judge must consider the facts with regard to the legal norm —the constraints and dictates of the applicable law—and reach a verdict or a decision. This decision is final and binding for both litigants. In criminal trials with jury, the judge must inform jury members of their responsibility and of the legal implications of the positions of both the Crown prosecutor and the accused, drawing their attention to the nature of evidence submitted by the two parties.

In rendering judgements, the sole requirement of Quebec judges is that they be totally impartial, acting only within the authority of the law. This independence, however, is not without its obligations: judges must never be heard to criticize the law; they must apply it in accordance with the legislators' intentions; and they must refrain from any involvement in politics.

In Quebec, judges cannot be removed by arbitrary government decision, but only if found guilty of grave ethical, moral, or behavioural breaches in carrying out their duties. Judges can remain in their jobs until age 75, though they may be assigned a lighter workload after 65. They are also guaranteed immunity from lawsuits for any action performed in their capacity as judges. Judges are offered generous remuneration so as to attract the best candidates and ensure their impartiality. A judge is not allowed to pursue any other profession.

Finally, a note on socioprofessional characteristics. Nine out of ten Quebec judges are male, French-speaking lawyers. Many have a bachelor's degree in a related field and can boast twenty years' experience in private practice. Prior to entering the judicature, most have been active members of the Quebec Bar. They have exercised their function as judges for eight years on average. Two-thirds of Quebec judges are from the professional or business class, and they often circulate within a professional network in which ex-partners and associates have become judges as well (Giard and Proulx 1985: 81–82).

12.4 THE JUDICIAL SYSTEM AND THE RELATIONSHIP BETWEEN CITIZENS AND THE STATE

One of the features of modern democratic theory is the equality before the law and the equal access to justice for all members of society. In Quebec, as in the rest of Canada, the state is not above the law. Although legal prescriptions and directives originate from the government, all its organizations and components are bound by the same statutes. Citizens and corporations who feel injured by a particular action or intervention can resort to the courts. In addition to the judiciary courts described in the preceding section, there exist administrative tribunals whose purpose is to hear litigations bearing on citizens' complaints against the administrative actions of the state.

The right to counsel is an integral part of a long constitutional and legal tradition in Canada, one that in recent years has been unequivocally supported and enhanced. By adhering to the 1966 International Agreement of Civil and Political Rights and to the Universal Declaration of Human Rights in 1978, by enacting the Bill of Rights in 1960, and by entrenching the Charter of Rights and Freedoms in 1982, Canada has demonstrated its commitment to legal rights for every individual. This includes the right to legal representation free of charge if it is beyond one's financial means and one's right under arrest or detention to retain and instruct counsel without delay. Every individual has the right to equal protection and benefit of the law without discrimination.

The true test of a legal system is not its structural complexity and sophistication but the quality and expediency with which it secures equality of treatment and access to justice. Recent developments show that such questions have been a central sociopolitical concern in Quebec

1. Administrative Tribunals

Quebec borrows the distinction between "courts" and "statutory tribunals" from English law. *Courts* are headed by non-removable judges with legal training whose responsibility it is to apply rules of the law. *Statutory tribunals*, often referred to as *administrative tribunals*, emerged largely as a result of numerous disputes occasioned by the implementation of new socioeconomic programs. Though they also make decisions on rules of law, their jurisdiction is limited and specialized. Members of an administrative tribunal are not necessarily jurists and they have neither the status nor the independence of regular court judges. The procedures and rules for admission of evidence are normally more flexible and simpler than those used in regular courts.

A broad definition of administrative tribunals would include all public authorities mandated to make decisions other than the courts of justice. Administrative tribunals can be structured as a board, commission, or bureau as well as a tribunal.

2. Legal Aid

The social reform movements of the 1960s and 1970s stimulated debates over the way legal assistance services should be delivered and deeply influenced the establishment of legal aid systems in Canada. Basically, two models were proposed. One, the "judicare" model, suggested that legal services be extended to the needy through private law firms. The other model involved the community clinic concept, and was viewed as a means of challenging the legal system in the interests of the poor. The latter model influenced the creation of experimental community legal clinics throughout Canada. These experiments and the attention they raised in the legal milieu laid the foundation for comprehensive legal aid system in Canada

Quebec legal aid merges elements of the two models: it operates both in the spirit of "judicare" and within the structural context of community legal clinics.

The Legal Aid Bureau, created by the Bar of Montreal, was Quebec's first legal aid service. In its early days, a full-time lawyer at the Bureau processed applications for aid: if an application was accepted, the client was referred to a private lawyer who provided services free of charge. Court costs were covered by members of the Bar through contributions to the Bureau.

Montreal's Palais de justice, *where most criminal and civil suits are contested.*
This building also houses the Legal Aid Bureau.

In an attempt to establish a broader service, the government of Quebec began granting funds to the Legal Aid Bureau in 1967. In 1971, legal aid clinics started to appear in economically disadvantaged areas.

One of these clinics—a demonstration project in Pointe St. Charles, Montreal called Community Legal Services Inc.—was particularly successful, and the first director of that project was appointed by the Quebec's Ministry of Justice to draft legislation for a new legal aid plan. When it appeared, the Quebec Bar opposed the draft legislation. However, two major compromises were reached: the client's right to choose a private rather than a staff lawyer was included, and local administrative control was deemphasized in favour of regional corporations to oversee the general functions of local offices. The Legal Aid Act was passed in 1972 and the Legal Services Commission was appointed in 1973. Coverage extends to both criminal and civil law.

The question of financial eligibility is central to the mission of any legal aid plan. As the current eligibility criteria are still those effective in 1985, the number of eligible people is diminishing every year. The financial criteria are too low and do not take into account increases in the cost of living, decreasing disposable income, and the new poverty line.

According to Statistics Canada, a family of three living in Montreal in 1990 is considered low-income if its weekly income is less than $471. The Canadian Council of Social Development states that with a weekly income of less than $492 a family of three lives below the poverty line. Yet, this same family will have access to legal aid only if its weekly income does not exceed $230. The discrepancy between eligibility criteria and the reality of poverty is such that an increasing number of low-income or poor people no longer qualify for legal aid. In the 1990 report of the Legal Services Commission, this situation was noted with alarm by the chairman of the commission; the percentage of requests for legal aid that had been accepted had increased only marginally (about 2 percent a year) since 1985. If criteria were not indexed, the chairman warned, only the very poorest welfare recipients will be able to qualify.

As it stands now, minimum-wage single workers (the working poor) no longer qualify, which runs counter to the original intent of the system. A legal aid program does not properly meet its mandate if it excludes de facto most poor people besides welfare recipients and people of no income.

As we see, although the judicial system in Quebec has been adapted to reflect the exigencies of democratic development, it is still lagging behind in some areas. The failure to adapt the legal aid system to changing socio-economic realities indicates clearly that further adjustments are needed.

KEY TERMS

Charter of Rights and Freedoms

Civil Code

Class-action suit

Court of Quebec

Court of the Sessions of the Peace

Legal Aid Bureau

Small claims court

REFERENCES AND FURTHER READING

Belleau, Charles. 1988. "Jalon d'une réforme globale de l'organisation judiciaire au Québec: la Cour du Québec." *Revue générale de droit*, 19 (December): 849–864.

Boisvert, Yves. "Généreuse à ses débuts, l'aide juridique est devenue chiche." 1992. *La Presse*, February 16. P. A–1.

Lemaître-Auger, Jacques. 1981. "L'Aide juridique au Québec." *Canadian Community Law Journal*, 5: 68–77.

Lemieux, Denis. 1989. "The Quebec civil law system in a common law world: the seven crises." *Juridical Review*, June: 16–31.

Giard, Monique and Marcel Proulx. 1985. *Pour comprendre l'appareil judiciaire québécois*. Sillery: Presses de l'Université du Québec.

Goulet, Jean. 1988. "The Quebec legal system." *Law Library Journal*, 73 (Spring): 354–381.

Sormany, Louis. 1989. "The creation of the Court of Quebec." *Commonwealth Law Bulletin*, 15 (January): 295–296.

Statistics Canada. 1985. *Civil Courts in Canada*. Catalogue 85–209.

Statistics Canada. 1986. *Legal Aid in Canada 1985*. (Ottawa: Supply and Services.)

Tremblay, Guy. 1989. *Une Grille d'analyse pour le droit du Québec*. 2nd ed. Montreal: Wilson et Lafleur Ltée.

PART IV

Making

Public

Policy

ECONOMIC
POLICY

The earlier discussion in this book of state-building dealt with the fundamental changes introduced by the Quiet Revolution. It was seen that the
economic sphere in particular had been targetted for major changes. This
led, among other things, to creation of a number of state-owned enterprises (SOEs) during the 1960s and 1970s, for the strategy was largely
based on state intervention.

The Quiet Revolution was not restricted to the short period from 1960
to 1966 (i.e., the two Liberal administrations). Most observers agree that
there was no significant rupture in policy after the Liberals were defeated
in 1966. The various governments that came to power during the next two
decades, pursued, irrespective of party denomination, the course initiated
by the Liberals. They shared a vision of Quebec's future as a distinct society, one that sought to rectify very specific economic problems:

1. The marginalization of the province's economy within Canada's
   global economy

2. Various structural problems of this economy, particularly in the manufacturing sector

3. Economic dependency in terms of investment capital and commercial trade

4. Regional disparities, both between Quebec and the rest of Canada and
   within Quebec itself

5. The marginal role played by francophones in ownership and management of the economy

This chapter looks at how well each of these problems have been addressed.

13.1 ADDRESSING QUEBEC'S ECONOMIC PROBLEMS

1. Marginalization of Quebec's Economy

This problem—also referred to by some authors as "peripheralization" of Quebec's economy relative to the Canadian and continental economies (Gagnon and Montcalm 1990)—is due to the simple geographical fact that its location has become peripheral to North America's economic centre of gravity, which in this century has been moving westward.

Yet, throughout the 1960s and 1970s, Quebec governments apparently believed they could circumvent this structural stumbling-block: their expressed desire throughout those decades was to develop a "wall to wall" economy. By creating a vastly diversified manufacturing sector, they hoped to ensure the province's presence in every economic sector. Thus, the emphasis was on developing sectors such as steel and automobile construction. It was this kind of thinking that motivated the Bourassa government in the 1970s. At a time when the North American steel industry was undergoing a severe crisis, Bourassa predicted that automobile makers would turn to aluminum as the main component in automobile chassis. He foresaw a bonanza for Quebec if the province could use cheap hydro-electric power to attract aluminum manufacturers, who would lure automobile makers. Bourassa, and after 1976 the Parti québécois, specifically targetted Ford Motor Company. But in vain: it eventually established its new plant in southern Ontario.

In 1978, the PQ spent huge amounts setting up *La société nationale de l'amiante*, an SOE involved in asbestos mining, the manufacture of related industrial products, and research and development for new asbestos products. Unfortunately, these schemes were all promoted at a time when, worldwide, this particular mineral was being banned, or its uses severely restricted. Only in the early 1980s was the idea of a "wall to wall" industrial sector finally abandoned in favour of specialization in high-tech industries (Gouvernement du Québec 1982) and consolidation of sectors in which Quebec was doing well, such as the aerospace industry, petrochemicals, transportation equipment, and so on. At the same time the strategy of chasing "smokestack" industries was dropped in favour of supporting innovative small and medium-sized businesses that could do well on the world market.

This new strategy came about with the 1979 publication of the PQ government's new economic development policy in the document *Bâtir le*

Québec (Challenges for Quebec): un énoncé de politique économique), followed in 1982 by Volume II of *Bâtir le Québec: le virage technologique* (The
Technology Conversion). Both reports recommended that Quebec concentrate on developing only those sectors in which it held comparative advantages, and ignore the sectors that would suffer from Quebec's peripheral
position in the continental economy. *Bâtir le Québec* acknowledged to
some extent the failure of public policies implemented since 1960.

*Claude Béland,
president of the*
Mouvement
Desjardins, *a
cooperative asso-
ciation to which
the banking
institutions of*
Les Caisses popu-
laires *belong.
[Courtesy Le
Devoir and Gilles
Paré, Librarian.
Photo: Jacques
Nadeau.]*

Despite numerous, serious governmental efforts between the 1960s
and the late 1980s to solve Quebec's fundamental economic problems,
various indicators attest to the marginalization of Quebec's economy
within the Canadian economy as a whole, and especially in comparison to
Ontario. Quebec's relative position within the Canadian economy has
actually regressed over the period:

1. **Quebec's share in Canada's GDP relative to Ontario's
   share in it**   Quebec's contribution to Canada's gross domestic
   product (GDP) in 1990 dropped to 87.1% of its 1961 contribution,
   while Ontario's relative share has remained more or less stable, shifting
   from 41.0% in 1961 to 41.5% in 1989 of total Canadian GDP. During

the same period, Quebec's share as a percentage of Ontario's contribution to the Canadian GDP has dropped by 11.2%.

Table 13.1

Quebec's Share of Canadian Gross Domestic Product (GDP) *(selected years)*

Year	Share of GDP (%)	Share of Ontario's Share of GDP (%)
1961	26.3	64.1
1971	24.8	59.3
1976	23.9	60.7
1981	22.7	60.3
1982	22.7	61.2
1983	22.5	59.6
1984	22.4	58.2
1985	22.4	58.3
1986	23.2	58.0
1987	23.5	58.0
1988	23.5	56.2
1989	23.0	55.0
1990	22.9	55.6

Sources: Bernier and Boily (1986: 70); Statistics Canada, *Provincial Economic Accounts*, cat. 13–213.

2. **Distribution of labour force as percentage of total labour force among the three economic sectors** The economy can be thought of as consisting of three sectors as follows:

- **The primary sector**, which comprises such economic activities as agriculture, mining, forestry, hunting, and fishery
- **The secondary sector**, essentially the manufacturing sector and construction
- **The tertiary sector**, which deals mainly with services and includes governmental and private corporation activities

Thus, public sector activities are part of the tertiary sector. In 1961, 54.0% of Quebec's labour force was accounted for by the tertiary sector. In 1991, the figure was 74.4%.

During the past three decades Quebec has lost ground in the primary and secondary sectors while gaining dramatically in the tertiary sector, keeping pace with the rise of the tertiary sector in Canada as a whole. Yet the blossoming of this sector presents some problems, as other data shows. The decline of the manufacturing sector has been steady since 1961, reaching its lowest point in 1985 (23% of the labour force). The last few years indicate a slight resurgence of the manufacturing sector, mainly as a result of the policies followed by the PQ and the second Bourassa government during the 1980s. These policies have sought to support, through various programs, the development of small and medium businesses. The Caisse de dépôt et placement alone has increased its total investments in small and medium businesses from $126.0 million in 1983 to $270.6 million in 1989.

3. **Quebec's and Ontario's respective shares in Canada's manufacturing sector**   Quebec's position has regressed in terms of the number of manufacturing establishments, number of employees, and value of shipments. Of special significance is the fact that Quebec's share in the value of shipments has fallen from 30.4% in 1960 to 23.1% in 1987. This represents a decline of 24% over the past 27 years. In some ways, Quebec is facing a problem of deindustrialization. During the past few years the number of establishments has stabilized and even increased during 1987. This is largely due to governmental action fostering the emergence of small and medium-sized businesses.

4. **Quebec's share of total exports and imports and international exports in the manufacturing sector**   Quebec's share in Canada's international trade has severely declined, especially in the field of exports. Whereas in 1965 Quebec accounted for 31.9% of Canada's exports, its share was down to 17.6% by 1991. The same phenomenon occurs in imports, though less drastically (26.7% in 1965; 18.7% in 1991). In the manufacturing sector, Quebec has increased its international exports relative to its exports to the rest of the Canadian provinces. Yet Quebec remains the greatest consumer of its own manufactured products. In 1984, for example, 52.3% of manufactured products were consumed in Quebec.

5. **The respective shares of total investments in Canada of Quebec**   Quebec's position remained relatively stable throughout the period except for the recession years of the early 1980s. Nonetheless, its share of total Canadian investments has always been lower than its share in the Canadian population. For instance, Quebec represented 25.8% of the Canadian population in 1986 but in 1992 was expected to receive only 21.3% of total investments in Canada.

6. **Quebec/Ontario ratio of global investments from 1962 to 1989 and their respective shares of investment**   Overall there has been a major change between 1962 and 1992 in Quebec's position relative to Ontario. The ratio of Quebec's to Ontario's

total investments went down from 69.2% to 54.2% during the period. However, there is a substantial difference between what went on during the PQ administration (1976– 1985) and what happened after the return of the Liberals in 1985. During the PQ's first term (1976–1981), the level of total investments relative to Ontario had more or less returned to the levels of the early 1960s. It only went down, never to return to its previous levels, during the recession of the early 1980s. Furthermore, things worsened under the Liberal administration. For one thing, public investments (i.e., the government and public institutions) dropped slightly between 1976 and the period following the Liberal takeover in 1985. Public investments represented 16.2% of total investments in 1976, but only 12.6% of total investments in 1989. The most dramatic decrease, which occurred in the field of public utilities, might help to explain the gap that now exists between the two provinces. Investments in that sector represented 25.7% of total investments in 1977, reached 32.2% in 1982, and plummetted to 17.2% in 1989. This difference can be largely explained by the completion of the various James Bay hydroelectric projects in the early 1980s.

One point worth noting is that in relative terms, among its total investments, Quebec's share in the manufacturing sector represents a greater proportion than similar figures for Ontario between 1985 and 1990. This is the first time such a phenomenon has happened since 1955.

The data unequivocally point to a decline in Quebec's economic performance since 1960. In the meantime, Ontario's position during the same period has either remained stable or gained ground. Efforts to rescue Quebec from its marginal status within the Canadian economy have so far proven to be unsuccessful.

2. Structural Problems of the Economy

Together, the decline of its manufacturing sector, the imbalances within it, and the rise of the tertiary sector may indicate the "deindustrialization" of Quebec's manufacturing sector and warrant a closer look at the composition of the tertiary sector.

Four indicators illustrate the big picture:

1. The steady decline of Quebec's manufacturing sector within Canada as observed in the previous section

2. The dominance of "soft" industries in the manufacturing sector, including such traditional areas as textiles, clothing, leather, furniture, wood, and lumber

   The presence and maintenance of the "soft" industries in the structure of Quebec's manufacturing sector has been a thorn in the side of successive governments from 1960 onwards, but while acknowledging the problem they have all ignored it in terms of policy.

These sectors face stiff international competition, but are highly protected by Canadian tariffs. They also offer very low productivity levels. As of 1988, these industries employed 33.5% of the total number of workers in the manufacturing sector while only contributing 17.8% of total value of manufacturing shipments. Quebec governments should have acted to slowly phase out these sectors.

(a) More energy and resources should have been put into developing alternative sectors, mainly in the field of high technology. This course of action, however, was not taken until the early 1980s.

(b) Programs should have been set up to encourage early retirement and create workforce training and retraining programs, even if it meant workers would probably not be able to reenter the labour force.

(c) The government and various SOEs should not have invested in and subsidized equipment modernization in those sectors.

(d) Finally, the Quebec government should not have pressured the federal government to maintain high tariffs on the goods produced by these traditional sectors.

Now that there has been an extension of the Free Trade Agreement to Mexico (NAFTA), competition with Mexico could jeopardize the economic viability of these sectors.

3. The high proportion of raw materials and non-treated products that make up Quebec's international exports, and the growing proportion of finished goods in its imports

Quebec's international trade structure is characterized on the exports side by raw materials and unfinished goods and on the imports side by the preponderance and growing proportion, since 1960, of finished goods. It is worth noting that among Quebec's exports, finished goods have increased substantially since the 1960s, having stood at a mere 13.8% of total exports in 1965 and increased to 40.3% in 1989. However, during the same period, imports of finished goods increased from 37.9% to 61.8%.

Conversely, on the exports side, raw materials and unfinished goods have declined slightly (from 63.3% in 1965 to 53.7% in 1989), while on the imports side the decrease has been more dramatic (from 47.5% in 1965 to 32.7% in 1989) in favour of finished goods.

While its general situation is improving, Quebec is still hindered by imbalances in its international trade. Its export structure is still dominated by raw materials and unfinished goods. Efforts should be made to process raw materials into industrial products within Quebec instead of shipping them out raw and buying them back as finished goods.

4. The disproportionate place taken up by the tertiary or services sector, and what is usually referred to as the "non-productive" subsector

Guy St-Pierre, president of SNC-Lavalin, the largest Canadian engineering firm. [Courtesy Le Devoir and Gilles Paré, Librarian. Photo: Jacques Nadeau.]

Quebec is suffering from hypertrophy in its tertiary sector, and particularly in its non-productive subsector. Tertiary activity contributed to 70.5% of Quebec's GDP in 1987, up from 56.5% in 1961. At first glance, this is in keeping with trends observed in most industrialized countries of the Western world. However, in Quebec, the situation appears to be somewhat different. For one thing, the growth of the tertiary sector has taken place largely as a result of "deindustralization." As one observer writes:

It would appear that the phenomenon of the rise of the tertiary sector within Quebec's economy has surpassed the optimum level. Far from demonstrating that Quebec's economy has entered the post-industrial era, the "ballooning" of the tertiary sector is rather the indicator of a worrisome anemia of the manufacturing sector. (Lamonde 1979: 351–352).

If one divides the tertiary sector into "productive" and "non-productive" subsectors, it is evident that the latter has experienced the faster growth rate. The *productive* subsector includes activities related to industrial production (e.g., finance, marketing) and private consumer services. The *non-productive* subsector includes all collective services such as public administration, education, health, and social services.

Current data on the subject are not readily available; the most recent figures go back to 1984. These show that between 1973 and 1984, the productive subsector had increased its input in Quebec's GDP by 6.8%, while the non-productive subsector's share grew by 16.4% (Bernier and Boily 1986: 80).

In terms of employment, the public and parapublic sectors (schools, hospitals, welfare institutions, SOEs, etc.) have grown tremendously over the past three decades. The number of civil servants working for the Quebec government and its agencies—excluding those working in the parapublic sector—went from 36,766 in 1960 to 70,006 in 1970. By 1985, the number of civil servants had gone up to 150,333. To put it another way, in 1960 there were 7.13 provincial civil servants per 1,000 people; by 1970 this figure had gone up to 11.6; and by 1985 it had reached 22.8 (Bernier and Boily 1986: 373).

As for all public servants working in Quebec—including those working for the federal government, municipalities, and SOEs at all levels, but excluding those in the services of the parapublic sector—their number went from 164,557 in 1965 to 448,831 in 1985. The fastest-growing subsector is that of municipal employees (Bernier and Boily 1986: 374ff.).

There have been few changes in the manufacturing sector since the 1960s. Quebec now faces intense international competition with diminishing chances of success. The technological challenge should have been met much earlier, especially given the fact that in the course of about twenty years (i.e., from the mid-1960s to the mid-1980s), Quebec's population evolved from being poorly educated to being one of the most educated in North America. But Quebec governments have not taken advantage of their vast human resources potential. As a result, a large portion of Quebec's manufacturing sector still rests on cheap labour and offers low productivity levels.

In international trade, Quebec's position has improved somewhat, but in the field of natural resources there awaits an opportunity to encourage foreign investment to stimulate the production of industrial products from raw materials within the province.

At first glance, the rise of the tertiary sector matches that of all advanced industrial societies. Data indicates that the non-productive sector is growing faster than the productive sector, but more research and data are necessary to fully analyze the implications of this for Quebec; it is possible, for example, that the apparent rise of the tertiary sector reflects widespread underemployment, as is the case in some Third World countries. The bloating of the public and parapublic sectors over the past thirty years or so would seem to point in that direction, but detailed analysis is required before reaching such a conclusion.

3. Economic Dependency

Like the rest of Canada, but to a lesser degree, Quebec is dependent on the United States in terms of both investment and trade. With regard to foreign investment, Quebec governments since 1960 have always been receptive to American capital—much more so than the rest of Canada, where economic nationalism was prevalent throughout the Trudeau years (1968–1979, 1980–1984). Such nationalism is still strong in English Canada, especially among the left, and led to vigorous opposition to the 1988 Free Trade Agreement with the United States. Quebec, on the other hand, hailed the agreement as the greatest development in Canada in the 20th century.[1] Trade dependency, too, is a trait shared with the rest of Canada. In terms of international exports and imports, the United States is by far Quebec's major trading partner.

Let us look at investment and trade dependency in more detail.

Investment Dependency

1. **Presence of foreign capital in manufacturing sector as measured by share of corporate income tax** Taxable income totals show that in the manufacturing sector, foreign capital has decreased since 1965. Then at 59.8%, its share of corporate income tax went down to 47.2% in 1987. Though the biggest change has been in the overall economy, the hardest-hit sectors have been (1) transportation, communications, and public utilities and (2) services. Foreign

---

1. Disagreements between Quebec and the rest of Canada have, at times, given rise to embarrassing situations internationally. On one occasion, Robert Bourassa, then Premier of Quebec, was in New York courting American investors, while at home, during a period of extreme Canadian nationalist sentiment, the federal government was setting up the Foreign Investment Review Agency (FIRA). During the 1988 federal election campaign, which was dominated by the free trade debate, Quebec's position was clearly at odds with that of most of English Canada, particularly Ontario. This has led some observers during the Meech Lake debate of the spring of 1990 to link Quebec's stance on free trade with English Canada's refusal to ratify the accord. Without going so far as to say that English Canada was getting even with Quebec, some observers postulated that anti-Quebec sentiment in the rest of Canada had been exacerbated by Quebec's position on free trade.

ownership in these two sectors respectively went from 41.0% and 24.9% in 1965 to 3.2% and 9.9% in 1987. (Bernier and Boily 1986: 154–155)

These figures indicate that Canadians, including francophones and anglophones from Quebec and the rest of Canada, have gained greater input in Quebec's economy, particularly in sectors other than manufacturing where foreign interests still account for almost half of generated taxable corporate income.

2. **Number of employees in firms controlled by foreign capital**   The presence and impact of foreign capital on the ten provincial economies have been measured in various ways. As of 1984, when Statistics Canada ceased to publish such detailed data (which had been of immense value to political economists), the only data on foreign capital are now offered at the aggregated level of Canada as a whole. The last year of reference for the detailed intraprovincial level was 1981.

In 1961, 31.3% of Quebec workers in the manufacturing sector were employed by foreign-controlled firms, whereas in 1981 this figure stood at 28.6%. Again, there is a presumption that French and English Canadians have gained some ground in the control of Quebec's manufacturing sector.

3. **Value added in firms controlled by foreign capital**   We see a slight drop over the two decades in the percentage of value added generated by foreign-controlled firms in the manufacturing sector. Whereas in 1961 foreign-controlled firms generated 41.8% of value added, the figure had fallen to 37.1% by 1981.

Yet, in comparison with other sets of data, these figures show that foreign-owned firms operate in the more dynamic sectors of the manufacturing sector where value added and productivity are high. For instance, in 1981 in Quebec foreign-controlled firms were responsible for 55.9% of value added in rubber and plastic products, 58.3% in machinery, 60.0% in transportation material, 48.0% in electrical appliances, 41.3% in nonmetallic mineral products, and 81.2% in chemical products (Bernier and Boily 1986: 139). Other, less productive sectors, such as the traditional sectors referred to earlier, are controlled by either French or English Canadians.

Trade Dependency   There is little point in using up space here to demonstrate that the United States is by far Quebec's largest trading partner in terms of both exports and imports. One interesting feature should be emphasized, however: while the United States' share of Quebec's exports continues to grow, its share as provider of imports to Quebec fluctuates.

Laurent Beaudoin, president of Bombardier. This engineering company specializes in all transportation materials, from snowmobiles to trains and airplanes. [Courtesy Le Devoir and Gilles Paré, Librarian. Photo: Jacques Grenier.]

In 1970, the United States received 58.2% of Quebec's exports; by 1990 this figure had reached 76.1% and has been on an upward trend since the mid-1980s. The high point of United States imports after 1976 was 53.1%, reached in 1983, a figure that has been decreasing since. In 1990, American imports stood at 46.3%. In this regard, Quebec's figures are much lower than those of Canada as a whole, which have ranged from 70.1% in 1980 to 68.7% in 1987.

With respect to composition of exports and imports, there is, as noted in the previous section, an imbalance, with Quebec trading raw materials and unfinished goods for manufactured products. But, as seen previously, there has been a strong effort since the mid-1960s to correct this imbalance.

Although Quebec seems to have lessened its dependency on American investments over the past thirty years, the United States is still a significant presence in its economy, especially in the areas of natural resources (and particularly mining) and manufacturing. In manufacturing, American capital controls the most productive sectors.

In terms of trade, over the past thirty years, Quebec has increased its dependency on the American market for its international exports, while its sources of imports have become more diversified, though the United States still accounts for about 50% of total imports.

Table 13.2

Quebec's Exports and Imports to the U.S., 1976–1989

Year	Exports (% of total exports)	Imports (% of total imports)
1976	62.8	41.2
1977	65.0	43.5
1978	65.0	45.6
1979	63.8	51.3
1980	59.9	51.5
1981	65.0	46.4
1982	64.5	47.1
1983	69.6	53.1
1984	75.1	52.7
1985	75.8	50.5
1986	77.5	49.0
1987	77.3	47.5
1988	75.3	45.0
1989	72.8	45.3
1990	76.1	46.3

Source: Bureau de la statistique du Québec, *Commerce international du Québec* (Quebec: Gouvernement du Québec, 1991).

4. Regional Disparities

Regional Disparities Between Quebec and Canada   From Quebec's standpoint, any discussion of regional economic disparities within the Canadian federation must take into account its own economy's marginalization. Closing the gap between regions was a major theme throughout the Quiet Revolution. Surprisingly, though, the most vociferous comments on the issue came not from Quebec but from the federal government, especially during the Trudeau years. For Prime Minister Trudeau, the one simple way to eliminate regional disparities and hinder "provincialism" —referred to by some as "province-building" (Young, Blais, Faucher 1984)—was to implement a host of redistribution programs: equalization payments, whereby the richer provinces transferred some of their wealth to the poorer provinces; the creation of a Department of Regional Economic Expansion (DREE); and transfer payments from the federal government to the provinces earmarked for public assistance, health care, higher education, shared-cost programs, and so on. Trudeau believed that Quebec's nationalism was caused and fuelled by unequal regional development within the Canadian federation. Thus, he reasoned, redistribution of national wealth would be the best way to quash the nationalism of Quebec and manifestations of province-building in the rest of Canada, especially in the western provinces.

To measure Quebec's economic regional disparity, Ontario has been the traditional yardstick. Below we will attempt to assess whether, during the past thirty years, Quebec has succeeded in closing the gap between itself and Ontario, using the following indicators:

1. **Personal income per capita**   There have been some improvements in the area of income and wages but on all counts Quebec still lags behind Ontario. For instance, in 1961, Quebec's personal income per capita was 76.1% of Ontario's; by 1990 it was 81.6% with data showing a decline in the latter part of the 1980s. A high point of 88.9% was reached in 1981. But monetary policy pursued by the Bank of Canada from 1988 to 1990 has had the effect of widening the gap again. A policy of high interest rates was implemented to curb the inflation rate in southern Ontario, where it was much higher than in the rest of Canada. One consequence was that labour settlements yielded substantially higher wage increases than in Quebec, or in the rest of Canada for that matter. Many observers contend that this policy of high interest rates brought on the recession of 1990–1992, which started at least six months earlier than in the United States.

   In comparison to Canada overall, Quebec has also made progress with regard to personal income. In 1961, Quebec's per capita personal income was 90.2% of the Canadian average. In 1981, it reached 99.4%, and by 1990, it stood at 93.1%.

Table 13.3

Per Capita Personal Income: Comparison Between Quebec, Ontario, and Canada—Selected Years

Year	Quebec ($)	Ontario ($)	Canada ($)
1961	1,489	1,954	1,651
1966	2,055	2,680	2,303
1971	3,028	4,020	3,414
1976	6,306	7,390	6,747
1981	11,340	12,757	11,413
1986	15,843	18,508	16,818
1988	18,511	21,853	19,484
1990	19,623	24,034	21,085

Sources: Statistics Canada, *Income Estimates for Subprovincial Areas*, cat. 13–216; Statistics Canada, *National Income and Expenditures Accounts: Annual Estimates*.

2. **Average hourly wage in the manufacturing sector**
   Again, the gap has closed somewhat since 1960. That year, Quebec's
   hourly wage was 85.1% that of Ontario. By 1990, it had reached 90.2%.
   In this instance, the gap was narrowed partly because of progressive
   social policy regarding minimum wages, especially under the PQ
   administration (1976–1985). The minimum wage is revised periodi-
   cally to keep up with inflation. As of October 1992, it stood at $5.70
   an hour. The level set for the minimum wage has a direct impact on
   hourly wages in the rest of the economy by pushing them upwards.
   Also to be reckoned with are the settlements in the public and para-
   public sectors over the past twenty-five years. They tended to be very
   generous until the late 1970s, thus also contributing to rising hourly
   wages in the private sector. Over the past few years, Quebec has lost
   some ground as collective bargaining settlements have tended to be
   higher in Ontario than in the rest of Canada.

3. **Average annual unemployment rate**   Quebec's problem of
   chronic high unemployment remains as serious as it was in the early
   1960s. Generally speaking, Quebec's annual unemployment rate is
   higher than Ontario's by more than 50%. And things have gotten
   worse in the past few years. Figures for 1988 and 1989 indicate that
   Quebec's unemployment rate was almost twice as high as Ontario's.
   This situation gives credence to the theory that Ontario's economic
   boom in the late 1980s has had a negative impact on the rest of
   Canada—that higher interest rates set by the Bank of Canada might
   have been warranted by the situation in Ontario, but such a measure
   was not advantageous for the rest of Canada.

4. **Federal transfer payments as part of total general revenues**   Transfer payments are a complex matter involving both
   unconditional and conditional programs. The first category includes
   equalization payments, which are transfers made by the federal government based on each province's capacity to raise revenues. They
   are intended to remedy regional economic disparities within Canada
   by having the richer provinces share their wealth with the less affluent
   provinces. The objective is to enable every province to provide the
   same level and quality of services without having to raise taxes to
   unreasonable levels. As of the early 1990s all but three provinces
   (Alberta, British Columbia, and Ontario) were receiving equalization
   payments. These are paid on a per capita basis.
      Conditional transfers cover shared-cost programs such as hospital-
   ization insurance, public assistance, and higher education. These
   programs cover provincial fields of jurisdiction. Federal transfers are

made on a uniform per capita basis to the provinces. The federal government, however, sets the regulations governing use of those funds even though they are intended for areas under provincial jurisdiction. Since the mid-1980s there have been fluctuations in the sums transferred to the provinces, but the trend is toward decreasing the amounts in this category.

In the early 1960s, Quebec opposed this system of transfer payments, and the federal government agreed that a province could opt out of it to set up its own programs and regulations as long as they met minimal national standards. Upon meeting these conditions, the province would receive some form of equivalent compensation such as tax points (i.e., a federal tax withdrawal equivalent to the sum of money the province would have received had it continued to participate in the shared-cost program). It was under this agreement that Quebec withdrew, in 1963, from the newly created Canada Pension Fund. Quebec's independent pension scheme eventually gave rise to the Caisse de dépôt et placement du Québec, which has become a major player in Quebec's economic development.

On top of all these arrangements is the added complication of a complete review of fiscal agreements every five years. Bargaining sessions between the federal government and the provinces have taken place in 1962, 1967, 1972, 1977, 1982, 1987, and 1992.

5. **Quebec's and Ontario's relative share of federal transfer payments**   Overall, transfer payments to Quebec have always represented a higher percentage of total general revenues than those to Ontario. More-detailed information is required before any general conclusions can be reached about the gap between the two provinces. The difference may stem from any of a number of factors. Quebec, for example, may receive more because it has opted out of more programs than Ontario, or it may be that the importance of equalization payments in Quebec's total general revenues has grown over the past few years. One trend is clear, however: since the late 1970s the federal government has steadily reduced the amounts it transfers to the provinces in terms of constant dollars, and in the process some provinces have suffered more than others. With regard to Quebec's and Ontario's relative share of transfer payments, part of the gap is due to the fact that Quebec receives equalization payments, while Ontario, as the richest province, does not.

The oft-heard claim that Quebec has been on the losing end of Canadian fiscal federalism is unfair. Support for such a claim would require a much more detailed analysis of the various components of fiscal federalism. It does seem clear, however, that, taking into account the difference in population between the two provinces (in 1986, 6.5 million for Quebec and 9.1 million for Ontario), Quebec has generated more general revenues from its own sources, in absolute numbers, than Ontario throughout most of the 1980s. The net result has been a greater fiscal burden on Quebec taxpayers. The brunt of this has been shouldered by individuals, as the percentage of total revenues from corporations is much lower in Quebec than in Ontario (e.g., for the fiscal year 1989, corporate income taxes in Quebec amounted to 1.7% of total general revenues in contrast to 6.4% in Ontario).

Regional Disparities Within Quebec   In regions outside metropolitan Montreal, there has been significantly less economic activity, especially in the manufacturing sector. Regional economic activity generally revolves around natural resources and raw materials (mining, lumber, etc.), most of which is destined for foreign markets. Only a few small centres of industrial production are based on processing of the natural resources found in the regions. These facts are borne out by the following indicators:

1. **Relative importance of the Montreal area in manufacturing**   Data regarding the manufacturing sector show that,

Bernard Lemaire, a member of the Lemaire family, who head Cascades, a company specializing in the transformation and manufacturing of products from pulp and paper. [Courtesy Le Devoir and Gilles Paré, Librarian. Photo: Louise Lemieux.]

depending on how the Montreal area is defined, it accounts for half to two-thirds of industrial activity in Quebec as measured by three indicators: number of employees, percentage of establishments, and value of shipments. The concentration increased between 1960 and 1985, and though there has been a slight drop in the number of employees, the percentage of establishments located in the Montreal area has increased by about 10%. When Montreal is broadly defined, the value of shipments has remained more or less steady, but when only the metropolitan census region is taken into account it seems to have suffered a significant drop between 1985 and 1986. More recent data is lacking to see if that trend has continued.

Since 1960 both the provincial and the federal government have injected considerable sums into programs aimed at decentralization of economic activity and regional development, but to little effect. Market laws have prevailed over prefabricated socioeconomic policies.

2. **Per capita personal income by administrative region as compared to Montreal** Per capita personal income by administrative region tends to follow the pattern of regional disparity described above. There are such tremendous disparities that the Quebec Council on Social Affairs has issued a report titled *Deux Québec dans un* (Two Quebecs in One) (Conseil des affaires sociales 1989). With the Montreal region as a yardstick (Montreal=100), in 1961 most other regions had a personal per capita income of roughly two-thirds that of Montreal. The gap has closed somewhat during the past two decades; most regions averaged around 80% of Montreal's personal per capita income in 1982 and the gap was narrower still according to figures for 1989. It is difficult to assess whether this points to a sort of economic dynamism in the regions—manifesting itself in sectors other than the manufacturing sector—or to Montreal's economic decline within the larger context of the North American continent. Given the data on regional disparities within Canada, the latter explanation seems more plausible.

3. **Unemployment rates by administrative region, 1975–1989** Though Montreal and the province of Quebec have high unemployment rates compared to Toronto and Ontario, within Quebec the Montreal region along with the Quebec and Ottawa valley regions —both governmental administrative centres—maintain the lowest levels of unemployment compared to the rest of the province. Other regions mostly show double-digit figures for the period 1975–1989. Regions that are especially vulnerable include the Gaspé and Lower St. Lawrence in the East, the Saguenay-Lac-Saint-Jean in north central Quebec, and Abitibi-Témiscamingue in the west. The economy of

these regions is based on natural resources (fisheries, mining, forestry, etc.). In all three regions, manufacturing accounts for less than 2% of total value of production in Quebec.

4. **Net migration by administrative region, 1961–1987**
   Population growth by administrative region for the period 1961–1987, expressed in terms of interregional migration, shows negative growth or depopulation in most regions, except for the Montreal metropolitan area and, at times, the Outaouais region (i.e., the westernmost part of Quebec near the Ottawa region). Many federal civil servants live on the Quebec side of the Quebec-Ontario border because of lower housing costs. The inner core of the island of Montreal is also steadily losing residents, who are moving to suburbs in the north and south of Montreal.

   Figures based on the Quebec government's now-abandoned model, which divided the province into ten administrative regions, showed that in 1983 the Montreal region accounted for 56.5% of Quebec's total population (Bureau de la statistique du Quebec 1985: 297). Using the more restrictive boundaries of metropolitan census region, the 1986 census results showed that Montreal made up 44.7% of Quebec's total population. The bulk of Quebec's economic activity is concentrated in the southwestern part of the province, the geographical area closest to the core of the continental economy.

   The objectives set forth by the pioneers of the Quiet Revolution have not been met on this front either. Quebec continues to lag behind Ontario, though to expect any more may be foolish given Ontario's undeniably superior geographical position relative to the core of the continental economy, not to mention the longstanding stability of its well-balanced economic structure. What progress Quebec has made in narrowing the gap has been at great cost to its citizens, with most of the catching up achieved through state intervention via subsidies or SOEs. The fact that the Quebec government lacks the necessary economic, monetary, and fiscal power needed to restructure its economy partly explains these minimal results.

   There is less excuse, however, for the failure to achieve a significant reduction in regional inequalities within Quebec itself. The government has some measure of control over regional economic development policy, yet over the past thirty years there has been far more talk and creation of "White Papers" than action toward economic decentralization. In the end, market forces have always prevailed over the bureaucracy's master plans, whether they be the planning projects of the 1960s or the decentralization programs devised at the numerous economic summits held during the 1970s and 1980s.

5. Marginal Role Played by Quebec Francophones

In 1960, of course, Quebec francophones controlled very little of their province's economy. The primary objective of the pioneers of the Quiet Revolution was to promote a greater francophone presence in Quebec's economy. Creation of SOEs would guarantee francophone control over the newly created institutions in the public sector. But what about the private sector? Unfortunately, it is difficult to statistically measure the amount of progress, or lack thereof, made in this area.

The Data   What is required are studies in which ownership is identified by ethnicity or nationality of the controlling capital, i.e., into three categories of ownership or control: French-Canadian, English-Canadian, and foreign. At present only approximations are available as to such ownership in Quebec. The best such sources are the various studies, conducted from the early 1960s on, by economist André Raynauld and his associates. The estimates are expressed in various terms, such as value added, value of production, export revenues, etc. Such data for the manufacturing sector exist for the years 1961 and 1978 from Raynauld and Vaillancourt (1984). A recent study (Vaillancourt and Carpentier 1989) covers the year 1987, but unfortunately it only deals with one indicator comparable to those used in the previous studies, namely ownership by nationality of controlling capital as measured by number of employees for establishments of 50 or more employees. The figure is available for various sectors of the economy, such as manufacturing, services, wholesale and retail trade, financial services, and so on.

Since the purpose of this section is to measure progress made by francophone Quebecers in the control of their economy using the most recent data, we will only use figures related to nationality of ownership in terms of number of employees, as was done in the 1987 study. Other approaches to quantifying data for the three studies have not been consistent (Raynauld 1974; Raynauld and Vaillancourt 1984; Vaillancourt and Carpentier 1989). And unfortunately, information based on number of employees by nationality of controlling capital is not as significant or revealing as information based on other data as mentioned above. For one thing, it tends to overemphasize the level of control exercised by French Canadians. In the manufacturing sector, for instance, if, instead of the number of employees indicator, the value-added indicator were used for 1961 and 1978, results would be much less favourable with regard to French Canadian control (see Table 13.4).

Similar data for the primary and tertiary sectors would be extremely useful; however, such data is scarce, with only the years 1961 and 1978 fully covered. The 1987 study examines these sectors only in terms of number of employees.

Table 13.4

French Canadian Control in the Manufacturing Sector

As Measured by Number of Employees

	French Canadian	English Canadian	Foreign
1961	21.7	47.0	31.3
1978	27.8	38.6	33.5

As Measured by Value Added

	French Canadian	English Canadian	Foreign
1961	15.4	42.8	41.8
1978	22.3	37.1	40.6

Analysis of the Data   Thus, in our discussion two sets of data will be used: one pertaining to the manufacturing sector and the other to the financial sector, both of them using the percentage-of-employees indicator. These will be distributed by nationality of controlling capital. In the manufacturing sector, internal variations by subsector, over the years, prove to be very significant.

Between 1961 and 1978, French Canadian gains were made at the expense of English Canadian capital, while between 1978 and 1987 the gains made by French Canadians came at the expense of foreign capital. Within the manufacturing sector, important shifts in ownership among the various subsectors occurred between 1961 and 1987. For example, in the food and beverage industry, the degree of French Canadian ownership measured as a percentage of employment increased between 1961 and 1987 from 35.1% to 54.2%. In printing and publishing, the French Canadian share went from 29.1% in 1961 to 60.8% in 1987. In metal fabrication, it went from 27.2% to 50.3%, while in nonmetallic mineral products, it went from 21.0% in 1961 to 51.2% in 1987. Those were the most dramatic shifts in ownership, but other sectors also need to be looked at closely.

As seen previously, when the nationality of ownership is measured by number of employees, French Canadians do much better than on other indicators. In 1987, 39.3% of all employees in the manufacturing sector were under French Canadian control. In this regard, French Canadians ranked first. However, one must be cautious in interpreting this particular set of data, as it has negative as well as positive implications.

On the positive side, since this measurement takes into account only firms with 50 or more employees, it shows that French-Canadian-controlled establishments have grown in size since 1961—a definite departure from the old mom-and-pop shops! On the negative side, comparison with the value-added figures shows that French-Canadian-controlled firms have much lower productivity levels than foreign- and English-Canadian-owned firms. Overall, however, French-Canadian-owned firms have made important headway in the manufacturing sector, a development reflected in the lists of the top 500 companies published by several financial magazines, all of which attest to the increasing presence of firms controlled by French Canadians.

Nowhere have French Canadians made greater gains than in the financial sector. Francophones control such financial juggernauts as the Caisse de dépôt et placement du Québec (the state-run Quebec pension plan) which has assets of more than $41 billion; Power Corporation; and the Mouvement Desjardins enterprises (i.e., the credit union movement, which has, as a result of federal and provincial deregulation, branched out into all sectors of financial services). There have been numerous mergers within the banking, insurance, real estate, and brokerage sectors. In some cases French-Canadian conglomerates have taken control of institutions formerly held by English Canadians (Bélanger and Fournier 1987: 134–181). An important francophone presence has also developed in the larger accounting firms, and in engineering consulting firms.

Direct government intervention (in the form of subsidies, guaranteed loans, fiscal incentives, the creation of SOEs, and so on) has done much to enhance the role of French Canadians in the control and management of their economy. In short, some twenty-five years of interventionist economic policies have yielded some of the results that can be observed today.

Along with direct economic intervention, there have also been noneconomic policies that have had a direct impact on the economy. First and foremost among these is Quebec's language legislation. Bill 22 and, especially, Bill 101 have led to individual socioeconomic promotion for thousands upon thousands of francophones. Combined with the boom in post-secondary education, language legislation has enabled francophones to obtain middle- and high-level management jobs all across the private sector, not only in that part controlled by French Canadians. There has, effectively, been an invasion of francophone managers into English-Canadian- and foreign-controlled enterprises and institutions.

Both collectively and individually, Quebec francophones have substantially increased their stake in the financial sector of their economy. They own more of it than they did in 1960, and their power as decision-makers has been vastly increased.

An important facet of the French Canadian presence in the manufacturing sector has yet to be mentioned: those corporations in the primary or secondary sectors owned by an SOE. Among them, the *Société générale de financement* (SGF), Sidbec, and Hydro-Québec are worth mentioning. Again this ensures French-Canadian control over enterprises that in the past might have been controlled by English-Canadian or foreign capital. It also has an impact in terms of providing high-level management jobs for francophones.

The Role of the Caisse   The major player in this field over the past twenty-five years has been the Caisse de dépôt et placement du Québec. The Caisse has been directly responsible for the creation or acquisition under francophone control of such giants as Provigo (a supermarket chain store), Videotron (a telecommunications, cable television, TV network), Cascades Inc. (a paper manufacturer), etc.

The Caisse was created in 1965 when Quebec opted out of the Canada Pension Plan and created its own. The Caisse de dépôt et placement du Québec now administers a number of pension funds, mainly those for several categories of public employees, on top of its principal source of revenue, *Le Régime des rentes du Québec* (Quebec's version of the Canada Pension Plan). It also manages the funds of *La Régie de l'assurance automobile du Québec* (a public automobile insurance plan), *Le Fonds d'assurance-prêts agricoles et forestiers* (an agricultural and forestry insurance and loan program), and *La Régie des marchés agricoles du Québec* (agricultural marketing boards). As of December 31, 1991 it had assets of some $41.1 billion at book value. Since its inception, the Caisse has played a major role in Quebec's economy through its investment policies, and significantly contributed to the formation and consolidation of a francophone bourgeoisie.

The investment strategies of the Caisse have varied greatly over the years. In evaluating those strategies, it is important to bear in mind that the Caisse's primary role is to invest the contributions of its depositors in such a way as to guarantee maximum benefits for those who receive their pension cheques from the Régime des rentes and other pension funds it administers.

In evaluating investment strategies, it must also be remembered that, by law, the Caisse faces two important limitations: its share in any given company is limited to 30% of the stock, and stocks may not account for more than 30% of its total portfolio. Yet, within these rather strict parameters, the Caisse's investment strategies have met with great success over the years. Up to the late 1970s, the Caisse had a relatively conservative investment policy. Most of its portfolio was held in the form of bonds, especially of the Quebec government, Hydro-Québec, Quebec municipalities and school boards, and the private sector. With the arrival in 1979 of Jean Campeau as the Caisse's chairman of the board and general director for a ten-year term, things changed dramatically, particularly in relation to the private sector.

First, the Caisse began to concentrate on stocks rather than bonds. While from 1980 to 1990 the value of bonds held in the private sector by the Caisse went from $945.9 million to $83.2 million, the value of stocks and other convertible securities went from $1.5 billion in 1979 to $12.3 billion in 1990. By 1989, when the Caisse reached its portfolio ceiling of 30% in stocks, it had become the most important investor in Canada (Pelletier 1989).

Between 1982 and 1990, the Caisse's annual report listed its investments, including the number of shares it held in each enterprise and the value of its interest in the stock market. The list is impressive, the Caisse holding shares and bonds in most large Canadian businesses. As mentioned earlier, the Caisse has also made important investments in French-Canadian-owned enterprises, enabling some of them to expand from medium-sized businesses to large enterprises. It has also provided some French-Canadian companies with enough capital to buy out firms previously owned by English Canadian or foreign capital.

In 1983, when the Caisse began to buy shares on foreign stock markets, its foreign stocks were worth $42.8 million at book value. By 1990, foreign stocks at book value in the Caisse's portfolio, represented $3.353 billion, a formidable increase over the period. The foreign stocks held in 1990 break down as follows: 38.3% in the United States, 17.5% in continental Europe, 13% in Great Britain, and 31.2% in Asia (Caisse de dépôt et placement du Québec 1991a, 1991b).

Though these represent only 9.4% of the Caisse's total portfolio (and 27.3% its holdings of stocks and convertible securities), the Caisse's trend to foreign investment poses a problem for some observers. From the point of view of economic nationalism, investments abroad represent a flight of capital that could be used constructively in Quebec or Canada. The Caisse's answer to this criticism is that its first obligation is to maximize the assets of its depositors, and that in recent years performance on foreign stock markets has been better than that on Canadian stock markets.

13.2 CONCLUSION

The biggest achievement of the Quiet Revolution has been to remedy to some degree the fact that Quebec francophones have only a marginal involvement in the province's economy, in terms of both ownership and occupation of high-level management jobs.

How has the Quebec economy fared over the past thirty years? We have seen that results are mixed. Some problems (e.g., the structural problems of Quebec's manufacturing sector and the disproportionate size of the traditional or "soft" sectors) remain as acute as they were thirty years ago.

Other problems (e.g., the marginalization of Quebec's economy within the Canadian economy as a whole) have worsened. Regional economic disparities within Canada are still a problem, while disparities within Quebec can be viewed as having either increased or remained steady, depending on the indicators used. Dependency on foreign investment seems to have decreased significantly, but Quebec is more dependent than ever on the American market for its exports; though sources of imports are more diversified, American imports account for almost half of total imports. Overall, the situation is ambiguous to say the least.

The question is: Why, with the tremendous efforts of the Quebec state over the past thirty years, has Quebec's economic situation not substantially improved? Why has so much effort yielded so few results? Various answers have been offered in the literature. A recent book (Gagnon and Montcalm 1990) theorized that "peripheralization" has proved to be an insurmountable problem for the State. This explanation has merit, but it fails to address one central fact of Quebec's situation during the past thirty years: the province has embarked on a developmental model as if it were an independent country, i.e., as if it controlled all the economic tools and levers necessary to achieve balanced economic development. The reality is that, by its very nature, the federal system puts limits on the kind of course Quebec has pursued. Canadian provinces have only limited powers in economic policymaking. Tools basic to economic policy and development—powers over fiscal and monetary policy, international trade, foreign investments, etc.—remain in the hands of the central government.

In a conference given on December 2, 1991 at the *École des HEC*, the French business school in Montreal, Industry Minister Gérald Tremblay proposed a new industrial policy for Quebec. Instead of a mass-production approach, he suggested an added-value approach to the economy. He also suggested that Quebec should favour the industrial sectors, where there were competitive advantages to develop. This idea has been regarded as a new departure: for the first time, a minister of industry and trade knew what he was talking about. Quebec's industrial development would consider the industrial groupings where the companies able to compete internationally could be found.

The fundamental assumption of this model was that industrial development cannot be successful in the modern world economy without joint ventures between the private companies working on related products. To date, thirteen such groupings have been identified. Among them, five are already competitive: aerospace equipment, pharmaceuticals, information technology, electricity, and transformation of minerals and metals. (The eight others, though not yet fully competitive, are crucial for regional development purposes and have tremendous growth potential: ground transportation, petrochemicals and plastics, food processing, housing, textiles and fashion, forest products, environment protection, and culture.)

Quebec has gone as far as it can: it has gained extra powers through such tactics as opting out of the Canada Pension Plan, discussed earlier, and setting up SOEs. At times, it resorted to programs such as the Quebec Stock Saving Program, which provided access to capital to small and medium-sized enterprises and income tax breaks to investors. In the final analysis, however, Quebec has never fully had the means to support its ambitious economic agenda.

This is not to say that Quebec would have succeeded as an independent country. There is no way of knowing how political independence might have influenced the five economic factors discussed in this chapter. The remarks on federalism are made to illustrate how Canada's constitutional system imposes certain constraints on provincial economic policymaking.

KEY TERMS

Active population	**Mixed economy**
Deindustrialization	**Peripheralization/marginalization**
Economic dependency	**Public policy**
Foreign investment	**Regional disparities**
Gross domestic product	**Unemployment rate**
Industrial policy	**Value added**

REFERENCES AND FURTHER READING

Bélanger, Yves and Pierre Fournier. 1987. *L'Entreprise québécoise: développement historique et dynamique contemporaine*. Montreal: Hurtubise HMH.

Bernier, Gérald and Robert Boily. 1986. *Le Québec en chiffres de 1850 à nos jours*. Montreal: ACFAS.

Bureau de la statistique du Québec. 1985. *Le Québec statistique*. 1985–1986 ed. Quebec: Les Publications du Québec.

Bureau de la statistique du Québec. 1989. *Le Québec statistique*. 59th ed. Quebec: Les Publications du Québec.

Caisse de dépôt et placement du Québec. 1991a. *États financiers et statistiques financières*. Montreal.

Caisse de dépôt et placement du Québec. 1991b. *Rapport annuel 1990*. Montreal.

Conseil des affaires sociales. 1989. *Deux Québec dans un: rapport sur le développement social et démographique.* Boucherville and Quebec: Gaêtan Morin, éditeur and Le Gouvernement du Québec.

Conseil exécutif, Gouvernement du Québec. 1991. "Liste des organismes gouverne-mentaux par ministre responsable et selon la catégorie." Mimeograph. Quebec: Secrétariat à la reforme administrative et aux emplois supérieurs.

Gagnon, Alain G. and Mary Beth Montcalm. 1990. *Quebec: Beyond the Quiet Revolution.* Scarborough: Nelson Canada.

Gouvernement du Québec. 1979. *Bâtir le Québec: un énoncé de politique économique.* Quebec: Ministère de l'industrie et du commerce.

Gouvernement du Québec. 1982. *Bâtir le Québec II: le virage technologique.* Quebec: Ministère de l'industrie et du commerce.

Lamonde, Pierre. 1979. "La Tertiarisation de l'économie québécoise." In Rodrique Tremblay (ed.), *L'Économie québécoise.* Montreal: Les Presses de l'Université du Québec. Pp. 347–354.

Lapalme, Georges-Emile. 1988. *Pour une politique: le programme de la Révolution tranquille.* Montreal: VLB éditeur.

Ministre délégué aux finances et à la privatisation. 1988. *Privatisation des sociétés d'état: rapport d'étape 1986–1988.* Quebec: Gouvernement du Québec.

Parizeau, Jacques. 1979. "Introduction à la première édition." In Pierre Fréchette, Rolland Jouandet-Bernadat, and Jean P. Vézina (eds.), *L'Économie du Québec.* Montreal: HRW. Pp. xx–xxv. Reproduced in Gérard Boismenu, Laurent Mailhot, and Jacques Rouillard (eds.), *Le Québec en textes.* Montreal: Boréal express. Pp. 236–243.

Pelletier, Mario. 1989. *La Machine à milliards: l'histoire de la Caisse de dépôt et placement du Québec.* Montreal: Québec/Amérique.

Raynauld, André. 1974. *La Propriété des entreprises au Québec: les années 60.* Montreal: Les Presses de l'Université de Montréal.

Raynauld, André and François Vaillancourt. 1984. *L'Appartenance des entreprises: le cas du Québec en 1978.* A study prepared for the Conseil de la langue française du Québec by the Centre de recherche en développement économique (Université de Montréal) Quebec: Éditeur officiel du Québec.

Romulus, Marc and Christian Deblock. 1985. "Politique économique et développe-ment industriel au Québec." *Interventions Economiques,* nos.14–15: 193–230.

Tremblay, Rodrigue. 1979. *L'Économie québécoise.* Montreal: Les Presses du l'Université du Québec.

Vaillancourt, François and Josée Carpentier. 1989. *Le Contrôle de l'économie du Québec: la place des francophones en 1987 et son évolution depuis 1961.* Quebec: Centre de recherche en développement économique and the Office de la langue française.

Young, R. A., Philippe Faucher, and André Blais. 1984. "The concept of province building: a critique." *Canadian Journal of Political Science,* 17(4)(December): 783–788.

CHAPTER 14

LANGUAGE
POLICY

Few issues have stirred more emotion and controversy in Quebec than the language question. After more than thirty years, it is still at the core of Quebec politics. In fact, an inordinately large part of the political game of the past three decades has been played out on the language issue. The so-called "politicization of language" has constantly mobilized the political energy of Quebecers and Canadians alike. Many of the institutional changes and policy orientations that have marked the recent history of the province are a direct function of Quebec's and Canada's collective reaction to language issues and the ethnocultural dynamics of modern Quebec. This chapter will review the history of politics and policies of language in Quebec in order to clarify the current situation.

14.1 THE SOCIOECONOMIC ROOTS OF THE LANGUAGE CONTROVERSY

[T]he French language is particularly characterized by inferior duties, small enterprises, low incomes, and low levels of education. The domain of the English language is the exact opposite, that of superior duties involving initiative and command, and large enterprises, and high levels of income and education. (Quoted in Levine 1990: 140)

Such was one of the observations in the report of the Commission of Inquiry on the Position of the French Language and on Language Rights in Quebec (also known as the Gendron Commission after its chairman). The findings of this commission, sponsored by Quebec, corroborated the conclusions of the federal Royal Commission on Bilingualism and Biculturalism (RCBB) (the Laurendeau-Dunton Commission), which only three years earlier, in 1969, had exposed the dismal socioeconomic disparities and inequalities that existed between Canadians of British and of French origin.

The growth and sudden surge of a radical nationalist movement in the early 1960s, combined with the new aggressiveness and political hunger of the Quiet Revolution, were serious enough to prompt the federal government, and later the provincial government, to investigate the social and economic ramifications of language. While everyone had been more or less aware of the implicit and perennial sociolinguistic hierarchy that segregated Canadian, and, even more so, Quebec society, the findings of both the Laurendeau-Dunton and the Gendron commission lifted the veil on what was perceived by many French-language and Quebec rights activists as an appalling socioeconomic iniquity that historically has been the lot of francophones in Quebec and Canada.

Of all the ethnic groups that make up the Canadian mosaic, French Canadians ranked among the least educated and the lowest paid—only slightly better than native peoples. In Canada outside Quebec, it was virtually impossible, despite constitutional guarantees, for French-speaking Canadians to receive an education in their own language. In contrast, the anglophone minority in Quebec had always had complete access to a full range of educational and social services dispensed in their own language. Finally, it was found that French Canadians were underrepresented in the federal public service in top- and middle-level decision-making positions.

Demonstration in October 1971 for "Defence of the French Language." This was known as the manifestation McGill français. *[Courtesy Archives nationales du Québec.]*

But it was the comparatively poor socioeconomic situation of French Canadians in their own province, where they constituted a majority, that raised the most concern and fuelled the anti-English resentment and pro-Quebec activism that animated the nationalism of the 1960s and 1970s. Key sectors of the Montreal and Quebec economies were controlled largely by English Canadian and foreign (mostly American) investors. In the early 1960s, anglophone economic power was undeniably a far-reaching and pervasive force. Drawing on the findings of the RCBB's background studies on the economic situation of francophones, and summing up the Commission's conclusions, Marc Levine[1] put the matter succinctly: Only 21.8% of the Quebec manufacturing labour force in 1961 worked in establishments owned by francophones; only 13% of Montreal's manufacturing establishments were owned by French Canadians. The value added in a francophone establishment, on average, was less than 25% that in an anglophone establishment and less than 15% that in a foreign-owned establishment. Francophone firms were still oriented mostly toward local markets: they sold only 22% of their output outside Quebec, in contrast to 49% by anglophone-owned establishments, and 60% by foreign-owned establishments (Levine 1990: 23).

By far the most frustrating aspect of this whole situation was the fact that francophone Quebecers, mostly in Montreal, could not work in their own language. They had to be fully bilingual if they aspired to well-paid jobs and managerial responsibilities, a requirement that was rarely, if ever, expected of their anglophone counterparts. The report of the RCBB was unequivocal on this score. In terms of opportunities to express themselves, to learn and to develop within a setting where their linguistic and cultural idiom was accepted and understood, francophones were seriously handicapped. English was overwhelmingly the language of work at the top levels. The relatively few francophones at this level had to work in a predominantly English-speaking milieu, but more importantly, the many francophones at lower levels were also forced to use English as their language of work (RCBB 1969: 469). In its own study of the situation, the Gendron Commission confirmed this pattern of linguistic relations and segregation at work. It went even further in its analysis and found that a francophone in a decision-making or managerial position was far less able than anglophone colleagues to impose his or her own language in dealings with subordinates. A francophone subordinate had to use English 63% of the time when dealing with an anglophone superior, while an anglophone subordinate would speak French to a francophone superior only 31% of the time (Gendron Commission 1972: 92ff).

---

1. Levine's book is to date the most comprehensive work in English on language issues in Quebec. This chapter draws in part from his work.

A new awareness of this treatment of the French language helped to spark the nationalistic discontent of the 1960s, and led directly to the politicization of language that marked the next three decades.

Until the 1960s, language had basically been a non-issue. Article 133 of the BNA Act (the Constitution) cited both French and English as the official languages of the legislature and courts of the province. Article 93 sanctioned the establishment of a dual school system along denominational, and thus for all practical purposes linguistic, lines. This provision operated as a de facto protection of English language rights in education throughout the province. The traditional distaste of Quebecers for state intervention before 1960 (Brunet 1964) prevented this particular linguistic dynamic from being altered for more than a century. The only exceptions were in 1910 when the provincial legislature passed the Lavergne Law (named after its proponent in the legislature) regulating the language practices of public utilities and requiring that written communications with the public (bills, signs, posters, tickets, contracts) by railway, telephone, and electric power companies use both languages. Similarly, in 1937, a law giving primacy to the French-language texts in interpretations of laws and regulations in the province was also passed. These two exceptions did not in any way serve as precedents for other reforms, however. They remained isolated incidents in the pre-1960 history of language policy in Quebec. Despite its rather modest objectives, the Lavergne Law went through, but with only the reluctant support of the governing (Liberal) party establishment, who expressed concern that the law would alienate the anglophone business community. As for the 1937 law, Premier Duplessis repealed it one year later, yielding to heavy pressure from the English-speaking business community (Bouthillier and Meynaud 1972: 326–328, 363; Levine 1990: 34).

To a large extent, linguistic geography accounts for the near-total absence of political concern over language prior to the Quiet Revolution. With only the notable exception of Montreal, where an ever-increasing proportion of English-speaking Quebecers have come to live, Quebec has always been solidly French-speaking. Even today, the number of immigrants who settle outside the Montreal metropolitan area remains minimal.

Over the years, the size of regions outside Montreal containing substantial English-speaking communities has been shrinking steadily. In 1871, it was possible to find in the Eastern Townships, south of Montreal, many predominantly anglophone townships. Brome, Compton, and Stanstead, for example, boasted populations of more than 75% English-speaking residents. Others, like Richmond, Sherbrooke, and Missisquoi, had populations of which nearly two-thirds were of British origin. By the middle of the 20th century, these once-proud bastions of British loyalism had undergone a complete reversal in their demographic situation: nine out of ten town-shippers were francophone. A similar pattern of English emigration occurred in all the other regions where anglophones were once found in appreciable numbers. Also, to make a stronger point, we could call attention to the fact that Montreal had an English-speaking majority until the 1850s, and that the first French-speaking mayor was elected during that decade.

In 1871, 22.6% of English-speaking Quebecers resided in Montreal; by 1961, 74.3% of them had made Montreal their home (Levine 1990: 10). The status of the city as a major Canadian economic and financial centre, as well as its largely English character and atmosphere until the 1960s, contributed significantly to this situation. With its already well established and economically dominant English-speaking community, Montreal was a natural pole of attraction for those Quebecers of British origin who resided outside Montreal. In addition, the waves of European immigrants who came to settle in the city, and adopted English as their language of daily public use, gradually swelled the number of English-speaking Montrealers.

In short, Quebec's demographics during the Quiet Revolution precluded direct ethnic and linguistic confrontations. The French and the English lived in separate quarters, and separate worlds that hardly ever intersected. The island of Montreal was, in fact, the only place where there existed any potential for ethnolinguistic conflicts. But a pattern of urban and sub-urban growth developed whereby the vast majority of each linguistic group simply chose to reside in self-contained areas where the other would rarely set foot. East of boulevard Saint-Laurent (Montreal's main street) were the francophone working-class neighbourhoods, and later on, lower-middle-class suburbs. On the western side was the anglophone-dominated finan-cial district; posh, mainly English-speaking neighbourhoods; and, later on, the middle-class suburbs of the West Island. As Marc Levine explains:

> there apparently was sufficient territorial separation on the Island through the 1960s to help keep potentially conflict-producing lin-guistic contacts to a minimum—tne consociational model of "good social fences" making "good social neighbors." (Levine 1990: 13)

But the geography of language does not tell the whole story. In addition, a well-oiled and effective system of elite accommodation—founded on an implicitly-agreed-upon division of labour between (1) the French-speaking, traditional, clergy-dominated middle class, and (2) the English-speaking industrial and financial elite—succeeded for well over a century in main-taining social peace and ethnolinguistic relations without major tensions. So long as it was allowed to keep its ideological and political dominion over its flock of Catholic and French-speaking labouring masses intact, the clerical elite provided anglophone industrialists and financiers with an ideal pool of docile and cooperative workers. This division of labour was also a division of power and societal jurisdiction: control of minds and politics went to the francophone elite; control of the economic realm went to its anglophone counterpart. This tacit entente reached its apogee under the premiership of Maurice Duplessis (McRoberts 1988: 108).

Though it was not without its occasional glitches, such an arrangement, developed over two hundred years of history, worked relatively well until after the Second World War. The miners' strike at the city of Asbestos in 1949 was the first in a chain of events that challenged the status quo. The following decade, though unequivocally dominated by the authoritarian and conservative government of Duplessis, saw a multitude of relentless attacks on the traditional order and system of elite accommodation. As we have seen, the combined action and joint efforts of labour organizations and an emerging technocratic middle class eventually led to the onset of that new era of socioeconomic management and institutional politics known as the Quiet Revolution (Roy 1976; Behiels 1985).

The buoyant and exciting sociopolitical atmosphere of the 1960s brought the refurbishing of the old structures of power and the abandonment of the values for which the traditional elites had stood. The perennial strategy of *la survivance* which the clergy had upheld was henceforth deemed inadequate. True, cooperation with the British conqueror had thwarted the assimilationist plans of the 19th century and eventually paid off in terms of political power and historical continuity; but to the rising guard of the revolution, the benefits of the survival strategy were negligible. Though francophones in Quebec had been allowed to keep their religion, language, and legal system, they lived as second-class citizens in their own province. Access to the levers of real social power—economic power—was denied them. They were a majority dominated by a minority. The findings of the RCBB and Gendron Commission only vindicated the sense of outrage that carried forward the emerging, renewed nationalism.

The philosophy of *Maîtres chez nous*, the central theme of the new age, left its imprint on the political conscience of Quebecers and the public policy agenda for the next three decades. It implied that the anglophone elite had to be dislodged, or at least that francophones had to be allowed to occupy as much room at the top of the economic hierarchy as their numbers warranted.

The political representatives of the new middle class who supported these views came to power in 1960 with the election of the Liberal party, and immediately began to replace the old political administrative structures and rebuild a new society. The growth of state functions and interventions that ensued were integral parts of a newly assertive strategy of both class and nationalism. While the expansion of the state primarily benefitted the new middle class, giving it technocratic and bureaucratic, and thus social, dominance (Guindon 1988; Simard 1979), it also provided

French-speaking Quebecers in general with much-needed tools to prop up their nationalist pride and develop their economic capabilities. Indeed, as we have seen, the Quebec state became during the 1960s and 1970s a major economic player, starting with the nationalization of Hydro-Québec and continuing with the creation of important financial and investment institutions (e.g., SGF and Caisse de dépôt et placement) (Gagnon and Montcalm 1990: 39–77).

The cultural explosion of the 1960s must also be mentioned—*chansonniers*, theatre, literature, etc. In this charged nationalistic atmosphere, language emerged as a potent symbol of French Canadian affirmation and emancipation. As the new leadership took a firm grip of the state and the tools of policymaking, as it sought more direct access to and control over the sites of social, economic, and political power, it saw no reason why everything could not be done in French. The establishment of French as the official language of Quebec's public affairs and business operations became an integral and programmatic part of the process of social and political redefinition that the new middle class was controlling and imposing on Quebec society.

14.2 AN OVERVIEW OF LANGUAGE POLICY SINCE 1960

Épanouissement vs. *Minorisation*

While it is true that language became an issue because of the political and cultural aspirations of the new leadership, it manifested itself in more-mundane ways. The sheer fear of cultural disappearance, and what was perceived by many as the stubborn tendency of immigrants to integrate themselves into the anglophone rather than the francophone community, prompted many activists to press for direct governmental intervention in language relations.

It was in Montreal, of course, that these threats were felt most intensely. In spite of the fact that the city's francophone population had remained a solid majority through the 1960s, Montreal still sported a predominantly English face, with English commercial signs and place names. But perhaps the most disturbing fact for many French-language activists and nationalists was the fact that 98% of immigrants' "linguistic transfers" involved adoption of English. (The fact that 53% of net linguistic transfers in the rest of the province favoured French was small consolation given that the bulk of immigrants landed and lived in Montreal.)

In addition, the English-language school system attracted nearly all non-French, non-English-speaking children. According to the Gendron Commission:

whereas in 1943, 52% of the Italian children under the jurisdiction of the Montreal Catholic School Board were enrolled in French schools, by 1972 this percentage had dropped to nine. (D'Anglejan 1984: 33)

By the late 1960s, nine in ten "allophone" children in Montreal were enrolled in English-language public schools, both Protestant and Catholic. The reasons usually cited included the poor quality of French-language compared to English-language education; the inadequate teaching of English as a second language in French schools; the feeling of rejection immigrant parents experienced in a number of French schools; and the definition of the school system along denominational lines, a situation that forced some non-Catholics to send their children to Protestant schools, where they then received schooling in English (D'Anglejan 1984: 33–34). One final reason, clearly, is that, given the dominance of English in North America, immigrants understood that English was without a doubt the language of upward mobility, even in Quebec (Levine 1990: 56–57).

Immigrant anglicization soon came to be perceived as a threat to francophone *épanouissement* (blossoming), a rejection of the language of the majority to which many took offence. The linguistic choices of immigrants and the massive enrollment of their children in English schools were "fraught with explosive cultural and economic implications" (Levine 1990: 61). The fear of *minorisation* began to grow and nationalists warned against the danger to French language and culture.

In 1962, the Société Saint-Jean-Baptiste de Montréal (SSJBM), a promoter of the French language and the nationalist movement, before the Commission of Inquiry on Education (the Parent Commission), urged that: (1) all graduates of Quebec schools possess "knowledge" of French; (2) in Quebec courts, the French texts of laws be considered the only authentic texts; (3) private enterprises in Quebec be required to have "francised" names (e.g., Eaton's should be *Eaton*; Smith's Hardware should be *Quincaillerie Smith*); and (4) the language of instruction in all public schools in Quebec should be French, with the exception of schools for children whose mother tongue is English, in which case instruction should be bilingual (Levine 1990: 52). Other political and para-political organizations, such as the Ralliement pour l'indépendance nationale (RIN), added their voices to that of the SSJBM and pressed for similar policies.

Partly in response to these calls for francisation and partly in accordance with its own objectives of cultural development, the Lesage government created in 1961 the Ministry of Cultural Affairs, which included an *Office de la langue française*, designed to oversee "the correctness and enrichment" of French in Quebec. But the government's initial commitment to French culture and language fizzled out as other policy priorities took centre stage. While the question of language and cultural reinforcement had quickly gained attention in mainstream francophone political circles, the government began to make it a central policy issue only after a major linguistic crisis broke out in 1968 in Saint-Léonard, an east-end suburban municipality of Montreal.

The Saint-Léonard Crisis

The town of Saint-Léonard had grown from a semi-rural, homogeneously French-speaking community of about 1,000 residents in the mid-1950s to an ever-developing, multiethnic suburb of more than 52,000 by the late 1960s. Attracted by affordable modern housing and convenient access to downtown Montreal and east-end factories, thousands of lower-middle-class francophones and large numbers of Italian immigrants moved to Saint-Léonard in the 1960s. By the end of the decade, the town's population was 60% francophone and 30% Italian immigrants; the remainder consisted of anglophones and a few other ethnic groups (Levine, 1990: 67).

In 1963, noticing the increasingly multiethnic character of the community, the local school board opened bilingual elementary schools in which classes would be taught in both French and English. What was conceived as an option designed to ensure mastery of the French language and still offer the quality of English-language instruction desired by immigrant parents almost became a rule among allophones. The innovation was tremendously popular. Four years later, over 90% of Saint-Léonard's allophone schoolchildren were enrolled in bilingual classes, thus providing a captive clientele for the English-language high schools of the districts: 85% of the students enrolled in bilingual elementary schools, in fact, went on to English secondary schools. This situation provoked serious concern among nationalists who saw their worst fears materializing: public schooling functioning as an instrument of anglicization. Even more disturbing to them was the fact that a number of francophone parents also took advantage of the bilingual schools.

Apprised of these unexpected results, the francophone-controlled Saint-Léonard school board decided in November 1967 to terminate its bilingual program as of the fall of 1968, though allowing those already enrolled to complete the program. This imposition of French unilingualism was deeply resented and negatively received by allophone parents who, through the Saint-Léonard Parents' Association, demanded that bilingual classes be restored and parental freedom of choice maintained. They threatened to take court action, withhold school taxes, and keep their children out of class. Startled by the intensity of the reaction, the school board postponed implementation of the policy for another year.

But the damage was done. Soon, activists were storming the barricades. A francophone organization, the *Mouvement pour l'intégration scolaire* (MIS), was created with the aim of making French the sole language of education in Saint-Léonard's public schools. Support for unilingualist action came from other national and local organizations such as the RIN, the SSJB, and the Montreal Teachers' Federation. The situation quickly deteriorated to an all-out war, each side resorting to court actions, sit-ins, public demonstrations, etc. The Saint-Léonard crisis eventually lost its purely local character and, in the following months, culminated in events of national significance that contributed to a sense of general linguistic crisis and symbolized the dissolution of linguistic peace: the bloody riots of the Saint-Jean-Baptiste parade on June 24, 1968, the separatist bombings of anglophone institutions and businesses, and various "urban guerilla" actions, such as the violent protest against the anglophone-controlled Murray Hill Company. All this, combined with perceived growing support for independence and unilingualism, and the creation of the PQ in October 1968, inexorably brought the language question into the centre of the political arena.

It was in this supercharged atmosphere that the government announced in November 1968 its intention to legislate in the area of language. The introduction of Bill 85 marked the first in a series of steps made by successive governments to intervene on the language issue. The bill advocated:

> the creation of a Linguistic Committee within the Superior Council of Education which would establish regulations governing the language of education. School boards would be obliged to provide instruction in either language if requested. However a working knowledge of French would be required of all pupils. The bill thus provided protection for the rights of parents to choose the language of instruction for their children, while proposing provisions to ensure that persons settling in the province would acquire a working knowledge of French and send their children to French schools. (D'Anglejan 1984: 36)

French-language rights activists and other nationalists were dissatisfied, and launched several fierce, public attacks on the government's proposal. The governing party (the Union nationale) was itself divided over the bill. In the end, the Premier simply withdrew Bill 85—but not without reiterating his support for open access to English-language schools.

Thus, the problem was left unresolved, and the crisis continued to dominate the news. Less than a year later, after mass demonstrations calling for the francisation of McGill University, boycotts, and counterdemonstrations culminating in riots in the streets of Saint-Léonard, Premier Bertrand presented and passed Bill 63 in the National Assembly. This new legislation, a revised version of Bill 85, essentially maintained the status quo with respect to bilingualism and freedom of choice. It did, however, establish the principle of priority of French in the public and private sectors, and recognize the fundamental right of francophones to work in French. It entrusted the Office de la langue française with the role of ensuring the priority of French in public postings and hearing complaints of workers and employees who felt their right to work in French was being denied.

While the legislation satisfied anglophones and allophones, it angered French unilingualists, who immediately called for its withdrawal. The issue of the anglicization of immigrants dominated the political agenda throughout the 1970s, as a vociferous francophone nationalist movement continued to campaign for the primacy of French in education and all other spheres of public and private life.

Bourassa and Bill 22

In the years that followed Bill 63, ethnolinguistic unrest reached new heights in the 1970 FLQ crisis, which symbolized the exasperation large segments of the francophone population were feeling, and showed that the concept of linguistic duality was no longer tenable for a growing number of French-speaking Quebecers. The new Liberal government, which under the leadership of Robert Bourassa had been elected only months before the FLQ crisis, was pressed to take stock and come up with a comprehensive solution to the language problem.

Its response was Bill 22, entitled the Official Languages Act, which addressed the two central issues in the language debate: the economy and language of education. Bill 22 was presented to the National Assembly in May 1974 and declared French the sole official language of the province, which meant that a working knowledge of it was now a prerequisite for

Demonstration against Bill 22 in 1974. [Courtesy Archives nationales du Québec.]

employment and advancement in the public service. Professionals—doctors, lawyers, nurses, social workers—would henceforth have to demonstrate their ability to work in French in order to be granted work permits. Contracts with the government would have to be drawn up in French. French would have to be the language of business at every level, in firm names, on product labels, on public signs, etc. However, the concurrent use of another language was not prohibited; thus, Bill 22 maintained the legitimacy of bilingualism (D'Anglejan 1984: 38).

Under the legislation, business establishments were encouraged to obtain "francisation certificates" in order to receive contracts, subsidies, concessions, or benefits from government. The certificates were to be issued only to businesses that met the following requirements related to language of work: (1) knowledge and use of French by management personnel; (2) presence of francophones in management; (3) availability in French of manuals, catalogues, written instructions, and other documents distributed to personnel; (4) the possibility for personnel to communicate in French among themselves and with superior officers (D'Anglejan 1984: 38). It was at this point that the *Régie de la langue française* was established to supervise, set up, implement, and assist firms in the francisation process, as well as generally enforce the law.

The fundamental logic of the bill was based on persuasion rather than coercion. Loath to interfere in the workings of private enterprise, the Bourassa government relied on incentives to promote the position of French in the economy. As Marc Levine explains:

> The only coercion in Bill 22 involved companies doing business with the government: if firms were willing to forgo provincial government contracts or subsidies, they could avoid the costs of francisation altogether. Although some Anglophone businessmen fretted over the discretion given the Régie, most understood that Bill 22 was not about to disrupt Anglophone control or the use of English in the Montreal economy. (Levine 1990: 101).

Insofar as public administration was concerned, all agencies of the provincial state were to operate in French, though individuals were allowed to choose either language in their dealings with government. Similarly, municipal and local institutions were permitted to draw up documents in both languages if a minimum of 10% of their clientele was anglophone (Gagnon and Montcalm 1990: 181).

Its approach to the language of education was the most controversial aspect of Bill 22. Bill 63 had made the choice of the language of instruction for one's children a legal right. Bill 22 limited this right by restricting access to English schools to children with sufficient knowledge of English to receive their instruction in that language. Language tests were to be administered by school boards to determine who would be allowed to register in English schools. The size of the English school system could be expanded only at the discretion of the minister of education, and only to accommodate the English-speaking community.

This measure was, obviously, intended to curb the flow of immigrant children into English schools and restrict existing allophone enrollment in the English system by limiting facilities (D'Anglejan 1984: 39; Gagnon and Montcalm 1990: 181). In spite of persuasion programs aimed at developing immigrants' fluency in French and fostering their natural attraction to and eventual assimilation of the language and culture of the majority, under Bill 63's freedom-of-choice clause, most immigrants continued to send their children to English schools. By 1973–1974, 88.6% of Montreal allophone school children were being taught in English. The share of total Montreal school enrollment claimed by the English-language sector had risen from 36.8% in 1970 to 40.3% in 1974. When the end of the baby boom and slowing immigration led to declining enrollment in Montreal schools, French-speaking schools underwent an 18.4% decline under Bill 63, but the English sector's reduction in enrollment was roughly a mere third of that, 5.7%. In some school districts, such as Saint-Léonard, the enrollment in English schools increased by 69.7% between 1970 and 1974, while French-school enrollment declined by 1.4% during the same period (Levine 1990: 101).

Lévesque and Bills 101, 57, and 58

Bill 22 pleased no one. It was opposed by nationalists as too timid, and anglophone groups were furious at the diminished status that English would henceforth have in Quebec. The law was denounced for its ambiguities; for the discretionary powers granted to the Minister of Education, school boards, and the Régie; for the language tests; and finally for the many loopholes that would allow its more stringent prescriptions to be circumvented.

During the two years it was in force, Bill 22 failed to resolve the language problem. Although the legislation helped slow down the depopulation of French schools on the Island of Montreal, enrollment in the anglophone school network continued to grow, from 40.3% to 41.2% (Levine 1990: 107). Bourassa promised to humanize the school assignment process, but in the November 1976 election he was defeated before he had the chance to amend the law.

The victory of the PQ was a turning point in the province's political history. For the first time, a group whose unequivocal aim was to promote Quebec's political independence and to make French the predominant language of public and private life in the province came to power. The PQ wasted no time. On August 26, 1977, less than a year after the party's ascent to power, Bill 101 (known in English as the Charter of the French Language) was passed in the National Assembly by a vote of 54 to 32 after heated public debate.[2]

Bill 101 reinforced the status of French as the official language of Quebec and, in Chapter II of the bill, delineated fundamental language rights, namely:

- The right of "every person to have the civil administration, the health and social services, the public utility firms, the professional corporations, the associations of employees, and all business firms doing business in Quebec communicate with him/her in French"

- The right to speak in French in deliberative assembly

- The right of workers to carry on their activities in French (which implied, as stipulated in Chapter VI of the law, a prohibition from dismissing, demoting, or transferring an employee on the basis of his/her insufficient knowledge of a language other than French. Similarly, it also prohibited an employer from making employment contingent upon the knowledge of a language other than French, unless it could be demonstrated that the nature of the duties required the knowledge of that other language.)

- the right of consumers of goods and services to be informed and served in French

- the right of every person eligible for instruction to receive that instruction in French

In addition, Bill 101 designated French as the language of the legislature and the courts, and declared that only the French versions of laws, regulations, or documents were official. The dispositions already found in Bill 22 regarding the use of French in business and commerce were intensified: instructions on products, catalogues, brochures, toys and games, contracts, application forms, and firm names all had to be in French. Similarly, only French could be used on public signs and posters (though several exceptions were allowed).

Bill 101 differed markedly from Bill 22 in the rigour with which it imposed the use of French in both public utilities and private enterprises, and at all levels. Bill 22 had relied on the goodwill of Quebec industry to increase the use of French. Bill 101 dictated deadlines and sanctions. Business establishments with more than 50 employees were forced to obtain

---

2. A prior, somewhat more radical version of the law, Bill 1, had been presented in April 1977. As hearings stretched into July, the government began to worry that the opposition might filibuster to prevent the bill from being passed in time for the beginning of school in September. The bill was withdrawn, purged of its more radical and authoritarian content, and reintroduced as Bill 101. Some of its more stringent components, such as the francisation program of public administrative bodies, had also been loosened up (Levine 1990: 118).

Camille Laurin, minister responsible for language policy under the Parti québécois government. He initiated Bill 1, which later became Bill 101. This bill made French the official language of Quebec. [Courtesy Archives nationales du Québec.]

their francisation certificates by 1983. Failure to comply led to one of three types of sanctions: ineligibility to receive government contracts or subsidies, substantial fines, and finally—this was a somewhat less tangible but nonetheless effective punishment—moral sanctions and public denunciation likely to result in a loss of clientele and revenue (D'Anglejan 1984: 40–41).

As far as the language of education was concerned, Bill 101 allowed only certain categories of children to receive instruction in English: children whose father or mother received his or her elementary instruction in English in Quebec; children whose father or mother, domiciled in Quebec on the date the law came into force, received his or her elementary instruction in English outside Quebec; children already enrolled in the English school system; and the younger siblings of the preceding. All other categories, including English-speaking migrants from other parts of Canada, had to receive their education in French.

Finally, three different boards were created to enforce the law and carry out functions formerly assigned to the Régie de la langue française:

1. The *Office de la langue française*, responsible for defining and conducting Quebec policy and research in linguistics and terminology, approving francisation certificates, administering French proficiency tests, setting up terminology committees, and supervising the introduction and use of French terminology in government organizations

2. The *Conseil de la langue française*, responsible for monitoring the progress of language planning and its implementation with respect to the status, use, and quality of the French language, and counselling the minister of education on all questions of the Bill's interpretation

3. The *Commission de surveillance et des enquêtes*, responsible for dealing with failures to comply with the law

At first, Bill 101 was greeted with bitterness by the anglophone community, whose leaders, who where mostly in the education sector, called for open defiance and civil disobedience (Levine 1990: 122–123). But by the early 1980s anglophones were showing signs that they had adapted politically and institutionally to the new linguistic reality under Bill 101. They abandoned efforts to restore freedom of choice in schooling, recognized French predominance, and focussed instead on loosening Bill 101's strictures regarding commercial signs and obtaining government services in English. While admitting that Quebec was a predominantly francophone society, *Alliance-Québec*, an anglo-right pressure group formed in 1982 and funded by federal monies, lobbied the provincial government for changes in language policy and supported legal challenges to selected aspects of Bill 101. In 1983, a SORECOM survey polling anglophones on their opinions on the French language showed that the vast majority considered it important for themselves (94%) and for their children (96%) to speak French. Nearly three-quarters (74%) felt anglophones whose mother tongue was English were making increased efforts to learn French. Finally, 80% of those surveyed thought it legitimate for the Quebec government to protect the French language (Gagnon and Montcalm 1990: 185–186).

The same survey measured francophone opinion with regard to language rights for anglophones, and found that 66% believed English-speaking persons should be able to communicate with Quebec's government institutions in English; 89% believed English-language institutions should be able to function internally in English (so long as they provided services in French), and 72% believed English-speaking people who came to Quebec, irrespective of their country of origin, should be able to send their children to English schools (Gagnon and Montcalm 1990: 186).

Clearly the tensions that pitted one linguistic community against the other barely a decade earlier had dramatically subsided. The PQ government demonstrated its goodwill by considering modifications to its language legislation. Calls from the French media for a softening of the law in the name of social peace, in combination with the abrogation of certain sections of Bill 101 by several Quebec courts and the Canadian Supreme Court, certainly played a role in bringing the government to a more tolerant and flexible stance. The court decisions in particular hit hard at both the spirit and content of Bill 101:

- In 1979, the Supreme Court declared the provisions making French the sole official language of the provincial legislature and the courts unconstitutional.

- In 1981, the new, patriated Canadian constitution included Article 23, guaranteeing access to English-language schools in Quebec to children of parents who had received their primary education anywhere in Canada, and clashing with provisions of Bill 101.

- In 1984, the Supreme Court upheld a Quebec lower court decision abrogating Article 73 of Bill 101 as incompatible with Article 23 of the new Constitution (Levine 1990: 130).

Eventually, the PQ government did make an effort to reach out to the anglophone community. Bill 57, passed in January 1984, and the final language legislation of the PQ, modified Bill 101 in response to the concerns of the anglophone community. The preamble was amended to give institutions of the English-speaking community explicit recognition. Prior to Bill 57, the law required that anglophone Quebecers be bilingual to work in English-speaking public institutions and administrations. With Bill 57, the onus of bilingualism was henceforth to be borne by the institution and

The anglophone community had always felt Bill 101 was aimed at them, and encroached on their rights. A demonstration on January 22, 1982 in front of the Montreal Stock Exchange. [Courtesy Le Devoir and Gilles Paré, Librarian. Photo: Jacques Grenier.]

not individuals; the law required that sufficient bilingual staff be available to offer services in the official language. Similarly ,whereas Bill 101 had stipulated that internal communications in English school boards, health and social service institutions, and English municipalities had to be in French, Bill 57 removed this restriction to allow employees to communicate with each other in their own language. Communications between institutions, required to be exclusively in French under Bill 101, could now be accompanied by an English translation. Finally, business establishments were allowed to negotiate their francisation program with the Office de la langue française so as to avoid adverse economic consequences.

Bill 57 was well received by the anglophone community, though there were some minor criticisms of the limited nature of the changes. Montreal's French press also praised the law as a sign of social maturity on linguistic matters. In November 1985, the Quebec electorate brought Robert Bourassa and the Liberal party back to power. Bourassa continued the rapprochement with the anglophone community, first by decreeing in December 1985 that no prosecution would be made of individuals or institutions for contravening Bill 101 until the courts had ruled on its validity. Then, in June 1986, the government passed Bill 58, a law granting amnesty to 1,013 "illegals" attending English schools in violation of the Charter of the French Language, i.e., Bill 101. The law allowed these children to continue their education, with the implication that all of their siblings and descendants were guaranteed access to English schools.

Bourassa and Bills 140, 142, and 178

In November 1986, the reelected Bourassa presented two more bills related to language policy: Bill 140, which outlined a radical streamlining of the linguistic bureaucracy created by Bill 101; and Bill 142, an act to guarantee anglophones the right to receive social and health services in English. Bill 140 was eventually abandoned in the face of strong opposition from both inside and outside the bureaucracy. As the intent of the bill was to "rein in the administrative arms of aggressive language policy" (Levine 1990: 132), critics claimed it would substantially weaken Bill 101. Bill 142, however, was passed in December 1986. Since the enactment of Bill 101, the dispensation of social services had evolved on a territorial-linguistic basis: in the anglophone enclaves of Montreal, health and social services institutions were given the right to offer services in English, provided that these be available in French as well; they were recognized by the Office de la langue française as anglophone institutions. In its original version, Bill 142 had extended English-language health and social services to *all* individuals who expressed themselves in English. This meant that the government might require health and social services to be available in English outside anglophone enclaves. Radical nationalists saw this as a step toward a return to a bilingual Quebec, and their mobilization against Bill 142 forced the government to retreat. In its final form, the law applied only to regions where the linguistic composition of the population justified the existence of services in English.

This relative truce brought about by Bill 57, Bill 58, and Bill 142 disintegrated over the question of commercial signs in late 1986. That year, the Quebec Court of Appeal ruled that the disallowance of any language other than French on commercial signs violated the guarantees of linguistic equality contained in the Canadian constitution, as well as the guarantees of freedom of expression contained in Quebec's own Charter. The Court's decision coincided with the reemergence of English in public communication in certain sectors of Montreal; this, plus the perceived laissez-faire attitude of government toward the situation, reignited linguistic tensions. Public denunciations and guerilla-like attacks on English business establishments occurred. Mass demonstrations were organized in Montreal to defend Bill 101 and preserve the French character of that city and of the whole province.

Once again Bourassa was caught between the two communities. On one side, francophone nationalists pressed him to maintain the integrity of Bill 101; on the other, anglophones demanded he make good on his 1985 electoral promise to relax the restrictions on commercial signs. In December 1988, the Supreme Court upheld the Court of Appeal's decision and ruled that Bill 101 illegally proscribed bilingual signs. Bourassa's response was Bill 178 and the recourse to the *notwithstanding clause*—one that allows a province to exempt itself from a constitutional disposition. Bill 178 demanded French-only signs on the outside of commercial establishments, but allowed languages other than French to be displayed inside stores, so long as French remained graphically predominant.

The legislation was decried by both communities. Francophone nationalists accused Bourassa of diluting Bill 101; anglophones, both within and outside Quebec, were outraged by the invocation of the notwithstanding clause. Three prominent English-speaking ministers resigned from Bourassa's cabinet: Richard French (Communications), Clifford Lincoln (Environment) and Herbert Marx (Justice). After months of further tensions and equivocation as to what the predominance of French signs really entailed, the government announced that in shopping malls, in all establishments with more than 50 employees, on mass transit vehicles, in large department stores, and in chains such as McDonald's, all signs, inside and out, had to be French-only. In the end, Bill 178 applied only to commercial establishments with fewer than 50 employees and "clear predominance" was defined as French signs twice as large or twice as numerous as those

After a decision of the Supreme Court in December 1988 and the Bourassa government's enactment of Bill 178, which dealt with the language used on signs, there was great bitterness, especially among the anglophone community. Here is a vandal's comment on the situation. [Courtesy Le Devoir and Gilles Paré, Librarian. Photo: Jacques Grenier.]

in the other language. Bill 178 turned out to be only slightly less stringent than Bill 101 on the question of language of commercial signs.

Bill 178 disturbed the relative linguistic peace achieved in the early 1980s. The anglophones in particular felt abandoned and discouraged by what they saw as Bourassa's reneging on his 1985 campaign promises. Their discontent was revealed in the 1989 election when the Equality Party, an English-rights party whose platform harkened back to the pre-1976 era, won four seats in the National Assembly, essentially on the linguistic issue. The strength of the Equality Party in Montreal was the result of a tremendously alienated anglophone community.

14.3 TAKING STOCK: WHAT LANGUAGE POLICIES REALLY ACHIEVED

The Charter of the French Language (Bill 101) had two primary objectives: (1) francising the economy to bolster the economic situation of French-speaking Quebecers; and (2) protecting the demographic position of francophones in Montreal by redirecting allophones and English-speaking children from outside Quebec to the French public schools (Levine 1990: 138).

The Economy

As far as the economy goes, while language policy alone cannot account for the relative strengthening of francophones in the Quebec and North American economies, there is no doubt that it reinforced the deliberate efforts of successive governments to enhance the economic role and position of French-speaking Quebecers. Just as government-sponsored economic initiatives, such as Hydro-Québec, the SGF, and the Caisse were instrumental in creating a new breed of successful francophone entrepreneurs (Gagnon and Montcalm 1990: 39–77, 102–132; Levine 1990: 149–176), French-language policies—the Charter of the French Language in particular—contributed directly to asserting the French character of the Quebec economy. As French increasingly became the lingua franca of economic relations, language policies helped to increase the prominence of francophones in their own economy. While some analysts have argued that francisation of the economy was well under way even before Bill 22, language policies probably accelerated that process. The fact remains: the socioeconomic position of both francophones and the French language have made significant progress since the days of the RCBB and the Gendron Commission. And many of the imbalances and injustices identified by those two commissions had, by the late 1980s, largely been corrected or at least appreciably improved upon.

French has undeniably asserted itself as the language of the workplace in particular. The percentage of Montreal francophones working almost exclusively in French increased from 48% in 1971 to more than 56% by the mid-1980s. During the same period, the percentage of Montreal anglophones working almost exclusively in English declined from 66.8% to 46.7%. By the late 1970s, Montreal's bilingual anglophones reported using French at work between 30% and 40% of the time. In fact, by the 1980s it had become markedly difficult for Montreal anglophones to make it in the labour market without at least a working knowledge of French. Increasingly, their economic welfare has come to depend on being bilingual: while in 1961, unilingual anglophones constituted 32% of Montreal's highest-paid workers, in 1985 they represented only 7.8%. In 1961, unilingual anglophones represented 57.1% of the best-paid *English-speaking* workers in Montreal; in 1985 their percentage had declined to 31.7%.

By comparison, the socioeconomic status of francophones had made impressive gains between 1961 and 1985. In 1961, for example, male anglophone Montrealers earned 51% more than francophones; by 1980, they earned only 14% more. Although francophones constituted over 67% of Montreal's labour force in 1961, they represented only 44% of the city's best-paid workers; by 1985, 75.4% of Montreal's best-paid workers were francophone, a percentage that corresponds roughly to the proportion of francophone workers in the overall labour force. Similarly, whereas 67.8% of Montreal francophones earned less than $25,000 a year in 1970 (in 1985 constant dollars), only 51.5% of Montreal anglophones fell into this income category. By 1980, the proportion of francophones in the lower end of the income scale had fallen to 53.5% with considerable increases in both middle- and upper-level earnings categories.

There is no doubt that factors other than language policy have contributed to the collective economic betterment of francophones in Montreal and in the rest of Quebec. An improved school system has produced better-educated francophones, thus broadening the middle class; increased unionization and labour movements in the 1960s and 1970s has improved the economic situation of many categories of workers; and finally, massive employment in the public sector, with wages that exceed those of the private sector for comparable jobs, have created large, privileged segments in the working and middle classes. But along with all of this, language policies encouraged francophone assertiveness in the workplace and opened opportunities for upward mobility that were virtually nonexistent before 1960.

The key achievement of the language policies—in particular the Charter of the French Language—was their success as morale boosters for French-speaking Quebecers. In this way, they served the main objective of the Quiet Revolution, that of the economic autonomization of francophones. As a tool of cultural development, language policies supported the *épanouissement* ideology implicit in much of Quebec politics since the 1960s. Although highly symbolic, the control over language and the concomitant mobilizing of ethnic and national pride of francophones formed the impetus for a tremendous effort toward economic self-reliance—something long perceived as the primary prerequisite for national and collective objectives. In this sense, language and economic autonomy go hand in hand.

Through the promotion of the French language and national character, language policies also aimed to promote the growth of francophone corporations and players in the Quebec economy. By the 1980s, the existence of a francophone economic elite was no longer in doubt. Rarely would a major investment be made without the participation of one or more francophone financial institutions. The *caisses populaires*, the *Banque nationale* (a private bank), and the *Groupe La Laurentienne* (a private insurance company) are now prominent players in the Quebec economy. Industrial conglomerates such as Bombardier and Cascades, and major engineering firms such as SNC-Lavalin, now have significant holdings on an international scale. In short:

> the evidence is clear that the linguistic segmentation of economic activity in Montreal has declined since the 1970s as Francophone firms have penetrated historically Anglophone sectors in finance,

heavy industry, high technology and advanced corporate services. (Levine 1990: 190)

Yet, despite these apparent successes and the gains made with respect to the French language, the battle for complete francisation of the economy has not yet been won. Studies have shown that while unilingual franco-phones' opportunities for well-paid employment have expanded over the years, bilingualism is still necessary for advancement in corporate Montreal. The status of French as a language of management has improved only because public-sector managerial employment has flourished along with the Quebec state; in firms controlled by English-Canadian or foreign capi-tal, francophone managers are still less likely to work exclusively in French. In fact, the progress of French has been mainly of a local nature. In head offices and corporate activities oriented toward non-Quebec markets, English continues to be the main language of communication. Similarly, while francophone control of capital is by any standard impressive, anglo-phone capital is still in command of the Montreal economy through major international corporations such as Seagrams, Pratt & Whitney, Bell Canada Enterprises, Imasco, and Alcan Aluminum. In spite of the emergence of substantial francophone corporations in Montreal and across Quebec, the bulk of francophone economic strength continues to be confined to locally oriented small and medium-sized companies. Finally, despite the tremen-dous leap forward made by francophone wage earners since the 1960s, more than one out of five French-speaking Montrealers continued to live below the poverty line during the 1980s.

The economic triumph of French-speaking Quebecers is not yet com-plete. For this reason it is unlikely the language issue will be laid to rest in the near future. The goal of making French the "normal and customary" language of work as envisioned by Bill 101, has yet to be accomplished. Para-doxically, as the Quebec economy seeks integration into the international economy, English-language work requirements will likely be imposed on upwardly mobile francophones and allophones. English is and probably will remain the dominant language of Montreal's, and by extension Quebec's, economy.

Education

Perhaps the greatest achievement of Bill 101 was its success in reversing the trend toward English-language schooling of allophone children. Bill 101 put an end to what was perceived by many as the threat of francophone marginalization in Montreal public schools. In 1977–1978, the English-language school network of Montreal attracted 41.5% of the Island's school children; by 1989–1990 that share had fallen to 29.0%. By the late 1980s, two-thirds of Montreal's allophone children were enrolled in French-language schools. In fact, Bill 101 has completely inverted the enrollment trends that characterized Montreal's school network until the mid-1970s: it has turned English-language education into a preserve for a narrowly defined community of anglophones, and slowed the depopulation of the city's French-language schools.

But its ultimate impact may be far more radical and not so desirable. In their book, *The English Fact in Quebec*, journalists Sheila McLeod Arnopoulos and Dominique Clift warned that the gift of Bill 101 might well be a Trojan horse. By forcibly integrating immigrants into the mainstream of Quebec society and supposedly guaranteeing francophone demographic survival, Bill 101 might recast French Québécois culture in ways that have little to do with its traditional characteristics (McLeod Arnopoulos and Clift 1980). While some see this as a positive contribution to Quebec's cultural dynamism, it may also lead to social tensions as the historical cultural homogeneity of schools is rapidly transformed by multiculturalism. By 1987, French-language schools comprised over 25% nonfrancophones and over 35% of their clientele were not of French Québécois ethnic origin. Grappling with this racial and ethnic diversity is proving to be a problem for the predominately francophone body of educators: they must teach in French to students with little or no mastery of the language; introduce "multicultural" education to the heretofore "homogeneous" French Canadian Catholic curriculum and personnel; and deal with the general problems of an influx of children from disadvantaged households (as many immigrant households are).

This reasoning appears to have been sound. Reports of conflict in the schools are not uncommon, and signs of xenophobia are rampant among certain segments of the francophone Québécois population (Levine 1990: 143–146).

14.4 WHITHER THE LANGUAGE QUESTION?

There is no doubt that the determination of French-speaking Quebecers to assert their majority status and make French the official language of the province has paid off. Greater collective self-confidence and a stronger grip on the socioeconomic destiny of the province are the obvious, positive outcomes of linguistic affirmation. It may even be said that Bill 101 in particular has contributed to a rapprochement between French- and English-language groups in Montreal and Quebec as a whole. Bilingualism among Montreal anglophones went from a mere 24% in 1960 to 53% in 1981, and some surveys even suggest that as many as two-thirds of Montreal anglophones under the age of 25 are now bilingual. The domineering and scornful behaviour the anglophone minority often exhibited towards francophones prior to the Quiet Revolution is definitely a thing of the past. Fear of *minorisation* in Montreal is less and less justified as the linguistic composition of the greater Montreal area increasingly favours the French language.

This is not to deny that certain aspects of the language question are bound to flare up again. Net "linguistic transfers" in Montreal still favour English, as more people report using English at home than there are people whose mother tongue is English (21.6% and 25.2% respectively, a difference of 3.6).

Similarly, allophones still tend to use English rather than French at home, and in the strongly English atmosphere of the West Island, the rate of francophone anglicization is fairly high considering the gains made by the French language elsewhere (in towns like Montreal West, more than a quarter of the persons whose mother tongue is French have reported speaking English only at home in the 1986 census, a percentage only slightly lower than that found among franco-Ontarians).

The influence of English remains undeniably strong in Quebec. The main threat to French may no longer come from a privileged anglophone minority, but English does remain the language of upward mobility in the corporate world—a fact appreciated by both francophones and allophones. In addition, the constant and indisputable influence of North America's English-language culture creates tremendous anglicization pressures that are further reinforced by the efforts of the business community to keep Quebec's economy in tune with the world economy and international technological advances.

In short, the French language remains vulnerable, though for different reasons than those that threatened the integrity of French culture and language prior to the 1960s. It seems more necessary than ever to step up efforts to maintain the predominance of French and preserve the victories gained over two decades of linguistic warfare. The threats to French are perceived as real, not only by activists, but also by large segments of the population.

In a 1987 survey, 60% of francophones interviewed labelled immigrants a serious threat to the French language, and overwhelming numbers favoured "making more babies" to deal with the depopulation problem (Levine 1990: 220). By bringing different cultures into the French fold, Bill 101 not only created a language threat; it also subjected French-speaking Quebecers to a cultural shock they were not prepared for, opening the door to all the attendant difficulties of intergroup accommodation.

Finally, in attempting to reduce their own vulnerability, French-speaking Quebecers have made the English-speaking community feel threatened. Resentment and distrust is running high, as the crisis over Bill 178 and the creation and electoral victories of the Equality Party show. At the convention of *Alliance-Québec*, in June 1991, delegates spoke in favour of a bilingual Quebec, exhorting English-speaking Quebecers to speak their language wherever and whenever they pleased; that kind of language activism is unprecedented in the history of this traditionally moderate lobby group.

After more than two decades of tension, the language question remains a central issue in Quebec politics.

KEY TERMS

Épanouissement

Minority rights

Notwithstanding clause

REFERENCES AND FURTHER READING

Behiels, Michael. 1985. *Prelude to Quebec's Quiet Revolution.* Montreal: McGill-Queen's University Press.

Bouthillier, Guy and Jean Meynaud. 1972. *Le Choc des langues au Québec.* Montreal: Les Presses de l'Université du Québec.

Brunet, Michel. 1964. "Trois Dominantes de la pensée canadienne-française : l'agriculturisme, l'anti-étatisme et le messianisme." In Michel Brunet, *La Présence anglaise et les canadiens: études sur l'histoire et la pensée des deux Canadas.* Montreal: Beauchemin. Pp. 113–166.

D'Anglejan, Alison. 1984. "Language planning in Quebec: an historical overview and future trends." In Richard Y. Bourhis (ed.), *Conflict and Language Planning in Quebec.* Clevedon: Multilingual Matters Ltd. Pp. 29–52.

Gagnon, Alain G. and Mary Beth Montcalm. 1990. *Quebec: Beyond the Quiet Revolution.* Toronto: Nelson Canada.

Gendron Commission. 1972. *La Langue de travail.* Quebec: Éditeur officiel.

Guindon, Hubert. 1988. *Quebec Society: Tradition, Modernity, and Nationhood.* Toronto: UTP.

Levine, Marc. 1990. *The Reconquest of Montreal:. Language Policy and Social Change in a Bilingual City.* Philadelphia: Temple University Press.

McLeod Arnopoulos, Sheila and Dominique Clift. 1980. *The English Fact in Quebec.* Montreal: McGill-Queen's University Press.

McRoberts, Kenneth. 1988. *Quebec: Social Change and Political Crisis.* 3rd ed. Toronto: McClelland and Stewart.

Royal Commission on Bilingualism and Biculturalism. 1969. *The Work World.* Ottawa: Queen's Printer.

Roy, Jean-Louis. 1976. *La Longue Marche des québécois.* Montreal: Leméac.

Simard, Jean-Jacques. 1979. *La Longue Marche des technocrates.* Montreal: Ed. Coop. Albert Saint-Martin.

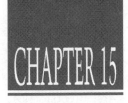

CHAPTER 15

ENERGY AND ENVIRONMENTAL POLICY

Energy is one of the key variables in economic development. Seventy-four governments worldwide have appointed themselves entrepreneurs in the oil industry rather than leave the business to the private sector (Klapp 1987). In Canada, from Atlantic to Pacific, the provinces have created their own electric power utilities. In the current Canadian political system, although natural resources are under provincial jurisdiction, policies concerning oil and international operations are greatly influenced by federal-provincial relations and by decisions of the Canadian federal government. Energy became a crucial issue after the 1973 oil shock. The world suddenly realized how fragile the supply of its primary energy source, oil, really was. An alternative source, nuclear energy, has proven to be a complex, expensive, and potentially dangerous technology that governments keep under strict regulations.

The kind of valuable oil reserves that could be transformed into a saleable commodity have never existed in Quebec. There is only one very small natural gas reserve, exploited by SOQUIP, a state-owned enterprise, and one nuclear plant, built twenty years ago, which operates mainly as a window to the industry.

The only major energy resource is hydroelectric power, controlled through the state monopoly Hydro-Québec. Some argue that this public enterprise has become a state within a state, an agency so autonomous that successive governments have been unable to control it. Hydro-Québec not only produces and distributes electricity, it also serves to foster economic development. In fact, Robert Bourassa (1985) has published a book in which he explains how electricity might be used to develop the Quebec economy.

Quebec's distinctive energy policy stems from the development of Hydro-Québec and the growing political and economic importance of this state enterprise over the years. Electricity is the only major source of energy that is locally produced. The promise of hydroelectric power yet to be developed allows the government to sell electricity to Ontario, New Brunswick, and the northeastern American states. Lately, native groups have bitterly opposed the construction of new projects in the James Bay area, demanding increased compensation for the environmental damages that will inevitably follow.

In this chapter we discuss the development of Hydro-Québec as a major instrument of energy policy. We will see that, besides use of Hydro-Québec for economic development purposes, energy policy in Quebec has been relatively limited.

15.1 THE INSTRUMENTS OF ENERGY POLICY

One of the features of economic policies over the past thirty years in Quebec has been their implementation through the use of state-owned enterprises (SOEs). In the early days of the Quiet Revolution, many of the reforms posed huge administrative problems in the various government departments managing those changes. SOEs, on the other hand, do not require the day-to-day supervision of the government and are able to intervene more deeply in the economy and in more sectors.

SOEs exist in a grey zone between the public and the private sectors, and so are subject to both economic and political considerations. From this perspective, they are more autonomous than most government organizations (Faucher and Bergeron 1988). Their autonomy is increased in a technology-intensive industry such as energy. The complexity of the tasks carried out by Hydro-Québec makes it difficult for people outside the organization to control it. Also, state enterprises that make a profit year after year, like Hydro-Québec, are able to borrow money on financial markets without support from the government.

On the other hand, because Hydro-Québec is an important economic institution, it is always in the public eye. This unrelenting public scrutiny in turn lessens the autonomy of the enterprise. Also, the healthy revenue Hydro-Québec generates is crucial for a government that has been running at a deficit since the mid-1970s. In 1981, the government passed Bill 16, which, theoretically, reduced Hydro-Québec's financial autonomy. With this bill, the government wanted to skim off profits not strictly needed for reinvestment. At the same time, it used rate increases to regulate the demand for electricity.

Now one of the highest-ranking enterprises in Canada, Hydro-Québec was created in 1944 when the Liberal government of Adélard Godbout nationalized the Montreal Light, Heat and Power company. Two Royal Commissions had found that, during the 1930s, private companies, and especially the Montreal Light, Heat and Power, were guilty of overcapitalization, of an artificial division of capital and shares, and of profit accumulation at the expense of their customers. The companies were not reinvesting enough profits to maintain and expand operations. There were signs that they would not be able to meet the growing demands of the Quebec market.

In 1944, the year Hydro-Québec came into being, Godbout was replaced by Duplessis, who had opposed the move to nationalization. Although the Duplessis administration did not actively promote the expansion of Hydro-Québec, it initiated the preliminary work for the construction of the

Manic 5 and the Daniel Johnson dam. [Courtesy Archives nationales du Québec.]

Manicouagan project. According to Faucher and Bergeron (1988), the list of Hydro-Québec's undertakings between 1944 and 1962 showed it to be an active and efficient company. In 1955, 75% of the electricity produced in Quebec was produced by private companies. As discussed below, in 1962, the government completed what Duplessis had started in 1944 and nationalized the remaining private companies.

Hydro-Québec had proven its ability to survive and modestly prosper between 1944 and 1962. It demonstrated that a public organization could be more efficient than a plethora of private companies. It was later used as an example of how state enterprises could be created to intervene in various economic sectors.

In 1967, Hydro-Québec created the *Institut de recherche sur l'électricité du Québec* (IREQ). Its purpose was to respond to the technical needs of Hydro-Québec and assure the scientific base needed for its development.

A second state enterprise on the same model, SOQUIP, was created to manage oil and natural gas operations for the government. SOQUIP might have become an important oil company with refining capacity and a network to sell the resulting products, as was initially suggested in a policy proposal, but the government decided not to make it anything more than a window on the industry. SOQUIP never ventured beyond a few limited partnerships in western Canada and several unsuccessful exploration projects in Quebec. Consequently, SOQUIP has played a marginal role, except perhaps in the reorganization of the natural gas distribution in Quebec. SOQUIP was mostly involved in joint ventures with various private companies (Laux and Molot 1988). Over the past five years, the Caisse dépôt has replaced SOQUIP as the Quebec-based partner in these joint ventures.

Hydro-Québec remains the most important instrument of Quebec's energy policy.

15.2 THE 1962 ELECTION AND ITS AFTERMATH

The 1962 provincial election in Quebec was fought by the Liberal party over one issue: the nationalization of companies producing electricity. As for the election results, it is not clear how the issue explains the Liberal victory. If Lesage had taken a poll before calling the election, he would have found that support for nationalization was low among Quebec's voters.

Although there were sound economic reasons to nationalize the private companies, it was political reasons that convinced the Premier to launch an election on the issue. After only two years in office, the Lesage government was showing signs of disintegration (Desbarats 1977: 22). Reformers and conservatives in the Cabinet were at each other's throats, and most of the reforms that would make the Quiet Revolution famous were still on the drawing board. At the end of a stormy Cabinet meeting at the Lac-à-l'Épaule governmental retreat, Jean Lesage decided to call an election on the issue. For Premier Lesage, it was an opportunity to end the infighting in his government and simply ask the people of Quebec for a decisive mandate to centralize control over the electric power system in the province. It was presented as the key to future industrialization, and as a precursor to economic liberation and full employment. Upon reelection, the government nationalized 11 companies at a total cost of $611 million. In the neighbouring province of Ontario, the same exercise had been carried out in 1906.

Nationalization made sense technically as well. The mixed system that existed at the time included Hydro-Québec and 46 private producers, 48 cooperatives, and 34 municipalities, each with its own distribution system. The power lines of the various companies actually crossed as they delivered electricity from the dams to distant markets. For example, dams were built on the Bersimis river on Quebec's north coast for the Montreal market, even though another company, the Shawinigan Power Company, was located in between. Hydro-Québec rationalized the production and standardized the distribution of electricity (Faucher and Bergeron 1988).

The unification through nationalization lowered and standardized rates. Production and transportation costs were cheaper in a rationalized system. In Abitibi, the electrical system that had operated at 25 cycles was brought up to 60, the same level as everywhere else in the province. The new Hydro-Québec was able to improve the training of local technicians and engineers. Finally, as a public enterprise, Hydro-Québec did not have to pay the $15 million in taxes that the private companies had paid annually to the federal government. The first stage of nationalization was far from complete: 40% of the electricity-generating capacity of the time remained in the hands of companies such as the Alcan Aluminum Company, which produced electricity for its own operations and sold the surplus to Hydro-Québec.

The owners fought hard against nationalization. McRoberts (1988: 167) writes that "as a class," Canadian business was bitterly opposed to the measure. Only when it became obvious that the project was to be financed mostly on the American markets regardless of their opposition did Montreal's financial institutions cooperate. There has been some speculation that the private electricity companies were simply trying to extract better compensation from the government, since it was clear to everyone that they were in no position to undertake the massive expansion of production capacity required to meet future demand (Jobin 1978).

Hydro-Québec's development between the 1962 nationalization and the 1982 recession was sustained by cultivating demand through various marketing techniques. Between 1964 and 1970, sales increased by 44%; 1971 and 1974, 48%; and 1975 and 1980, 38%. Then, between 1980 and 1983, demand increased by 7% a year. In its current forecasts for the next 20 years, Hydro-Québec estimates the growth at around 2.7% annually (Faucher and Bergeron 1988: 274).

15.3 HYDRO-QUÉBEC IN THE 1990s

The two oil shocks in the 1970s and the problems with nuclear energy accidents at Three Mile Island and Chernobyl have made the field of energy especially newsworthy over the past two decades. In Quebec, energy consumption climbed yearly from the early 1960s until the 1980s. In the early 1980s, overall consumption stabilized and then decreased, back to early-1970s levels. It is also interesting to note that the relative importance of the different sources of energy has changed. Reliance on oil has decreased in favour of locally produced electricity and natural gas imported from western Canada. Coal has become negligible as a source of energy. As Table 15.1 illustrates, it took until 1988 before energy consumption in Quebec returned to the levels of 1981. After 1982, the level of oil consumption was lower than it had been in 1967.

Because the production of electricity requires long-term planning (15 years for some projects), accurate long-term estimates about consumption are essential. For example, initial research for the James Bay project was done in the 1950s, construction started in the early 1970s, and production began at the end of the 1970s. However, despite its best efforts at prediction, in 1982 Hydro-Québec saw a net decline in its electricity deliveries (Carpentier 1988). The combined recession, inflation, and high interest rates of 1982 reduced the demand for electricity and forced the company to revise its estimates for future energy consumption. All its forecasts had been proved wrong, and the company capital spending program plummeted from $65 billion to $18 billion.[1]

Over the rest of the 1980s a new management philosophy was implemented at Hydro-Québec, one geared toward a reduction of the administrative costs. Headquarters and regional offices were reorganized in order to reduce the number of managers, and operations were decentralized

---

1. The 1980 development plan had predicted that 26,000 MW (megawatts) would have to be added between 1985 and 1997. In the 1988 plan, this number was revised to only 6,500 additional megawatts for the same period. Hydro-Québec, after two decades of new projects, had no new power plants planned for the period between 1984 and 1995.

Table 15.1

Energy Consumption in Quebec, 1962–1988

Year	TEPs[1]	Per Capita
1962	23,085,413	4.30
1963	22,940,602	4.19
1964	22,575,172	4.04
1965	23,029,972	4.05
1966	23,055,317	3.99
1967	24,462,487	4.17
1968	25,896,247	4.37
1969	27,602,064	4.61
1970	29,052,447	4.83
1971	28,702,195	4.76
1972	29,979,785	4.95
1973	31,949,325	5.26
1974	32,731,935	5.35
1975	31,984,402	5.18
1976	32,688,532	5.24
1977	31,839,277	5.07
1978	33,114,589	5.25
1979	33,561,921	5.29
1980	33,484,898	5.24
1981	32,045,479	4.98
1982	29,047,496	4.48
1983	28,143,387	4.32
1984	28,954,504	4.42
1985	29,331,221	4.46
1986	29,898,101	4.57
1987	30,091,928	4.56
1988	31,955,790	4.86
1989	32,807,238	4.94

1. TEPs = 4.1868×10^{10} J (10^{10} calories).

Source: Ministère de l'Énergie et des ressources, *L'Énergie au Québec, Édition 1989* (Quebec: Éditeur officiel du Québec), p. 10.

(Carpentier 1988). It took Hydro-Québec ten years to adjust to the very unstable energy market. Consumer demand and growing competitiveness in oil and natural gas had made planning more difficult.

Hydro-Québec also had to adjust to major changes in its governmental environment. The Ministry of Natural Resources became the Ministry of Energy, a shift that signalled increased interest from the government in energy supply. Suddenly, the company had to accommodate a trend toward

Table 15.2

Quebec Energy Consumption by Source, 1962–1988

Year	Oil (%)	Electricity (%)	Natural Gas (%)	Coal (%)
1962	69.7	18.7	2.5	9.1
1963	69.9	18.7	2.8	8.6
1964	67.7	21.7	3.0	7.6
1965	67.3	21.3	3.6	7.7
1966	70.6	19.5	3.6	6.3
1967	72.3	19.1	3.6	4.9
1968	72.6	18.5	4.3	4.6
1969	72.7	18.8	4.7	3.9
1970	73.6	19.2	4.4	2.7
1971	73.9	19.3	4.8	2.0
1972	73.2	20.1	4.8	1.8
1973	72.8	20.2	5.0	2.0
1974	70.5	21.8	6.0	1.7
1975	70.7	21.5	6.3	1.5
1976	70.3	21.7	6.3	1.7
1977	66.6	25.1	6.8	1.6
1978	67.6	26.8	7.1	1.8
1979	66.1	25.2	7.4	1.4
1980	63.6	27.2	7.6	1.5
1981	60.0	29.8	8.9	1.3
1982	57.3	32.1	9.2	1.4
1983	53.2	33.9	11.6	1.3
1984	48.8	36.7	13.1	1.4
1985	44.6	38.9	15.2	1.2
1986	43.6	40.1	14.9	1.3
1987	42.1	41.7	14.8	1.4
1988	43.2	40.4	15.0	1.4
1989	44.7	39.4	14.6	1.3

Source: Ministère de l'Énergie et des ressources, *L'Énergie au Québec, Édition 1988* (Quebec), p. 10.

energy conservation and exports, a radical adjustment for an organization used to filling a demand that doubled every decade.

Hydro-Québec has handled this major turnaround well. Costs that were climbing at a rate of 20.5% per year between 1976 and 1982 increased by only 5% per year from 1982 to 1987. Between 1982 and 1987, the workforce was reduced from 19,721 to 18,702 employees.

Marketing and sales became a top priority. For prices to remain competitive with those of other sources of energy and consumption, sales had to increase. Hydro-Québec, with its large surpluses, tried to make sales in New England, and agreed to sell to aluminum producers according to a cost- and risk-sharing system. Now, in the early 1990s, these surpluses are gone, and Hydro-Québec is encouraging energy conservation.

Estimates for long-term consumption patterns remain difficult to calculate. Though for the next 15 to 20 years, production of electricity in Quebec will be based on hydroelectric power, conservation of energy will only delay the inevitable. Eventually, Hydro-Québec will have to consider nuclear or other forms of energy.

15.4 ENERGY AND ECONOMIC DEVELOPMENT

Energy became a priority during the 1970s when availability of cheap energy resources was thrown into doubt for the first time. Later, between the Iranian revolution and the war in the Arab gulf, the security of supply and decreasing prices turned this issue around. Today, the question for Hydro-Québec is how to use the economic advantages related to hydroelectricity.

This question was at the heart of the energy policy proposed by the Quebec government in 1988. In the policy document, the government set seven objectives: (1) to use energy to stimulate economic development and help regional development; (2) to maximize the use of hydroelectric power; (3) to ensure the dependability of the oil supply; (4) to secure access to Canadian resources in order to develop the petrochemical industry in Quebec; (5) to encourage competition between the different sources of energy in order to maintain low prices and provide alternatives to consumers; (6) to encourage research into new sources of energy and energy preservation; and (7) to protect the environment. It remains to be seen how well these objectives are achieved in years to come.

In this section, we address three aspects of this energy policy that are based on the fact that hydroelectric power is cheap and easily available to the Quebec government: attracting foreign capital to energy-intensive sectors of the economy; exporting energy surpluses abroad; and generating jobs, research, and industrial development.

1. Attracting Foreign Investment

The low cost of hydroelectric power has been used by the Quebec government to attract international investments. Since the early 1980s thirteen companies have signed contracts with Hydro-Québec to obtain substantive cost reductions over long periods for energy-intensive industries.

2. Exporting Electricity

Since more hydroelectric power is available than is required by the Quebec market, the government sells it, earning revenue that pays for part of the production facilities. In the early 1960s, it was decided that Hydro-Québec would sell some of its surpluses on the American market. After experimenting with temporary contracts, Hydro decided to sell electricity on a more regular basis over long periods.

When the recession worsened in 1982, Hydro-Québec was already committed to an ambitious construction project launched in the early 1970s under Bourassa, the James Bay Hydro Electric Development Project. Because the work was in an advanced stage, the installations under way were completed. Hydro-Québec was then faced with dwindling growth in yearly sales, a generating capacity in excess of Quebec's needs for years to come, and heavy financing charges for the construction. With a newly completed natural gas network competing for the same provincial market, the obvious solution seemed to be to sell electricity to U.S. neighbouring states (Forces 1984).

Hydro-Québec was in a weak negotiating position and, according to some observers, did not negotiate a high enough price for its electricity. So what began as a strategy to obtain a rapid increase in revenues became the basis for long-term exports to the United States. Critics have pointed out that if demand in Quebec increases faster than expected, the contracts that guarantee energy to U.S. markets will make it impossible for Hydro-Québec to meet the needs of its domestic market. Also, dams have a limited life—between 25 and 50 years for the concrete ones. Once the American contracts terminate, they ask, how much longer will the dams be able to serve the Quebec market?

According to Pierre Lamonde (1987), there is no clear evidence that these contracts will generate profits for Hydro-Québec. Exporting energy could be problematic for another reason, namely, that these exportation contracts may not, in the end, generate profits. Some contracts run into the next century—a contract with Maine, for example, does not expire until 2019—and the bottom line is difficult to predict. Another variable is the relative value of Canadian and U.S. currency. Also, assessing the true cost of the energy exported depends on figuring out such details as which dams are attached to which exports.

Planning a timetable is very complex. As mentioned, if the domestic market begins to demand more energy, Hydro-Québec may have problems producing the amounts required. Construction on all Hydro's power plant

Opposite page: Map representing the Great Whale (Grande baleine) project. [Courtesy Hydro-Québec.]

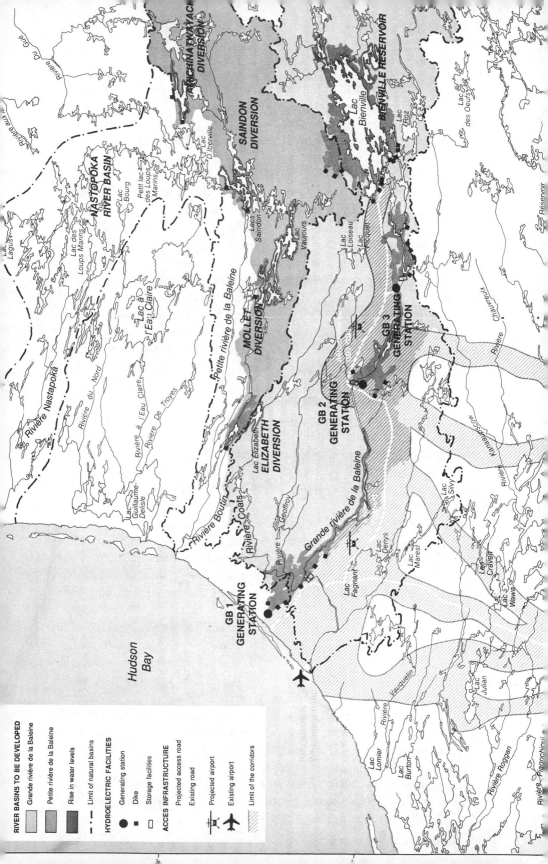

RIVER BASINS TO BE DEVELOPED

Grande rivière de la Baleine
Petite rivière de la Baleine
Rise in water levels
Limit of natural basins

HYDROELECTRIC FACILITIES

Generating station
Dike
Storage facilities

ACCES INFRASTRUCTURE

Projected access road
Existing road
Projected airport
Existing airport
Limit of the corridors

NASTAPOKA RIVER BASIN

MOLLET DIVERSION

LAFLAMME-WYAC DIVERSION

SAINDON DIVERSION

BIENVILLE RESERVOIR

Lac Bienville

Lac D'Iberville

Lac Saindon

Lac Vaujours

Lac Loiseau

Lac Pocquet

GB 3 GENERATING STATION

GB 2 GENERATING STATION

Lac Elizabeth

ELIZABETH DIVERSION

GB 1 GENERATING STATION

Hudson Bay

Grande rivière de la Baleine

Petite rivière de la Baleine

Rivière Nastapoka

Rivière du Nord

Rivière à l'Eau Claire

Rivière De Troyes

Rivière Guillaume-Delisle

Lac à l'Eau Claire

Lac des Loups Marins

Petit lac des Loups Marins

Lac Bourg

Lac des Loups Marins

Lac Laguisi

Rivière aux F...

Rivière du Gué

Rivière Boutin

Rivière Coats

Rivière Geoffroy

Lac Silvy

Lac Denys

Lac Marest

Lac Fagnant

Lac Craven

Lac Wawa

Lac Julian

Lac Burton

Lac Lomier

Rivière Vauquelin

Rivière Roggan

Rivière Piagochioui

Rivière Kwakwatanikapistikw

Rivière Chauvreux

Réservoir...

Rivière...

Lac des Oeufs

projects, except phase one of James Bay, was delayed several years because of shrinking demand. By early 1985, with phase one of James Bay completed, Hydro-Québec had a 24% power surplus. But the American buyers knew Hydro-Québec had to sell and were able to obtain a bargain.

3. Energy and Economic Policy

Hydro-Québec has been used to foster economic development. Over the years, the enterprise has become one of the largest employers in Quebec and the second-largest public utility in North America (McRoberts 1988: 174). In this regard, Hydro has been a more successful undertaking than the attempts made during the 1960s to plan regional economic development. Various economic development strategies have sought to cash in on this comparative advantage. Hydro-Québec is an important economic player, with more than 18,000 employees and annual investments of around $2 billion (Canadian). According to Faucher and Bergeron (1988), Hydro's pricing, financial, and administrative policies must be analyzed in order to understand how it has served as an instrument not only for energy policy, but also for economic policy.

In the field of engineering, Hydro-Québec was used to help desegregate English-speaking and French-speaking Quebecers. Although French-speaking engineers had been available for twenty years, in 1963, the time of nationalization, at one of the biggest private hydroelectric power companies in Quebec only 20 engineers out of 175 were francophone, whereas at Hydro-Québec 190 engineers out of 243 were francophone (McRoberts 1988: 97)

Hydro-Québec has also helped numerous local engineering firms develop an internationally recognized expertise. Instead of developing its own concentrated pool of engineering expertise, Hydro-Québec has relied on private firms, which has enabled them to develop an internationally competitive advantage. Hydro-Québec also has an international branch through which it markets its own expertise.

The economic performance of Hydro-Québec has been impressive. Pricing policies have been vastly improved. For example, preferential rates have been used to foster economic development and have been far more effective than other means of doing so (Faucher and Bergeron 1988). A significant proportion of Quebec's growth will continue to rely on Hydro-Québec.

Hydro-Québec has developed products that are sold around the world. It is currently working with Japanese firms to develop a new type of battery. Hydro-Québec has also considered bringing Japanese firms into Quebec to manufacture the products it needs for its own development.

The enterprise has also borrowed more money on the world financial markets than any other Quebec-based organization. Through conservative

management, Hydro-Québec has been able to maintain a favourable interest rate for its borrowing despite the lower reputation of the province (a
situation that has recently improved) relative to Ontario (Faucher and
Bergeron 1988).

15.5 ENERGY AND ENVIRONMENT

The production of electricity in Quebec has been based almost entirely on
hydroelectric power. However, there is increasing opposition to the use of
such power because of environmental concerns. For example, resistance to
towers and power lines has increased over the past decade, and some studies have raised concerns about the potential health hazards posed by the
magnetic fields around transmission lines.

In 1982, Hydro-Québec created a division staffed by over 300 employees to handle environmental questions. This division also supervises the
levels of PCBs and other chemicals contained in Hydro's equipment. In
addition, Hydro-Québec is obliged to consider the environmental impact
of its projects on areas it develops (Hydro-Québec 1989).

Demonstration in April 1991 against phase two of the James Bay project.
[Courtesy Le Devoir and Gilles Paré, Librarian. Photo: Jacques Nadeau.]

In Portneuf, an area near Quebec City, citizens have extracted a promise from the public utility to replace a planned high-power transmission line over the St. Lawrence River with a tunnel, although it is not clear that the technology to do so is currently available.

Cree Indians living in the James Bay area, where Hydro-Québec plans to build more dams in phase two of the James Bay project, have been successful in mobilizing environmental groups to oppose future projects, some of which are intended to export electricity to the northeastern United States. Thus, contracts already signed with some New England states and New York public utilities may be jeopardized.

A coalition of environmentalists and native peoples has been very active lately in opposing the Great Whale project, whose purpose is to expand existing facilities. The potential buyers in New England and New York have been forced to postpone their decision because of questions raised about pollution in the basins and impact on the native people's traditional way of life. Though scientific results have so far been inconclusive about the impact on wildlife and the territory, this opposition has had the unfortunate effect of helping American utilities renegotiate a lower price from Hydro-Québec.

Public hearings on the Great Whale project. The Quebec government held several meetings with the Inuit and native populations to get their views. [Courtesy Le Devoir and Gilles Paré, Librarian. Photo: Jacques Nadeau.]

The recession of the early 1990s has reduced demand for public utilities in the American northeast for electricity from Hydro-Québec for the next few years. Presumably, energy consumption will eventually rise, and demand for cheap energy from James Bay will follow. The environmentalist lobby's concerns might then be overwhelmed by consumers' demand.

The James Bay and Northern Quebec Agreement

It is possible that the current native opposition to the second phase of the James Bay development is a bargaining tactic for obtaining a better compensation package along the lines of the 1975 James Bay and Northern Quebec Agreement.

The James Bay and Northern Quebec Agreement is Canada's first, and to date only, major modern land claim settlement. An extremely complex document, it details a unique scheme for the social, cultural, economic, and environmental management and development of the James Bay and Northern Quebec Territory. The Agreement provides for several dozen committees, municipal corporations, authorities, boards, and other legal entities through which native people can exert control over their affairs.

Energy Minister John Ciaccia. He was one of the key actors in 1975 in the signing of the James Bay agreement between Inuit, native peoples, and the Quebec government. This agreement might be cited as an example of the innovative program of devolution given to Inuit and native peoples in Canada. [Courtesy Le Devoir and Gilles Paré, Librarian. Photo: Jacques Nadeau.]

The Agreement was signed November 11, 1975 by the Quebec government, the *Société d'énergie de la Baie James*, the *Société de développement de la Baie James*, the *Commission hydroélectrique du Québec* (Hydro-Québec) and the Northern Quebec Inuit Association, the Grand Council of the Crees (of Quebec), and the Government of Canada. It provides the native parties with: specified land rights; hunting, fishing, and trapping rights; promises of hydro development project modifications and remedial measures; promises of future development and environmental considerations; provision for local and regional government authority; establishment of native-controlled health and education authorities; measures relating to policing and administration of justice; continuing federal and provincial benefits; and promises of native development and economic measures. The Agreement also provides for cash compensation for use of the Territory of approximately $232.5 million, divided proportionally between the Crees and the Inuit and paid out over a maximum period of 21 years. Canada's share of the payments is $32.75 million. In consideration of these rights and benefits, the native parties agreed to "cede, release, surrender and convey all their Native claims, rights, titles and interests" (Section 2.1) to the 400,000-square-mile Territory.

The James Bay and Northern Quebec Agreement, which was necessary to permit construction of the James Bay project, resulted in approximately 4,386 Inuit and 6,650 Cree people, living in fifteen Inuit and eight Cree communities, being registered as beneficiaries entitled to all the rights and benefits provided in the Agreement. The Agreement was approved, given effect, and declared valid by the Parliament of Canada and the National Assembly of Quebec.

Though some progress has been made in reducing domestic consumption of hydroelectric power, some difficult questions will have to be addressed soon. Nuclear energy and other potential sources may have to be considered. Solar and wind sources have not gone any further than the experimental stage in Quebec. Currently being tested are batteries that can be charged during nightly down times, then used to supplement the supply during peak hours. The possibility of producing hydrogen cheaply from the existing facilities is also under investigation.

15.6 ENERGY AND INTERGOVERNMENTAL RELATIONS

In Canada, energy exports fall under the jurisdiction of the federal government's National Energy Board. The federal government also has an Environment Protection Board involved in the environmental impact assessment of the upcoming phase two of the James Bay project. Hydro-Québec has, consequently, become increasingly involved in intergovernmental relations.

Hydro-Québec has been in dispute with the Newfoundland government since the 1969 agreement that authorized Hydro-Québec to buy between 69% and 95% of the electricity produced by the Churchill Falls plant in Labrador (between 31 and 43 billion kW·h of the 45 billion kW·h produced). According to its *Annual Report*, 1987, Hydro-Québec produces 29,759 MW; 22,794 MW come from its 53 hydroelectric facilities, 1,740 from 26 thermal power plants and 5,225 from Churchill Falls. Newfoundland agreed then to sell the electricity at a fixed price for the next 45 years, to be lowered for the following 20 years. In 1985, Hydro-Québec was selling this electricity for ten times as much at 3.6 cents per kW·h. (Faucher and Bergeron 1988: 274). Understandably, Newfoundland has gone to court in a bid to revise the terms; so far it has been unsuccessful. Recently, however, the two governments have begun to discuss a new power project that could eliminate the previous source of conflict.

In 1981, the federal government, in a move that affected only Quebec, amended the National Energy Act to create a right-of-way across Quebec territory for the transmission of electrical power from Labrador to the United States. This was intended to undermine Hydro-Québec's long-standing contract with Newfoundland (McRoberts 1988: 352). The idea has since been abandoned.

15.7 ENVIRONMENTAL POLICY

The environmental impact of energy projects represents an important aspect of environmental concerns in Quebec. But there is more. The field of environmental policy has been developing for twenty years and today attracts increasing public attention.

A crucial environmental issue in Quebec is water pollution. About 75% of environmental-department budgetary expenses go toward curing this problem. It is also an issue for intensive intergovernmental discussions. For example, the main waterway in Quebec, the St. Lawrence River, has to be cleaned; but control of pollution in the river is only possible with the co-operation of the governments around the Great Lakes and the River. Similarly, carbon dioxide control can only be achieved through international cooperation. The Montreal Protocol on Substances That Deplete the Ozone Layer (1987) is one example of the kind of international agreement required.

The first legislative action concerning the environment in Quebec goes back to the 1972 Environment Quality Act. This act was the first attempt to coordinate existing regulations concerning water, land, and air environmental protection.

The Department now implements 12 laws. Some of these laws are defined according to product, such as the law on pesticides; some according to people, such as the regulation banning smoking in public buildings; others according to the function of the policy instrument, such as the "Loi sur les réserves écologiques" or the "Loi sur la Société québécoise d'assainissement des eaux." Other laws specify the object protected (trees or water) or attempt to be global, such as the law concerning endangered species or the law concerning the quality of the environment. To implement these laws, the government has established various programs that specify particular issues. For example, the water protection act is applied through three programs dealing with pollution coming from farms, from cities, and from industries. Regulation is also divided along the lines of industrial sectors, such as pulp and paper, aluminum, etc. Regulation has to be written to be applied to these various possibilities. Such diversity makes policy difficult to successfully implement. Environment policy is still a growing field where a lot of fine-tuning has to be done, as Quebec came rather late at addressing these problems.

Moreover, the Department of the Environment has been traditionally difficult to manage. Successive ministers have complained that their civil servants have not kept them informed of potential hazards or that exemptions were made to regulations without their knowledge. Lately, reforms to regulation have been discussed through the Department but excluding

The increasing environmental concern of citizens has made recycling a daily habit in our modern life. Many cities, including Montreal, have their own programs to recycle everything from paper to bottles and cans. [Courtesy Le Devoir and Gilles Paré, Librarian. Photo: Louise Lemieux.]

the minister's office (see Francoeur 1992). The comptroller general has noted that the information available to the Department is still too limited.

The Department was established in 1979 to take charge of various existing programs. More specifically, the ministry is charged with developing knowledge on the environment and its evolution; preventing deterioration of the environment; and to restoring air, water, and land quality. While the total budget of the Quebec government only doubled for the period, the Department's budget multiplied by five: in current dollars, from $83 million in 1981 to $415 million in 1990.

Outside the Department, different governmental bodies have been created to deal with specific angles of the issue. In 1978, the *Bureau d'audiences publiques sur l'environnement* (BAPE) was established. The BAPE allows public participation in decision-making, making inquiries following ministerial requests on environmental issues, and, more importantly, evaluating the environmental impact of projects.

The process is as follows: A promoter of a project has to submit to the minister a description of it for approval. The minister sends this document to the BAPE and makes it public according to an established procedure. After 45 days of consultation, the BAPE sends a note to the minister and sets up public hearings if this is judged necessary. Two 21-day periods are given to the hearings. Then, a second note, summarizing the BAPE's analysis, is sent to the minister, who informs the Cabinet of his or her decision, and if necessary what modifications to the project must be made.

The BAPE has 19 employees to fulfill its mandate: 5 members nominated for five years, and 14 staffers for technical, scientific, and administrative work.

In 1988, the *Conseil de la conservation et de l'environnement* replaced the 15-year-old *Conseil consultatif sur l'environnement*, a consultative body established to conduct studies and give policy advice to the minister. In the Conseil a round table has been established to bring the interested groups—cities, industries, unions, etc.—together.

Another issue of growing importance is waste management. Dumpsites are becoming an important problem in Quebec, as elsewhere in the industrial and urbanized world. Cleaning old dumpsites and finding safe new ones has become an important issue mobilizing local populations. In the Montreal area, the *Défi déchets* programs have been initiated with the goal of diminishing the garbage dumped by 50% over a 20-year period. These programs, still at the experimental stage, will involve composting organic garbage, recycling metal, paper, plastic, and glass, and incinerating what is left.

In October 1987 the government published an environment policy proposal *Un nouveau cap environnemental*, and in 1988 a survey of the environmental problems in Quebec, *L'Environnement au Québec: un premier bilan*. Addressing the difficulties of formulating and implementing regulations, the government has initiated a more coherent process and has been able to compare the importance of different sources of pollution. One of the points emphasized in the survey was the importance of pollution resulting from mining. Another was the fact that the pulp and paper industry in Quebec produced as much water pollution as a population of eight million people. On the other hand it also noted that, in the industrial sector in general, modern technologies have made possible the reduction of pollution.

In summary, environment policy in Quebec is a rapidly developing field that will probably become a major issue in the years to come, with more pressure coming from interest groups forcing the government to improve its intervention.

15.8 CONCLUSION

What the Quebec government can do in the area of energy is basically restricted to electricity. The creation of SOQUIP has not produced a reliable supply of oil and natural gas. By selling its Alberta assets, SOQUIP is less directly involved than it used to be in energy policy. Only through the Caisse de dépôt et placement has the Quebec government retained some decision-making power in its former subsidiary. Oil deals are managed by central states in many countries and by a small group of international companies. Perhaps the Quebec government was well advised to get out of an industry where it could have played only a very minor role. Energy in Quebec means electricity and thus is the domain of Hydro-Québec. Though now somewhat settled after its tumultuous beginnings, Hydro-Québec remains the foremost example of successful state intervention in the Quebec economy.

Over the years, the government has reduced the autonomy of Hydro-Québec. For instance, in 1978, Bill 41 gave the government power to appoint the enterprise's board of directors and president. In 1981, Bill 16 in theory forced Hydro-Québec to pay annual dividends to the government up to a maximum of 75% of the available surplus (McRoberts 1988: 366).

Hydro-Québec has been facing hard times. Consumers' electricity bills have risen, a situation made worse by the public's perception that they are subsizing Hydro's sales to New England or multinational companies in Quebec. For Hydro-Québec, it has become increasingly hazardous to predict when new projects should be initiated. Pricing of exports has been difficult to calculate. Also, relations with employees have become troubled.

Collective agreement renewals have become painful for Hydro, customers, and employees.

In a 1988 policy proposal, the government reiterated that Hydro-Québec should remain the main instrument of intervention in the energy sector. SOQUIP, on the other hand, was relegated to a more background position, participating in projects on an ad hoc basis. In theory, Hydro-Québec, as the main instrument for the implementation of the government energy policy, is under governmental control. In practice, the government has not used its power over Hydro-Québec as often as it might—largely, perhaps, because the policy intentions of the department of energy have never been clear enough to be put into operation.

KEY TERMS

Concentrated pool

Joint ventures

Nationalization

Public policy

REFERENCES AND FURTHER READING

Bourassa, Robert. 1985. *Power from the North*. Toronto: Prentice-Hall.

Carpentier, Jean-Marc. 1988. "Hydro-Québec: more than ever an instrument for economic development." *Forces*, 80: 27–29.

Desbarats, Peter. 1977. *René: A Canadian in Search of a Country*. Toronto: Seal Book.

Faucher, Philippe and Johanne Bergeron. 1988. "Hydro-Québec." In Allan Tupper and Bruce G. Doern, *Privatization, Public Policy and Public Corporations in Canada*. Halifax: Institute for Research on Public Policy. Pp. 265–327.

Francoeur, Louis-Gilles. 1992. "Paradis désavoue ses fonctionnaires." *Le Devoir*, April 22. Page A-2.

Gouvernement du Québec. Développement économique. 1980. *L'Électricité, facteur de développement industriel au Québec*. Preliminary report to *Bâtir le Québec*. Quebec: Éditeur officiel du Québec.

Gouvernement du Québec. Ministère de l'Énergie et des ressources. 1988. *L'Énergie, force motrice du développement économique: politiqué énergétique pour les années 1990*. Quebec: Éditeur officiel du Québec.

Government of Canada. Indian and Northern Affairs. 1982. *James Bay and Northern Quebec Agreement Implementation Review*, February.

Hafsi, Taieb and Christiane Demers. 1989. *Le Changement radical dans les organisations complexes: le cas d'Hydro-Québec.* Montreal: Gaétan Morin.

"Hydro-Québec." 1984. *Forces,* 68: (Special issue.)

Jobin, Carol. 1978. *Les Enjeux économiques de la nationalisation de l'électricité (1962–1963).* Montreal: Les Éditions coopératives Albert St-Martin.

Klapp, Merrie Gilbert. 1987. *The Sovereign Entrepreneur: Oil Policies in Advanced and Less Developed Capitalist Countries.* Ithaca: Cornell University Press.

Lamonde, Pierre. 1987. *Rentabilité des exportations d'énergie et puissance garanties: nouveau test sur le scénario de 6000 MW.* Mimeograph. Montreal: INRS-Urbanisation.

Laux, Jeanne Kirk and Maureen Appel Molot. 1988. *State Capitalism: Public Enterprise in Canada.* Ithaca: Cornell University Press.

Sauriol, Paul. 1962. *La Nationalisation de l'électricité.* Montreal: Éditions de l'homme.

CHAPTER 16

SOCIAL
POLICY

The development of the Quebec *welfare state*, intertwined as it was with
the policies of the federal government until the beginning of the 1970s, has
been singularly complicated. Now, in the aftermath of the Quiet Revolution, the Quebec state has enlarged its role in the field of welfare to the
point where it accounts for nearly two-thirds of Quebec's total expenditures.
In this chapter, we will trace this development, focussing on the nature of
federal-provincial relationships and how Quebec has reacted to different
interventions by creating a social security structure whose features make
it virtually unique in North America.

We will see why several Quebec governments have fought to retain a
provincial jurisdiction over the social security system as set out in the
BNA Act, and how Quebec has developed its own particular expertise in
this field.

16.1 DEVELOPMENT OF THE QUEBEC
WELFARE STATE: 1600–1960

There is comparatively little information about the various private and
local agencies that preceded the first forays into the whole field of social
welfare by the Quebec state (Guest 1980; Splane 1965). We do know that
the first agency formed to help the poor in Canada was in Quebec: it was
called the *Bureau des pauvres* (Poor House). The Bureau was founded in
1688 when the *Conseil souverain* (Sovereign Council, the highest colonial
court) acted on a suggestion from the rich merchants of Quebec City to

create an agency to help the poor and sick of the city and to provide shelter for vagrants. Impoverished citizens could receive help from the *bureaux des pauvres* (local offices of the *Bureau*) on the condition that they had been living in the city for at least three months.

The existence of this agency was constantly threatened by the paucity of its financial resources, which derived from church boxes and door-to-door solicitation for food, clothes, and money. However, various *bureaux* continued to operate in the province of Quebec right up until 1960, when they were replaced by parish committees (Poulin 1949: 61). The most important aspect in the history of the original *bureaux des pauvres* is that they had owed their existence to the efforts of the city's merchant class, to the great dissatisfaction of the Church.

Over time, Quebec and English Canada developed two very different perspectives on the role of the state in matters of social assistance. The Quebec population, predominantly Catholic and dominated by the Church, remained, almost until the beginning of the 1960s, reluctant to consider any secular approaches. Citizens in the other provinces, meanwhile, supported the creation and development of secular institutions, both public and private. Quebec's attitudes were reinforced by a tendency, especially after the Conquest (1763), to distrust and reject the behaviour of the English community and obey the authority of the Church. For its part, the Church's intent was to preserve both the Catholic character of the province and its own powerful position (Guillemette 1966: 10).

The Church was a powerful opponent for any Quebec politician who favoured intervention by the State into the field of public assistance. It represented the prevailing ideology which argued that the freedom of the individual had to be respected and any government intervention would restrict and impede the development of this freedom; and furthermore, that any person or group for whom the state took responsibility would be driven into a form of psychological infantilism, lessening personal social responsibility. The argument also held that any public assistance programs had to be considered carefully, with many studies to demonstrate their necessity, for there loomed the risk of the welfare state turning into a dictatorship. However, it appears that what the Church in Quebec actually feared was that increasing government intervention would threaten its own hegemony in society (Angers 1944: 355).

Until the end of the Second World War, there were major differences in the way social programs were carried out from province to province. While most of the Canadian provinces developed their own policies and sought to increase their control of the economy, Quebec continued to restrict itself to the responsibilities traditionally allotted to the state. Manitoba (in 1916) and Saskatchewan, for example, showed a clear determination to

Table 16.1

Development of Quebec Welfare State, 1871–1992

(legislation and events)

For People Out of Work	For People Who Cannot Work	For Women, Children, and the Family	For Maintaining the Labour Force
BNA Act, in article 92.7 gives the provinces responsibility for health and welfare services (1867)	Act Respecting Industrial Accidents (1909)	Spread of Children's Aid Societies in various cities and provinces (1895–1915)	Public Health Act (1886)
Code Municipal (1871)	Workmen's Compensation Act (1926)	Public Charities Act (1921)	Agricultural schools established (1922)
Civic Relief Commission, Montreal (1933)	Taschereau government rejects idea of federal unemployment insurance (1933)	Foundling Act (1921)	Sanitary Unit Act (1928)
Creation of Department of Health and Welfare (1941)	Quebec opts into Old Age Pensions Act (1936)	Adoption Act (1924)	Public Health Act (1932)
	Federal-provincial mental health grant (1947)	Quebec Social Insurance Commission (1930)	Agreement between Quebec and federal government on unemployment assistance (1959)
	Boucher Report on social assistance (1963)	Social welfare courts established (1937)	Hospital Insurance Act (1961)
	Quebec Pension Plan (1965)	Mother's Allowance (1938)	Report on education (1966)
		Children's Protection Act (1944)	Castonguay-Nepveu report on health (1971)
		Blind Persons Act (1952)	
		Tremblay Commission on the Constitution (1956)	
		First municipal social welfare service in Quebec, Montreal (1957)	
		Schooling allowances (1961)	
		Boucher Report on social assistance (1963)	
		Castonguay-Nepveu report on health (1971)	
		Harnois Report on mental health (1987)	
		Rochon Report on social and health services (1988)	

Source: Adapted from Allan Moscovitch, *The Welfare State in Canada: A Selected Bibliography, 1840 to 1978* (Waterloo, Ont.: Wilfrid Laurier University Press, 1983), Appendix V.

widen the scope of their social policies by being the first provinces to introduce measures to help poor mothers (mothers' allowances). As a consequence, the social expenditures of these two provinces grew more rapidly
than those of the other provinces, and especially Quebec.

Quebec clearly lagged behind all the other Canadian provinces in the
devlopment and expansion of its social policies. As Stewart Bates points
out, the Church successfully blocked all forms of government intervention,
leaving control of economic development in the hands of private enterprise,
and control of welfare and education in the hands of a nongovernmental
agency, namely the Catholic Church (Bates 1939: 146–147).

Even the Quebec Public Charities Act of 1921, introduced under the
Taschereau government, which was primarily a move to save the religious
and charity institutions at the municipal level from the financial crisis that
struck after the First World War (Vigod 1979: 61), was opposed by some.
Political and business leaders were usually the first to insist upon maintaining the hegemony of the religious institutions and the Catholic character of the welfare and health care system. However, despite repeated
assurances by Premier Taschereau that the state's intervention in the welfare and health care sectors was designed only to save the traditional institutions of Quebec society, several reporters criticized the Act, chief among
them *Le Devoir* publisher Henri Bourassa, for whom this "poor act" was a
serious threat to the structure of the hospital system.

The Quebec Public Charities Act was a first, albeit timid, step toward
the principle of state responsibility for financial management of welfare and
health care institutions in Quebec. But the tough years of the economic
crisis of the 1920s and 1930s wrought a decisive change in the attitude of
Quebec governments. With the number of unemployed workers increasing
as quickly as Quebec's revenues were diminishing, and the debts of all the
provinces growing by leaps and bounds, the fiscal strength of Canadian
federalism was badly shaken. Other provinces, mainly in western Canada,
asked the federal government to ensure the survival of their welfare programs, but Quebec governments, especially Taschereau's, continued to take
the position that social security was outside its jurisdiction. Furthermore,
the Quebec government maintained that establishing a national old age
pension scheme would necessitate higher taxes, which would be a serious
blow to the social and moral character of the people (Vigod 1979). But the
fiscal situation of municipalities in Manitoba and Alberta was so critical
that Ottawa yielded to the demands of these provinces, and in 1927 introduced the Old Age Pension Act. Quebec was the last province to accept
this program, in 1936.

The 1940s ushered in a period during which the federal government
attempted to regain control over social policies through various constitu-

tional amendments and legal battles. The political mood at this point is indicated by the publication of two federal reports, both aimed at establishing the basis of a real Canadian welfare state, but by different means: (1) the Rowell-Sirois Report (1940) and (2) the Marsh Report on social security in Canada (1943), which was immediately characterized as Canada's Beveridge Report. The aggressive foray into welfare and social security matters by the federal government after the Marsh Report was astonishing; it flew directly in the face of the Rowell-Sirois Report, which had recommended the opposite course of acknowledging provincial jurisdiction in these matters. Two other reports were published on this theme (Cassidy 1943).

The federal government believed that centralization of power was the only way to ensure a complete social security program, one that guaranteed an equal level of service from province to province. The federal arguments consisted in three basic points: first, the provinces did not have the financial resources to adequately fullfil all their social obligations; second, social security was an integral part of economic policy, and therefore essential to the search for greater economic stability in Canada; and third, it was clearly better to have uniform legislation throughout Canada.

Quebec and the other provinces objected most strenuously to the recommendation that the federal government retain total control over planning and development of social policy. Prime Minister Mackenzie King was well aware that his proposals—i.e., the Marsh, Heagerty, and Cassidy reports—might jeopardize relations with the Quebec Liberals and the overall political climate in Canada. However, the Quebec government's mistrust of the reports was not just the result of its traditional opposition to greater centralization of power in Ottawa. For Quebec, and many agencies, these reports represented a new socializing tradition that threatened the social and cultural values of the population. Quebecers were always very distrustful of any form of socialism or any massive intervention by the state, and the Quebec government now declared that it would not:

> sacrifice the direction of its social policy for motives of technical, administrative or even economic order. In this matter more than in any other, except in the cultural and education sectors, provincial autonomy must be totally respected, as guaranteed in the Constitution of 1867. (Tremblay 1956: vol. 2, 317)

The first universal welfare program in Canada was instituted by the 1944 Family Allowance Act, which provided a stipend to mothers of children under 16 years old and attending school. Several political reasons prompted Mackenzie King to propose such a program. First of all, the Liberal party was threatened in Saskatchewan and Ontario by the C.C.F. In 1944, Saskatchewan elected the first C.C.F. government in Canada, headed by T. C. Douglas. Quebec, still bitter over conscription (imposed in 1942), seemed a rather fragile ally to King's government. With Quebec's birthrate the highest in the country, the Family Allowance Act would represent financial compensation and a profitable political move.

Nevertheless, the provinces were resisting federal policies more and more. Major political changes were emerging that promised to significantly hinder the centralizing initiatives of the federal government. The conservative nationalism of Quebec Premier Maurice Duplessis, for whom provincial autonomy was not negotiable, posed the biggest obstacle to a greater centralization, one that persisted up to the end of Prime Minister Louis St-Laurent's reign (1948–1957). During the constitutional conference of 1950, the question of security for the elderly was raised. The federal government wanted jurisdiction in this matter, but getting it would require a constitutional amendment. The plan was to introduce such an amendment into Part VI of the BNA Act, which is related to agriculture and immigration, but in which an act of Parliament took precedence over any provincial act. For Maurice Duplessis this meant granting control of the whole old age pension system to the federal government. Also, the idea of the federal government imposing a supplementary tax to finance such a project seemed to him absolutely unreasonable and a direct threat to the provinces' powers. The Union nationale leader, nonetheless, favoured the idea of an old age pension program as long as provincial powers were respected.

In June 1951, the federal government adopted bills creating the Old Age Security Act and the Old Age Assistance Act (see Article 94a of the BNA Act). This set the tone for the 1950s, a period during which federal government policies focussed on creating laws concerned with the health and welfare of Canadians. However, faced with the centralizing objectives of the federal government, the Duplessis government created the Tremblay Commission in 1954; its mandate was to focus on the evolution of Canadian federalism and on federal-provincial relations since the beginning of the 1940s (Tremblay 1956). In its report, the Commission made recommendations to the federal government that it should acknowledge provincial jurisdiction in certain matters, including welfare, health, and education, and to provide each province with the financial means to meet all their responsibilities. In its opinion, too great a centralization of power in the hands of the federal government would have an adverse effect on the Canadian political structure. The Tremblay Commission also recommended that greater fiscal power and the allocation of responsibility for welfare and health care programs be given to the provinces, particularly to Quebec (Tremblay 1956: 312).

The attitude of the Commission was essentially accommodating, and implied that if Quebec was not ready to accept the federal government's "new federalism," it was free to separate from the Canadian federation (Lamontagne 1954: 284–285). The Commission recommended instead that all the provinces, and especially Quebec, put aside their autonomist demands, and develop more-coherent policies in cooperation with the federal government if they wished to preserve the federal pact (Tremblay 1956: vol. 2, 318).

But the main criticisms of the Tremblay Commission relating to this "new federalism" centred around three areas of federal power: (1) to legislate, (2) to tax and spend, and (3) to emphasize and impose its control over provincial policies.

1. With its power to legislate, the federal government appropriated, without the support of all provinces, the power to legislate in exclusively provincial matters.

2. By the extension of its power to tax in Section 91.3 of the BNA Act, the federal government interfered in matters of direct taxation, which are an exclusive right of the provinces (Section 92.2).

3. Though the revenue might be used to finance provincial welfare and education programs, the process would contravene the spirit of the Canadian constitution. Pierre Trudeau also vigorously denounced this type of manipulation in *Cité libre*, arguing that, according to the Constitution, the federal government cannot use funds levied for provincial purposes.

What the "new federalism" did elucidate was acceptable spending patterns for the federal government in matters of provincial jurisdiction. The strategy was clear-cut: by spending in such areas as welfare, health, and education, and by giving grants to hospital and postsecondary educational institutions, the federal government earned a certain degree of control over the use of funds and consequently in orienting the policies of various agencies. The use of this power by the federal government was to be the object of controversy over the next decades.

The "new federalism" ended with the election of John Diefenbaker's Conservative party in 1958, a party that favoured the decentralization of power. The Tories proved to be more receptive to provincial demands. During this period Quebec sought to defend its autonomy, and not only in welfare matters. This changed as the 1960s ushered in a new political orientation.

16.2 THE QUIET REVOLUTION AND "COOPERATIVE FEDERALISM": 1960–1970

The election of Jean Lesage in Quebec signalled the start of a health care and social security program specific to Quebec. The introduction of the Hospitalization Act in 1961 represented for Quebec the beginning of a new era in health care legislation that culminated in the creation of a health insurance plan by the Bourassa government ten years later. The Hospitalization Act was far more important than one might first imagine. Not only did it reorganize medical services in Quebec, some held that it was a key policy at the beginning of the Quiet Revolution.

At the start of the 1960s, Quebec had been the only province without a hospitalization insurance program for its citizens. The majority of hospitals in Quebec had still been owned by religious institutions. After the Hospitalization Act, faced with a decrease in their effectiveness and imminent nationalization of the operation of health care services, these institutions agreed to partially withdraw in exchange for monetary compensation.

In social security matters, Quebec continued to play an auxiliary role, leaving the entire sector in private hands. Most of the private agencies, such as the Société St-Vincent-de-Paul established in 1846, belonged to the Church. Not only did Quebec regress almost back to where it was in 1921, after the Public Charities Act was adopted, but the role of helping sick people was still regarded as a charititable function.

In 1961, facing an increase in unemployment assistance costs, the Lesage government created the Boucher Commission to review the whole social security system. After documenting the lack of response to the needs of the population by successive Quebec governments from Taschereau to Duplessis, the Boucher Report made four suggestions. First, it said that social security and assistance should be considered, not as charity, but as a right to which all persons in need are entitled. Second, social policies could be combined with economic policies. Third, a general philosophy should rule social programs in Quebec. Finally, the report strongly recommended that the Quebec government acknowledge its responsibilities, and take a more dynamic and creative role in social security matters.

The Boucher Report reinforced the arguments of Claude Morin, a social sciences professor at Laval University, who in a series of articles had denounced the federal social security programs, charging that they did not attend to the real social problems facing Quebec. Morin had also criticized the programs for creating an atmosphere of competition between the federal government and the provinces, for increasing the fiscal burden of the poorer provinces, and for keeping the allowances too low. He had gone on to urge the withdrawal of the federal government from social security, leaving the field to the provinces, who were closer to the people, and more apt to recognize their real needs and to develop satisfactory solutions (Morin 1961: 19–23).

At the federal level, Parliament, in 1961, created the Hall Commission on health care services to address the criticisms and demands from various consumer groups and political parties, and to make recommendations for the modification of Canada's health care services. However, it appears the idea for a task force surfaced after the Canadian Medical Association wrote a letter stating that its interests were being threatened by such demands. At the time of the Commission, the provinces were being left to manage their own health insurance programs in cooperation with the federal government. In its report, made public in June 1964, the Hall Commission strongly recommended the creation in each province of health insurance programs, similar to Saskatchewan's and subsidized by the federal government.

But by the time the Hall Commission published its report, a new Liberal government had come to power in Ottawa. Its leader, Lester B. Pearson, faced escalating demands for greater control over social and cultural development not only from Quebec but from all the provinces. The Pearson government's response was to present the idea of "cooperative federalism," the objective of which was to establish "a strong central system and strong provinces." Many attempted to define "cooperative federalism," but the best description was that of Jean-Luc Pépin, member of parliament for Drummond-Arthabaska and parliamentary secretary to the minister of trade and commerce. In a speech delivered on December 12, 1965 to the members of the Canadian Institute of Public Affairs, Pépin said that "cooperative federalism" would facilitate a solution for two major political problems in Canada: the troubled relations between the federal government and the provinces (Quebec in particular), and the equally rocky relationship between the French and English populations. He believed "cooperative federalism" was not just a simple technical mechanism, but rather the result of a certain vision of Canada that would lead to more-harmonious relations between the two founding cultures.

However, in certain federal and provincial jurisdictions, Prime Minister Pearson believed the federal government had to be careful not to give privileges to some provinces that were unfairly denied to other provinces, or which might exacerbate regional differences. Contrary to the opinion of many legal writers, he thought welfare, health care, and social security matters should remain under double jurisdiction. Furthermore, according to Pearson, "cooperative federalism" could work only if the federal government agreed to modify certain rules of Canadian federalism, and only if Quebec in particular showed a firm commitment to Canadian unity.

Pearson's brand of federalism was quickly tested. The proving ground was, first, a Canadian pension plan, announced in the Speech from the Throne on May 16, 1963, and second, the creation of the Canadian Assistance Plan in 1966, which arose from federal-provincial discussions. These two developments, which had important implications for social security policies in Quebec and the rest of Canada, are often characterized as examples of "cooperative federalism." However, in view of how these programs were implemented in Quebec, this interpretation has perplexed many observers. Claude Morin, for one, saw the ultimate outcome as rather a victory for the Quiet Revolution and the Lesage administration.

The universal pension plan proposed by the Pearson government was intended to replace all existing programs. In July 1963, Quebec Premier Jean Lesage unequivocally declared at a federal-provincial conference that Quebec would never accept the federal proposal, and that Quebec would create its own pension plan. As Lesage pointed out, a universal pension plan would mean the intrusion of the federal government into a field in which the Boucher Commission had just recommended a greater role for the Quebec government. Its own plan would require a rapid accumulation of capital, and because of the sums involved it was recommended that a para-governmental agency manage the funds under the control of the Quebec government. Thus, on the basis of a report presented by Claude Castonguay, the idea for the Caisse de dépôt et placement was developed. In the heat of the conflict, the actual purpose of the pension plan—to ensure greater security for retired people—quickly became secondary.

Discussions between the Quebec and the federal government largely superseded discussions between the federal government and the other provinces, mainly because only Quebec and Ottawa had any real expertise on pension plans, and partly because the other provinces showed comparatively little interest (Bella 1979: 451). Quebec was ready to accept an amendment to Section 94a of the Canadian Constitution in 1951, following the discussions on old age pensions, to permit the federal government to establish a pension plan with benefits for widows and children. In return, the Quebec government asked for recognition of its power to create its own pension plan, arguing that Section 94a granted the province such power. The federal government replied that the English version of the Canadian Constitution did not have the same meaning as the French. Quebec's fears of the federal government widening its jurisdiction in matters of social policy were realized.

At the famous federal-provincial conference from March 31 to April 2, 1965, the Quebec and federal governments were mutually antagonistic. It was only after secret discussions between federal minister Maurice Sauvé and a highly placed civil servant of Quebec, Claude Morin, that an agreement was reached, on April 20, creating two pension plans in Canada: one for Quebec and a federal one for the other provinces. The *Quebec Pension Plan* is managed entirely by the Quebec government; the *Canada Pension Plan* is administered by the federal government. The idea that this turn of events represents a victory for "cooperative federalism" is somewhat far-fetched; it appears rather to constitute a firm acknowledgement of the "legislative primacy" of Quebec in social security matters.

During the federal-provincial discussions, the provinces appear to have played a decisive role. In Quebec, for example, the minister for family and welfare, René Lévesque, fought for greater autonomy in social security and communicated Quebec's intention, in January 1966, to withdraw from the social assistance joint programs, taking advantage of the opting-out clause promised by the Pearson government in 1963. The Bélanger Commission, created by the Quebec government in March 1963 to study Quebec fiscal issues, noted that the formula of financial compensation for provinces not participating in federal shared-cost programs provided an opportunity for Quebec to achieve greater autonomy. However, administrative backwardness in Quebec's public health and education sectors created a special sense of urgency in Quebec's goal of modernization (Bélanger 1965: 21).

After the Union nationale's publication of the political manifesto *Égalité ou indépendance* in 1965 the "cooperative federalism" formula was unequivocally rejected by subsequent Quebec governments. According to Union nationale leader Daniel Johnson, the formula represented just one more step toward the centralization of power in the federal government, and in net effect the institution of federal-provincial conferences had resulted in Quebec having no more rights than any other Canadian province.

To everyone's surprise, the Union nationale was elected in June 1966 with 40.8% of the vote and 56 of the 108 seats in the Quebec National Assembly. Now in charge, Johnson was obliged to embark upon the reform of the entire social security system, in accordance with the campaign platform. That same year, he appointed a task force on health and social welfare headed by Claude Castonguay. In one of its reports, the Castonguay Commission emphasized that social security could be used to mitigate the effects of an economic crisis, and could contribute to the social as well as the economic development of the state (Castonguay 1967: 24). Clearly, the Quebec government wanted to assume full responsibility for social welfare. During a federal-provincial conference held in February 1968, Premier Johnson asked for nothing less than total control in this area, and in particular over family allowances, unemployment, and old age pensions.

The combination of the sudden death of Premier Johnson in 1968, the creation of the Parti québécois, and the election of Pierre Elliott Trudeau as Prime Minister led to an overhaul of federal-provincial relations. From

1968 to 1971, the efforts of the federal government were directed toward reform of the Constitution, and the struggle for control over social security was the basis of political discussions between Ottawa and Quebec. In answer to Quebec's demand for total control over family allowances and old age pensions, the federal government published in 1969 a document completely rejecting Quebec's position. It even threatened to take back from the provinces the gains made during the 1965 negotiations on the Quebec/ Canada Pension Plans (Leman 1980: 62). The discussions seemed destined to fail, as the Quebec government stood firm. This led to the constitutional dead end of the 1971 Constitutional conference at Victoria.

16.3 THE "PROFITABLE FEDERALISM" OF ROBERT BOURASSA: 1970–1976

At the beginning of the 1970s, the Castonguay-Nepveu Commission presented its final report to the Quebec government. This report, with its innovative suggestions for reforms that placed the Quebec governments in a preeminent position, had a significant impact on subsequent strategies adopted by the federal and Quebec governments. Rick Van Loon writes:

> more important from the federal government's perspective, the publication of the highly innovative Castonguay-Nepveu Report left social policy initiative in Canada squarely with the government of Quebec, a situation that was difficult to countenance for members of the federal government. (Van Loon 1979: 475)

The recommendations of this report served to facilitate the establishment of the Quebec health insurance plan, which aimed to provide universal free health care for all citizens of Quebec. Meanwhile, Claude Castonguay became Minister of Social Affairs in the Robert Bourassa government elected on April 29, 1970.

Premier Bourassa was confronted with a formidable challenge. With the growth of the nationalist movement, which succeeded in electing seven MNAs under the banner of the Parti québécois, he had to prove that Canadian federalism could still be "profitable" for Québécois. This was one of his major electoral campaign themes. But it was a few months after his election that Quebec was shaken by the October Crisis, and these events succeeded in drawing attention to the issue of poverty in Quebec, and that the federal programs launched at the beginning of 1966 had done little to alleviate the problem.

The Economic Council of Canada had predicted the urgency of the situation in 1968, and requested that a Senate committee be created to look into the issue of ever-worsening poverty in Canada (Economic Council,

*Claude Castonguay,
who co-chaired the
Castonguay-Nepveu
Commission in the
1960s, is considered
the father of Quebec's
Medicare system.
[Courtesy Le Devoir
and Gilles Paré,
Librarian. Photo:
Jacques Nadeau.]*

1968: 127–136). Several eminent Canadian experts accused the federal government of being directly responsible for the October Crisis, because of its refusal to acknowledge that economic growth had increased the gap between rich and poor. The federal government's negligence was denounced in 1971 by the Senate Special Committee on poverty.

In Quebec, Bourassa's government was in a difficult predicament. How could it prove to Quebec and Canada the advantages of federalism when such extreme disparities existed and were worsening? In search of a solution, the Bourassa government wanted to adopt several of the recommendations of the Castonguay-Nepveu Report regarding Quebec's social policy. At preliminary talks at the constitutional conference in Victoria in June 1971, the Bourassa cabinet requested that the issue of power-sharing in social matters be placed on the agenda. In February, Quebec had clearly indicated that it was going to ask for nothing less than exclusive jurisdiction in this area. To argue its case, the Quebec government had appointed Claude Castonguay, who had already stated publicly the necessity to establish the primacy of Quebec and the provinces in this field.

The other provinces, however, were somewhat perplexed by Quebec's stance, since they did not experience any major difficulties in the existing division of powers in the field. Furthermore, the Trudeau government did

Table 16.2

Health Expenditures in Selected Provinces, 1977, 1981, and 1985

(per capita)

	Public	Private	Total	% of GDP
Quebec:				
1977	543	110	653	6.5
1981	866	215	1,081	6.8
1985	1,205	316	1,521	7.2
Ontario:				
1977	528	180	708	5.2
1981	779	305	1,084	5.1
1985	1,159	477	1,636	5.7
Alberta:				
1977	525	146	671	4.1
1981	931	246	1,177	4.2
1985	1,465	266	1,731	5.5
Nova Scotia:				
1977	447	131	578	7.6
1981	746	216	962	8.6
1985	1,088	358	1,146	8.1
Canada:				
1977	521	153	674	5.6
1981	838	265	1,103	5.7
1985	1,210	380	1,590	6.4

Source: Bureau de la statistique, Gouvernement du Québec, *Le Québec statistique,* 59th ed. (Quebec: Éditeur officiel du Québec, 1989), p. 885.

nothing to seek an an alternative arrangement with Quebec, choosing instead to ignore Quebec's demands for federal constitutional proposals, which appeared to simply reaffirm federal power.

At the Victoria Conference the federal government and the premiers were faced with the challenge of drafting a new constitutional charter with an amending formula. The Conference was the culmination of three years of negotiation and discussion. In no uncertain terms, Quebec requested that Section 94a of the BNA Act be amended to allow the provinces to legislate in matters such as family allowances and old age pensions, and allow the federal government to legislate in social security matters only with the agreement of the provincial governments. However, several provinces were against such an amendment: they were not interested in gaining new powers, especially when the federal government had not promised to deliver the financial support necessary to carry out these new responsibilities.

The federal government gave the provinces 12 days to accept or refuse the Victoria Charter in its entirety, which did contain a modified version of Section 94a. All provinces accepted the Charter except Quebec, which claimed that it lacked the guarantees Quebec required for total responsibility over social policy. The Bourassa government argued that the provinces could better ascertain their citizens' needs, and that individually they could perform this function in a more equitable manner. In May 1972, the federal government responded to Quebec's refusal by increasing benefits for the guaranteed income supplement and old age pensions, but it still refused to give Quebec control over family allowances.

This incited Quebec's minister of social affairs, Claude Castonguay, to demand that Bourassa force the federal government to respect Quebec's jurisdiction. The ways things were, the overlapping jurisdictions made it impossible for Quebec to carry out a thorough reform of its social security system. Claude Castonguay accused the federal government of trying to act unilaterally without consulting Quebec, because it had refused to accept the Victoria Charter. He also emphasized how he had insisted during the October events on the urgent need to reach an agreement that would allow Quebec to fully assume responsibility over social, cultural, economic, and political matters, which would have resolved the conflicts that were at the origin of that crisis (Castonguay 1972).

During the annual conference of the premiers of August 2–5, 1972 in Halifax, Nova Scotia, Bourassa stated that "profitable federalism" had been, as far as social security was concerned, a failure and that the provinces should henceforth block the spending power of the federal government in all areas. The federal government, witnessing its diminishing control over social policy in Canada and realizing that the Castonguay-Nepveu Commission report had given Quebec a certain edge in this matter, proposed in April 1973 a reform of the social security system in Canada, the main elements of which were borrowed from Castonguay-Nepveu.

From 1973 to 1977 serious discussions took place between the federal and provincial ministers of welfare, making this period one of the most intensive attempts ever at cooperation between the federal government and the provinces (Leman 1980: 113). And although the election of the Parti québécois in 1976 stopped all such initiatives, some progress was made, despite the fact that a complete integration of provincial and federal welfare policies was not achieved.

16.4 THE CONSTRAINTS OF THE ECONOMIC CRISIS: 1976–1992

Since the 1973 oil crisis, increased expenditures and inflation had affected the federal budget and the revenues of the provinces to such an extent that the implementation of numerous social programs had become jeopardized. One of the most important achievements of the entire program of social security review in Canada was the introduction of the Social Services Act on June 22, 1977. This act was the result of intensive negotiations that culminated in the provinces' acceptance of "block funding" from the federal government to cover their expenditures on social security.

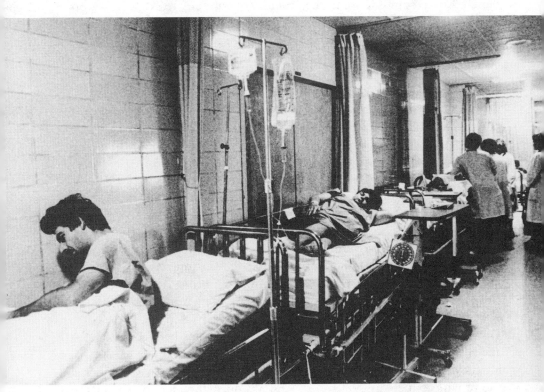

The emergency room at Hôpital Notre-Dame in Montreal. Citizens have to wait several hours in emergency rooms before they can be seen by a doctor. [Courtesy Le Devoir and Gilles Paré, Librarian. Photo: Jacques Grenier.]

For the Quebec government, this proposition meant less revenue, but greater control. For the federal government, such a solution enabled it to better protect itself against inflation; after years of fighting for increased control over the provinces' social policies, it now seemed prepared to abandon this agenda. As the economic situation deteriorated, the provinces, too, were less interested (Hepworth 1977).

If there had been a "War on Poverty" in Canada, it was clear that the new war was against increases in public expenditures on welfare, and that the poor would be the first to suffer from the governmental choices. It became more and more evident, at the end of the 1970s, that under the current division of powers Canada was not equipped to ensure job security and adequate public services to every citizen. To be sure, Quebec and the other provincial governments were in a better position than they had been during the economic crisis of the 1930s, but the crucial problem of ensuring similar services to all reappeared. The economic crisis shook the old theory that governments could ensure that citizens had adequate services and means to withstand an economic crisis.

The provinces adopted different strategies, from rationalization to extra-billing for services, in an attempt to eliminate their deficits. These measures created discontent among social agencies. The introduction by the federal government of the Canadian Health Act seemed to be a compensatory measure, showing that the division of powers between Quebec, the provinces, and the federal government was still a matter for debate—and that the economic crisis was just an interlude.

Prior to the Budget speech of 1981, in which the federal government had announced this bill, Monique Bégin, minister of national health and welfare, had waged an incessant and energetic campaign against what were in her view the twin plagues of overbilling and patients' contributions, which she charged were eroding the Canadian health system. Then, after a gestation period during which the federal government had deliberately avoided any discussions on the subject with Quebec and the other provinces, the federal government tabled on December 12, 1983 its first draft of Bill C-3—the Canadian Health Act—before the House of Commons, simultaneously forwarding a copy to all the provincial ministers of social affairs. Opposition to the bill grew fast, especially in Quebec, where it was quickly realized that if the bill were passed the federal government, whatever its intentions, would acquire more powers in the planning, rationalization, and programming of health services.

Bégin countered that she had no such intention, but sought only to penalize those provinces that had decided, after the financial difficulties of the early 1980s, to ask users of health services to pay. For example, in some provinces hospital patients had to pay different fees for various services; also, some provinces permitted extra-billing. Remember that in Canada, according to the Medical Care Act of 1966, Canadians paid for health services via the income tax and then received hospital services partially or totally free, depending on the province (as in Quebec and Manitoba).

With Bill C-3, the federal government threatened to hold back one dollar in federal grants for every dollar the province took from the hands of its citizens.

Obviously, the Quebec government agreed in principle, since it was one of the first to acknowledge the concept of free, equal, universal access in its 1969 Health Insurance Act. However, (1) the Quebec government did not see the necessity of such a bill, since the management and operation of health services differed from one province to the next; and (2) Quebec's particular objection to Bill C-3 was that it gave the federal government sweeping powers to intervene in and directly influence health matters in the provinces through the exercise of its spending power.

Marc-Yvan Côté, Minister of Social Affairs (including health) in the Bourassa government. His reform project led to the doctors' strike in the summer of 1990. The issues of quality service and doctors' autonomy remain central elements of the conflict. [Courtesy Le Devoir and Gilles Paré, Librarian. Photo: Jacques Grenier.]

Seven provinces (Quebec, Ontario, British Columbia, Alberta, New Brunswick, Newfoundland, and Prince Edward Island) reacted by presenting a memorandum to the House of Commons Permanent Committee on Health, Social Welfare, and Social Affairs. Quebec's objections were focussed on Sections 4 and 9 of the initial version of Bill C-3: under Section 4, the provinces, in their new role as mere dispensers of services, would lose all control over the development and establishment of health policy; Section 9 reserved for the federal government the power to define which services would be covered by hospitalization insurance. In the memorandum, the minister of social affairs under the PQ, Pierre-Marc Johnson, while stating his agreement with the principles behind the proposed legislation, expressed regret that the federal government had to use means that invaded a jurisdiction exclusive to the provinces.

Faced with widespread opposition, both from provinces and from numerous agencies, Bégin was forced to make many amendments to her bill in order to reassure critics that it was not meant to invade the area of health. The revised version of her bill stated:

> ...it is not the intention of the government of Canada that any of the powers, rights, privileges or authorities vested in Canada or the provinces under the provisions of the BNA Act, or any amendments thereto, or otherwise, be by reason of this Act abrogated or derogated from or in any way impaired.

This was not enough, and the provinces made an unprecedented collective gesture by going to the Senate, on April 4, 1984, requesting that it not adopt Bill C-3. But to no avail: the bill was adopted on its third reading on April 9. Invited to speak in front of the Senatorial Committee on social affairs, the former minister of social affairs under the Bourassa government, Claude Castonguay, spoke for all the provinces in his criticism of this encroachment into a provincial jurisdiction.

More recently, on August 15, 1991, the Supreme Court of Canada has ruled that the federal government has the power to end an existing agreement and limit its tranfer payments to the provinces for welfare programs. This decision affects Ontario, British Columbia, and Alberta more severely than Quebec. In its unanimous ruling, the Court said the basic principle of parliamentary sovereignty allows the federal government to end its 1967 agreement to pay 50% of the cost of social assistance programs in the three provinces. The Court argued that the Canadian Assistance Plan contains no guarantee that the 50-50 cost-sharing formula should remain frozen forever. The message sent to all provinces by this decision was that the federal government could decide unilaterally to break any agreement with the provinces.

After this decision, the three wealthiest provinces (Ontario, British Columbia, and Alberta) wanted the federal government to take more responsibility in the field of fiscal federalism, but the pressures that came from Quebec were different. The Quebec government was insisting that Ottawa withdraw from any role in the field of health, arguing that it should have the right to impose some form of user fee on hospital patients, an approach deemed contrary to the Canada Health Act by federal officials.

16.5 THE MODERN QUEBEC WELFARE STATE

As we have seen, Quebec's social programs had their beginnings in the Quiet Revolution, when Quebec underwent a momentous social, economic, and cultural awakening. Today, as part of its income security program, the

Quebec government spends over $10 billion annually in long- and short-term assistance, allowances, and benefits of various kinds to some two million citizens.

Since 1961, when hospital insurance was introduced, successive Quebec governments have contributed to the development of a social security program that is unique in North America. The state provides a variety of services to cope with illness, unemployment, old age, poverty, or disability. All Quebecers, regardless of their financial situation, are entitled to hospital insurance and health insurance. This means free medical and surgical services. For the elderly and the disabled, and for some young people, it also means free medication, prostheses, orthopedic devices and treatment, and dental care.

Quebec's social security program also provides for income support or replacement. Social aid benefits are paid to individuals and heads of families who are unable to afford the basic necessities. Quebec's employment centres assist those who are looking for work or seeking employment counselling or services. Quebec's employers and employees contribute to the unemployment insurance fund, which is administered by the federal government. Both the Canadian and the Quebec government offer job placement, complementary training, retraining, and upgrading programs.

When workers' flow of regular income is interrupted by the retirement, disability, or death of a spouse, Quebec's pension plan provides financial protection for them and their dependants. All Quebecers between 18 and 65 whose income exceeds a certain amount contribute to the plan. For low-income workers, assistance is available in the form of a work income supplement: benefits increase in accordance with the number of dependants.

Persons aged 65 and over receive an old age pension and a guaranteed income supplement. If they are unable to live alone or with their families, they may choose to live in one of a number of public and private retirement homes in Quebec, for a small rental fee.

Families with one or more children under 18 receive family allowance payments; the amount depends on a variety of factors, including the number of children and the age of each child. Quebec also has a network of partially subsidized public and private day-care centres. These are open to all families, regardless of whether the mother works outside the home.

All employers contribute to Quebec's workers' compensation fund, set up in 1931. This fund is administered by a para-governmental body, which works in the field of prevention and provides accident victims with the care and services they require. The same agency provides financial, psychological, and other assistance to crime victims.

Finally, Quebec has a government-administered, no-fault automobile insurance plan. Compensation is paid to those who, because of an accident,

The recognition of social rights is a good indicator of generosity of any society. Here, older people belonging to the Association pour la défense des droits sociaux *(Association for the Defense of Social Rights) are asking for reduced fares in public transportation. [Courtesy Archives nationales du Québec.]*

suffer bodily injury, incur a temporary loss of income, or face the loss of a family member. Owners of motor vehicles must be insured for property damage.

After the economic crisis of the early 1980s, the Bourassa government attempted, in 1988, during its first mandate, to control the ever-increasing welfare payments to citizens. Part of the strategy included sending social services employees to the homes of recipients in order to verify the information received about their economic situations. The press immediately

Table 16.3

Poverty Rates and Number of Poor Citizens in Quebec, 1975–1986

Years	Total (000)	%	Household (000)	%	Family (000)	%	Single	%
1975	1206	20.3	550	26.5	266	17.7	284	50.8
1977	1129	18.7	511	24.0	259	16.4	251	46.1
1979	1059	17.6	516	23.5	241	15.0	274	46.6
1981	1135	17.9	567	24.0	253	14.8	314	48.5
1982	1203	18.7	598	24.6	272	15.6	326	47.6
1984	1297	20.1	639	25.4	304	16.9	335	46.4
1985	1226	19.0	614	24.3	290	15.8	324	46.4
1986	1192	18.1	615	23.6	286	15.3	329	44.5

Source: Richard Langlois, *S'Appauvrir dans un pays riche* (Montreal: CEQ—Éditions Saint-Martin, 1990), p.104.

labelled these employees the *bou-bou macoutes* (i.e., Bourassa's brown shirts), and the Bourassa government was widely criticized for its treatment of the poor. Today, the state of Quebec is shrinking at the same time that demands from the unemployed and poor citizens are on the rise. In the future, the Quebec welfare state will have to take a close look at how it will continue to provide a safety net to all citizens.

KEY TERMS

Assurance-maladie (medicare system)   Intergovernmental relations

Conseil souverain (Sovereign Council)   Overbilling

Constitutional amendment   Public policy

Cooperative federalism   Social security

Equalization payments   Welfare state

FOR REFERENCES AND FURTHER READING

Angers, François-Albert. 1944. "French Canada and social security." *Canadian Journal of Economics and Political Science*, 10(3): 355–364.

Bates, Stewart. 1939. *Financial History of Canadian Governments*. Study prepared for the Royal Commission on Dominion-Provincial Relations. Ottawa.

Bélanger, Marcel. 1965. *Commission royale d'enquête sur la fiscalité*. (Quebec: Gouvernement du Québec.

Bella, Leslie. 1979. "The provincial role in the Canadian welfare state: the influence of provincial social policy initiatives on the design of the Canadian Assistance Plan. *Canadian Public Administration*, 22(3): 439–452.

Boucher, J.-Émile. 1963. *Rapport du comité d'étude sur l'assistance publique*. Quebec: Gouvernement du Québec.

Cassidy, Harry M. 1943. *Social Security and Reconstruction of Canada*. Toronto: Ryerson Press.

Castonguay, Claude. 1967. *L'Assurance-maladie: rapport de la Commission d'enquête sur la santé et le bien-être social*. Quebec: Gouvernement du Québec.

Castonguay, Claude. 1972. "Bloqué par Ottawa: le Québec ne peut plus assumer ses responsabilités." *Le Devoir*, May 15, 17.

Economic Council of Canada. 1968. *Fifth Annual Review: The Challenge of Growth and Change*. Ottawa: Queen's Printer.

Guest, Dennis. 1980. *The Emergence of Social Security in Canada*. Vancouver: University of British Columbia Press.

Guillemette, André M. 1966. "Welfare in French Canada." *Canadian Welfare*, 42(1): 8–13.

Hepworth, H. Philip. 1977. "Personal social services: an uncertain future." *Perception*, 1(1): 44–45.

Lamontagne, Maurice. 1954. *Le Fédéralisme canadien: évolution et problèmes*. Quebec: Presses de l'Université Laval.

Leman, Christopher. 1980. *The Collapse of Welfare Reform: Political Institutions, Policy and the Poor in Canada and the United States*. Cambridge, Mass.: MIT Press.

Mackenzie King, Hon. W. L. 1949. "Welfare and the modern state." *Canadian Welfare*, 24(7): 2–3.

Morin, Claude. 1961. "La Sécurité sociale canadienne : problèmes et perspectives." *Relations industrielles*, 16(1): 3–25.

Pépin, Jean-Luc. 1968. "Co-operative federalism." In Peter Meekinson (ed.), *Canadian Federalism: Myth and Reality*. Toronto: Methuen Publications. Pp. 320–329.

Poulin, Gonzalve. 1949. "Evolving social services in the province of Quebec." *Canadian Welfare*, 24(7): 59–62.

Reid, Allana G. 1964. "The first poor-relief system of Canada." *Canadian Historical Review*, 27(4): 424–431.

Rowell-Sirois Commission (1940). *Report of the Royal Commission on Dominion-Provincial Relations*. Ottawa: Government of Canada.

Splane, Richard B. 1965. "Towards a history of social welfare." *Canadian Welfare*, 4(2): 56–59.

St-Pierre, Arthur. 1955. "La Sécurité sociale." *L'Actualité économique*, 31(2): 195–217.

Tremblay, Thomas. 1956. *Rapport de la Commission royale d'enquête sur les problèmes constitutionnels*. Quebec: Gouvernement du Québec.

Vaillancourt, Yves. 1988. *L'Évolution des politiques sociales au Québec, 1940–1960*. Montreal: Presses de l'Université de Montréal.

Van Loon, Rick. 1979. "Reforming welfare in Canada." *Public Policy*, 27(4): 470–504.

Vigod, B. L. 1979. "The Quebec government and social legislation during the 1930s: a study in political self-destruction." *Journal of Canadian Studies*, 14(1): 56–69.

Wallace, Elizabeth. 1950. "The origin of the social welfare state in Canada, 1867–1900." *Canadian Journal of Economics and Political Science*, 16(3): 383–393.

White, Charles A. 1981. "Development of our welfare state: self care to state care." *Canada and the World*, 46(8): 14–15.

PART V

Conclusion

QUEBEC:
A
MODERN
SOCIETY

It is the political modernization of Quebec that has put this provincial state in competition with the federal government and given rise to the need to redefine the Canadian constitution. The essence of this political modernization has been the transfer of authority to the State. In Quebec, the provincial state has replaced the Catholic Church as the authority in social, educational, and welfare matters, and it has established a network of powerful state-owned enterprises that have fostered economic development and helped small enterprises to grow. But further development of the Quebec state now rests on a transfer of more powers from the federal to the Quebec government; this transfer has been requested by all Quebec governments since 1960.

After the so-called Quebec round of constitutional discussions, which had led to the Meech Lake agreement (reached in 1987 and rejected in June 1990), the Quebec government, through legislation, forced the federal government and the provinces to hold a referendum on either Quebec sovereignty or a renewed federalism. Several provinces also voted to hold a referendum in case a constitutional accord was signed and had to be ratified by the people.

On July 7, 1992, after 11 hours of intense negotiation, the federal government and the premiers of the anglophone provinces agreed upon a new constitutional package that recognized a veto right for Quebec. Two days later, the Quebec Premier, Robert Bourassa, opened the door for his comeback to the negotiating table by saying that even if his government had some reservations about this agreement, he would study it very carefully.

At the beginning of August, Bourassa participated for the first time in two years in an informal meeting with his federal and provincial colleagues. On August 22, he reached an agreement that gave back to Quebec its veto right and recognized linguistic minority rights. This agreement was endorsed on July 28 in Charlottetown; and all premiers agreed to hold a referendum on October 26, 1992.

Actually, there were two referendums: one in Canada under the supervision of the Federal Electoral Officer and one in Quebec under the terms of the Directeur général des élections. The question asked was the same: "Do you agree that the Constitution of Canada should be renewed on the basis of the agreement reached on August 28, 1992?" The verdict surprised most federal and provincial leaders who supported the Charlottetown agreement, since a No vote was endorsed by 54.4% of Canadians, including the Quebec vote; and in Quebec, where the participation rate was 82.8% —about 10 points higher than the average for the rest of Canada—the No side won by 56.7%. Such a low number is also a bad sign for the sovereigntists, who would have to increase their share of the vote.

Although there will be exhaustive analysis of what the vote actually means, it is already a unique indicator of what divides and defines both Quebec and Canadian society. If the Charlottetown agreement was supposed to build consensus and enable Quebec to rejoin the Canadian family, today's situation makes it unclear what Quebec's future decision will be. This agreement was the third attempt by English Canada (the 1982 constitutional accord and the Meech Lake accord being the first two) to persuade Quebec to sign the 1982 constitutional accord. The next Quebec election, which will probably occur in 1994 after a federal election, will be crucial, for PQ leader Jacques Parizeau has stated that it will be a referendum election, a vote for the PQ being a vote for sovereignty.

When the Meech Lake accord finally failed after three years of discussions, the Quebec Premier stated that an acceptable solution would have to include the five demands of the accord: recognition of Quebec as a distinct society, a greater Quebec role in immigration, greater control over appointments to the Supreme Court of Canada, limitations to the federal government's spending power and capacity to intervene in provincial jurisdictions, and a veto over constitutional amendments.

At the other end of the constitutional spectrum, the PQ suggests that Quebec should become a sovereign country, hopefully but not necessarily linked to Canada in an economic association. Over the years one of the main objections to the "sovereignty-association" option has been its economic cost. Two reports published before the referendum by the Royal Bank and the Canadian Imperial Bank of Commerce stressed that the political uncertainty following a No vote would be devastating for the Canadian economy.

However, Merrill Lynch, the Fraser Institute, the Toronto Dominion Bank, and others have over the past few years published reports explaining that though there would be costs, they would be limited and bearable and that moreover, through economic response to the ongoing political uncertainty, Quebec has already paid part of this cost.

After Meech's failure, various scenarios were developed. The Liberal party of Premier Bourassa, in the Allaire Report, proposed that relations between Quebec and Canada should consist in a loose confederation and that in Quebec Ottawa should only exercise a very limited number of powers: money, defence, customs, equalization payments, and debt management. This report—later opposed by Bourassa—was a clear indication of how much change Quebecers wanted.

The Bélanger-Campeau Commission reached the conclusion that a new agreement with the rest of Canada was impossible, and that Quebec's independence should be prepared. Its report gave rise to two other parliamentary commissions, one on the federal offers and one on the costs of sovereignty. This led, after further hearings, to the Commission's recommendation that a referendum on sovereignty-association or on "acceptable" federal offers should be held in Quebec by October 26, 1992.

Despite all the pressure toward more autonomy—from his own party, from the Bélanger-Campeau Commission, and from journalists, trade unions, and important segments of the business community—Bourassa maintained that the Charlottetown offer was the best he could get from English Canada. He desperately wanted to avoid a referendum on sovereignty-association.

If the October referendum cannot be interpreted as a vote from Quebec in favour of independence, since it was mainly a rejection of the Charlottetown deal, it is certainly a clear signal that Quebec will not settle for less than what was proposed. Among Quebecers who voted No, many simply thought it was a bad deal, even if the Quebec government *could* promote its distinct society, unique culture, and civil law tradition, and Ottawa *could* let Quebec decide how to spend federal money in housing, urban affairs, recreation, tourism, forestry, and mining.

One of the key difficulties in the latest discussions was that there was no shared philosophy about Quebec's and Canada's future. In Quebec, the BNA Act of 1867 (modernized in 1982) was considered a pact between *two nations*, one of French and one of British origin. Such a status was required so that the "national state" could foster the development of the only French-speaking civilization in North America. There was also concern about the assimilation of French Canadians outside Quebec, which reinforced the feeling that the French language needed protection. To many sovereigntists, recognition of the Quebec people as a nation is much more important than concepts such as the distinct society, or even giving special status to

Quebec, and they feel that years have eroded this "two nations" aspect of the Canadian fabric.

Another difficulty stemmed from the fact that the rest of Canada does not fully accept the particular notion of collective rights that underlies the Quebec vision of society. Nor is the idea of special status popular; rather, it is generally believed that federal institutions should be strengthened and that all provinces should have the same status.

Though the Quebec and Canadian visions are drifting apart, the Charlottetown agreement attempted to blend the two in a bewildering document: while the Canada clause recognized the specificity of the Quebec society, another article of this clause stated, "Canadians confirm the principle of the equality of the provinces at the same as recognizing their diverse characteristics." Putting these two visions together in the same clause seemed risky to Quebecers, and for other provinces this was giving too much to Quebec.

From the official and legal documents of the accord, released a week before the end of the referendum campaign, it was hard to tell how resulting conflicts would eventually be resolved by the Supreme Court of Canada. Moreover, several issues—linguistic duality, the economic union, power over regional development, etc.—were still to be negotiated, meaning that separate accords would have to be reached well after the referendum. The October 26 vote was more on the general outlines of an agreement than on a definite constitutional package.

Quebec's demands will not fade away. The social and political transformations of the past thirty years require drastic changes to the Canadian constitution, and expectations have been created, especially under Bourassa's regime, that such changes would be made. The rejection of the Charlottetown accord is a clear indication that the deal did not satisfy these expectations.

General elections are scheduled shortly, both at the federal and at the provincial level. Traditionally, general elections in Canada are called every four years. The Conservative government, reelected in 1988, is required to hold an election no later than November 1993. The Liberals in Quebec, elected in 1989, could hold on until 1994. Prime Minister Mulroney has announced that no constitutional talks will be held before the next general federal election. Restoration of the economy will be the major issue on the agenda between now and the election. The next decisive date for the constitutional future of Canada might well be the next general election in Quebec. The PQ has announced that if elected it would initiate the process for sovereignty regardless of the issue of economic association with the rest of Canada.

This book has recounted the evolution of Quebec society since the 1960s. We have seen the historical and sociological constraints that shaped the evolution and the structural and institutional characteristics of Quebec's political system, and looked at central policy issues in the light of all these elements. The aim has been to offer the student new ways of looking at policymaking in Quebec, and to show that central democratic principles have become fundamental values shared by all Québécois.

Throughout its early history Quebec had faced many challenges, and had always surmounted them; but the election of the Liberals in 1960 gave Quebec the chance to build a modern society that could stand on its own. The many social, economic, and institutional reforms launched testifies to a deep feeling shared by Québécois that the future was in their hands. Some of the institutional changes, including creation of the Department of Education, made it possible for all Quebecers to pursue higher education. Young Quebecers could acquire knowledge and skills necessary to face and respond to the social, political, and economic needs of their society. The growth of the bureaucracy created a new technocratic class that was instrumental in formulating these new challenges. Their momentum sent a signal to the other sectors of the economy that from now on it was necessary to adapt the economic structure to internal and external demands. A new partnership was established between the state and the private sector.

Environmental issues have become a major concern. Over the past twenty years, since the James Bay agreement, efforts have been made to ensure that hydroelectric projects have as little impact as possible on the environment and do not threaten native peoples' way of life. Though the Great Whale project will continue, protection of the ecosystem and of aboriginal cultures will be a priority.

When it was ratified, the Free Trade Agreement (FTA) with the United States challenged Quebec industry to compete in today's global marketplace and offered new opportunities for Quebecers to help bring the world closer together. Now, with the North American Free Trade Agreement (NAFTA), which includes Mexico, there will be even greater access to, and competition in, goods, services and construction. Though in 1991 Quebec exports to Mexico represented $88 million, and imports were close to $440 million, Quebecers are committed to reversing this trade deficit.

Quebec nationalists do not seek to break economic ties with Canada or the United States; on the contrary, the dismantling of all barriers to trade among Canadian provinces is a key goal. Furthermore, no other province has spoken out so loudly in favour of the FTA. It might seem contradictory to argue for more open internal trade while promoting autonomy, but as long as it stays in the Canadian federation, Quebec wants to improve its economic performance.

In the light of the vote on the Charlottetown agreement, the question of distribution of resources between the federal and the provincial government will remain at issue. If Quebec wants to stay in the Canadian political system, it will have to reach agreements that achieve a better coordination of federal and provincial policies, and it will have to concede certain advantages to other provinces. The debate over Quebec's relative autonomy and sharing of responsibilities and fiscal powers remains tied to various political and economic circumstances.

Whatever happens in the next ten years, Quebec is by any standard a modern society, and its concerns are the same as those of other political entities and countries in the world. More institutional changes, and more social and political questions, are on the horizon. On the economic front, Quebec will have to restructure its economy in order to adjust to the advent of a global economy. If the past is any indication, Quebec will not flinch from these new challenges.

Appendices

APPENDIX 1

QUEBEC CHARTER OF HUMAN RIGHTS AND FREEDOMS[1]

Whereas every human being possesses intrinsic rights and freedoms designed to ensure his protection and development;

Whereas all human beings are equal in worth and dignity, and are entitled to equal protection of the law;

Whereas respect for the dignity of the human being and recognition of his rights and freedoms constitute the foundation of justice and peace;

Whereas the rights and freedoms of the human person are inseparable from the rights and freedoms of others and from the common well-being;

Whereas it is expedient to solemnly declare the fundamental human rights and freedoms in a Charter, so that they may be guaranteed by the collective will and better protected against any violation;

Therefore, Her Majesty, with the advice and consent of the National Assembly of Quebec, enacts as follows:

Fundamental Freedoms and Rights

1. Every human being has a right to life, and to personal security, inviolability and freedom.

   He also possesses juridical personality.

2. Every human being whose life is in peril has a right to assistance.

   Every person must come to the aid of anyone whose life is in peril, either personally or by calling for aid, by giving him the necessary and immediate physical assistance, unless it involves danger to himself or a third person, or he has another valid reason.

3. Every person is the possessor of the fundamental freedoms, including freedom of conscience, freedom of religion, freedom of opinion, freedom of expression, freedom of peaceful assembly and freedom of association.

4. Every person has a right to the safeguard of his dignity, honour and reputation.

5. Every person has a right to respect for his private life.

6. Every person has a right to the peaceful enjoyment and free disposition of his property, except to the extent provided by law.

7. A person's home is inviolable.

---

1. The text is not a complete reproduction of the Charter of Human Rights and Freedoms, but an extract of those sections that set out the rights of citizens.

8. No one may enter upon the property of another or take anything therefrom without his express or implied consent.

9. Every person has a right to non-disclosure of confidential information.

   No person bound to professional secrecy by law and no priest or other minister of religion may, even in judicial proceedings, disclose confidential information revealed to him by reason of his position or profession, unless he is authorized to do so by the person who confided such information to him or by an express provision of law.

   The tribunal must, *ex officio*, ensure that professional secrecy is respected.

9.1 In exercising his fundamental freedoms and rights, a person shall maintain a proper regard for democratic values, public order and the general well-being of the citizens of Quebec.

   In this respect, the scope of the freedoms and rights, and limits to their exercise, may be fixed by law.

Right to Equal Recognition and Exercise of Rights and Freedoms

10. Every person has a right to full and equal recognition and exercise of his human rights and freedoms, without distinction, exclusion or preference based on race, colour, sex, pregnancy, sexual orientation, civil status, age except as provided by law, religion, political convictions, language, ethnic or national origin, social condition, a handicap or the use of any means to palliate a handicap.

   Discrimination exists where such a distinction, exclusion or preference has the effect of nullifying or impairing such right.

10.1 No one may harass a person on the basis of any ground mentioned in section 10.

11. No one may distribute, publish or publicly exhibit a notice, symbol or sign involving discrimination, or authorize anyone to do so.

12. No one may, through discrimination, refuse to make a juridical act concerning goods or services ordinarily offered to the public.

13. No one may in a juridical act stipulate a clause involving discrimination.

   Such a clause is deemed without effect.

14. The prohibitions contemplated in sections 12 and 13 do not apply to the person who leases a room situated in a dwelling if the lessor or his family resides in such dwelling, leases only one room and does not advertise the room for lease by a notice or any other public means of solicitation.

15. No one may, through discrimination, inhibit the access of another to public transportation or a public place, such as a commercial

establishment, hotel, restaurant, theatre, cinema, park, camping ground or trailer park, or his obtaining the goods and services available there.

16. No one may practise discrimination in respect of the hiring, apprenticeship, duration of the probationary period, vocational training, promotion, transfer, displacement, laying-off, suspension, dismissal or conditions of employment of a person or in the establishment of categories or classes of employment.

17. No one may practise discrimination in respect to the admission, enjoyment of benefits, suspension or expulsion of a person to, of or from an association of employers or employees or any professional corporation or association of persons carrying on the same occupation.

18. No employment bureau may practise discrimination in respect of the reception, classification or processing of a job application or in any document intented for submitting an application to a prospective employer.

18.1 No one may, in an employment application form or employment interview, require a person to give information regarding any ground mentioned in section 10 unless the information is useful for the application of section 20 or the implementation of an affirmative action program in existence at the time of the application.

18.2 No one may dismiss, refuse to hire or otherwise penalize a person in his employment owing to the mere fact that he was found guilty or that he pleaed guilty to a penal or criminal offence, if the offence was in no way connected with the employment or if the person has obtained a pardon for the offence.

19. Every employer must, without discrimination, grant equal salary or wages to the members of his personnel who perform equivalent work at the same place.

A difference in salary or wages based on experience, seniority, years of service, merit, productivity or overtime is not considered discriminatory if such criteria are common to all members of the personnel.

20. A distinction, exclusion or preference based on the aptitudes or qualifications required for an employment, or justified by the charitable, philanthropic, religious, political or educational nature of a non-profit institution or of an institution devoted exclusively to the well-being of an ethnic group, is deemed non-discriminatory.

Similarly, under an insurance or pension contract, a social benefits plan or a retirement, pension or insurance plan, or under a public pension or public insurance plan, a distinction, exclusion or preference based on risk determining factors or actuarial data fixed by regulation is deemed non-discriminatory.

Political Rights

21. Every person has a right of petition to the National Assembly for the redress of grievances.

22. Every person legally capable and qualified has the right to be a candidate and to vote at an election.

Judicial Rights

23. Every person has a right to a full and equal, public and fair hearing by an independent and impartial tribunal, for the determination of his rights and obligations or of the merits of any charge brought against him.

    The tribunal may decide to sit in camera, however, in the interests of morality or public order.

    Furthermore, in proceedings in family cases, sittings in first instance are held in camera unless the tribunal decides otherwise on the motion of any person and if it deems it expedient in the interests of justice.

24. No one may be deprived of his liberty or his rights except on grounds provided by law and in accordance with prescribed procedure.

24.1 No one may be subjected to unreasonable search or seizure.

25. Every person arrested or detained must be treated with humanity and with the respect due to the human person.

26. Every person confined to a house of detention must be treated with humanity and with the respect due to the human person.

27. Every person confined to a house of detention while awaiting the outcome of his trial has the right to be kept apart, until final judgment, from prisoners serving sentence.

28. Every person arrested or detained has a right to be promptly informed, in a language he understands, of the grounds of his arrest or detention.

28.1 Every accused person has a right to be promptly informed of the specific offence with which he is charged.

29. Every person arrested or detained has a right to immediately advise his next of kin thereof and to have recourse to the assistance of an advocate. He has a right to be informed promptly of those rights.

30. Every person arrested or detained must be brought promptly before the competent tribunal or released.

31. No person arrested or detained may be deprived without just cause of the right to be released on undertaking, with or without deposit or surety, to appear before the tribunal at the appointed time.

32. Every person deprived of his liberty has a right of recourse to *habeas corpus*.

32.1 Every accused person has a right to be tried within a reasonable time.

33. Every accused person is presumed innocent until proven guilty according to law.

33.1 No accused person may be compelled to testify against himself at his trial.

34. Every person has a right to be represented by an advocate or to be assisted by one before any tribunal.

35. Every accused person has a right to a full and complete defense and has the right to examine and cross-examine witnesses.

36. Every accused person has a right to be assisted free of charge by an interpreter if he does not understand the language used at the hearing or if he is deaf.

37. No accused person may be held guilty on account of any act or omissions which, at the time when it was committed, did not constitute a violation of the law.

37.1 No person may be tried again for an offence of which he has been acquitted or of which he has been found guilty by a judgment that has acquired status as *res judicata*.

37.2 Where the punishment for an offence has been varied between the time of commission and the time of sentencing, the accused person has a right to the lesser punishment.

38. No testimony before a tribunal may be used to incriminate the person who gives it, except in a prosecution for perjury or for the giving of contradictory evidence.

Economic and Social Rights

39. Every child has a right to the protection, security and attention that his parents or the persons acting in their stead are capable of providing.

40. Every person has a right, to the extent and according to the standards provided for by law, to free education.

41. Parents or the persons acting in their stead have a right to require that, in the public educational establishments, their children receive a religious or moral education in conformity with their convictions, within the framework of the curricula provided for by law.

42. Parents or the persons acting in their stead have a right to choose private educational establishments for their children, provided such establishments comply with the standards prescribed or approved by virtue of the law.

43. Persons belonging to ethnic minorities have a right to maintain and develop their own cultural interests with the other members of their group.

44. Every person has a right to information to the extent provided by law.

45. Every person in need has a right, for himself and his family, to measures of financial assistance and to social measures provided for by law, susceptible of ensuring such person an acceptable standard of living.

46. Every person who works has a right, in accordance with the law, to fair and reasonable conditions of employement which have proper regard for his health, safety and physical well-being.

47. Husband and wife have, in the marriage, the same rights, obligations and responsibilities.

    Together they provide the moral guidance and material support of the family and the education of their common offspring.

48. Every aged person and every handicapped person has a right to protection against any form of exploitation.

    Such a person also has a right to the protection and security that must be provided to him by his family or the persons acting in their stead.

Special and Interpretative Provisions

49. Any unlawful interference with any right or freedom recognized by this Charter entitles the victim to obtain the cessation of such interference and compensation for the moral or material prejudice resulting therefrom.

    In case of unlawful and intentional interference, the tribunal may, in addition, condemn the person guilty of it to exemplary damages.

50. The Charter shall not be so interpreted as to suppress or limit the enjoyment or exercise of any human right or freedom not enumerated herein.

51. The Charter shall not be so interpreted as to extend, limit or amend the scope of a provision of law except to the extent provided in section 52.

52. No provision of any Act, even subsequent to the Charter, may derogate from sections 1 to 38, except so far as provided by those sections, unless such Act expressly states that it applies despite the Charter.

53. If any doubt arises in the interpretation of a provision of the Act, it shall be resolved in keeping with the intent of the Charter.

54. The Charter binds the Crown.

55. The Charter affects those matters that come under the legislative authority of Quebec.

Affirmative Action Programs

86. The object of an affirmative action program is to remedy the situation of persons belonging to groups discriminated against in employment, or in the sector of education or of health services and other services generally available to the public.

    An affirmative action program is deemed non-discriminatory if it is established in conformity with the Charter.

87. Every affirmative action program must be approved by the Commission,[2] unless it is imposed by order of a tribunal.

    The Commission shall, on request, lend assistance for the devising of an affirmative action program.

88. If, after investigation, the Commission confirms the existence of a situation involving discrimination referred to in section 86, it may propose the implementation of an affirmative action program within such time as it may fix.

    Where its proposal has not been followed, the Commission may apply to a tribunal and, on proof of the existence of a situation contemplated in section 86, obtain, within the time fixed by the tribunal, an order to devise and implement a program. The program thus devised is filed with the tribunal which may, in accordance with the Charter, make the modifications it considers appropriate.

89. The Commission shall supervise the administration of the affirmative action programs. It may make investigations and require reports.

90. Where the Commission becomes aware that an affirmative action program has not been implemented within the allotted time or is not being complied with, it may, in the case of a program it has approved, withdraw its approval or, if it proposed implementation of the program, it may apply to a tribunal in accordance with the second paragraph of section 88.

91. A program contemplated in section 88 may be modified, postponed or cancelled if new facts warrant it.

    If the Commission and the person required or having consented to implement the affirmative action program agree on its modification, postponement or cancellation, the agreement shall be evidenced in writing.

    Failing agreement, either party may request the tribunal to which the Commission has applied pursuant to the second paragraph of section 88 to decide whether the new facts warrant the modification, postponement or cancellation of the program.

    All modifications must conform to the Charter.

---

2. The *Commission des droits de la personne du Québec* is the Charter's trustee.

92. The Government must require its departements and agencies to implement affirmative action programs within such time as it may fix.

   Sections 87 to 91 do not apply to the programs contemplated in this section. The programs must, however, be the object of a consultation with the Commission before being implemented....

138. The Minister of Justice has charge of the application of this Charter.

THE MEECH
LAKE ACCORD

Constitution Amendment, 1987

Following is the text of the Constitutional Accord approved by the Prime Minister and all provincial Premiers on June 3, 1987, which provided the basis for submitting a resolution to Parliament and the provincial legislatures, seeking approval of the *Constitution Amendment, 1987*.

1987 CONSTITUTIONAL ACCORD

WHEREAS first ministers, assembled in Ottawa, have arrived at a unanimous accord on constitutional amendments that would bring about the full and active participation of Quebec in Canada's constitutional evolution, would recognize the principle of equality of all the provinces, would provide new arrangements to foster greater harmony and cooperation between the Government of Canada and the governments of the provinces and would require that annual first ministers' conferences on the state of the Canadian economy and such other matters as may be appropriate be convened and that annual constitutional conferences composed of first ministers be convened commencing not later than December 31, 1988;

AND WHEREAS first ministers have also reached unanimous agreement on certain additional commitments in relation to some of those amendments;

NOW THEREFORE the Prime Minister of Canada and the first ministers of the provinces commit themselves and the governments they represent to the following:

1. The Prime Minister of Canada will lay or cause to be laid before the Senate and House of Commons, and the first ministers of the provinces will lay or cause to be laid before their legislative assemblies, as soon as possible, a resolution, in the form appended hereto, to authorize a proclamation to be issued by the Governor General under the Great Seal of Canada to amend the Constitution of Canada.

2. The Government of Canada will, as soon as possible, conclude an agreement with the Government of Quebec that would
    (a) incorporate the principles of the Cullen-Couture agreement on the selection abroad and in Canada of independent immigrants, visitors for medical treatment, students and temporary

workers, and on the selection of refugees abroad and economic criteria for family reunification and assisted relatives,

(b) guarantee that Quebec will receive a number of immigrants, including refugees, within the annual total established by the federal government for all of Canada proportionate to its share of the population of Canada, with the right to exceed that figure by five per cent for demographic reasons, and

(c) provide an undertaking by Canada to withdraw services (except citizenship services) for the reception and integration (including linguistic and cultural) of all foreign nationals wishing to settle in Quebec where services are to be provided by Quebec, with such withdrawal to be accompanied by reasonable compensation,

and the Government of Canada and the Government of Quebec will take the necessary steps to give the agreement the force of law under the proposed amendment relating to such agreements.

3. Nothing in this Accord should be construed as preventing the negotiation of similar agreements with other provinces relating to immigration and the temporary admission of aliens.

4. Until the proposed amendment relating to appointments to the Senate comes into force, any person summoned to fill a vacancy in the Senate shall be chosen from among persons whose names have been submitted by the government of the province to which the vacancy relates and must be acceptable to the Queen's Privy Council for Canada.

MOTION FOR A RESOLUTION TO AUTHORIZE AN AMENDMENT TO THE CONSTITUTION OF CANADA

WHEREAS the *Constitution Act, 1982* came into force on April 17, 1982, following an agreement between Canada and all the provinces except Quebec;

AND WHEREAS the Government of Quebec has established a set of five proposals for constitutional change and has stated that amendments to give effect to those proposals would enable Quebec to resume a full role in the constitutional councils of Canada;

AND WHEREAS the amendment proposed in the schedule hereto sets out the basis on which Quebec's five constitutional proposals may be met;

AND WHEREAS the amendment proposed in the schedule hereto also recognizes the principle of the equality of all the provinces, provides new arrangements to foster greater harmony and cooperation between the Government of Canada and the governments of the provinces and requires that conferences be convened to consider important constitutional, economic and other issues;

AND WHEREAS certain portions of the amendment proposed in the schedule hereto relate to matters referred to in section 41 of the *Constitution Act, 1982;*

AND WHEREAS section 41 of the *Constitution Act, 1982* provides that an amendment to the Constitution of Canada may be made by proclamation issued by the Governor General under the Great Seal of Canada where so authorized by resolutions of the Senate and the House of Commons and of the legislative assembly of each province;

NOW THEREFORE the (Senate) (House of Commons) (legislative assembly) resolves that an amendment to the Constitution of Canada be authorized to be made by proclamation issued by Her Excellency the Governor General under the Great Seal of Canada in accordance with the schedule hereto.

SCHEDULE
CONSTITUTION AMENDMENT, 1987

CONSTITUTION ACT, 1867

1. The *Constitution Act, 1867* is amended by adding thereto, immediately after section 1 thereof, the following section:

   "**2.** (1) The Constitution of Canada shall be interpreted in a manner consistent with

   (a) the recognition that the existence of French-speaking Canadians, centred in Quebec but also present elsewhere in Canada, and English-speaking Canadians, concentrated outside Quebec but also present in Quebec, constitutes a fundamental characteristic of Canada; and

   (b) the recognition that Quebec constitutes within Canada a distinct society.

   (2) The role of the Parliament of Canada and the provincial legislatures to preserve the fundamental characteristic of Canada referred to in paragraph (1) (a) is affirmed.

   (3) The role of the legislature and Government of Quebec to preserve and promote the distinct identity of Quebec referred to in paragraph (1) (b) is affirmed.

   (4) Nothing in this section derogates from the powers, rights or privileges of Parliament or the Government of Canada, or of the legislatures or governments of the provinces, including any powers, rights or privileges relating to language."

2. The said Act is further amended by adding thereto, immediately after section 24 thereof, the following section:

   "**25.** (1) Where a vacancy occurs in the Senate, the government of the province to which the vacancy relates may, in relation to that vacancy, submit to the Queen's Privy Council for Canada the names of persons who may be summoned to the Senate.

   (2) Until an amendment to the Constitution of Canada is made in relation to the Senate pursuant to section 41 of the Constitution Act, 1982, the person summoned to fill a vacancy in the Senate shall be chosen from among persons whose names have been submitted under subsection (1) by the government of the province to which the vacancy relates and must be acceptable to the Queen's Privy Council for Canada."

3. The said Act is further amended by adding thereto, immediately after section 95 thereof, the following heading and sections:

"Agreements on Immigration and Aliens

95A. The Government of Canada shall, at the request of the government of any province, negotiate with the government of that province for the purpose of concluding an agreement relating to immigration or the temporary admission of aliens into that province that is appropriate to the needs and circumstances of that province.

95B. (1) Any agreement concluded between Canada and a province in relation to immigration or the temporary admission of aliens into that province has the force of law from the time it is declared to do so in accordance with subsection 95C(1) and shall from that time have effect notwithstanding class 25 of section 91 or section 95.

(2) An agreement that has the force of law under subsection (1) shall have effect only so long and so far as it is not repugnant to any provision of an Act of the Parliament of Canada that sets national standards and objectives relating to immigration or aliens, including any provision that establishes general classes of immigrants or relates to levels of immigration for Canada or that prescribes classes of individuals who are inadmissible into Canada.

(3) The *Canadian Charter of Rights and Freedoms* applies in respect of any agreement that has the force of law under subsection (1) and in respect of anything done by the Parliament or Government of Canada, or the legislature or government of a province, pursuant to any such agreement.

95C. (1) A declaration that an agreement referred to in subsection 95B(1) has the force of law may be made by proclamation issued by the Governor General under the Great Seal of Canada only where so authorized by resolutions of the Senate and House of Commons and of the legislative assembly of the province that is a party to the agreement.

(2) An amendment to an agreement referred to in subsection 95B(1) may be made by proclamation issued by the Governor General under the Great Seal of Canada only where so authorized

(a) by resolutions of the Senate and House of Commons and of the legislative assembly of the province that is a party to the agreement; or

(b) in such other manner as is set out in the agreement.

95D. Sections 46 to 48 of the *Constitution Act, 1982* apply, with such modifications as the circumstances require, in respect of any declaration made pursuant to subsection 95C(1), any amendment to an agreement made pursuant to subsection 95C(2) or any amendment made pursuant to section 95E.

95E. An amendment to sections 95A to 95D or this section may be made in accordance with the procedure set out in subsection 38(1) of the *Constitution Act, 1982*, but only if the amendment is authorized by resolutions of the legislative assemblies of all the provinces that are, at the time of the amendment, parties to an agreement that has the force of law under subsection 95B(1)."

4. The said Act is further amended by thereto, immediately preceding section 96 thereof, the following heading:

"General"

5. The said Act is further amended by adding thereto, immediately preceding section 101 thereof, the following heading:

"Courts Established by the Parliament of Canada"

6. The said Act is further amended by adding thereto, immediately after section 101 thereof, the following heading and sections:

"Supreme Court of Canada

101A. (1) The court existing under the name of the Supreme Court of Canada is hereby continued as the general court of appeal for Canada, and as an additional court for the better administration of the laws of Canada, and shall continue to be a superior court of record.

(2) The Supreme Court of Canada shall consist of a chief justice to be called the Chief Justice of Canada and eight other judges, who shall be appointed by the Governor General in Council by letters patent under the Great Seal.

101B. (1) Any person may be appointed a judge of the Supreme Court of Canada who, after having been admitted to the bar of any province or territory, has, for a total of at least ten years, been a judge of any court in Canada or a member of the bar of any province or territory.

(2) At least three judges of the Supreme Court of Canada shall be appointed from among persons who, after having been admitted to the bar of Quebec, have, for a total of at least ten years, been judges of any court of Quebec or of any court established by the Parliament of Canada, or members of the bar of Quebec.

101C. (1) Where a vacancy occurs in the Supreme Court of Canada, the government of each province may, in relation to that vacancy, submit to the Minister of Justice of Canada the names of any of the persons who have been admitted to the bar of that province and are qualified under section 101B for appointment to that court.

(2) Where an appointment is made to the Supreme Court of Canada, the Governor General in Council shall, except where the Chief Justice is appointed from among members of the Court, appoint a person whose name has been submitted under subsection (1) and who is acceptable to the Queen's Privy Council for Canada.

(3) Where an appointment is made in accordance with subsection (2) of any of the three judges necessary to meet the requirement set out in subsection 101B(2), the Governor General in Council shall appoint a person whose name has been submitted by the Government of Quebec.

(4) Where an appointment is made in accordance with subsection (2) otherwise than an required under subsection (3), the Governor General in Council shall appoint a person whose name has been submitted by the government of a province other than Quebec.

101D. Sections 99 and 100 apply in respect of the judges of the Supreme Court of Canada.

101E. (1) Sections 101A to 101D shall not be construed as abrogating or derogating from the powers of the Parliament of Canada to make laws under section 101 except to the extent that such laws are inconsistent with those sections.

(2) For greater certainty, section 101A shall not be construed as abrogating or derogating from the powers of the Parliament of Canada to make laws relating to the reference of questions of law or fact, or any other matters, to the Supreme Court of Canada."

7. The said Act is further amended by adding thereto, immediately after section 106 thereof, the following section:

"106A. (1) The Government of Canada shall provide reasonable compensation to the government of a province that chooses not to participate in a national shared-cost program that is established by the Government of Canada after the coming into force of this section in an area of exclusive provincial jurisdiction, if the province carries on a program or initiative that is compatible with the national objectives.

(2) Nothing in this section extends the legislative powers of the Parliament of Canada or of the legislatures of the provinces."

8. The said Act is further amended by adding thereto the following heading and sections:

"XII—CONFERENCES ON THE ECONOMY AND OTHER MATTERS

148. A conference composed of the Prime Minister of Canada and the first ministers of the provinces shall be convened by the Prime Minister of Canada at least once each year to discuss the state of the Canadian economy and such other matters as may be appropriate.

XIII—REFERENCES

149. A reference to this Act shall be deemed to include a reference to any amendments thereto."

Constitution Act, 1982

9. Sections 40 to 42 of the *Constitution Act, 1982* are repealed and the following substituted therefor:

"**40.** Where an amendment is made under subsection 38(1) that transfers legislative powers from provincial legislatures to Parliament, Canada shall provide reasonable compensation to any province to which the amendment does not apply.

41. An amendment to the Constitution of Canada in relation to the following matters may be made by proclamation issued by the Governor General under the Great Seal of Canada only where authorized by resolutions of the Senate and House of Commons and of the legislative assembly of each province:

(a) the office of the Queen, the Governor General and the Lieutenant Governor of a province;

(b) the powers of the Senate and the method of selecting Senators;

(c) the number of members by which a province is entitled to be represented in the Senate and the residence qualifications of Senators;

(d) the right of a province to a number of members in the House of Commons not less than the number of Senators by which the province was entitled to be represented on April 17, 1982;

(e) the principle of proportionate representation of the provinces in the House of Commons prescribed by the Constitution of Canada;

(f) subject to section 43, the use of the English or the French language;

(g) the Supreme Court of Canada;

(h) the extension of existing provinces into the territories;

(i) notwithstanding any other law or practice, the establishment of new provinces; and

(j) an amendment to this Part."

10. Section 44 of the said Act is repealed and the following substituted therefor:

> "**44.** Subject to section 41, Parliament may exclusively make laws amending the Constitution of Canada in relation to the executive government of Canada or the Senate and House of Commons."

11. Subsection 46 (1) of the said Act is repealed and the following substituted therefor:

> "**46.** (1) The procedures for amendment under sections 38, 41 and 43 may be initiated either by the Senate or the House of Commons or by the legislative assembly of a province."

12. Subsection 47 (1) of the said Act is repealed and the following substituted therefor:

> "**47.** (1) An amendment to the Constitution of Canada made by proclamation under section 38, 41 or 43 may be made without a resolution of the Senate authorizing the issue of the proclamation if, within one hundred and eighty days after the adoption by the House of Commons of a resolution authorizing its issue, the Senate has not adopted such a resolution and if, at any time after the expiration of that period, the House of Commons again adopts the resolution."

13. Part VI of the said Act is repealed and the following substituted therefor:

> ## "PART VI
> ## CONSTITUTIONAL CONFERENCES
>
> **50.** (1) A constitutional conference composed of the Prime Minister of Canada and the first ministers of the provinces shall be convened by the Prime Minister of Canada at least once each year, commencing in 1988.
>
> (2) The conferences convened under subsection (1) shall have included on their agenda the following matters:
>
> (a) Senate reform, including the role and functions of the Senate, its powers, the method of selecting Senators and representation in the Senate;
>
> (b) roles and responsibilities in relation to fisheries; and
>
> (c) such other matters as are agreed upon."

14. Subsection 52(2) of the said Act is amended by striking out the word "and" at the end of paragraph (b) thereof, by adding the word "and" at the end of paragraph (c) thereof and by adding thereto the following paragraph:

> "(d) any other amendment to the Constitution of Canada."

15. Section 61 of the said Act is repealed and the following substituted therefor:

   "**61.**   A reference to the *Constitution Act 1982*, or a reference to the *Constitution Acts 1867 to 1982*, shall be deemed to include a reference to any amendments thereto."

General

16. Nothing in section 2 of the *Constitution Act, 1867* affects section 25 or 27 of the *Canadian Charter of Rights and Freedoms*, section 35 of the *Constitution Act, 1982* or class 24 of section 91 of the *Constitution Act, 1867*.

Citation

17. This amendment may be cited as the *Constitution Amendment 1987*.

Signed at Ottawa,　　　　　　　　　　　　　　　　　　*Fait à Ottawa*
June 3, 1987　　　　　　　　　　　　　　　　　　　　*le 3 juin 1987*

APPENDIX 3

THE BNA ACT AND CANADIAN CONSTITUTION

CONSTITUTION ACT, 1982*

PART I
CANADIAN CHARTER OF RIGHTS AND FREEDOMS

Whereas Canada is found upon principles that recognize the supremacy of God and the role of Law:

Guarantee of Rights and Freedoms

1. The *Canadian Charter of Rights and Freedoms* guarantees the rights and freedoms set out in it subject only to such reasonable limits prescribed law as can be demonstrably justified in a free and democratic society.

Fundamental Freedoms

2. Everyone has the following fundamental freedoms:
    (a) freedom of conscience and religion;
    (b) freedom of thought, belief, opinion and expression, including freedom of the press and other media of communication;
    (c) freedom of peaceful assembly; and
    (d) freedom of association.

Democratic Rights

3. Every citizen of Canada has the right to vote in an election of members of the House of Commons or of a legislative assembly and to be qualified for membership therein.

4. (1) No House of Commons and no legislative assembly shall continue for longer than five years from the date fixed for the return of the writs at a general election of its members.
    (2) In time of real or apprehended war, invasion or insurrection, a House of Commons may be continued by Parliament and a legislative assembly may be continued by the legislature beyond five years if such continuation is not opposed by the votes of more than one-third of the members of the House of Commons or the legislative assembly, as the case may be.

5. There shall be a sitting of Parliament and of each legislature at least once every twelve months.

---

*Enacted as Schedule B to the Canada Act 1982 (U.K.) 1982, c. 11, which came into force on April 17. 1982. Reproduced with permission of the Minister of Supply and Services Canada.

Mobility Rights

6. (1) Every citizen of Canada has the right to enter, remain in and leave Canada

   (2) Every citizen of Canada and every person who has the status of a permanent resident of Canada has the right
   - (a) to move to and take up residence in any province; and
   - (b) to pursue the gaining of a livelihood in any province.

   (3) The rights specified in subsection (2) are subject to
   - (a) any laws or practices of general application in force in a province other than those that discriminate among persons primarily on the basis of province of present or previous residence; and
   - (b) any laws providing for reasonable residency requirements as a qualification for the receipt of publicly provided social services.

   (4) Subsections (2) and (3) do not preclude any law, program or activity that has as its object the amelioration in a province of conditions of individuals in that province who are socially or economically disadvantaged if the rate of employment in that province is below the rate of employment in Canada.

Legal Rights

7. Everyone has the right to life, liberty and security of the person and the right not to be deprived thereof except in accordance with the principles of fundamental justice.

8. Everyone has the right to be secure against unreasonable search or seizure.

9. Everyone has the right not to be arbitrarily detained or imprisoned.

10. Everyone has the right on arrest or detention
    - (a) to be informed promptly of the reasons therefor;
    - (b) to retain and instruct counsel without delay and to be informed of that right; and
    - (c) to have the validity of the detention determined by way of *habeas corpus* and to be released if the detention is not lawful.

11. Any person charged with an offence has the right
    - (a) to be informed without unreasonable delay of the specific offence;
    - (b) to be tried within a reasonable time;
    - (c) not to be compelled to be a witness in proceedings against that person in respect of the offence;
    - (d) to be presumed innocent until proven guilty according to law in a fair and public hearing by an independent and impartial tribunal;
    - (e) not to be denied reasonable bail without just cause;

(f) except in the case of an offence under military law tried before a military tribunal, to the benefit of trial by jury where the maximum punishment for the offence is imprisonment for five years or a more severe punishment;

(g) not to be found guilty on account of any act or omission unless, at the time of the act or omission, it constituted an offence under Canadian or international law or was criminal according to the general principles of law recognized by the community of nations;

(h) if finally acquitted of the offence, not to be tried for it again and, if finally found guilty and punished for the offence, not to be tried or punished for it again; and

(i) if found guilty of the offence and if the punishment for the offence has been varied between the time of commission and the time of sentencing, to the benefit of the lesser punishment.

12. Everyone has the right not to be subjected to any cruel and unusual treatment or punishment.

13. A witness who testifies in any proceedings has the right not to have any incriminating evidence so given used to incriminate that witness in any other proceedings, except in a prosecution for perjury or for the giving of contradictory evidence.

14. A party or witness in any proceedings who does not understand or speak the language in which the proceedings are conducted or who is deaf has the right to the assistance of an interpreter.

Equality Rights

15. (1) Every individual is equal before and under the law and has the right to the equal protection and equal benefit of the law without discrimination and, in particular, without discrimination based on race, national or ethnic origin, colour, religion, sex, age or mental or physical disability.

(2) Subsection (1) does not preclude any law, program or activity that has as its object the amelioration of conditions of disadvantaged because of raced, national or ethnic origin, colour, religion, sex, age or mental or physical disability.

Official Languages of Canada

16. (1) English and French are the official languages of Canada and have equality of status and equal rights and privileges as to their use in all institutions of the Parliament and government of Canada.

(2) English and French are the official languages of New Brunswick and have equality of status and equal rights and privileges as to their use in all institutions of the legislature and government of New Brunswick.

(3) Nothing in this Charter limits the authority of Parliament or a legislature to advance the equality of status or use of English and French

17. (1) Everyone has the right to use English or French in any debates and other proceedings of Parliament.

(2) Everyone has the right to use English or French in any debates and other proceedings of the legislature of New Brunswick.

18. (1) The statutes, records and journals of Parliament shall be printed and published in English and French and both language versions are equally authoritative.

(2) The statutes, records and journals of legislature of New Brunswick shall be printed and published in English and French and both language versions are equally authoritative.

19. (1) Either English or French may be used by any person in, or in any pleading in or process issuing from, any court established by Parliament.

(2) Either English or French may be used by any person in, or in any pleading in or process issuing from, any court of New Brunswick.

20. (1) Any member of the public in Canada has the right to communicate with, and to receive available services from, any head or central office of an institution of the Parliament or government of Canada in English or French, and has the same right with respect to any other office of any such institution where
    (a) there is a significant demand for communications with and services from that office in which language; or
    (b) due to the nature of the office, it is reasonable that communications with and services from that office be available in both English and French.

(2) Any member of the public in New Brunswick has the right to communicate with, and to receive available services from, any office of an institution of the legislature or government of New Brunswick in English or French.

21. Nothing in sections 16 to 20 abrogates or derogates from any right, privilege or obligation with respect to the English and French languages, or either of then, that exists or is continued by virtue of any other provision of the Constitution of Canada.

22. Nothing in sections 16 to 20 abrogates or derogates from any legal or customary right or privilege acquired or enjoyed either before or after the coming into force of this Charter with respect to any language that is not English or French.

Minority Language Educational Rights

23. (1) Citizens of Canada

(a) whose first language learned and still understood is that of the English or French linguistic minority population of the province in which they reside,
or
(b) who have received their primary school instruction in Canada in English or French and reside in a province where the language in which they received that instruction is the language of the English or French linguistic minority population of the province,
have the right to have their children receive primary and secondary school instruction in that language in that province.

(2) Citizens of Canada of whom any child has received or is receiving primary or secondary school instruction in English or French in Canada, have the right to have all their children receive primary and secondary school instruction in the same language.

(3) The right of citizens of Canada under subsections (1) and (2) to have their children receive primary and secondary school instruction in the language of the English or French linguistic minority population of a province

(a) applies wherever in the province the number of children of citizens who have such a right is sufficient to warrant the provision to them out of public funds of minority language instruction; and

(b) includes, where the number of children so warrants, the right to have them receive that instruction in minority language educational facilities provided out of public funds.

Enforcement

24. (1) Anyone whose rights or freedoms, as guaranteed by this Charter, have been infringed or denied may apply to a court of competent jurisdiction to obtain such remedy as the court considers appropriate and just in the circumstances.

(2) Where, in proceedings under subsection (1), a court concludes that evidence was obtained in a manner that infringed or denied any rights or freedoms guaranteed by this Charter, the evidence shall be excluded if it is established that, having regard to all the circumstances, the admission of it in the proceedings would being the administration of justice into disrepute.

General

25. The guarantee in this Charter of certain rights and freedoms shall not be construed so as to abrogate or derogate from any aboriginal, treaty or other rights or freedoms that pertain to the aboriginal peoples of Canada including

    (a) any rights or freedoms that have been recognized by the Royal Proclamation of October 7, 1763; and

    (b) any rights or freedoms that now exist by way of land claims agreements or may be so acquired. *

26. The guarantee in this Charter of certain rights and freedoms shall not be construed as denying the existence of any other rights or freedoms that exist in Canada.

27. This Charter shall be interpreted in a manner consistent with the preservation and enhancement of the multicultural heritage of Canadians.

28. Notwithstanding anything in this Charter, the rights and freedoms referred to in it are guaranteed equally to male and female persons.

29. Nothing in this Charter abrogates or derogates from any rights or privileges guaranteed by or under the Constitution of Canada in respect of denominational, separate or dissentient schools.

30. A reference in this Charter to a province or to the legislative assembly or legislature of a province shall be deemed to include a reference to the Yukon Territory and the Northwest Territories, or to the appropriate legislative authority thereof, as the case may be.

31. Nothing in this Charter extends the legislative powers of any body or authority.

Application of Charter

32. (1) This Charter applies

    (a) to the Parliament and government of Canada in respect of all matters within the authority of Parliament including all matters relating to the Yukon Territory and Northwest Territories; and

    (b) to the legislature and government of each province in respect of all matters within the authority of the legislature of each province.

  (2) Notwithstanding subsection (1), section 15 shall not have effect until three years after this section comes into force.

33. (1) Parliament or the legislature of a province may expressly declare in an Act of Parliament or of the legislature, as the case may be, that the Act or a provision thereof shall operate notwithstanding a provision included in section 2 or sections 7 to 15 of this Charter.

  (2) An Act or provision of an Act in respect of which a declaration made under this section is in effect shall have such operation as it would have but for the provision of this Charter referred to in the declaration.

  (3) A declaration made under subsection (1) shall cease to have

---

* As amended June 21, 1984.

effect five years after it comes into force or on such earlier
date as may be specified in the declaration.

(4) Parliament or a legislature of a province may re-enact a declaration made under subsection (1).

(5) Subsection (3) applies in respect of a re-enactment made under
subsection (4).

Citation

34. This Part may be cited as the *Canadian Charter of Rights and
Freedoms.*

PART II
RIGHTS OF THE ABORIGINAL PEOPLES OF CANADA

35. (1) The existing aboriginal and treaty rights of the aboriginal
peoples of Canada are hereby recognized and affirmed.

(2) In this Act, "aboriginal peoples of Canada" includes the Indian,
Inuit and Métis peoples of Canada.

(3) For greater certainty, in subsection (1) "treaty rights" includes
rights that now exist by way of land claims agreements or may
be so acquired. *

(4) Notwithstanding any other provision of this Act, the aboriginal
and treaty rights referred to in subsection (1) are guaranteed
equally to male and female persons. *

35.1 The government of Canada and the provincial governments are
committed to the principle that, before any amendment is made
to Class 24 of section 91 of the *Constitution Act 1867*, to section
25 of this Act or to this Part,

(a) a constitutional conference that includes in its agenda an item
relating to the proposed amendment, composed of the Prime
Minister of Canada and the first ministers of the provinces,
will be convened by the Prime Minister of Canada; and

(b) the Prime Minister of Canada will invite representatives of the
aboriginal peoples of Canada to participate in the discussions
on that item. *

PART III
EQUALIZATION AND REGIONAL DISPARITIES

36. (1) Without altering the legislative authority of Parliament or of
the provincial legislatures, or the rights of any of them with
respect to the exercise of their legislative authority, Parliament
and the legislatures, together with the government of Canada
and the provincial governments, are committed to

---

*Subsections 35(3) and 35(4) and section 35.1 were added to the original *Constitution Act, 1982*
by amendments proclaimed on June 21, 1984.

(a) promoting equal opportunities for well-being of Canadians;

(b) furthering economic development to reduce disparity in opportunities; and

(c) providing essential public services of reasonable quality to all Canadians.

(2) Parliament and the government of Canada are committed to the principle of making equalization payments to ensure that provincial governments have sufficient revenues to provide reasonable comparable levels of public services at reasonably comparable levels of taxation.

PART IV.1*
CONSTITUTIONAL CONFERENCES

37.1 (1) In addition to the conference convened in March 1983, at least two constitutional conferences composed of the Prime Minister of Canada and the first ministers of the provinces shall be convened by the Prime Minister of Canada, the first within three years after April 17, 1982 and the second within five years after that date.

(2) Each conference convened under subsection (1) shall have included in its agenda constitutional matters that directly affect the aboriginal peoples of Canada, and the Prime Minister of Canada shall invite representatives of those peoples to participate in the discussions on those matters.

(3) The Prime Minister of Canada shall invite elected representatives of the governments of the Yukon Territory and the Northwest Territories to participate in the discussions on any item on the agenda of a conference convened under subsection (1) that, in the opinion of the Prime Minister, directly affects the Yukon Territory and the Northwest Territories.

(4) Nothing in this section shall be construed so as to derogate from subsection 35(1).

PART V
PROCEDURE FOR AMENDING
CONSTITUTION OF CANADA

38. (1) An amendment to the Constitution of Canada may be made by proclamation issued by the Governor General under the Great Seal of Canada where so authorized by

(a) resolutions of the Senate and House of Commons; and

---

*Part IV.1 was added by amendment on June 21, 1984. The former Part IV, which provided for the 1983 constitutional conference, was automatically repealed on April 17, 1983.

(b) resolutions of the legislative assemblies of at least two-thirds of the provinces that have, in the aggregate, according to the then latest general census, at least fifty per cent of the population of all the provinces.

(2) an amendment made under subsection (1) that derogates from the legislative powers, the proprietary rights or any other rights or privileges of the legislature or government of a province shall require a resolution supported by a majority of the members of each of the Senate, the House of Commons and the legislative assemblies required under subsection (1).

(3) An amendment referred to in subsection (2) shall not have effect in a province the legislative assembly of which has expressed its dissent thereto by resolution supported by a majority of its members prior to the issue of the proclamation to which the amendment relates unless that legislative assembly, subsequently, by resolution supported by a majority of its members, revokes its dissent and authorizes the amendment.

(4) A resolution of dissent made for the purposes of subsection (3) may be revoked at any time before or after the issue of the proclamation to which it relates.

39. (1) A proclamation shall not be issued under subsection 38(1) before the expiration of one year from the adoption of the resolution initiating the amendment procedure thereunder unless the legislative assembly of each province has previously adopted a resolution of assent or dissent.

(2) A proclamation shall not be issued under subsection 38(1) after the expiration of three years from the adoption of the resolution initiating the amendment procedure thereunder.

40. Where an amendment is made under subsection 38(1) that transfers provincial legislative powers relating to education or other cultural matters from provincial legislatures to Parliament, Canada shall provide reasonable compensation to any province to which the amendment does not apply.

41. An amendment to the Constitution of Canada in relation to the following matters may be made by proclamation issued by the Governor General under the Great Seal of Canada only where authorized by resolutions of the Senate and House of Commons and of the legislative assembly of each province:

(a) the office of the Queen, the Governor General and the Lieutenant Governor of a province;

(b) the right of a province to a number of members in the House of Commons not less than the number of Senators by which the province is entitled to be represented at the time this Part comes into force;

(c) subject to section 43, the use of the English or the French language;

(d) the composition of the Supreme court of Canada;

(e) an amendment to this Part.

42. (1) An amendment to the Constitution of Canada in relation to the following matters may be made only in accordance with subsection 38 (1):

(a) the principle of proportionate representation of the provinces in the House of Commons prescribed by the Constitution of Canada;

(b) the powers of the Senate and the method of selecting Senators;

(c) the number of members by which a province is entitled to be represented in the Senate and the residence qualifications of Senators;

(d) subject to paragraph 41(d), the Supreme Court of Canada;

(e) the extension of existing provinces into the territories; and

(f) notwithstanding any other law or practice, the establishment of new provinces.

(2) Subsections 38(2) to (4) do not apply in respect of amendments in relation to matters referred to in subsection (1).

43. An amendment to the Constitution of Canada in relation to any provision that applies to one or more, but not all, provinces, including

(a) any alteration to boundaries between provinces, and

(b) any amendment to any provision that relates to the use of the English or the French language within a province,

may be made by proclamation issued by the Governor General under the Great Seal of Canada only where so authorized by resolutions of the Senate and House of Commons and of the legislative assembly of each province to which the amendment applies.

44. Subject to sections 41 and 42, Parliament may exclusively make laws amending the Constitution of Canada in relation to the executive government of Canada or the Senate and House of Commons.

45. Subject to section 41, the legislature of each province may exclusively make laws amending the constitution of the province.

46. (1) The procedures for amendment under sections 38, 41, 42 and 43 may be initiated either by the Senate or House of Commons or by the legislative assembly of a province.

(2) A resolution of assent made for the purposes of this Part may be revoked at any time before the issue of a proclamation authorized by it.

47. (1) An amendment to the Constitution of Canada made by proclamation under section 38, 41, 42 or 43 may be made without a resolution of the Senate authorizing the issue of the proclamation if, within one hundred and eighty days after the adoption by the House of Commons of a resolution authorizing its issue, the Senate has not adopted such a resolution and if, at any time after the expiration of that period, the House of Commons again adopts the resolution.

(2) Any period when Parliament is prorogued or dissolved shall not be counted in computing the one hundred and eighty day period referred to in subsection (1).

48. The Queen's Privy Council for Canada shall advise the Governor General to issue a proclamation under this Part forthwith on the adoption of the resolutions required for an amendment made by proclamation under this Part.

49. A constitutional conference composed of the Prime Minister of Canada and the first ministers of the provinces shall be convened by the Prime Minister of Canada within fifteen years after this Part comes into force to review the provisions of this Part.

PART VI
AMENDMENT TO THE CONSTITUTION ACT, 1867

50. The *Constitution Act, 1867* (formerly named the *British North America Act, 1867*) is amended by adding thereto, immediately after section 92 thereof, the following heading and section:

"Non-Renewable Natural Resources, Forestry Resources and Electrical Energy

92A. (1) In each province, the legislature may exclusively make laws in relation to

(a) exploration for non-renewable natural resources in the province;

(b) development, conservation and management of non-renewable natural resources and forestry resources in the province, including laws in relation to the rate of primary production therefrom; and

(c) development, conservation and management of sites and facilities in the province for the generation and production of electrical energy.

(2) In each province, the legislature may make laws in relation to the export from the province to another part of Canada of the primary production from non-renewable natural resources and forestry resources in the province and the production from facilities in the province for the generation of electrical energy, but such laws may not authorize or provide for discrimination in prices or in supplies exported to another part of Canada.

(3) Nothing in subsection (2) derogates from the authority of Parliament to enact laws in relation to the matters referred to in that subsection and, where such a law of Parliament and a law of a province conflict, the law of Parliament prevails to the extent of the conflict.

(4) In each province, the legislature may make laws in relation to the raising of money by any mode or system of taxation in respect of

(a) non renewable natural resources and forestry resources in the province and the primary production therefrom, and

(b) sites and facilities in the province for the generation of electrical energy and the production therefrom,

whether or not such production is exported in whole or in part from the province, but such laws may not authorize or provide for taxation that differentiates between production exported to another part of Canada and production not exported from the province.

(5) The expression "primary production" has the meaning assigned by the Sixth Schedule.

(6) Nothing in subsection (1) to (5) derogates from any powers or rights that a legislature or government of a province had immediately before the coming into force of this section."

51. The said Act is further amended by adding thereto the following Schedule:

"THE SIXTH SCHEDULE

Primary Production from Non-Renewable Natural Resources

1. For the purposes of section 92A of this Act,

(a) production from a non-renewable resource is a primary production therefrom if

(i) it is in the form in which it exists upon its recovery or severance from its natural state, or

(ii) it is a product resulting from processing or refining the resource, and is not a manufactured product or a product resulting from refining crude oil, refining upgraded heavy crude oil, refining gases or liquids derived from coal or refining a synthetic equivalent of crude oil; and

(b) production from a forestry resource is primary production therefrom if it consists of sawlogs, poles, lumber, wood chips, sawdust or any other primary wood product, or wood pulp, and is not a product manufactured from wood."

PART VII
GENERAL

52. (1) The Constitution of Canada is the supreme law of Canada, and any law that is inconsistent with the provisions of the Constitution is, to the extent of the inconsistency, of no force or effect.

(2) The Constitution of Canada includes
   (a) the *Canada Act*, including this Act;
   (b) the Acts and orders referred to in Schedule I; and
   (c) any amendment to any Act or order referred to in paragraph (a) or (b).

(3) Amendments to the Constitution of Canada shall be made only in accordance with the authority contained in the Constitution of Canada.

53. (1) The enactments referred to in Column I of Schedule I are hereby repealed or amended to the extent indicated in Column II thereof and, unless repealed, shall continue as law in Canada under the names set out in Column III thereof.

(2) Every enactment, except the *Canada Act*, that refers to an enactment referred to in Schedule I by the name in Column I thereof is hereby amended by substituting for that name the corresponding name in Column III thereof, and any British North America Act not referred to in Schedule I may be cited as the *Constitution Act* followed by the year and number, if any, of its enactment.

54. Part IV is repealed on the day that is one year after this Part comes into force and this section may be repealed and this Act renumbered, consequential upon the repeal of Part IV and this section, by proclamation issued by the Governor General under the Great Seal of Canada.

54.1 Part IV.1 and this section are repealed on April 18, 1987.*

55. A French version of the portions of the Constitution of Canada referred to in Schedule I shall be prepared by the Minister of Justice of Canada as expeditiously as possible and, when any portion thereof sufficient to warrant action being taken has been so prepared, it shall be put forward for enactment by proclamation issued by the Governor General under the Great Seal of Canada pursuant to the procedure then applicable to an amendment of the same provisions of the Constitution of Canada.

56. Where any portion of the Constitution of Canada has been or is enacted in English and French or where a French version of any

---

*Section 54.1 was added by amendment on June 21, 1984.

portion of the Constitution is enacted pursuant to section 55, the English and French versions of that portion of the Constitution are equally authoritative.

57. The English and French versions of this Act are equally authoritative.

58. Subject to section 59, this Act shall come into force on a day to be fixed by proclamation issued by the Queen or the Governor General under the Great Seal of Canada.

59. (1) Paragraph 23(1)(a) shall come into force in respect of Quebec on a day to be fixed by proclamation issued by the Queen or the Governor General under the Great Seal of Canada.
    (2) A proclamation under subsection (1) shall be issued only where authorized by the legislative assembly or government of Quebec.
    (3) This section may be repealed on the day paragraph 12(1)(a) comes into force in respect of Quebec and this Act amended and renumbered, consequential upon the repeal of this section, by proclamation issued by the Queen or the Governor General under the Great Seal of Canada.

60. This Act may be cited as the *Constitution Act, 1981*, and the Constitution Acts 1867 to 1975 (No. 2) and this Act may be cited together as the *Constitution Acts, 1867 to 1981*.

61. A reference to the *Constitution Acts, 1867 to 1982* shall be deemed to include a reference to the *Constitution Amendment Proclamation, 1983*.*

---

*Section 61 was added by amendment on June 21, 1984.

SCHEDULE 1

to the

CONSTITUTION ACT, 1981
MODERNIZATION OF THE CONSTITUTION

Item	Column I Act Affected	Column II Amendment	Column III New Name
1.	British North America Act, 1867, 30-31 Vict., c. 3 (U.K.)	(1) Section 1 is repealed and the following substituted therefor: "1. This Act may be cited as the *Constitution Act, 1867.*" (2) Section 20 is repealed. (3) Class 1 of section 91 is repealed. (4) Class 1 of section 92 is repealed.	Constitution Act, 1867
2.	An Act to amend and Continue the Act 32-33 Victoria chapter 3; and to establish and provide for the Government of the Province of Manitoba, 1870, 33 Vict., c. 3 (Can.)	(1) The long title is repealed and the following substituted therefor: "*Manitoba Act, 1870.*" (2) Section 20 is repealed.	Manitoba Act, 1870
3.	Order of Her Majesty in Council admitting Rupert's Land and the North-Western Territory into the Union, dated the 23rd of June, 1870		Rupert's Land and North-Western Territory Order
4.	Order of Her Majesty in Council admitting British Columbia into the Union, dated the 16th day of May, 1871		British Columbia Terms of Union
5.	British North America Act 1871, 34-35 Vict., c. 28 (U.K.)	Section 1 is repealed and the following substituted therefor: "1. This Act may be cited as the *Constitution Act, 1871.*"	
6.	Order of Her Majesty in Council admitting Prince Edward Island into the Union, dated the 26th day of June, 1873		Prince Edward Island Terms of Union
7.	Parliament of Canada Act, 1875, 38-39 Vict., c.38 (U.K.)		Parliament of Canada Act, 1875

Item	Column I Act Affected	Column II Amendment	Column III New Name
8.	Order of Her Majesty in Council admitting all British possessions and Territories in North America and islands adjacent thereto into the Union, dated the 31st day of July, 1880		Adjacent Territories Order
9.	British North America Act, 1886, 49-50 Vict., c. 35 (U.K.)	Section 3 is repealed and the following substituted therefor: "3. This Act may be cited as the *Constitution Act, 1886.*"	Constitution Act, 1886
10.	Canada (Ontario Boundary) Act, 1889, 52-53 Vict., c. 28 (U.K.)		Canada (Ontario Boundary) Act, 1889
11.	Canadian Speaker (Appointment of Deputy) Act, 1895, 2nd Sess., 59 Vict., c.3 (U.K.)	The Act is repealed.	
12.	The Alberta Act, 1905, 4-5 Edw. VII, c.3 (Can.)		Alberta Act
13.	The Saskatchewan Act, 1905, 4-5 Edw. VII, c.42 (Can.)		Saskatchewan Act
14.	British North America Act, 1907, 7 Edw. VII, c. II (U.K.)	Section 2 is repleaded and the following substituted therefor: "2. This Act may be cited as the *Constitution Act, 1907.*"	Constitution Act, 1907
15.	British North America Act, 1915, 5-6 Geo. V, c. 45 (U.K.)	Section 3 is repealed and the following substituted therefor: "3. This Act may be cited as the *Constitution Act, 1915.*"	Constitution Act, 1915
16.	British North America Act, 1930, 20-21 Geo. V, c. 26 (U.K.)	Section 3 is repealed and the following substituted therefor: 3. This Act may be cited as the *Constitution Act, 1930.*"	Constitution Act, 1930
17.	Statute of Westminster, 1931, 22 Geo. V. c. 4 (U.K.)	In so far as they apply to Canada, (a) section 4 is repealed; and (b) subsection 7(1) is repealed.	Statute of Westminster, 1931

Item	Column I Act Affected	Column II Amendment	Column III New Name
18.	British North America Act, 1940, 3-4 Geo. VI, c. 36 (U.K.)	Section 2 is repealed and the following substituted therefor: "2. This Act may be cited as the *Constitution Act, 1940.*"	Constitution Act, 1940
19.	British North America Act, 1943, 6-7 Geo. VI, c. 30 (U.K.)	The Act is repealed.	
20.	British North America Act, 1946, 9-10 Geo. VI, c. 63 (U.K.)	The Act is repealed.	
21.	British North America Act, 1949, 12-13 Geo. VI, c. 22 (U.K.)	Section 3 is repealed and the following substituted therefor: "3. This Act may be cited as the *Newfoundland Act.*"	Newfoundland Act
22.	British North America (No. 2) Act, 1949, 13 Geo. VI, c. 81 (U.K.)	The Act is repealed.	
23.	British North America Act, 1951, 14-15 Geo. VI, c. 32 (U.K.)	The Act is repealed.	
24.	British North America Act, 1952, 1 Eliz. II, c. 15 (Can.)	The Act is repealed.	
25.	British North America Act, 1960, 9 Eliz. II, c. 2 (U.K.)	Section 2 is repealed and the following substituted therefor: "2. This Act may be cited as the *Constitution Act, 1960.*"	Constitution Act, 1960
26.	British North America Act, 1964, 12-13 Eliz. II, c. 73 (U.K.)	Section 2 is repealed and the following substituted therefor: "2. This Act may be cited as the *Constitution Act, 1964.*"	Constitution Act, 1964
27	British North America Act, 1965, 14 Eliz. II, c. 4, Part I (Can.)	Section 2 is repealed and the following substituted therefor: "2. This Part may be cited as the *Constitution Act, 1965*"	Constitution Act, 1965
28.	British North America Act, 1974, 23 Eliz. II, c. 13, Part I (Can.)	Section 3, as amended by 25-26 Eliz. II, c. 28, s. 38(1) (Can.), is repealed and the following substituted therefor: "3. This Part may be cited as the *Constitution Act, 1974.*"	Constitution Act, 1974

Item	Column I Act Affected	Column II Amendment	Column III New Name
29.	British North America Act, 1975, 23-24 Eliz. II, c. 28, Part I (Can.)	Section 3, as amended by 25-26 Eliz. II, c. 28, s. 31 (Can.), is repealed and the following substituted therefor: "3. This Part may be cited as the *Constitution Act (No. 1), 1975*.	Constitution Act (No. 1), 1975
30.	British North America Act, (No. 2), 1975, 23-24 Eliz. II, c. 53 (Can.)	Section 3 is repealed and the following substituted therefor: "3. This Act may be cited as the *Constitution Act (No. 2), 1975.*"	Constitution Act (No. 2), 1975

CONSTITUTION ACT, 1867*

[THE BRITISH NORTH AMERICA ACT, 1867]

30 & 31 Victoria, c. 3.
(Consolidated with amendments)

An Act for the Union of Canada, Nova Scotia, and New Brunswick, and the Government therefore; and for Purposes connected therewith.

(29th March, 1867.)

WHEREAS the Provinces of Canada, Nova Scotia and New Brunswick have expressed their Desire to be federally united into One Dominion under the Crown of the United Kingdom of Great Britain and Ireland, with a Constitution similar in Principle to that of the United Kingdom:

And whereas such a Union would conduce to the Welfare of the Provinces and promote the Interest of the British Empire:

And whereas on the Establishment of the Union by Authority of Parliament it is expedient, not only that the Constitution of the Legislative Authority in the Dominion be provided for, but also that the Nature of the Executive Government therein be declared:

And whereas it is expedient that Provision be made for the eventual Admission into the Union of other Parts of British North America:

I.—PRELIMINARY

1. This Act may be cited as the Constitution Act, 1867.

VI.—DISTRIBUTION OF LEGISLATIVE POWERS

Powers of the Parliament

91. It shall be lawful for the Queen, by and with the Advice and Consent of the Senate and House of Commons, to make Laws for the Peace, Order, and good Government of Canada, in relation to all matters not coming within the Classes of Subjects by this Act assigned exclusively to the Legislatures of the Provinces; and for greater Certainty, but not so as to restrict the Generality of the foregoing Terms of this Section, it is hereby declared that (notwithstanding anything in this Act) the exclusive Legislative Authority of the Parliament of Canada extends to all Matters coming within the Classes of Subjects next hereinafter enumerated; that is to say,—

    1. Repealed.
    1A. The Public Debt and Property.

---

*As amended by the *Constitution Act, 1982*. Reproduced with permission of the Minister of Supply and Services Canada.

2. The Regulation of Trade and Commerce.

2A. Unemployment insurance.

3. The raising of Money by any Mode or System of Taxation.

4. The borrowing of Money on the Public Credit.

5. Postal Service.

6. The Census and Statistics.

7. Militia, Military and Naval Service, and Defence.

8. The Fixing of and providing for the Salaries and Allowances of Civil and other Officers of the Government of Canada.

9. Beacons, Buoys, Lighthouses, and Sable Island.

10. Navigation and Shipping.

11. Quarantine and the Establishment and Maintenance of Marine Hospitals.

12. Sea Coast and Inland Fisheries.

13. Ferries between a Province and any British or Foreign Country or between Two Provinces.

14. Currency and Coinage.

15. Banking, Incorporation of Banks, and the Issue of Paper Money.

16. Savings Banks.

17. Weights and Measures.

18. Bills of Exchange and Promissory Notes.

19. Interest.

20. Legal Tender.

21. Bankruptcy and Insolvency.

22. Patents of Invention and Discovery.

23. Copyrights.

24. Indians, and Lands reserved for the Indians.

25. Naturalization and Aliens.

26. Marriage and Divorce.

27. The Criminal Law, except the Constitution of Courts of Criminal Jurisdiction, but including the Procedure in Criminal Matters.

28. The Establishment, Maintenance, and Management of Penitentiaries.

29. Such Classes of Subjects as are expressly excepted in the Enumeration of the Classes of Subjects by this Act assigned exclusively to the Legislatures of the Provinces.

And any Matter within any of the Classes of Subjects enumerated in this Section shall not be deemed to come within the Class of Matters of a local or private Nature comprised in the Enumeration of the Classes of Subjects by this Act assigned exclusively to the Legislatures of the Provinces.

Exclusive Powers of Provincial Legislatures

92. In each Province the Legislature may exclusively make Laws in relation to Matters coming within the Classes of Subject next hereinafter enumerated; that is to say,—

   1. Repealed.
   2. Direct Taxation within the Province in order to the raising of a Revenue for Provincial Purposes.
   3. The borrowing of Money on the sole Credit of the Province.
   4. The Establishment and Tenure of Provincial Offices and the Appointment and Payment of Provincial Officers.
   5. The Management and Sale of the Public Lands belonging to the Province and of the Timber and Wood thereon.
   6. The Establishment, Maintenance, and Management of Public and Reformatory Prisons in and for the Province.
   7. The Establishment, Maintenance, and Management of Hospitals, Asylums, Charities, and Eleemosynary Institutions in and for the Province, other than Marine Hospitals.
   8. Municipal Institutions in the Province.
   9. Shop, Saloon, Tavern, Auctioneer, and other Licences in order to the raising of a Revenue for Provincial, Local, or Municipal Purposes.
   10. Local Works and Undertakings other than such as are of the following Classes:—
       (a) Lines of Steam or Other Ships, Railways, Canals, Telegraphs, and other Works and Undertakings connecting the Province with any other or others of the Provinces, or extending beyond the Limits of the Province;
       (b) Lines of Steam Ships between the Province and any British or Foreign Country;
       (c) Such Works as, although wholly situate within the Province, are before or after their Execution declared by the Parliament of Canada to be for the general Advantage of Canada or for the Advantage of Two or more of the Provinces.
   11. The Incorporation of Companies with Provincial Objects.
   12. The Solemnization of Marriage in the Province.
   13. Property and Civil Rights in the Province.
   14. The Administration of Justice in the Province, including the Constitution, Maintenance, and Organization of Provincial Courts, both of Civil and of Criminal Jurisdiction and including Procedure in Civil Matters in those Courts.
   15. The Imposition of Punishment by Fine, Penalty, or Imprisonment for enforcing any Law of the Province made in relation to any Matter coming within any of the Classes of Subjects enumerated within this Section.

16. Generally all Matters of a merely local or private Nature in the Province.

Non-Renewable Natural Resources, Forestry Resources and Electrical Energy

92A. (1) In each province, the legislature may exclusively make laws in relation to

  (a) exploration for non-renewable natural resources in the province;

  (b) development, conservation and management of non-renewable natural resources and forestry resources in the province, including laws in relation to the rate of primary production therefrom; and

  (c) development, conservation and management of sites and facilities in the province for the generation and production of electrical energy.

(2) In each province, the legislature may make laws in relation to the export from the province to another part of Canada of the primary production from non-renewable natural resources and forestry resources in the province and the production from facilities in the province for the generation of electrical energy, but such laws may not authorize or provide for discrimination in prices or in supplies exported to another part of Canada.

(3) Nothing in subsection (2) derogates from the authority of Parliament to enact laws in relation to the matters referred to in that subsection and, where such a law of Parliament and a law of province conflict, the law of Parliament prevails to the extent of the conflict.

(4) In each province, the legislature may make laws in relation to the raising of money by any mode or system of taxation in respect of

  (a) non-renewable natural resources and forestry resources in the province and the primary production therefrom, and

  (b) sites and facilities in the province for the generation of electrical energy and the production therefrom,

whether or not such production is exported in whole or in part from the province, but such laws may not authorize or provide for taxation that differentiates between production exported to another part of Canada and production not exported from the province.

(5) The expression "primary production" has the meaning assigned by the Sixth Schedule.

(6) Nothing in subsections (1) to (5) derogates from any powers or rights that a legislature or government of a province had immediately before the coming into force of this section.

Education

93. In and for each Province the Legislature may exclusively make laws in relation to Education, subject and according to the following Provisions:—

    (1) Nothing in any such Law shall prejudicially affect any Right or Privilege with respect to Denominational Schools which any Class of Persons have by Law in the Province at the Union:

    (2) All the Powers, Privileges, and Duties at the Union by Law conferred and imposed in Upper Canada on the Separate Schools and School Trustees of the Queen's Roman Catholic Subjects shall be and the same are hereby extended to the Dissentient Schools of the Queen's Protestant and Roman Catholic Subjects in Quebec:

    (3) Where in any Province a System of Separate or Dissentient Schools exist by Law at the Union or is thereafter established by the Legislature of the Province, an Appeal shall lie to the Governor General in Council from any Act or Decision of any Provincial Authority affecting any Right or Privilege of the Protestant or Roman Catholic Minority of the Queen's Subjects in relation to Education:

    (4) In case any such Provincial Law as from Time to Time seems to the Governor General in Council requisite for the due Execution of the Provisions of this Section is not made, or in case any Decision of the Governor General in Council on any Appeal under this Section is not duly executed by the proper Provincial Authority in that behalf, then and in every such Case, and as far only as the Circumstances of each case require, the Parliament of Canada may make remedial Laws for the due Execution of the Provisions of this Section and of any Decision of the Governor General in Council under this Section.

APPENDIX 4

BENCHMARKS IN THE HISTORY OF QUEBEC

1534	Jacques Cartier lands in bay of Gaspé and takes possession of the territory in the name of François I, King of France. This act marks the discovery of Canada.
1608	On July 3, Samuel de Champlain drops anchor along the north shore of the St. Lawrence River at a place the Indians call *Kébec* (Quebec).
1634	At the request of Champlain, Laviolette establishes a post at the confluence of the Saint Maurice and the St. Lawrence Rivers, upstream from Quebec. This post becomes Trois-Rivières.
1642	Paul de Chomedey de Maisonneuve founds Ville-Marie, a small colony comprising a fort, a hospital, a chapel, and a residence housing 70 people. The settlement later became Montreal.
1759	During the Seven Year War, Wolfe's armies lay siege to Quebec City and defeat Montcalm's troops on September 13 at the battle on the Plains of Abraham.
1760	Despite Lévis' victory in Sainte-Foy, Montreal also falls to British troops, and the British Conquest is over.
1763	Under the Treaty of Paris, the King of France ceded Canada and all of its dependencies to the King of England. The Royal Proclamation of 1763 institutes Quebec's government bodies.
1791	The Constitution Act makes possible the establishment of the parliamentary system in Canada and grants French Canadians their own homeland. For this purpose, the country is divided into two provinces: Upper Canada, mainly English-speaking with York (Toronto) as its capital, and Lower Canada, mainly French-speaking with Quebec City as its capital.
1837– 1838	The English army quells the Rebellion of the Lower Canada *Patriotes*. This marks the end of a constitutional, social, and economic crisis.
1840	The Act of Union unites Upper and Lower Canada under a single government.
1867	The British North America (BNA) Act is proclaimed, creating the federation of Ontario, Quebec, Nova Scotia, and New Brunswick.
1917	Women vote for the first time in federal elections. They will obtain the right to vote in Quebec in 1940. Quebecers oppose overseas service to fight in the First World War. Riots take place in Quebec City.
1936	Liberal premier Taschereau resigns and is succeeded by Adélard Godbout. Maurice Duplessis becomes Quebec's premier for the first time on August 17. His party, the *Union nationale*, is a coalition of the former Conservatives and dissident Liberals.
1939	Liberal Adélard Godbout becomes premier, defeating Duplessis.
1942	Second conscription crisis. For the second time, Quebecers oppose overseas service while English Canada is strongly in favour.

1944	Duplessis becomes premier for the second time. He remains in power until his death in 1959, winning the 1948, 1952, and 1956 elections. The *Bloc populaire*, a party created in reaction to the conscription crisis, headed by André Laurendeau, wins four seats.
1948	The *Union nationale* (UN) wins the July 28 election. The current official Quebec flag is selected.
1952	The *Union nationale* wins the July 16 election.
1956	The *Union nationale* wins the June 20 election.
1958	Jean Lesage replaces Georges-Émile Lapalme as the Liberal leader.
1959	Duplessis dies on September 7. His successor, Paul Sauvé, initiates the first reforms, a prelude to the Quiet Revolution. Sauvé dies on January 2 after only 100 days in power. Antonio Barette becomes premier.
1960	Jean Lesage's Liberal party is elected on June 22.
1961	Claire Kirkland-Casgrain becomes the first woman to be elected to the National Assembly in Quebec after winning a byelection. Jean Lesage visits Paris and is greeted like a head of state.
1962	The Liberal party wins the election fought on the issue of nationalization of the electricity companies. Following the election, the modern Hydro-Québec is created.
1964	The Department of Education is created and Paul Gérin-Lajoie becomes the first minister of education.
1965	The *Caisse de dépôt et placement du Québec* is created.
1966	In the June 5 election the *Union nationale*, under Daniel Johnson's premiership, returns to power with a majority of seats but a minority of votes.
1967	France's president, Charles de Gaulle, shouts "*Vive le Québec libre*" from Montreal's city hall balcony. The *Mouvement souveraineté-association* (MSA) is created.
1968	Daniel Johnson dies in power and is replaced by Jean-Jacques Bertrand. The *Mouvement souveraineté-association* becomes the *Parti québécois* (PQ) in a merger with the *Ralliement national* and the *Rassemblement pour l'indépendance nationale* (RIN). Pierre Elliott Trudeau becomes Prime Minister of Canada.
1969	Bill 63, the *Union nationale* legislation allowing parents to choose the language of education of their children, is tabled.
1970	Robert Bourassa and the Liberal party win the April 29 election. In October, James Richard Cross and Pierre Laporte are kidnapped by the *Front de libération du Québec* (FLQ). The federal government decides to apply the War Measures Act and about 450 people are arrested, though the FLQ numbered only about 35. James Cross is freed but Pierre Laporte is murdered.
1971	After a strong public campaign, Bourassa rejects the Victoria Charter, an agreement to patriate and amend the constitution.
1972	The *Front commun* (Common Front), a coalition of public sector unions, launches a general strike that ends with a year in prison for the three union leaders.
1973	On October 29, Robert Bourassa is reelected, his party winning 102 of the 108 seats of the National Assembly.

1974	Bill 22, the Liberals' linguistic policy is adopted by the National Assembly.
1976	The *Parti québécois*, whose aim was to achieve Quebec sovereignty, wins the election on November 15. René Lévesque becomes premier.
1977	Bill 101, the *Parti québécois'* language legislation, is adopted.
1980	During the May 20 referendum, Quebecers refuse to grant their government a mandate to negotiate sovereignty-association with the federal government. The No vote wins with 59.6% and the Yes vote obtains 40.4%.
1981	The *Parti québécois* is reelected on April 13. In November, the First Ministers Conference on the Constitution in Ottawa ends with an agreement reached after an all-night private session from which Quebec is excluded. Quebec refuses to sign.
1982	Under severe financial constraints, the government decides to vote the collective agreements including 21% pay cuts for the period January to March 1983.
1984	Trudeau retires as prime minister of Canada. Except for nine months in 1979, he had been in power since 1968. On September 4, the Progressive Conservatives, headed by Brian Mulroney, win the federal election. René Lévesque welcomes the Conservative victory and says that there is a risk in dealing with the Conservative government, but that it is a "beautiful risk."
1985	Robert Bourassa's Liberal party (in power from 1970 to 1976) is reelected on December 2.
1989	The Liberal party is elected for a second consecutive mandate on September 29.
1990	In June, the Meech Lake accord is rejected. The accord was to settle Quebec's exclusion from the 1982 constitutional deal.
1991	The unions agree to negotiate with the government a salary freeze for the first six months of 1992.
1992	On October 26, the Charlottetown agreement is rejected by a majority of Canadians. Six provinces and the Yukon Territory vote against it; Quebec also votes no, in the proportion of 55.6% to 44.4%.

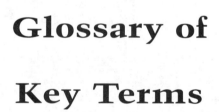

Glossary of
Key Terms

Active population   Members of the civilian population 15 years and older, employed or looking for employment during a given week. (Chapter 13)

Administrative regions   The ten regions into which the Quebec territory is divided for statistical, administrative, and economic purposes. (Chapter 11)

Affirmative action   The idea behind programs in the public service aimed at eliminating discrimination based on race, ethnicity, or sex, not only by ending certain hiring practices, but also by actively increasing employment of members of these groups. (Chapter 11)

Assemblée nationale   See **National Assembly**.

***Assurance-maladie* (medicare system)**   A program of health security for Quebec enacted in 1970 following the work of the Castonguay-Nepveu Commission. It provided both hospital and physician coverage. (Chapter 16)

Bicameralism   Existence of a two-house legislature. In contrast to *unicameralism*, in which there is only one house, usually a popularly elected assembly. (After abolition of the Legislative Council in 1968, the Quebec legislature became a unicameral one.) (Chapter 9)

Bill/law   Proposed legislation—i.e., legislation that is still in the process of being adopted. After adoption, the legislation is referred to as a *law* or *Act of Parliament*. In English, the term *bill* may sometimes be retained even after the legislation has been passed, as is the case with Bill 101; but in French the term *loi* (law) must always be used after passage. (Chapter 9)

Bipartism   A situation in which two major political parties compete for control of the government. Bipartism exists in the Quebec political system. (Chapter 5)

Cabinet   The group of advisors to the Premier consisting of a *Directeur de cabinet* (Chief of Staff) and several others who head the ***Conseil exécutif*** (Executive Council). The word, imported from France, is the same in French and English. In the Quebec parliamentary system, this concept is rather confusing, for it can describe the ***Conseil exécutif des ministres***. (Chapter 10)

Capitalism   An economic system in which individuals and corporations own the principal means of production and seek profits. (Chapter 1)

Capitalist mode of production   A certain historically conditioned way for an individual to obtain means of livelihood, in which the labourer has been dispossessed of the ownership of his or her means of production (as occurs when, for example, an artisan no longer owns his or her tools) because new machinery has replaced old-fashioned methods, and therefore sells his or her labour for wages to the person who now owns the tools and machinery necessary for production. (Chapter 1)

Caucus   A group of **MNAs** all belonging to the same political party. A *parliamentary caucus* is a meeting of all MNAs from the same party or **parliamentary group**. (Chapter 9)

Centralism   The tendency of the federal government to appropriate and control fields of policymaking that could or should otherwise be left to the discretion of the provinces. (Chapter 2)

Charter of Human Rights and Freedoms   Legislation passed in 1975 that came as a response to some of the concerns about individual liberties and collective rights. Later, the Canadian Charter of Rights and Freedoms was enacted in 1982. (Chapter 12)

Civil Code   A systematically arranged collection of laws on which legislation and court decisions are based. (Chapter 12)

Class-action suit   A legal action brought by a person or group on behalf of a number of people with similar claims or defences. (Chapter 12)

Class conflict   Political conflict due to the contending interests of social classes, such as the business class, the middle class, the working class, etc. (Chapter 7)

Collective bargaining   Negotiations, between representatives of labour unions and either government officials or private sector representatives, to determine salaries and working conditions. (Chapter 11)

Confederation   An association of independent states in which the states agree to confer certain limited authority upon the central government while retaining their full sovereignty individually. The Canadian political system was at its origin in 1867 a confederation, since four provinces (including Quebec) signed the BNA Act. (Chapter 2)

Concentrated pool   An association of large corporations and managers who have some control over the primary products. (Chapter 15)

***Conseil de presse du Québec* (Quebec Press Council)**   A private journalists' organization, founded on February 20, 1973, whose membership is voluntary. The *Conseil* has 19 members, six from press enterprises, six from the *Fédération professionnelle des journalistes du Québec* (Quebec Journalists' Professionnal Federation), and seven from the public at large. (Chapter 8)

***Conseil exécutif/des ministres* (Executive Council)**   The Premier's executive aides and their staffs, who are in charge of the Premier's relationships with the Cabinet members, officials of the party, the press, and the public. (Chapter 10)

***Conseil souverain* (Sovereign Council)**   The highest colonial court in Quebec, created in 1663. It was made up of the governor, the bishop, the intendant, and five councillors. But by the 1670s all important regulations were drafted by the intendant before they were made public at sittings of the council. (Chapter 16)

Consensus-building   Attempts, through various procedures, to alleviate the partisan nature of business conducted in the **National Assembly**. (Chapter 9)

Constituents   Persons who live and vote in an official electoral district. (Chapter 6)

Constitutional amendment   A formal change made to the Canadian constitution. (Chapters 2 and 16)

Consultant   A person from outside the government who is hired by a government agency to conduct research, collect data, and perform policy analysis. (Chapter 7)

Cooperative federalism   A concept of government under which powers are shared between federal and provincial levels. According to this concept, the Canadian constitution was an agreement between two founding nations. This idea was put forward by Jean-Luc Pépin in the early 1960s, who believed with others that this system was the most suitable one for Canada. An example of cooperative federalism in action would be the Canadian Assistance Plan, created in 1965. (Chapter 16)

Corporatism   A tripartite relationship between government, labour unions, and the private sector, in which governments seek the support of, or consult, business and labour organizations only, giving rise to a kind of corporate state. (Chapter 7)

Coureurs des bois   Fur traders who, as independent traders, travelled great distances to meet with the native peoples who trapped and prepared the pelts. Coureurs des bois usually exchanged goods for these pelts and brought them back to Montreal, where they sold them to French merchants representing metropolitan interests. Coureurs started being resorted to during the French regime as sources of supply began moving westward of Montreal, which was the main trading centre. Today, one of the oldest fur trade posts can be visited by the public in Lachine, on Montreal Island. (Chapter 1)

Court of Quebec   A court formed by merging the former Provincial Court, **Court of the Sessions of the Peace**, and Youth Court, which performs all the duties of these courts. Established June 17, 1988 by the Act to Amend the Courts of Justice and Other Legislation. (Chapter 12)

Court of the Sessions of the Peace   Abolished when the **Court of Quebec** was established by an act of the Quebec legislature on June 17, 1988. The act, which took effect on August 31, merged into a single judicial body the former Provincial Court, the Court of the Sessions of the Peace, and the Youth Court. (Chapter 12)

***Coutume de Paris* (Custom of Paris)**   The prevailing body of law during the French regime. Its prescriptions presided, among others, over the establishment and functioning of the seigneurial system. It regulated economic and social relations between *seigneur* and *censitaire*. (Chapter 1)

Cultural isolationism   The tendency of a society to close itself off from external cultural influences. A characteristic of Quebec mostly before the Quiet Revolution. (Chapter 3)

Cultural sovereignty A political goal proclaimed by Premier Robert Bourassa during the 1970 constitutional conference held in Victoria. The concept symbolized Quebec's quest for full control over communications and cultural policy on its territory. (Chapter 8)

Deindustrialization An absolute decline of the manufacturing sector in terms of employment and contribution to GDP. There occurs a shift of resources out of the domestic manufacturing operations, either to somewhere outside the area in question (a highly unlikely outcome in Quebec's case) or to the service sector. The term often has negative connotations, implying a lack of dynamism in the industrial sector and a tendency industry to be concentrated in traditional and low-productivity fields. (Chapter 13)

Delegated ministers See **state ministers**.

Democracy A system of government under which, in theory, the people rule, either directly or indirectly, and power is held by the many (polyarchy). (Chapter 1)

Deregulation A reduction in the number and scope of rules affecting the private economy. The movement to deregulation in Quebec began with the election of Robert Bourassa's Liberal government in 1985. Deregulation has proceeded in such industries as energy and the airlines. (Chapter 4)

Direct lobbying An attempt to influence an MNA's vote through personal contact with him or her. (Chapter 7)

***Directeur de cabinet* (Chief of Staff)** This person organizes the agenda of the Premier, responds to citizens' letters, and monitors the Premier's relationship with his or her administration, the **MNAs**, and the media. (Chapter 10)

Disavow An action of the federal government under Article 56 of the 1867 British North America (BNA) Act (the constitution act creating the Canadian federation), whereby it can disallow a bill passed by a provincial legislature within two years. This is done through an elaborate procedure involving the Governor General as representative of the Queen. With regard to Quebec, this right fell into disuse in the late 1890s. (Chapters 1 and 2)

***Discours inaugural* (Opening Speech)** An opening speech (called the Speech from the Throne in other legislatures) made at each new parliamentary session, in which the Government presents the key policy measures it is planning to introduce in the following months. (Chapter 10)

Discreet respondents Eligible voters who answer "I don't know" in public opinion polls. They are not undecided voters, since many might have an undeclared opinion. (Chapter 6)

Distribution or division of power The allocation of administrative, legislative, and political responsibility between the different levels of government. (Chapter 2)

Double majority principle   Under the Union Act, between 1840 and 1867, Lower Canada (Quebec) and Upper Canada (Ontario) were equally represented in a legislature comprising 84 members (until 1853, when the number of representatives was raised to 130). To have the force of law, a bill had to receive a majority vote by both delegations—a "double majority." (Chapter 1)

Economic dependency   A situation in which a significant proportion of a country or province's economy is owned and controlled by foreign interests—i.e., non-resident foreign nationals. (Chapter 13)

Elite theory   The belief that the few govern the many. These few, by holding key public and private sector positions, occupy positions of power and control. Both elite and class theory believe that elites control policymaking and government. (Chapter 7)

Enumeration   The process of naming all Quebec voters in each district on an official list before each election, in accordance with the Election Act. The door-to-door census is made by two persons, called *enumerators*, one named by the party in office and the other named by the opposition party. There are more than 20,000 active enumerators during each election. (Chapter 5)

Épanouissement   "Blossoming"; refers to the process of social, political, and economic emancipation of French-speaking Quebecers after 1960. (Chapter 14)

Equalization payments   Payments made by the federal government to provincial governments based on the needs of each province. The equalization formula takes into account several **tax fields**. (Chapters 2 and 16)

Federalism   A system of government under which two levels of authority cover the same area. Under a federal system (such as Canada's), provinces and the federal government both have full control over some specific jurisdictions; in other matters, power is shared by both levels. (Chapter 2)

Filibuster   An instance of the delaying tactic, that consists in speech-making to prevent progress on the passage of a piece of legislation. Often used in the **National Assembly**. (Chapter 9)

Fiscal federalism   The patterns of spending, taxing, and grants between levels of government. (Chapter 2)

Foreign investment   In this book, investments made in Quebec by non-resident foreign nationals. (Investments made by non-resident Canadians are considered domestic investment.) (Chapter 13)

Franchise   The right to vote. (Chapter 6)

Gender gap   The different outlooks and attitudes held by women and men as revealed in voting and participation patterns. (Chapter 6)

General election (in Quebec)   The elections in which Quebec voters select the 125 members of the **National Assembly**. (Chapters 5 and 6)

Grassroots lobbying Lobbying activities of rank-and-file members and would-be members of interest groups. (Chapter 7)

Gross domestic product (GDP) A measure of the total value of goods and services produced during a given year. The value of imports and the income from investments abroad are not included. In Quebec, GDP also excludes the value of goods and services produced by Quebecers outside Quebec. (Chapter 13)

Hyperpluralism A perverted system of government characterized by a proliferation of demanding groups, with the result that government cannot work efficiently. (Chapter 7)

Ideology A set of logically or historically related political beliefs and values. (Chapter 3)

Independence A political option considered by more-radical Quebec nationalists whereby Quebec would obtain fully separate political status as a bona fide state. (Chapters 2 and 6)

Independentist Said of those who favour political independence of Quebec from the rest of Canada. Also *sovereignist* and, in a negative sense, *separatist*. (Chapters 2 and 6)

Industrial policy In modern Quebec, an approach to economic policy that blends an emphasis on stimulating economic growth with an enlarged role for government, especially in promoting the conditions for growth. (Chapter 13)

Interest group An organization of people who organize to enter the policy-making process for the purpose of advancing certain goals. (Chapter 7)

Intergovernmental relations The workings of the federal system, i.e., the entire set of interactions between provincial and federal officials, and between various units of government. (Chapter 16)

Joint ventures Projects in which several enterprises or corporations invest together. (Chapter 15)

Jurisdiction The right to exercise authority, or the district or territorial limits within which authority may be exercised. (Chapter 2)

Law See **bill/law**.

Leadership convention Mass meetings where members of a political party choose their leader. (Chapter 10)

Legal Aid Bureau Quebec's first legal aid service, created by the Bar of Montreal. (Chapter 12)

Liberals Members of the Quebec Liberal Party, whose political ideology has evolved over the years, favouring at the beginning of the 1960s a broad scope of government activities, and later adopting to a much more "conservative" attitude. (Chapter 3)

Lieutenant Governor   The Queen's representative in Quebec. With the **National Assembly**, the Lieutenant Governor constitutes Parliament. (Chapter 10)

Lobbying   Communicating, usually on behalf of some **interest group**, with government decision-makers in hopes of exerting an influence. (Chapter 7)

Lobbyist   A representative of an **interest group**. (Chapter 7)

Majority leader   The head of the majority party in the **National Assembly**. More often called the *Government House Leader*. (Chapter 9)

Marginalization   See **peripheralization/marginalization**.

Mass media   The means of communicating with or providing information to large numbers of people in a society. Often divided into *print* and *broadcast* media. (Chapter 8)

***Médias communautaires* (community media)**   Radio and TV stations that target specific audiences, such as "the francophone community outside of Quebec" or "the Italian community." We have seen in the recent years a proliferation of such stations in Quebec. (Chapter 8)

Mercantilism   Economic theories and practices that developed in Europe in the mid-15th century and lasted well into the 18th. Mercantilism sought to further a nation's superiority over other states by securing a monopoly over precious metals and other valuable, often exotic goods. To this end, colonies were created to supply the metropolis with exclusive natural products. The colonies' economic development was closely monitored and controlled by the imperial government. Accumulation and self-sufficiency were sought by exporting as much product as possible while importing as little as possible. (Chapter 1)

Merit system   A set of administrative procedures for hiring, promoting, and dismissing government employees based on professional or technical performance. (Chapter 11)

***Ministère du Conseil éxécutif* (Department of the Executive Council)**   A department under the leadership of the premier that has close to 250 permanent employees and assists the Premier. (Chapter 10)

Ministers without portfolio   See **state ministers**.

Minority party   A political party that gets the support of few voters. (Chapter 6)

Minority rights   A guarantee in the Constitution that all citizens of Canada have the right to be served in either French or English, as they choose. (Chapter 14)

Mixed economy   A partly free-market economy, in which government is a leading economic actor and deeply involved in decisions affecting the economy. (Chapter 13)

MNAs   Members of the **National Assembly**. (Chapter 9)

National Assembly (*Assemblée nationale*)   Quebec's legislative branch. It took on this name in 1968. Prior to that it was called the Legislative Assembly like the legislatures of all other Canadian provinces. At the federal level the legislature is called the House of Commons. The National Assembly has 125 members. (Chapters 5 and 9)

National interest   A nation's well-being. In the case of Quebec, the fact that, constitutionally, Canada is considered a binational country gives a different meaning to the word "national." Quebec's national interest differs from that of Canada as a whole. (Chapter 2)

Nationalism   A political **ideology** based on celebration of the shared social, cultural, and institutional characteristics of members of a nation. (Chapter 3)

Nationalization   Purchase or appropriation by the state of private industrial corporations. (Chapters 4 and 15)

Nation-building   The view, in contrast to the concept of **province-building**, that the federal government should use all possible means to establish national policy and that provinces should meet federally determined national standards. The federal government can use its fiscal and taxation powers to curb provincial autonomy. (Chapter 4)

Notwithstanding clause   A clause that permits a province to omit or limit the application of federal legislation in certain matters, such as language policy. Such a clause applies for five years, after which the provincial government must proclaim it again. (Chapter 14)

Office of the Premier   A body consisting in a *Directeur de cabinet* (Chief of Staff), an *Adjoint au directeur de cabinet* (Adjuct Chief of Staff), and several advisors. (Chapter 10)

Overbilling   The practice of doctors of charging citizens for medical services covered by *Assurance-maladie*, the Quebec medicare system. (Chapter 16)

Parliamentary group   Elected members of the **National Assembly** who are too few in number to be called representatives of a political party. (Chapter 9)

Parliamentary system   A system of government in which the chief executive is that leader whose party holds the majority in the legislature after an election or whose party forms a major part of the ruling coalition. (Chapter 9)

Party identification   Voters' preference for, psychological attachment to, or loyalty to a political party. (Chapter 6)

Patronage   The granting of jobs, contracts, and other political favours by the party in power. (Chapter 5)

Péquiste   Any member, militant, or follower of the Parti québécois. (Chapter 6)

Peripheralization/marginalization   These interchangeable terms refer to Quebec's constantly decreasing influence, relative to its share of the population, in the overall Canadian economy. Geographically speaking, throughout the 20th century Quebec has suffered from the westward displacement of North America's centre of economic gravity. (Chapter 13)

Pluralist   Said of a theory which contends that Quebec's political system is made up of competing **interest groups** fairly representing different religious, economic, and cultural interests. (Chapter 7)

Political culture   The attitudes, norms, and values shared by the members of a community with regard to the way they perceive and experience their relations with each other and their political system. (Chapter 3)

Political participation   Includes all activities by which citizens take part in the selection of political officeholders. (Chapter 6)

Political socialization   The complex process by which people acquire their political values. (Chapter 3)

Private bills   Bills introduced by members of the **National Assembly** whose content is for the particular interest of a person, organization, or locality. Not to be confused with **private members' bills**. (Chapter 9)

Private members' bills   Bills introduced by individual members of the **National Assembly** rather than, as is usually the case, by the Premier or a Cabinet member. These bills, which are actually *public bills*, are rarely put to a vote, as priority is given to the government's legislative agenda. Nonetheless, the MNA sponsoring such a bill will have scored points with his or her constituents, which is usually the intent of such bills. Not to be confused with **private bills**. (Chapter 9)

Privatization   Full or partial sale by governments of **state-owned enterprises**. (Chapter 4)

Province-building   A tendency of a province to call for more responsibility and powers in some or all fields of policymaking. (Chapters 2 and 4)

Provincial Court   See **Court of Quebec.**

Public opinion   The collective attitudes and beliefs of citizens concerning social issues, or the distribution of such attitudes and beliefs. (Chapter 3)

Public policy   A general course of action adopted by the government in response to some social pressure. (Chapters 13 to 16)

Radio-Québec   A state-owned television enterprise whose mandate is essentially educational, being similar to that of Radio-Ontario or PBS in the United States. Created on February 22, 1968 by the Quebec government. (Chapter 8)

Realignment election   A critical election that produces a sharp change in existing patterns of party loyalty among groups of voters, a change that does not end with the election. (A lessening of the importance of party loyalties in voting decisions is called a *dealignment.*) (Chapter 6)

Redistributive measures Refers to various social programs established during the the 1930s as a followup to adoption of Keynesian economic theory by the certain governments. In Canada, some redistributive measures were: unemployment compensation, public assistance, compensation, pensions of various sorts, and transfer payments from the federal to the provincial governments in the fields of health, public assistance, and postsecondary education. Other examples are the **equalization payments** program whereby the richer provinces, through a formula designed and administered by the federal government, share their wealth with the poorer ones, assuring the latter of sufficient revenues to provide reasonably comparable levels of public services at reasonably comparable levels of taxation. (Chapter 1)

Referendum A popular consultation on a specific issue, usually a constitutional matter in Canada, requiring a "yes or no" vote. Such an electoral procedure is not widely used in Quebec.

The question asked in the 1980 Quebec referendum was whether to give the Quebec government the mandate to negotiate **sovereignty-association**—in other words, to initiate the process toward Quebec **independence**. (Chapter 6)

Regional disparities Substantial differences in income, employment, standard of living, industrial development, and other economic indicators between different regions of a country or province. (Chapter 13)

Responsible government A type of elected government in which the Premier and his or her Cabinet members are fully responsible and accountable for their actions and those of their subordinates in the administration before the representatives of the people in the **National Assembly**. This notion of responsibility of the Executive vis-à-vis the legislature came into being in 1848. (Chapter 9)

Secrétaire exécutif (Executive Secretary) A member of the Premier's office whose main task is to serve as liaison between the Premier and members of the **National Assembly**. (Chapter 10)

Secrétaire général (General Secretary) The head of the **Ministère du Conseil exécutif** (Department of the Executive Council). His or her role is to keep all ministers informed about the Government's legislative schedule. (Chapter 10)

Secularization The process by which a society's orientation is no longer determined or defined by the clerical authorities. (Chapter 3)

Separatism The advocacy of Quebec **independence**. (Chapter 3)

Small claims court A court dealing with minor claims, created in 1972 by the Legal Aid Act. Coverage extends to both criminal and civil law. (Chapter 12)

Social security Insurance that provides economic assistance to persons faced with unemployment, disability, or old age. (Chapter 16)

Solliciteurs Militants of a political party who canvass in its district to solicit funds and political support for the party. (Chapter 5)

Sovereignty-association   A political concept expounded by the PQ and Quebec nationalists whereby Quebec would yield all or a portion of its jurisdiction over its own **tax fields** to the federal government, and in return the federal government would manage redistribution of revenues to all the provinces in the form of services and programs. (Chapters 2 and 6)

Standing committees   The nine permanent legislative committees of the **National Assembly**, of which eight oversee the various departments of the Executive and one deals with the **National Assembly** itself. (Chapter 9)

Standing orders   Fixed rules governing the procedures of the **National Assembly**. (Chapter 9)

State ministers   Ministers who have legislative, administrative, and political roles to play in advising the Premier in special areas. Currently, there are four state ministers, who cover the following areas: the status of women, aboriginal affairs, electoral reform, and Canadian intergovernmental relationships. Also called *delegated ministers* or *ministers without portfolio*. (Chapter 10)

State-owned enterprises (SOEs)   Public enterprises that provide a service which could be handled by the private sector, and that typically charge for their services. Hydro-Québec and REXFOR are examples. (Chapter 4)

Tax fields   Bases of taxation (sales, income) over which a government (federal or provincial) exercises its administrative authority. (Chapter 2)

Tax-rental agreements   Administrative deals negotiated between the federal and the provincial governments whereby the province yields all or part of its jurisdiction over **tax fields** to the federal government. In return, the federal government manages the redistribution of revenues to the province in the form of services and programs. (Chapter 2)

Ultramontanism   A system of sociopolitical thought, which dominated Quebec for the better part of the 19th century, that essentially advocated the unquestionable authority of the Church in all social and political matters. (Chapter 3)

Unemployment rate   The proportion of the labour force actively seeking work but unable to find jobs. (Chapter 13)

Universal suffrage   The general right to vote in an election irrespective of sex, creed, colour, or race, and not subject to any minimal property value requirements. In Quebec, all individuals over 18 years of age have the right to vote in elections at every level of government. (Chapter 9)

Valid votes   Votes that are indicated correctly on the ballot by the voter and may be counted. On average, 1 to 2% of ballots are rejected for any one of several reasons that make it impossible to know which candidate was chosen by the voter. (Chapter 5)

Value added The difference between the final value of a product and that of all other goods which have entered into the production process. For example, the cost of energy required for the fabrication of the product from raw materials represents value added to those raw materials. (Chapter 13)

Welfare state A concept of the role of government as a basic provider of individual economic security and well-being. The idea underlies the complex array of social programs developed in Quebec since the 1960s. (Chapter 16)

Whips Leadership positions of the party in power in the **National Assembly**. Whips work with the party leader by carrying the word to party troops, and making sure as many members as possible are present whenever a vote is taken. (Chapter 9)

Youth Court See **Court of Quebec**.

Index

- - - - - - - - - - - *cut here* - - - - - - - - - - - -

STUDENT REPLY CARD

You can help us to develop better textbooks. Please answer the following questions about Lachapelle/Bernier//Salée/Bernier: *The Quebec Democracy: Structures, Processes, and Policies* and return this form via Business Reply Mail. Your opinions matter: thank you in advance for sharing them with us!

Name of your college or university: _____

Major program of study: _____

Course title: _____

Were you required to buy this book? _____ yes _____ no

Did you buy this book new or used? _____ new _____ used ($_____)

Do you plan to keep or sell this book? _____ keep _____ sell

Is the order of topic coverage consistent with what was taught in your course?

Are there chapters or sections of this text that were not assigned for your course? Please specify:

- - - - - - - - - - - · *fold here* - - - - - - - - - - -

Were there topics covered in your course that are not included in the text? Please specify:

What did you like most about this text?

What did you like least?

Please add any comments or suggestions: